Praise for *Doing Objects in Visual Basic 2005*

"*Doing Objects in Visual Basic 2005* is one of the few books that I've seen that lays the proper object-oriented foundation to make new Visual Basic.NET developers as well as VB6 veterans successful in moving to the .NET Framework."
—**Paul Ballard, *President, Rochester Consulting Partnership, Inc***

"Deborah Kurata's *Doing Objects in Visual Basic 2005* is ⌐
beached on the forbidding isle of .NET object-oriente
she says, leading you confidently into that vaguely men⌐   ⌐ep.
Suddenly the daunting and unfamiliar become doable and   ⌐ productive again. My goodness, you're actually enjoying yourself!"
—**Ward Bell, *V.P., Product Management, IdeaBlade, Inc***

"When is comes to advice on programming objects in Visual Basic, nobody could be better qualified than Deborah Kurata. She's been doing *Doing Objects* since VB4, and she doesn't let us down as we move our classic VB code to the Microsoft.NET platform. From initial analysis and design, through to the final implementation, you'll find everything you need here to take on the Visual Basic 2005 development environment. This book is a must have for every VB.NET developer!"
—**Kel Good, *MCT, MCITP, MCPD, Custom Software Development Inc.,* (*www.customsoftware.ca*)**

"I've long been frustrated that I couldn't recommend a book on object-oriented fundamentals in .NET. Sure, there were plenty of books on OO syntax. But what good is explanation of syntax if you don't already understand the concepts? At last, we have the successor to the *Doing Objects* series for classic VB, from which so many of us learned how to think about objects and object design, completely rewritten for .NET. If you're a VB 2005 developer who needs to add object orientation to your skill set, this is the book you need."
—**Billy Hollis, *author/consultant, Next Version Systems***

"Deborah Kurata does her *Doing Objects* thing again! This is the newest book from Deborah which has been completely rewritten from the ground up for the Visual Basic .Net 2005 developer. Anyone needing a solid foundation in object technology, Visual Basic .Net 2005, and Visual Studio .Net 2005 should read this book. Deborah's presentation of core topics such as class design, object state management, exception handling, events, data binding, validation, data access techniques, and many others is clear, concise, and direct. The clarity of the content, coupled with the hands-on examples make this book an easy read and a must have."
—**Ron Landers, *Senior Technical Consultant, IT Professionals, Inc.***

DOING OBJECTS IN
VISUAL BASIC 2005

DOING OBJECTS IN VISUAL BASIC 2005

THE ADDISON-WESLEY MICROSOFT TECHNOLOGY SERIES

Deborah Kurata

✦✦ Addison-Wesley

Upper Saddle River, NJ • Boston • Indianapolis • San Francisco
New York • Toronto • Montreal • London • Munich • Paris • Madrid
Cape Town • Sydney • Tokyo • Singapore • Mexico City

Many of the designations used by manufacturers and sellers to distinguish their products are claimed as trademarks. Where those designations appear in this book, and the publisher was aware of a trademark claim, the designations have been printed with initial capital letters or in all capitals.

The author and publisher have taken care in the preparation of this book, but make no expressed or implied warranty of any kind and assume no responsibility for errors or omissions. No liability is assumed for incidental or consequential damages in connection with or arising from the use of the information or programs contained herein.

The publisher offers excellent discounts on this book when ordered in quantity for bulk purchases or special sales, which may include electronic versions and/or custom covers and content particular to your business, training goals, marketing focus, and branding interests. For more information, please contact:

U.S. Corporate and Government Sales
800-382-3419
corpsales@pearsontechgroup.com

For sales outside the United States, please contact:

International Sales
international@pearsoned.com

 This Book Is Safari Enabled

The Safari Enabled icon on the cover of your favorite technology book means the book is available through Safari Bookshelf. When you buy this book, you get free access to the online edition for 45 days. Safari Bookshelf is an electronic reference library that lets you easily search thousands of technical books, find code samples, download chapters, and access technical information whenever and wherever you need it.

To gain 45-day Safari Enabled access to this book:
    Go to http://www.awprofessional.com/safarienabled.
    Complete the brief registration form.
    Enter the coupon code WCRU-JYTP-GMXK-DAPG-ZGVY.
If you have difficulty registering on Safari Bookshelf or accessing the online edition, please e-mail customerservice@safaribooksonline.com.

Visit us on the Web: www.awprofessional.com

Library of Congress Cataloging-in-Publication Data:
Kurata, Deborah.
  Doing objects in Visual basic 2005 / Deborah Kurata.
      p. cm.
  ISBN 0-321-32049-2 (pbk. : alk. paper) 1. Object-oriented programming (Computer science) 2. Microsoft Visual BASIC. I. Title.
  QA76.64.K872 2007
  005.1'17--dc22

ISBN-10 0-321-32049-2
ISBN-13 978-03-2132049-2
Text printed in the United States on recycled paper at R.R. Donnelley in Crawfordsville, IN
Second printing September, 2007

To my daughters, Jessica and Krysta. Thank you for listening to me read the entire Lord of the Rings *trilogy out loud, and for dressing up as Middle Earth characters for the midnight movie showing—even if it meant being half asleep through school the next day.*

CONTENTS

FOREWORD

Object-oriented technology has been working its way into the mainstream consciousness for a long time now—decades, in fact. It really started to gain momentum for business development in the mid-90s with the widespread use of the COM/DCOM and CORBA technologies. Object orientation (OO) got a big boost around the turn of the century with the introduction of the object-oriented Java and Microsoft .NET development platforms.

As far back as 1994, with VB 3.0, advanced Visual Basic developers were trying to exploit the ideas of OO by using instances of forms as "objects." This was a hack to work around the lack of OO support in VB at that time, but the technique was useful and, I think, influenced how Microsoft shaped the language from that point forward.

VB 4.0 was the real beginning of OO support in VB due to its support for COM and its ability to create real class files. Deborah Kurata's 1995 book, *Doing Objects in Microsoft Visual Basic 4.0*, rapidly became one of the must-have books for any serious VB developer. She followed up with a VB 6.0 edition in 1998, continuing to guide untold numbers of developers toward the use of OO concepts and practices.

The challenge with classic VB, and with the COM/DCOM development platform, is that they weren't *truly* object-oriented. Although they supported the concepts of abstraction, encapsulation, and polymorphism, neither VB nor COM supported the idea of inheritance. Missing this pillar of OO seriously restricted important design and programming patterns.

Microsoft .NET represents a major shift toward OO. Not only do the flagship programming languages (VB and C#) support inheritance, but the *platform itself* supports the concept. In .NET everything is an object. Every application written in .NET continually uses objects to do its work.

This doesn't automatically make *your code* object-oriented, but it does mean that the use of objects is inescapable. A side effect is that becoming a good .NET developer requires a solid understanding of at least the basic OO concepts and how they were used to create .NET itself. And to truly exploit the power of .NET, a developer must move past being an object *user* and become an object *author*.

Such a shift is a big step, and there's a lot to learn. At the same time, we all have work that must be done, so it is important that we can apply concepts as rapidly as possible. As with her previous books, Deborah's new book is pragmatic, teaching OO concepts within the context of building real applications that use the features of .NET. I strongly support this idea of teaching such important concepts within a practical and pragmatic context.

Rockford Lhotka
Magenic Technologies

PREFACE

Welcome to the latest in the series of *Doing Objects* books. This series started in 1995 with Visual Basic 4.0, when VB could first do objects. At that time, little had been discussed about using object-oriented design and development techniques with Visual Basic. To help improve that situation, almost half of each book in the series was dedicated to helping developers think in object-oriented terms and design an object-oriented application. The other half presented a full-featured solution for building an object-oriented application.

As with each of the other books in this series, this book is about designing and developing great applications for Visual Basic using object-oriented principles. However, today's Visual Basic developer is much more versed in design concepts, so only one chapter of this book is dedicated to design. The remaining chapters provide techniques for building an object-oriented application *and* a reusable application framework.

Unlike other books that provide reference-type information and short examples with no context, this book presents each topic in a logical sequence, illustrating the techniques by designing and developing a full-featured application. This allows you to readily see how each technique fits into your development activities.

This book also demonstrates how to build an application framework you can reuse in every application you build. With an application framework you can significantly increase your productivity and that of your team.

This new edition of the book was completely rewritten to use the features of Visual Basic 2005, Visual Studio 2005, and the .NET Framework. It makes no assumptions about your experience with .NET. It provides tips for experienced .NET developers and those new to .NET. There are even some tips specifically for developers moving from VB6 to .NET.

Why Do Objects?

Everything in .NET is basically an object. You cannot really do anything in .NET without doing objects. But Visual Basic 2005 still allows you to create modules, and it provides default form instances. Thus, you can still pretend to code without objects. So why make the move to using object-oriented techniques in your Visual Basic applications?

- Objects help you think about an application in terms of real-world things, aiding in the design process.
- Objects define all their data and processing in one programming unit. All of the code having to do with customers is in one code file, all of the code having to do with products is in another code file, and so on. This makes it much easier to develop, test, and maintain your code and to manage the complexities of software development. It also simplifies multiprogrammer development.
- Objects allow for building an application framework with base form classes and base business object classes. Common code resides in these base classes and not within every form or code file. This can drastically reduce the amount of code you have to write, test, and maintain.
- Objects allow you to work with other high-productivity features in .NET, such as object binding.

This book expands on these topics to help you know when, how, and why to do objects in Visual Basic 2005.

Who Should Read This Book?

The goal of most Visual Basic developers is to get the job done. You have existing code to maintain, enhancements to implement, and new applications to write—all with limited time and other resources. You need to be as productive as possible. Learning a new version of your programming language and development environment takes away from that productivity. So you need a way to learn the new tools and techniques as rapidly and efficiently as possible.

This book is for developers who need to quickly learn the key features of Visual Basic 2005, Visual Studio 2005, and the .NET Framework and incorporate the new techniques into their daily design and development activities. Specifically, if you are interested in learning how an object-oriented approach and these new tools and techniques can minimize the complexity of software design and development and improve your productivity, this book is for you.

I have many opportunities to talk with software developers at conferences, via newsgroups and e-mail, and through my consulting company. The key concern for many developers is how to come up to speed quickly on the many new features. Bookstores have shelves full of books, but it is hard to know where to begin, how the features interrelate, or even how to find time to do that much reading. The goal of this book is to provide details on the key features in one place and all within the context of designing and building a full-featured application.

This book assumes you are familiar with some version of Visual Basic, even if it is only a classic version like VB3 or VB6. It assumes you know how to write programming logic and put controls on forms. This book is not for people new to programming. Nor is it for developers who have never used a visual programming tool, such as Visual Basic. After you learn the basics, come back to this book to learn best practices for building great Visual Basic 2005 applications.

About This Book

This book begins with an overview of object-oriented terms and techniques. It then covers a pragmatic approach to application design, including the design of an application framework. The majority of the book details how to use the tools and techniques in Visual Basic, Visual Studio, and the .NET Framework to build great object-oriented applications.

This book is organized as follows:

- **Chapter 1, "Introduction to OO in .NET":** Basic object-oriented terminology and concepts are covered in this first chapter, including specifics on how these concepts are realized in Visual Basic. It also provides an in-depth discussion about the benefits of an object-oriented approach.
- **Chapter 2, "Designing Software":** When designing an application, you have many design aspects to consider, such as user interface, business objects, and database. Managing all these aspects is

easier if you follow a design methodology. This chapter presents the GUIDS Methodology, a pragmatic approach to object-oriented design.

- **Chapter 3, "Building Projects":** This chapter covers the basics of building a solution with associated projects for the user interface, business logic, and data access layers. It includes a discussion of productivity enhancers such as templates and using the built-in Windows application framework.
- **Chapter 4, "Building the User Interface Layer":** The user interface of a .NET application is composed of two parts. The outside is the part of the application that the user sees and interacts with. The inside is the code behind the forms. This chapter shows you how to build both parts with reuse and changeability in mind. It also introduces base form classes and programmatic interfaces.
- **Chapter 5, "Building the Business Logic Layer":** The business logic layer includes all of the functionality of the application. This chapter details how to build classes with appropriate properties and methods. It also introduces base business object classes and generics.
- **Chapter 6, "Class Tools and Techniques":** Visual Studio has many fun tools to help you build your application. This chapter covers the Class Designer, Object Test Bench, code snippets, and unit tests. It also covers more advanced techniques such as building master/detail classes.
- **Chapter 7, "Binding the User Interface to the Business Objects":** Visual Studio provides enhanced features for binding your user interface elements to business object properties. This chapter describes binding and details how to perform object binding. It also covers how to write code to validate user-entered values.
- **Chapter 8, "Building the Data Access Layer":** Most applications require some type of data. This chapter details how to build a database. It then covers how to build a data access component that uses ADO.NET to retrieve and save data in a database.

"Building Along" Activities

It is often easier to learn by doing. So this book provides "building along" activities in each development chapter. You can build along with these activities to construct the sample application.

By the time you reach the end of the book, you will have a full-featured Windows application that demonstrates many of the techniques presented in this book. You will also have the basics of an application framework that you can reuse in all your applications.

In addition, each chapter includes a "Try It!" section. If you don't have time to build the entire sample application, you can download the sample code and extend several features using the "Try It!" sections. This provides a facility for you to practice what you are reading without the commitment of building the entire sample application. Note, that many of the "Try It!" exercises build on prior "Try It!" exercises to demonstrate how the techniques build on one another and work together to form a complete application.

What You Need to Use This Book

To work through any of the techniques, "building along" activities, or "Try It!" section exercises, you must have some edition of Visual Basic 2005. You can download the free Visual Basic 2005 Express Edition or use any other edition of these tools. In some cases the Express Edition does not provide a feature discussed in this book. These cases are clearly indicated in the text.

When you launch Visual Studio 2005 for the first time, you are asked to select your default development settings. The settings you select affect the names of many of the menu options, the layout of some of the dialogs, and other features of Visual Studio. This book uses the General Development settings, because they are the most common settings used by .NET developers.

NOTE: If you have your Visual Studio set to use the Visual Basic Development settings instead of the General Development settings, many of your Visual Studio options and some of the dialogs will be different from those in this book. You can continue to use your settings and work with the differences, or you can change your settings.

To set your Visual Studio settings so that your environment matches the one used in this book, select **Tools** | **Import and Export Settings**. Select **Reset All Settings** and click **Next**. Choose whether to save your current settings, and click **Next**. Select **General Development Settings**, and click **Finish**.

Although you could use any database product, to work through all the techniques in Chapter 8 you should also have access to a version of SQL Server. You can use SQL Server 2000 or any edition of SQL Server 2005. If you don't have SQL Server, you can download the free SQL Server 2005 Express Edition. If you want to use Microsoft Access instead, notes are provided in Chapter 8 about the features of Visual Studio 2005 that do not work with Access.

Downloading the Code

You can build all of the code for the sample application from instructions in this book by following the "building along" activities. However, you may not have time to work through every example. If you want to download the code, you can find it at http://www.insteptech.com.

Errata

I have made every effort to describe the concepts presented in this book in a clear and concise fashion. I have tried to ensure that the book is up to date as of this writing. And I have worked with the technical reviewers and technical editors to confirm that there are no errors in the text or code. However, mistakes are possible, and improvements are always welcome.

If you have suggestions for improving the content of the book, or if you find something that is incorrect or unclear, I would like to hear from you. I can then incorporate your comments in future editions of this book. You can reach me via e-mail at deborahk@insteptech.com.

ACKNOWLEDGMENTS

This book had several starts and stops over a ten-month period. During this time, I have had help from many different people at Addison-Wesley. I'd like to especially thank Joan Murray for her work as the acquisitions editor and for her infinite patience. I'd also like to thank Gayle Johnson for copy editing the book and Kristy Hart for taking the manuscript through production.

I also had a great set of technical reviewers. I'd like to thank Richard Ainsley, Mary Jane Beddow, Ward Bell, James Butler, Sam Gill, Julia Lerman, Robert Ranck, Bill Sarris, and Fred Yano, who all gave of their free time to review and comment on chapters. I'd also like to thank the technical editors: Paul Ballard, Mark Dunn, Ken Getz, Kel Good, Ron Landers, and Ethan Roberts. Special thanks to Robin Shahan for her assistance in reading each chapter and trying each set of "building along" activities, all in a very short time frame. I appreciate all of your time!

Finally, I would like to thank my family for their understanding and support. To my husband and partner, Jerry, thanks for working at home so I could crank through chapters at the office without interruption. To my 17-year-old daughter, Jessica, thank you for running all of my errands so that I could focus here. To my 14-year-old daughter, Krysta, thank you for bugging your sister when you needed a ride to the mall. And to my parents, Jerre and Virginia Cummings, thank you for buying the books!

—Deborah Kurata, October 2006

ABOUT THE AUTHOR

Deborah Kurata is cofounder of InStep Technologies Inc. (http://www.insteptech.com), a professional consulting firm that focuses on turning your business vision into reality using Microsoft .NET technologies. InStep provides premier software design, development, and consulting services to the most successful companies in Silicon Valley, the San Francisco Bay area, and other locations nationwide. You can reach InStep at 925-730-1000 or at info@insteptech.com.

Deborah has more than 15 years of experience in architecting, designing, and developing successful applications. She has authored several books, including the *Doing Objects in Visual Basic* series (Sams), *Best Kept Secrets in .NET* (Apress), and *Doing Web Development: Client-Side Techniques* (Apress). She also writes for MSDN and *CoDe* magazine (http://www.code-magazine.com/).

Deborah speaks at .NET user groups all over the country as a member of the INETA Speaker's Bureau (http://www.ineta.org/) and at conferences such as VSLive, DevDays, and TechEd. For her work in support of software development and software developers, she has been recognized with the Microsoft Most Valuable Professional (MVP) award. After a hard day of coding and taking care of her family, Deborah enjoys blowing stuff up (on the XBox, of course).

Deborah holds degrees in physics and mathematics from the University of Wisconsin–Eau Claire and an MBA from the College of William and Mary.

CHAPTER 1

INTRODUCTION TO OO IN .NET

I amar prestar aen . . . the world is changed.
—Galadriel, The Lord of the Rings

You may recognize this quote as the first words from the movie *The Lord of the Rings: The Fellowship of the Ring*. These words are just as true in the world of software development as they are in Middle Earth. Our world is changed.

In the days of VB1 and VB2, it was truly possible to be a Visual Basic expert. Everything we needed to know was in one handbook-sized manual. Then came VB3 with its data access; VB4 with objects; and VB5 and VB6 with ActiveX, ActiveX Data Objects (ADO), and Distributed Component Object Model (DCOM). Suddenly it was impossible to be an expert in all things Visual Basic.

Then Microsoft took everything we knew, shook it up, turned it upside down, and gave us VB.NET. It felt vaguely familiar, but it definitely was not the VB we knew. Yes, it was different. It was also bigger, more powerful, and fully object-oriented (OO).

The VB integrated development environment (IDE) was replaced with Visual Studio, which supports Visual Basic and several other programming languages such as C# (pronounced "C sharp"). This new IDE has an overwhelming number of features to help us create, build, test, and debug our applications.

Along with a new VB, we got the .NET Framework. The .NET Framework includes a *huge* class library that provides thousands of features we can use to create applications, including prebuilt data types, Windows features, Web features, debugging features, access to the file system, and operating system functions. Just about any code that we wrote in VB6 that accessed the Windows API can now be written using the .NET Framework class library instead.

Since the .NET Framework and the new Visual Basic are based on object-oriented concepts, understanding OO has become crucial for fully understanding our new VB and for getting the most from the .NET Framework.

1

This chapter introduces fundamental object-oriented concepts and the key features of the new Visual Basic that support these concepts.

What Is OO?

Today's world of software design and development is all about managing complexity. Computer-savvy users want more and more features. Software products, such as Microsoft Word and Excel, set high expectations. The business environment requires software to react quickly to shifting corporate needs. And tools and technologies are changing faster than ever. It is easy to become overwhelmed by the complexity.

The key to successful software is managing this complexity—and managing complexity is one of the goals of object orientation (OO). **Object-oriented** means looking at a software system in terms of the things, or *objects*, that are relevant to that system and how those objects interact. As you design and then build your application, you can focus on one object at a time, temporarily ignoring the complexities of the rest of the system.

OO concepts are used in many professions. For example, when designing an office, an architect thinks about working spaces, foundations, frameworks, and plumbing systems. These are the real-world objects. The architect does not concentrate on the process of pouring the foundation, hammering nails, or connecting the plumbing, nor on the details of the data, such as how much concrete or how many nails. These lower-level processes and details are important but not applicable to the high-level design of an office building. And without the high-level design, the processes and data details are irrelevant.

Object orientation does not ignore the data or the process. It combines the best of a procedure-oriented view (where the focus is on the process) and a data-centric view (where the focus is on the data) and adds productivity concepts such as reuse, testability, and, of course, managing complexity.

Consider a time sheet. Using a data-centric view, the key data elements are the employee name, date, and hours worked. But just looking at the data does not provide the full picture of time sheet processing. Using a procedure-oriented view, the focus is on the process of generating the time sheet. But this does not consider the bigger picture of how the time sheet fits into an overall system.

From an object-oriented perspective, the time sheet has data (called **properties**) and processes (called **methods**). It also has relationships to other objects in the system, such as an employee object, a logging object, a data access object, and so on.

Thinking about an application in an object-oriented way makes it easier to break the application into its parts (objects), focus on the most important aspects of each part, and look at the relationships between those parts. And since Visual Basic is now a fully object-oriented programming language, using an object-oriented approach to thinking about your application makes it easier to map these thoughts into object-oriented code.

Introduction to Object-Oriented Concepts

Object-oriented concepts and terminology are crucial to understanding Visual Basic and the .NET Framework. This section provides an overview of each key OO concept and introduces the associated Visual Basic 2005 syntax. If you already know OO and Visual Basic 2005, you may want to skip this section.

If you are new to these concepts, it's okay if you don't feel comfortable with all this terminology and syntax right away. These introductory examples are meant to give you an idea of the syntax. As you progress through this book, you will see these object-oriented terms and techniques used in the design and again in implementation. Starting in Chapter 3, "Building Projects," the examples provide step-by-step details to help you build along and try out the syntax if desired. Each time you see the terms and syntax used, they will seem more familiar. Soon they will become a permanent part of your vocabulary and programmer's toolbox.

What Are Objects?

Objects are things. People, companies, employees, time sheets, and ledger entries are all types of objects. In object-oriented terms, the word **object** is used to describe one specific thing, such as Sam Smith the carpenter at 3322 Main Street and the May 15th time sheet for Jessica Jones.

Objects have data associated with them called **properties**. Sam Smith has a name, occupation, and address. The time sheet has an employee name, time period, and hours worked.

NOTE: In object-oriented literature, properties are sometimes called **attributes**, **resources**, or even just **data**.

Objects also *do* things. The time sheet is filled out, validated, and submitted for payment. In real life, we fill out time sheets, validate them, and submit them for payment. In a computer system, the time sheet can perform these operations for itself. The things an object can do are defined with **methods**.

NOTE: In object-oriented literature, methods are also called **behaviors**, **services**, **operations**, or **responsibilities**.

Objects can be real-world things, such as an employee or time sheet. Objects can be conceptual things, such as an engineering process or payroll. Objects can also be implementation-specific things, such as forms, controls, and DataSets. The same object-oriented concepts apply regardless of whether the object is based on the real world, on a concept, or on the implementation.

Since objects are fundamental to understanding object orientation, it is important that you can recognize objects and define their appropriate properties and methods. So take a moment to think about the things around you. What objects do you see? How would you define their properties and methods?

Your phone has properties such as color, volume, and mute. It has methods such as increase volume, decrease volume, turn on mute, turn off mute, dial, answer, and transfer. An employee has properties such as name, address, and occupation. An electronic time sheet has properties such as employee name, date, and hours. It has methods such as calculate pay.

If you want to form a mental picture of an object, it would look something like Figure 1.1. Each specific time sheet object is identified by the values of the properties shown at the center of the object. The methods are shown around the properties.

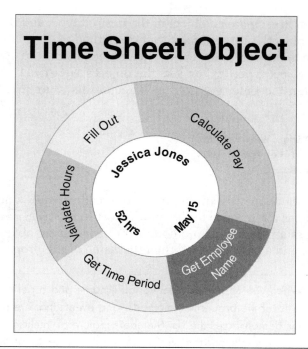

Figure 1.1   The time sheet object encapsulates the properties within the object and exposes them through methods.

This depiction indicates that an object's property values should not be directly accessed by something outside the object. For example, the time period should not be adjusted except through the get time period method, and the employee name would not be retrieved except through the get employee name method. This concept of hiding the internal data is a part of what is called **encapsulation** and is a key premise of object-oriented programming. (See the "What Are Classes?" section for a coding example demonstrating this feature of encapsulation.)

Every object is of a specific type. For example, the object defined as Sam Smith the carpenter at 3322 Main Street is an employee object type, and the May 15th time sheet for Jessica Jones is a time sheet object type. All the objects of a particular type have the same set of properties and methods.

From a programming perspective, you can define your own object types using classes, as described in the "What Are Classes?" section. Or you can use the object types provided in the .NET Framework. In either case, you first create an object of the desired type, and then you can set or get the object's properties and call its methods.

The following code creates an object using the .NET Framework `Timer` object type. It then sets the object's `Interval` property to define how often the timer goes off and executes its `Start` method to start the timer.

```
Dim myTimer As New Timer
myTimer.Interval = 1000
myTimer.Start()
```

The `New` keyword in the first line of code creates a new `Timer` object and assigns a reference to that new object to the `myTimer` object variable. To access a property or method of the new `Timer` object, use the object variable and a period (.) and then the name of the property or method.

NOTE: When you type the object variable name and a period in Visual Studio, you see a list of the properties, methods, and events that are appropriate for that object. This demonstrates the List Members feature of Intellisense. **Intellisense** provides auto-completion and display of class documentation within Visual Studio as you are coding. Other Intellisense features are demonstrated in later chapters.

Everything in Visual Basic can be accessed as an object: forms, strings, even integers. Check out this code:

```
Dim i As New Integer
Dim s As String
i = 5
s = i.ToString
```

The first line creates a new `Integer` object and assigns it to `i`. The variable `i` is then assigned a value of `5`. The last line calls the `ToString` method of the `Integer` object to convert the number to a string.

NOTE: Even though you can use the `New` keyword to create integers, it is not necessary and is not commonly done in practice. It is shown in this example to illustrate that you *can* work with simple data types as objects.

In .NET, an integer and other primitive data types, such as Boolean and decimal, are called **value types**. Value types store and pass their contents by their actual value. Technically speaking, value types are allocated either on the stack or inline in a structure. A standard set of value types are built into the .NET Framework, such as integer and decimal. You can also create your own value types. You do not need to use the `New` keyword for any value type.

More complex data types in .NET, such as strings and arrays, are **reference types**. Reference types store and pass their contents as a reference to the value's memory location. Technically speaking, reference types are allocated on the memory heap. The .NET Framework provides a set of built-in reference types, such as string and array. Classes that you create (as described in the "What Are Classes?" section) are reference types.

.NET automatically creates a **boxed value type** for each value type. Boxed value types allow value types to be accessed like reference types (such as the preceding integer example). In addition, boxed value types allow you to convert value types to reference types. For example, adding to the preceding code example, you could assign the integer to an object. This converts the integer value type to an object reference type.

```
Dim o As Object
o = i
```

This conversion of value types to reference types and vice versa is called **boxing**. Boxing has a performance hit, so you want to minimize the amount of boxing in your application wherever possible.

Variables that are value types each have their own copy of the data. Therefore, operations on one variable do not affect other variables. Variables that are reference types, such as object variables, can refer to the same object. Therefore, operations on one variable can affect the same object referenced by another variable. Check this out:

```
Dim myTimer As New Timer
myTimer.Interval = 1000

Dim myTimer2 As Timer
myTimer2 = myTimer
myTimer2.Interval = 500

Debug.WriteLine(myTimer.Interval)     ' Displays 500
Debug.WriteLine(myTimer2.Interval)    ' Displays 500
```

This code creates a new `Timer` object, assigns it to the `myTimer` object variable, and sets its `Interval` property to `1000`. It then defines a second `myTimer2` object variable, assigns it to the same `Timer` object, and sets the `Interval` property to `500`.

Since `myTimer` and `myTimer2` are object variables, they are reference types. Assigning one object variable to another object variable sets both variables to reference *the same object*. Changing the properties using either object variable makes the changes to the underlying object. Hence, the sample code results in `500` for both `myTimer.Interval` and `myTimer2.Interval`.

The one exception to this behavior is strings. Even though strings are a reference type, assigning one string to another string copies the data so that both strings do not reference the same data. This provides a more natural use of strings in your application. For example:

```
Dim employeeName As String
employeeName = "Jessica Jones"

Dim employeeName2 As String
employeeName2 = employeeName
employeeName2 = "Sam Smith"

Debug.WriteLine(employeeName)     ' Displays "Jessica Jones"
Debug.WriteLine(employeeName2)    ' Displays "Sam Smith"
```

Even though `employeeName2` is assigned to `employeeName` and then `employeeName2` is changed, `employeeName` remains unchanged. The sample code results in the display of `Jessica Jones` and then `Sam Smith`.

Notice also that the `New` keyword is not required for strings. Strings were designed as a special case to make it easier and more natural to work with string variables.

Understanding how to create an object and call its properties and methods is crucial to any development with Visual Basic. Chapter 5, "Building the Business Logic Layer," provides many more examples of creating and using objects.

What Are Scenarios?

To understand an object within a particular context, and to define the appropriate set of properties and methods, it is important to look at how the object will be used. That is the purpose of scenarios.

Scenarios describe the processes that use the objects. For example, a payroll scenario has a set of steps for defining the payroll period, validating the time sheets, summing the hours from each time sheet, determining the correct pay using calculations that depend on the type of employee, and so on.

NOTE: You may see scenarios called **use cases** or user **stories**.

By defining the scenarios and looking at how the objects are used in each scenario, you can ensure that the appropriate properties and methods are defined for each object. For each property, the scenarios provide the business rules detailing the validation for the property. For each method, the scenarios clarify the needed logic.

Scenarios are defined during the design phase, as detailed in Chapter 2, "Designing Software." You then use the scenarios during development as you code the business rules and logic. You can also use the scenarios as the basis of your test plans.

What Are Classes?

Humans like to classify things, to find similarities in things, and to group them accordingly. Things with similar attributes (properties) and behaviors (methods) are grouped. In object-oriented terminology, the definition of the properties and methods that describe a particular classification is called a **class**. A class defines a particular object type. You can think of a class as a blueprint, providing the details of how objects of that type are made.

A cookie cutter is another analogy often used to illustrate the relationship between objects and a class. The cookie cutter is the class and provides the definition; it specifies the size and shape. The cookies are the objects created from the cookie cutter class.

For example, an employee class can have name, address, and occupation properties. Sam Smith and Jessica Jones are both objects from the employee class. Likewise, a time sheet class can have employee, date, and hours properties and a calculate pay method. Each person's weekly time sheet is then an object from the time sheet class.

A specific object created from a class is called an **instance** of the class. Each instance can have values for the defined set of properties and can perform the defined methods. So Sam is an instance of the employee class, and Jessica's time sheet for last week is an instance of the time sheet class.

The set of properties and methods described by a class are often called class **members**. A class defines the members, including the actual code to maintain the property values and perform the methods. Each object that is an instance of that class can execute the methods and retain values for each property.

Figure 1.2 shows a time sheet class and two time sheet objects created from the time sheet class: Jessica Jones's time sheet and Sam Smith's time sheet, both from May 15.

A class itself normally does not maintain state, meaning that it normally does not have any property values. Nor does it normally execute the class methods. Instead, the class defines the properties and contains the implementation of the methods that are used by each object created from the class. Each object has values for the properties and performs the methods. You do not eat the cookie cutter or fill out a time sheet class. You eat each cookie and fill out each individual time sheet.

The .NET Framework itself is composed of a set of classes. For example, the button in the Visual Studio Toolbox represents a `Button` class. Each time you add a button to a form, you create an instance of that `Button` class. The `Button` class has specific defined methods, such as `Focus`, and properties, such as `Name` and `Text`. The `Button` class itself does not have a value for the `Name` or `Text` properties. Nor can it have focus. Instead, it contains the implementation of the `Name` and `Text` properties and the `Focus` method. The `Button` objects that you create as instances of that `Button` class have values for the `Name` and `Text` properties and perform the `Focus` method.

In Visual Basic, any code you write resides in a class. If you type some code in a form, your code is in the form's class. Even if you write code in a module, the code compiles as a class!

If you have never created a class, the following example may help you visualize the code for a `TimeSheet` class:

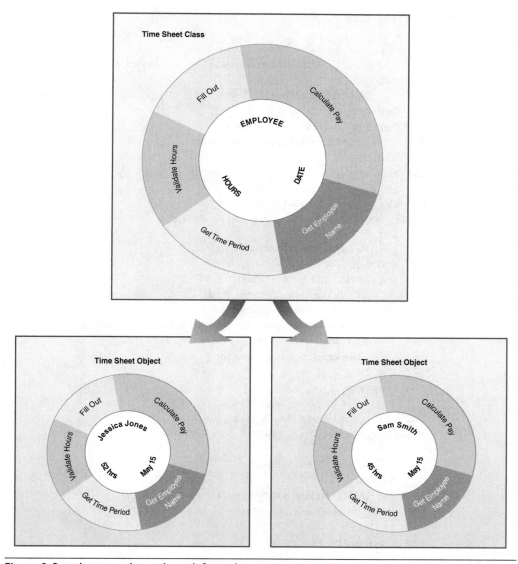

Figure 1.2   The time sheet class defines the properties and methods for each object from the class. The objects created from the time sheet class have values for the properties and can execute the methods.

```vb
Public Class TimeSheet

    Private _currentEmployee As Employee
    Public Property CurrentEmployee() As Employee
        Get
            Return _currentEmployee
        End Get
        Set(ByVal value As Employee)
            _currentEmployee = value
        End Set
    End Property

    Private _weekEndingDate As Date
    Public Property WeekEndingDate() As Date
        Get
            Return _weekEndingDate
        End Get
        Set(ByVal value As Date)
            If value > Now.Date Then
                Throw New Exception( _
                    "Date must be on or before today's date")
            End If
            _weekEndingDate = value
        End Set
    End Property

    Private _totalHours As Decimal
    Public Property TotalHours() As Decimal
        Get
            Return _totalHours
        End Get
        Set(ByVal value As Decimal)
            _totalHours = value
        End Set
    End Property

    Public Function CalculatePay() As Decimal
        Return CurrentEmployee.HourlyRate * TotalHours
    End Function
End Class
```

NOTE: If this code looks foreign to you, don't worry. The steps for creating classes with properties and methods, along with "building along" activities, are detailed later in this book. The purpose of this example is to give you a feel for what a class looks like.

The first line defines the class's scope and name. In this case, the class is named `TimeSheet` and is public.

The next set of code defines the private data and public accessors that provide access to that data. This follows the concept of encapsulation that was shown in Figure 1.1. For example, the private `_weekEndingDate` variable contains the value of the time period property. Since this variable is private, it is hidden and cannot be accessed except from within this class. The public `WeekEndingDate Property` statement implements the get time period and set time period functionality. Any code that needs to set or get the time period uses this public property.

NOTE: Even though the get time period and set time period functionality was described earlier as methods, they are implemented as `Property` statements. See Chapter 5 for more information on using `Property` statements.

By implementing properties using private variables and public `Property` statements, you can associate code with the setting or retrieval of the data value. In the `WeekEndingDate` example, the code that sets the date validates the date before assigning it.

The code at the end of the class in the preceding example demonstrates a method—in this case, a function that calculates the pay. In Visual Basic, methods are implemented with functions or subroutines.

To access the properties and use the methods of a class, you normally begin by creating an instance of the class and storing a reference to that instance in an object variable. You then use that object variable to get or set properties and execute methods on the resulting object.

The following code uses the `New` keyword to create a new object from the `TimeSheet` class. It then sets the properties on the object and executes the `CalculatePay` method on the object.

```
Dim totalPay As Decimal
Dim ts As New TimeSheet
ts.CurrentEmployee = Jessica 'Jessica is an Employee object
ts.WeekEndingDate = #8/15/2006#
ts.TotalHours = 51
totalPay = ts.CalculatePay
```

The New keyword creates a new instance of the TimeSheet class, and a reference to that instance is stored in the defined object variable (ts). Using the object variable and a period, the remainder of the code sets the object's properties and calls the method to calculate the pay.

As stated earlier in this section, objects normally maintain state (property values) and execute methods. The class itself *normally* does not maintain state or execute methods. However, Visual Basic does support static class data and static class methods.

Static class data (also called **shared data**) is data that the class retains, independent of any object. Use static class data any time you want to retain data that is shared between all objects, such as to keep a count of the total objects created from a class.

A **static class method** (also called a **shared method**) is a method that can be executed independent of any object. Static class methods are good for utility functions when you don't need to perform a process on any particular object. The MessageBox and Debug classes in the .NET Framework both have static class methods, so you don't need to create an instance of the class to use the methods. See Chapter 5 for more information on using the Shared keyword to create static class data and static class methods.

NOTE: If you write code in a module instead of a class, all the properties and methods in the module are static. You cannot create an instance from a module.

Building code as individual classes logically separates the code, with each class defining its own data and implementing its own methods. Having code organized into logical classes makes finding code for maintenance and enhancements effortless and produces a system that is much easier to extend. It also simplifies testing and debugging, because you can test each class as an independent unit. By using OO, you can manage the complexity of your application.

What Is Inheritance?

In object-oriented terms, inheritance defines an "is a" relationship between two or more classes. A beagle *is a* dog, and a poodle *is a* dog, so both beagle and poodle inherit from dog. Both beagle and poodle have dog attributes and exhibit dog behaviors. A dog class in this example is called the **parent class** or **base class**, and the classes that inherit from it (beagle and poodle) are called **child classes** or **derived classes**.

Likewise, think about your phone. All types of phones have basic phone attributes and behaviors, such as volume, dial, answer, and disconnect. Your desk phone may have additional, specialized behaviors, such as transfer features. Your cell phone has amazing features such as taking pictures and playing movies.

Even though each type of phone may have specialized behaviors, your desk phone *is a* phone, and your cell phone *is a* phone, so both desk phone and cell phone inherit their basic functionality from phone. Phone is the parent (or base) class, and desk phone and cell phone are the child (or derived) classes. You could draw this relationship as shown in Figure 1.3.

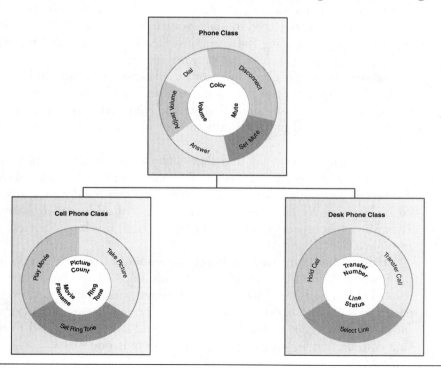

Figure 1.3   Inheritance extracts common functionality into a base class, promoting reuse.

When you inherit from a class, all the properties and methods in the base class are available to the derived class, just as if the properties and methods were in the derived class. So the desk phone can perform the answer method, as can the cell phone, even though the implementation for answer is defined in the base phone class.

Any class in the .NET Framework that is not intentionally sealed (marked as not inheritable) can be a used as a base class. So you can inherit the functionality of the .NET Framework classes in your application. You can also use any class in your application as a base class and inherit from it.

You can see inheritance in action as soon as you create your first form. When you create a form, Visual Studio creates a designer.vb file and generates the following code in that file:

```
Partial Class TimeSheetWin
    Inherits Windows.Forms.Form
```

The `Inherits` keyword specifies that your form inherits from the .NET Framework's `Windows.Forms.Form` class. This `Form` class provides all the common code required to make your form work like a Windows form. See Chapter 4, "Building the User Interface Layer," for more information on viewing designer.vb files and on form inheritance.

As you define the classes for your application, you may find that some classes have a number of the same properties and methods but also have some properties and methods that are different. You can extract the common properties and methods into another class and then use that class as a base class.

For example, you may find that each of your business object classes (such as `Employee` and `TimeSheet`) requires a property to keep track of the dirty state (added, updated, deleted). You can build a business object base class that contains this property instead of adding it to every class. Every business object class can then inherit from this base class and therefore have this property.

Using inheritance can minimize the amount of repeated code in your application. Common code is written only once in the base class and is reused by every derived class. Inheritance also makes your derived classes easier to build and maintain, because the derived classes focus exclusively on the features that make them unique. And if you ever need to change that common code, you have to change it in only one place.

What Is an Interface?

When talking about OO, the term "interface" has nothing to do with your user interface. An **interface** defines a list of properties and methods that a class can implement. But if the class implements a particular interface, it must implement all properties and methods defined by that interface.

For example, you can think of a phone as implementing a dial interface, `IDial`. (By convention, interfaces begin with the letter I.) This interface defines connect and make tone methods but does not implement them. This allows each phone to define how it connects and makes tones. Every phone that implements the `IDial` interface must provide an implementation for both the connect and make tone methods.

An interface is different from a base class in that an interface defines the list of properties and methods with no implementation. The implementation is left to the class that implements the interface. A base class contains both the list of properties and methods and their implementation. The class that inherits from the base class does not need to provide any implementation.

In your application, you can implement interfaces provided in the .NET Framework or define and implement your own interfaces. For example, if you want to ensure that every MDI child form in your application provides a standard set of methods, you could define an `IMDIChild` interface as follows:

```
Public Interface IMDIChild
    Function ProcessDelete() As Boolean
    Function ProcessNew() As Boolean
    Function ProcessSave() As Boolean
End Interface
```

To implement an interface in a class, use the `Implements` keyword. For example, if the `TimeSheetWin` class implements the `IMDIChild` interface, it would look like this:

```
Public Class TimeSheetWin
    Implements IMDIChild
```

Each form that implements this interface must provide an implementation for all three of the interface methods. See Chapter 4 for more information on implementing an interface.

Implementing an interface allows a class to be more formal about the behavior it promises to provide. Interfaces form a contract between the class and the rest of the application, and the compiler enforces this contract. If your class claims to implement an interface, all methods defined by that interface must be implemented before the class successfully compiles.

What Is a Namespace?

A namespace provides a mechanism for organizing classes in a logical manner. Conceptually, you can think of namespaces like the folders on your computer. Not all of your files are in the root directory. You create folders and subfolders to organize and easily find your files.

The .NET Framework is organized into namespaces under the `System` namespace. All features of the .NET Framework having to do with windows are under the `System.Windows` namespace, Windows forms features are under `System.Windows.Forms`, data features are under the `System.Data` namespace, debugging features are under `System.Diagnostics`, and so on. Can you imagine what it would be like to find a particular class in the thousands .NET Framework classes if it were not logically divided into namespaces?

By default, each project of your application is defined in its own namespace. But you can organize your classes into namespaces any way you like. See Chapter 3 for more information on defining namespaces.

The Basic Elements of an Object-Oriented System

The four basic elements of an object-oriented system are abstraction, encapsulation, inheritance, and polymorphism. This section defines these terms and describes why they are important to software design and development.

Abstraction: Focusing on What Is Important

Abstraction is a technique that we all use to manage the complexity of the information we collect every day. It allows us to recognize how things are similar and ignore how they are different, to think about generalities and not specifics, and to see what things are without thinking about what makes them that way. You can abstract important characteristics at any given time and for any particular purpose and ignore all other aspects.

How you develop an abstraction depends on both its purpose and your perspective. For example, on a warm summer day I look at a tree and abstract it as a shade provider. My young daughter abstracts it as a place to climb. One tree, two different abstractions.

Abstraction is used to identify the objects involved with a particular application. In developing a payroll system, you would think about Jessica Jones and abstract her as an employee, thinking only about her salary and how she gets paid. When working on the company softball league application, you would abstract Jessica as a player and be more concerned with her position and batting average. One object, two completely different abstractions.

Scenarios can ensure that the correct abstraction is used in a particular application. They provide context for the objects, giving them a purpose.

Using abstraction, you can focus on the objects and not on the implementation. This lets you think about what needs to be done and not how the computer will do it. It allows you to pull the design out from behind the technological wall of computer processing and bring it out to where the users can participate. The users, or **domain experts**, become key participants in the design process.

This seems so obvious, yet before current object-oriented methodologies existed, the user's participation all but stopped after the requirements definition phase and did not pick up again until the completion of the user-interface prototype. The design process, which had involved flowcharting and data flow diagramming, was considered too technical and inundated with jargon. So the users were ignored throughout the design and then were surprised with a prototype.

When object-oriented methodologies first appeared, the same was still true. Object-oriented techniques were for the academic crowd. The preferred object model diagramming techniques were complex and full of jargon and rules. The next chapter provides a straightforward methodology that uses abstraction to provide an elegant yet simple and practical approach that keeps the users involved throughout the design process.

Encapsulation: Hiding Your Private Parts

Most organizations have independent units, usually called departments. The sales department makes the sales, the production department produces the item, the shipping department ships it, and so on. Each department is responsible for its own procedures and internal information. For example, the sales department has procedures for calling prospects, evaluating the opportunity, sending sales materials, following up with current customers, maintaining prospect information, and so on.

You could say the departments are **encapsulated** because the internal information (properties) and standard operating procedures (methods) are contained within the department. These are figuratively hidden from other departments except through defined interfaces. Anyone who needs the department's procedures or information goes to that department to ask for it.

If a shipping clerk acquires the name of a prospect, the clerk knows better than to handle the prospect directly. Instead, the clerk collaborates with the sales department by using the publicly accessible defining prospects feature and sends the name to them.

The same principles are used in object-oriented applications to encapsulate each object's properties and methods. When an object needs to perform a procedure that is encapsulated in another class, it does not perform the procedure directly. Instead, it collaborates with an object belonging to the other class to perform the procedure.

Encapsulation aids in abstraction by hiding the internal implementation of an object within the class. You then can use an object without understanding how its class is implemented. So the shipping clerk can define a prospect to the sales department without knowing how the sales department actually handles the prospect.

You may already use encapsulation, but refer to it as data hiding. By creating private variables and public `Property` statements within a class, as shown in the "What Are Classes?" section earlier, you are encapsulating that data.

Inheritance: Attaining Reuse

Things that are similar still have some differences, and things that are different often have some similarities. Reviewing the prior inheritance example, both your desk phone and your cell phone can be classified as phones. Looking at their differences, your desk phone can transfer calls, and your cell phone can take pictures.

Say you are asked to create phone emulator software. You could implement all properties and methods for a cell phone into a cell phone class. This class would include volume and picture count properties and dial, answer, disconnect, and take picture methods. Likewise, you could implement all properties and methods for a desk phone into a desk phone class.

This class would include volume and transfer number properties and dial, answer, disconnect, and transfer methods. This duplicates the common phone information and functionality in both classes.

You can remove the property and method redundancy and attain reuse by using **inheritance**. You can remove the common phone properties and methods from the specialized classes and put them in a higher-level phone class. The cell phone class and desk phone class can then inherit from the phone class, attaining all its properties and methods. This "is a" relationship is depicted in Figure 1.3.

If a new type of phone class, such as a Web phone, were added to the class hierarchy shown in Figure 1.3, objects of the new class would automatically have all the properties and methods defined for the base phone class, greatly simplifying the development of the new class.

Inheritance is a powerful tool for code reuse. It is demonstrated in detail later in this book.

Polymorphism: Same Behavior, Different Implementation

Two or more classes can have methods that are named the same and have the same basic purpose but different implementations. This is **polymorphism**. The `Text` property of the .NET Framework is an example of polymorphism. Although the basic purpose of the `Text` property is the same, how the property works depends on whether you are setting the `Text` property of a `Form`, a `Label`, or a `TextBox`.

In the phone example, say the implementation of the `Dial` method needed to be different in the cell phone class and the desk phone class. The cell phone class would then need its own `Dial` method, and a desk phone class would need its own `Dial` method. You can request the `Dial` method by an object from either class without knowing how either class plans to implement that request. Both the cell phone class and the desk phone class have the `Dial` method, but the implementation of that behavior can be completely different.

Polymorphism can be implemented using inheritance. The base phone class would retain a `Dial` method, but the implementation would be empty (or would provide a default implementation). Each derived class would then override the base class `Dial` method by implementing the method. The result is that the desk phone class and cell phone class each have a `Dial` method, but the implementations are different. See Chapter 5 for more information on overriding base class members.

Polymorphism can also be implemented using an interface. In the phone example, the `Dial` method would be removed from the base phone class. An `IDial` interface would define the properties and methods for handling dialing. Both the desk phone class and cell phone class implement this interface so that they both have the same properties and methods for dialing but different implementations. See Chapter 4 for more information on implementing an interface.

The benefit of polymorphism is that you don't need to know the object's class to execute the polymorphic behavior. For example, you may have many classes in an application, each with its own save method. When the application is saved, each object knows the class it belongs to and automatically calls the correct save routine.

Object Orientation as a Process

Object orientation is basically a way to think about a particular software system or application in terms of the objects that the application needs and how they interact. You can apply this way of thinking through all the phases of the software development process.

OO is frequently broken into three phases: OO analysis (OOA), OO design (OOD), and OO programming (OOP). This section outlines these phases.

OOA: Analysis or Domain Model

Object-oriented analysis is looking at an entire system, often called a **domain**, and modeling it as a set of objects. The behavior of a particular object is defined with methods. The behavior of the entire system is identified through collaboration between the objects, each object calling the methods of other objects to complete a process. The state of a particular object is retained using properties. The state of the entire system is the combined state of all objects.

To attain a complete picture of the system, you need to define the classes that detail the objects involved with the system and the set of scenarios that describe how the objects collaborate to achieve an objective.

There are basically two ways to approach this task:

- Identify the classes, and then define the scenarios to describe how the objects from those classes work together.
- Define the scenarios and then use them to define the classes.

In practice, you may find that you interchange these approaches. You may begin the process by identifying some classes. Then you define several scenarios and find you need additional classes. As you define those classes you identify more scenarios, and so on.

At this stage in the process, the classes you define should be recognizable to anyone associated with the domain. This allows you to work more closely with those domain experts to collect the application requirements.

As an example, you can model a sales system as a set of classes such as `Customer`, `Lead`, `Product`, `Purchase`, and so on. Each of these class names should be familiar to the domain experts. The descriptions of the properties and methods associated with these classes should also be in domain terms.

The scenarios should also be phrased in terms of the domain, meaning in business terms and not programming terms. For example, a scenario for a sales system is as follows:

1. A person calls who is interested in your products but who is not a current customer.
2. The call center collects the person's name, company name, contact information, and information on products of interest.
3. The call center routes the information to the correct salesperson based on the lead's zip code.
4. The salesperson is notified of the new lead.
5. The salesperson collects information on products that are of interest to the new lead.
6. The salesperson performs a follow-up call and provides information on the products to the new lead.
7. The salesperson records the results of that call and schedules another follow-up call.

If you ignore implementation details during the analysis, it is easier to collect requirements without getting bogged down in details. You don't need to decide at this point if it is Web or Windows, how the salesperson is notified (with text messaging?), what the database looks like, and so on.

This makes it easier to look at implementation options later, because you know the underlying requirements.

The result of this phase is a set of scenarios that define a desired group of features and a model depicting the appropriate high-level objects to support those features.

Some companies expand the definition of "domain" and, wanting to gain more reuse, attempt to model their entire corporate process as part of OOA. The idea was to create one über `Customer` object that could be used by every application, one `Product` object, one `Purchase` object, and so on. If you have ever worked in a corporate environment, you can imagine the difficulty of getting everyone in the company to agree on one model. Plus, having one object be everything to every application negates many of the benefits of single focused object abstractions and adds to the complexity of every application.

Because of the significant cost and minimal return involved with these types of über efforts, the pendulum swung the other way, and methodologies such as Extreme Programming (XP) were implemented, minimizing the amount of information included in each analysis phase. (See the "Additional Reading" section for more information on Extreme Programming.)

In a perfect world, a complete domain-wide object-oriented analysis would be an excellent first step for any software development project. However, we don't live in a perfect world. The possibility of collecting accurate and detailed information for a complete system in a timely manner is just not feasible in most cases.

Most successful software projects have moved to a methodology that involves analyzing a small set of features at a time to get better information more quickly and efficiently. When you interview managers and domain experts, it is often easier to get good requirements if you focus the conversation on two or three features instead of an entire system.

OOD: Design Model

Object-oriented design begins with the domain model defined during the object-oriented analysis phase and breaks it into specific classes with clearly defined properties and methods. It then adds implementation details, such as security, serialization, and logging.

In cases where the OOA phase includes a large system, the OOD phase picks portions of the system and provides the details. Now that most development organizations are selecting fewer features to analyze at a time, there is more of an overlap between OOA and OOD and the transition from OOA to OOD is blurred.

The important thing that OOD does include that OOA does not is implementation details. OOD defines the classes, including the implementation details for properties and methods. It incorporates implementation constraints, such as security, logging, load, and performance. It includes architectural assumptions such as the location of the application's tiers (will there be an application server? database server? server farm? and so on).

Because of its technical nature, much of this step normally is done by the technical team, without much participation from the domain experts. Most domain experts don't care *how* you implement security or obtain the desired performance levels, only that you do implement security and have a highly performant application.

This phase often makes use of design patterns. A **design pattern** is a general, repeatable solution to a commonly occurring problem in software design. For example, the need to have a class that can provide one and only one object has a design pattern called a Singleton. The Singleton design pattern defines the set of classes needed to implement that pattern and solve that problem. (See the "Additional Reading" section for more information on design patterns.)

The result of this phase is a model that can readily be converted into code.

OOP: Programming

Each class defined in the OOD phase is developed as a class in the application. This process of converting the design into an application is object-oriented programming.

As you develop an application following OO principles, it is best to think of the classes as being independent entities that work together. For example, instead of a sales system application saving customer data, an object from the `Customer` class saves customer data. Instead of the sales system application printing a sales receipt, an object from the `Purchase` class prints the receipt.

Following an OO approach, you can focus on one class at a time, implementing all its properties and methods. For example, you could begin with the `Customer` class and implement all the properties and methods to collect customer data, save that data, and retrieve that data.

You could then fully test the `Customer` class without concern for the rest of the application.

The next chapter covers software design; the remaining chapters are dedicated to the object-oriented programming phase.

Benefits of an Object-Oriented Approach

Using an object-oriented approach to software design and development has many benefits. Frequently, they are described in vague terms. To make the benefits more concrete, let's examine common issues in the software life cycle and review how an object-oriented approach can help address them.

Speaking the Same Language

How are your meetings with your domain experts? The domain experts are the experts in the business function, and you are the expert in software design and construction. Why can't they just tell you what they want? Why do they instead tell you how many toolbar icons to put on the screen and how the Enter key should work? Does it ever seem that you just can't communicate with them?

Let's look at this problem from the domain experts' viewpoint. The domain experts are shown prototype after prototype, and each time they are asked if it meets their requirements. It should be no surprise that their biggest comment is that this button should be moved and that menu option renamed. But without the prototype, how can you discuss the requirements?

You need a common language to help you communicate. You need a language that keeps the domain expert focused on the problem that the application should solve, not on the user interface. With the object-oriented concept of abstraction and the process of building scenarios, you can discuss high-level business issues without regard for implementation. Therefore, you can discuss the design in terms of the business and not the technology.

Devising Real-World Models

Ever draw a flowchart? If you have ever taken a computer class, you have probably created a procedural model of a software project in the form of a flowchart or data flow diagram, like the model shown in Figure 1.4.

Drawing this type of flowchart or data flow diagram defines what a program needs to do, but it does not provide a model of the business. As businesses and the applications needed to support them become more and more complex, the procedural design model becomes too cumbersome and inflexible. Even minor changes to the business procedures can result in major changes to the flow.

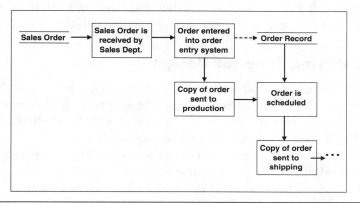

Figure 1.4   The procedural model used in structured design is too cumbersome and inflexible.

Businesses tend to deal with things: customers, sales orders, and widgets. These things, or objects, have certain behaviors: customers place orders, sales orders need to be filled, and widgets need production. The objects also have properties: customers have addresses, sales orders have quantities and prices, and widgets have styles and colors.

The basic premise of an object-oriented approach is to model real-world things and real-world concepts. This approach keeps the real-world issues in focus and results in a design that forms a closer fit with the real world.

Estimating How Long It Will Take

You finally get some domain information from the domain experts and obtain consensus on the project requirements. Now the project manager insists that you estimate how long it will take to develop this system. You look through your scribbled notes. In your head you are thinking, "I have no idea," but you say "three weeks," even though you know you have little to base the estimate on at this point in the project. But programmers are basically optimistic.

At its best, software scheduling is a difficult process. At its worst, it is a meaningless guess or is based on an arbitrarily imposed deadline. It is impossible to look at a system as a whole and establish a meaningful estimate of the work required. How can the project be broken down and estimated accurately? The object-oriented approach provides a way to abstract a project into classes that can be easily identified, understood, and reasonably estimated. You can then use your past experience with similar classes to set milestones and derive a more realistic schedule.

Justifying Time for Design

The project manager walks in, sees that you are not coding, and asks why you are scribbling notes and penciling cryptic diagrams when you should be at the keyboard. The schedule indicates that you should have the first set of features coded, but you have not yet begun.

You know you need to design the underlying structure for your application. But how do you get management to understand the importance of this architecture and put it on the schedule? How do you tell management that any time (and therefore money) saved by developing features quickly is lost later because of the complexity of working with code that has no underlying structure? How can you start building modules when you have no structure to attach them to? It would be like trying to put a tub in a second-floor bathroom when the foundation had not yet been poured.

The next chapter defines a clear set of steps for developing the architecture and framework of your application so that there is a structure into which all the classes of your design can be implemented. Each architecture step is defined as a task on the schedule and provides tangible results to show your progress, making it easier for you to define and schedule the architecture phase of your projects.

Preventing the Prototype Surprise

The domain experts want to see how the system looks to make sure that they have communicated their requirements successfully, so you complete a prototype of the system. At the presentation of the prototype, the group expresses its appreciation. You've spent many late hours to get to this point and are glad to hear the domain experts are happy with it. Your happiness turns sour, however, when they tell you how glad they are that you are almost finished. They had read about how easy Visual Basic is to use, and just knew the project estimate you had given was bloated. The pressure is now on you to throw more code onto the prototype to complete the project.

For some insight here, let's look back on our construction metaphor. Would anyone ask a building contractor to take the architectural model and just tack a bit more plywood onto it to create an office building? What would happen? A little wood could be tacked on here and there, and things would be fine. Then a little more wood, and it wouldn't take too long for the roof to wobble and the walls to fall in. Why? Because no internal structure exists to correctly hold the pieces together. The same happens with the software. Some amount of code can be added to the prototype with no problem. As more and more code is added, however, it becomes increasingly difficult to modify and manage the routines. Soon it seems the code is falling in on you.

You need to explain to the domain experts that they are looking at a prototype with nothing really holding it up, like a great facade on a soundstage. Why were they misled by the prototype?

The object-oriented approach presents ways to include the domain experts throughout the analysis phase. Doing so allows them to learn more about the complexities of software development and the required processes. This helps you manage domain expert expectations and prevents the prototype surprise.

Managing the Complexity of Programming

Now for the fun part. You get to write code.

You have it all in your head. You know exactly where everything is. You write more code. Things are starting to get messy. Days go by as you write more and more code. Now you can't remember which code file has which routine. Functions are calling functions that call other functions. Something you added broke another routine. Now you are no longer confident that the next change will not break something else. The code is falling down around you, and you start to wonder whether you need to redesign and start the coding over. But the deadline...

An object-oriented approach to development helps you manage the complexity of programming. It provides logic and order in how the pieces of an application are put together: a place for every routine, and every routine in its place. This makes the development process more efficient, because you know where code should be developed and what that code should do.

Simplifying Multiprogrammer Development

Management is worried about meeting scheduling commitments, so more programmers have been added to the project. You ask yourself, "Which parts of this mess can be divided up and given to someone else? How will they know when to call which of my routines?" Maybe you can just give these additional programmers that dreaded piece called "reports." Nothing else seems easily separated from the whole.

You need a clean way to segment the application. To ensure effective use of multiple programmers, these segments must be independent so that the programmers don't end up interfering with each other (and with you) as they develop their parts of the application. The application's internal structure needs walls between the segments—walls with doors.

Walls keep the segments from interfering with each other, and doors provide a mechanism for communication between the segments. The object-oriented approach builds the walls by defining independent, encapsulated classes. The objects from these classes interact with other objects only through the public interfaces that are defined as the doors, thus simplifying multiple-programmer development.

Adapting to Change

Ever have any requirements change during a project? Yesterday the vice president of sales met with Acme Widget Company, so the goal of your application was to manage the production of widgets. Today she met with ABC Paper Company, so now the goal of the application is to build a paper production management system.

Okay, maybe your requirements don't change that much, but they do change. You are then asked to assess the scope of the change. How do you tell the difference between a minor change and a major one? How can you determine which routines are affected?

Any changes in requirements often result in large amounts of rework or attempts to adapt the code to do something for which it just wasn't designed. This would be easier if the design were more clearly defined and therefore more adaptable.

The classes in an object-oriented design describe independent, well-defined entities. Making those classes encapsulated keeps the implementation hidden from the rest of the system, so it is more flexible and can more easily be adapted to change.

Managing Special Orders

The vice president of sales is back. This time she wants you to implement one database structure for users who buy the single-user version of the product and a different database for users who buy the multiuser version. You start thinking about the configuration nightmare of keeping two sets of code current.

Regardless of the client-specific change that is needed, you'd rather have one set of code. That code would have to be smart enough to include the correct routines based on those client-specific requirements. Using an object-oriented approach (and the architectural structure defined in the next chapter), you can make your application that smart and manage those special orders.

Preparing Interim Deliveries

The quality assurance/quality control group is starting to ask for completed pieces. You try to explain that nothing is really ready to be tested. You tell them they will get something as soon as the system is operational.

The documentation group files into your office next. They want some pieces that work so that they can begin the online help and user documentation. They cannot wait until everything is finished before they start, or they won't have the manuals ready in time for the first customer ship date.

The object-oriented approach allows you to build independent classes that can be combined for an interim delivery. This allows you to provide incremental deliveries for independent testing and documentation.

Measuring Progress

The project manager comes in for a status check. You report that the application is 80% complete. The project manager frowns and asks why it has been 80% complete for two weeks. You explain that you had to build some other parts and those required additional changes to the system. The project manager goes back to update the schedule, wondering which scheduled task should include the time required for these new parts. You guessed at the schedule, and now it is coming back to haunt you. Your project plan was unable to anticipate all the work that needed to be done.

The object-oriented approach allows you to define classes of your application and map these classes to identifiable and measurable tasks on the schedule. You can then more accurately estimate the time required to develop each of these classes and can more easily assess your progress.

Managing Maintenance

The application has finally shipped! Now you are assigned to a new project. Three months later your boss tells you that minor but critical maintenance must be done on your previous project. You look at the finished code and wonder whether you were really the person who wrote most of it. It is messy and difficult to follow.

The revisions are moving along slowly, and you are getting frustrated. Because the code is so disorganized, you are far into the changes before you realize that this supposedly minor fix will be a major effort. You are lost in the code's details. You make changes here and there, realizing that this means the entire application must be retested.

The classes in an object-oriented design describe independent, well-defined entities. Encapsulating the classes keeps the implementation hidden from the rest of the system, so it is more flexible and can be more easily adapted to change. You can then make modifications with minimal effect on the entire system, simplifying the change and the retesting.

Reusing Code

Back on your current project, you find that you need to include a few features in your new application that you had developed in your old one. Instead of rewriting these, you decide to copy them to this project, but now you have two identical sets of code to maintain.

Following an object-oriented approach, your common code can be built once and then reused in every application that needs it. Taking this a step or two further, you can buy or build an entire framework to define the basic infrastructure of your application and use all this code in every application you build.

A framework can include a base form class that defines the basic processing that every form in your application needs to support. For example, if the domain experts want each control to turn color when the control gets focus, you can write this code in a base form class, and every form that inherits from this base form gets this behavior. A base form class that supports this feature is detailed in Chapter 4.

A framework can also include base classes for your business objects, providing basic functionality that all your business objects need, such as tracking business object state (new, updated, deleted) and handling validation. A base business object class is detailed in Chapter 5.

The other key element of a framework is a common code library. For example, code to perform logging can be included in a code library.

Finally, a framework can include productivity tools. You can add your own code snippets to the built-in snippet library or build your own data visualizers to easily view complex data during debugging.

With Visual Basic, you can create your own reusable code, framework, and tools. In addition, a large, third-party vendor community provides all kinds of frameworks, tools, and add-ons. These include controls such as grids, database objects for manipulating data, code-generation tools, and other productivity add-ons. The third-party products and your own code are object-oriented, making them easy to reuse in your application. This can provide significant time savings in getting an application operational.

Conclusion

What Did This Chapter Cover?

This chapter introduced object-oriented concepts and terminology. It then demonstrated some basics of using object-oriented concepts in Visual Basic.

This chapter covered the following key topics:

- Visual Basic for .NET is significantly different from prior versions of Visual Basic.
- Since Visual Basic and the .NET Framework follow object-oriented principles, understanding object orientation is crucial to fully understanding these tools.
- Using an object-oriented approach to designing and building an application focuses on the objects relevant to that application and how they interact within the system. This focus allows you to manage the complexities of today's software.

- An object can be thought of as an actor with a distinct role (defined with properties) and responsibilities (defined with methods). The actor performs with other actors, each with their own roles and responsibilities, to present an organized and cohesive result.
- A scenario describes the process within which the objects are used. This helps you define the appropriate set of properties and methods, and recognize the object relationships. Carrying on the acting metaphor, you can think of the scenarios as the script, defining how the actors of the production interact.
- A class is a template, defining all the properties and methods associated with objects from the class, including their implementation.
- Abstraction focuses on the objects important for the application, not on their implementation. This approach allows you to perform the high-level design using the language of the business instead of using programming terminology.
- Encapsulation involves hiding the private properties and the implementation of the methods. The properties and methods are then accessed through a defined public interface.
- Inheritance provides a mechanism for attaining reuse by defining common functionality and extracting it into a base class.
- Polymorphism allows object members that perform similar functions to have the same name but different implementations.
- Object-oriented analysis involves developing a high-level model of the domain. This requires working with the domain experts to define the objects and scenarios.
- Object-oriented design converts the logical domain model into an implementation model providing the class-level detail needed to develop the application.
- Object-oriented programming involves building your application as a set of classes. Objects from these classes act together to perform all desired processing. This is different from a traditional view, in which a program is viewed as a collection of functions that perform a process. In OOP, each object performs actions, processes data, and works with other objects.
- An object-oriented approach has many benefits. The best way to realize these benefits is to work through the remainder of this book!

The next chapter provides a methodology to help you through the process of software analysis and design.

Building Along

It is often easier to learn by doing rather than by just reading. This book includes "building along" activities that allow you to work through the concepts and techniques.

The next chapter introduces and designs a Purchase Tracker application. The subsequent chapters detail each step of building the Purchase Tracker application with explanations, examples, and "building along" activities. Each "building along" activity provides step-by-step instructions for building a particular feature of the application or using a particular technique.

If you work through the entire book, you will have an operational Purchase Tracker application that you can use as a starting point for other applications you build.

Additional Reading

Beck, Kent. *Extreme Programming Explained: Embrace Change*. Upper Saddle River, NJ: Addison-Wesley, 2000.

This is the classic book on Extreme Programming. It defines techniques for development that allow you to define your application as small sets of functionality, which you can rapidly develop and test.

Booch, Grady. *Object-Oriented Analysis and Design with Applications*, Second Edition. Redwood City, CA: The Benjamin/Cummings Publishing Company, 1994.

Booch provides an academic discussion of object-oriented design concepts. He then presents a specific notation and methodology for object-oriented design and applies them to several case studies implemented in C++.

Fowler, Martin. *Patterns of Enterprise Application Architecture*. Boston, MA. Addison-Wesley, 2002.

Enterprise projects often contain similar design ideas that have proven effective in dealing with the inevitable complexity of enterprise applications. This book is a starting point to capture these design ideas as patterns. The book is organized in two parts, with the first part a set of narrative chapters on a number of important topics in the design of enterprise applications. These chapters introduce various problems in the architecture of enterprise applications and their solutions. The details of the solutions are in the second part, organized as patterns.

Freeman, Eric, Elisabeth Freeman, Kathy Sierra, and Burt Bates. *Head First Design Patterns*. Sebastopol, CA: O'Reilly, 2004.

If you are new to design patterns, this book provides a very easy-to-understand description of patterns and provides both good and bad examples of implementing patterns.

Gamma, Erich, Richard Helm, Ralph Johnson, and John Vlissides. *Design Patterns: Elements of Reusable Object-Oriented Software*. Reading, MA: Addison-Wesley, 1995.

This book, fondly referred to as the "gang of four book" after the four authors, presents a collection of common object-oriented design problems, along with patterns for solving those problems. This is the *classic* book on design patterns. It defines the concept of design patterns and then catalogs the set of Creational, Structural, and Behavioral patterns.

Taylor, David. *Object-Oriented Technology: A Manager's Guide*, Second Edition. Reading, MA: Addison-Wesley, 1997.

Taylor provides a good description of object-oriented techniques from a manager's perspective. If your boss just does not get OO, this is a great book to start with. And its fun style and small size make it manageable, even for someone too busy to read technical books.

Wells, Don. "Extreme Programming: a Gentle Introduction." 17 January, 2006. http://www.extremeprogramming.org/.

This Web site is a good place to start if you are interested in learning more about Extreme Programming.

Try It!

Here are a few suggestions for trying some of the techniques presented in this chapter:

1. The next time you get into your car, think about object-oriented concepts:
   - Notice that the gas pedal is an abstraction for the complex process of converting gasoline into forward motion.
   - Think about how the objects that comprise the car are encapsulated. Look at the radio. It provides behaviors such as finding a station, playing music, and increasing or decreasing the volume. The last selected volume and station are properties of the radio object. Identify other objects in the car, and define the behaviors and properties of those objects.

- The brake has a push behavior, as does the gas pedal. What other polymorphisms can you find in the car?
- The car has many reusable components. That was the revolution that resulted in the Model T and most automobile manufacturing and repair since then. Think about the benefits of reusable components.

2. Look around you, and think about other real-world objects and how they follow object-oriented principles.
3. Try visualizing one of your current applications in terms of objects and classes.

CHAPTER 2

DESIGNING SOFTWARE

Therefore, we may reasonably conclude that no matter how sophisticated the design method, no matter how well-founded its theoretical basis, we cannot ignore the practical aspects of designing systems for the real world.
—**Grady Booch, *Object-Oriented Design with Applications***

It is not enough to understand the theoretical aspects of object-oriented analysis and design. You need to consider practical aspects of the software process as well. A perfectly formed object model is useless if it takes so long to define that the business changes before you complete the model. A fully-detailed design is worthless if it takes so long that, to meet the schedule, development starts concurrent with the design. ("Sam, you go talk to the users; Jessica, you start the coding.")

Then there are the steps that are often not considered to be part of object-oriented analysis (OOA) and object-oriented design (OOD), such as user interface design and database design. These too need to be thought out, preferably before a significant amount of development is under way.

This chapter presents a pragmatic software design methodology to help you quickly and efficiently analyze and design your applications for the real world. This methodology provides easy-to-follow steps to help you and your project team collect requirements, perform the design (including user interface, database, and classes), define an architecture, and prepare for development. To illustrate the design process, this chapter introduces a sample application that is then built throughout the remaining chapters.

The Purpose of Design

Visual Studio and Visual Basic make it easy to develop an application without any real forethought. You can just add forms to your project, double-click on the forms and add code, then keep modifying the code until it works, and modify it further until it actually performs the required tasks. This may work if your application is very small (two or three forms). But this technique can become very impractical very quickly.

Without a design, you have no plan or strategy for the application's development. Without a design, you are building the application based on guesses about what the users need. When you deliver a guess-based application, you then need to modify it until it really does what the users need. This can lead to extended development times and much frustration for you and your users.

Thinking through the design before you build ensures that you are building the right application. It helps you understand what the application is supposed to do. It assists you in communicating with the domain experts about the application requirements. It helps you select the appropriate architecture and set of technologies for the application. It identifies the data that the application needs and how to work with it. And it sets you on a path that allows you to build more in less time.

The amount of time you spend on the application's design depends on the application's complexity. You would spend a great deal of time and money designing a new home, for example, but not much time or money designing a tree house for the kids. The same applies to your application. You may not spend much time designing the application to track the team scores for your bowling league, but you will want to take the time to do a careful design of your company's order entry/inventory/invoicing application.

Remember, however, that small projects don't always stay that way. Designing small projects with the same care as large ones can pay off with a foundation that supports future enhancements. Otherwise, you could reach that dreaded quagmire called rewrite and find that you need to start the whole process over!

You may be thinking you really don't have time for design. Management wants the application finished in weeks, not months. But it is possible to work through the design process very quickly if you follow a good design methodology.

A design methodology helps you develop a plan for defining the design. Using a methodology, you can logically and efficiently think through all aspects of the design. A methodology is not a cookbook in which you follow specific instructions and have a design when you are finished. A methodology provides guidelines and a path. As you proceed down that path, you use your experience and knowledge to create the design.

Many design methodologies assume you need to design all aspects of every possible feature of an application before you can begin to build it. This is not necessarily true. If you can define an architecture for your application that supports change and allows future modifications to be easily implemented, you can design and build the application in small pieces. Because each piece is relatively small, you can deliver it quickly.

In actuality, the software design process involves incomplete information at every step. It would be great if design were deterministic from beginning to end, if you could know every detail before you begin. But this is not practical. If your design process insists that complete information be collected at every step, your project will quickly experience analysis paralysis.

If you design smaller pieces and implement an architecture that easily supports change, you can readily accept that information is incomplete. Your project then becomes nimble, and you achieve progress much more quickly.

You can design the first piece of the application with the information you collect and then develop it, design the second piece of the application and then develop it, and so on. If you have separate teams working on the design and development, the steps can overlap. So, the developers on the team can begin developing the first piece while the designers are working on the design of the second piece. The developers can then build the second piece while the designers are designing the third piece, and so on.

Much of these just-in-time design, build for change, and iterative development concepts stem from what has become known as Extreme Programming (XP). The following quote summarizes the basics of XP:

> "So you code because if you don't code, you haven't done anything. You test because if you don't test, you don't know when you are done coding. You listen because if you don't listen you don't know what to code or what to test. And you design so you can keep coding and testing and listening indefinitely." —Kent Beck

For more information on XP, see the "Additional Reading" section of Chapter 1, "Introduction to OO in .NET."

The GUIDS Methodology

The list of application requirements may seem unattainable, and the user interface (UI) possibilities can seem infinite. It may not be obvious how to convert the requirements into a design and then the design into code. But these tasks are not difficult if you have a methodology for working through this process.

The GUIDS (pronounced "guides") Methodology is a pragmatic approach to software analysis and design. It incorporates object-oriented principles and other real-world concepts such as user interface design. It is independent of language or toolset, so it can be used with any software project.

The GUIDS Methodology is so named because each letter of GUIDS represents a phase in the process:

- **Goal-centered design** defines the basic goal of the application, the scenarios required to meet that goal, and the associated business objects.
- **User interface design** details the look and feel.
- **Implementation-centered design** describes the architecture and detailed class design.
- **Data design** specifies the database, including the tables and fields, and any other data stores.
- **Strategies for construction** outlines the strategies for the construction phase, including project planning and scheduling, source code control, testing, and so on.

The following sections provide details on each of these phases.

NOTE: Although this chapter refers frequently to the design of a new application, the steps of the GUIDS Methodology are equally valid when designing new features for an existing application.

Goal-Centered Design

Software development would be so easy if the users could just tell you what they want. Then you could go back to your office and, without further interruption, code it and deliver the completed application to them. It would be exactly what they had asked for. They'd love it, and everyone would live happily ever after. Well, life doesn't work that way, and neither does software development.

Users cannot tell you what they want. They can tell you what they do and what they think a software application should do, but they cannot tell you what they really want. Have you ever delivered an application that followed a defined specification, only to have the users say, "That wasn't exactly what I was looking for"?

The purpose of the goal-centered design ("G") phase of the GUIDS Methodology is to help you figure out what the users really want. Because the users cannot adequately tell you want they want, you have to convert what the users tell you into the actual application requirements.

NOTE: Although it's called goal-centered *design*, this phase is often considered an analysis phase because its focus is analyzing the application requirements.

The "G" phase is composed of the following steps:

- Define the primary goal of the application.
- Define the use cases based on the goal.
- Break the application into manageable feature sets.
- Detail the scenarios included in the current feature set.
- Identify the business objects and optionally build a domain model.

The remainder of this section details these steps. When these steps are complete, you will have a better understanding of the application's purpose and the tasks that the user must perform when using the application.

The result of the "G" phase is a design document that defines the goal statement, scenarios, business objects, and an optional domain model. The scenarios in this document are used during the user interface design phase to define the appropriate user interface required to perform each task.

They are used in the implementation-centered design phase to define all the classes the application requires. They are used in the data design phase to ensure that the data stores support all the required scenarios. And they provide the outline for a functional test plan.

NOTE: Historically, the document resulting from this type of analysis phase has been called a requirements specification, project analysis document, functional specification, or problem statement. Regardless of its name, this document forms the basis of the application's design.

By defining the goal and scenarios for your application, you can ensure that you understand what to build before you build it.

Defining the Primary Goal

When you start on a software project, someone gives you a brief description of the project. "We need a new application that does x" or "Modify the abc application so it does that" or "The users from accounting put in a request for a new application" or (rarely) "Here is the completed specification for the xyz application." Regardless of the level of detail you receive at this point, the first thing you need to understand is the purpose of the application you are building.

Start with the information you are provided, contact the appropriate domain experts as needed, and write a goal statement. The goal statement is normally short (one or two sentences) and reflects the application's main purpose.

Don't expect the domain experts or users to write the goal statement for you. In the words of Alan Cooper in *About Face: The Essentials of User Interface Design*:

> "Contrary to what you might suspect, few users are consciously aware of their goals: While it is the user's job to focus on tasks, the designer's job is to look beyond the task to identify the user's goals. Therein lies the key to creating the most effective software solutions."

Let's walk through an example.

You are asked to develop a Purchase Tracker application to track all the company's customers and their purchases. It tracks customer information so that the company knows who its customers are. It tracks products so that the company knows what products it has available for purchase. And it tracks which customers purchased which products. This information supplies the sales team with details on the products purchased by different customers, indicating what other products the customer may be interested in purchasing.

After discussions with the domain experts, you define the application's primary goal as follows:

> The primary goal of the Purchase Tracker application is to track customers and products and allow the sales department to view the set of products purchased by a customer.

When you have a draft of the primary goal, review it with the project sponsors and domain experts. This ensures that there is no miscommunication as to the application's main purpose. The goal statement sets the project's scope by defining the high-level set of features that the application will support.

Defining the Use Cases

The goal is a good place to start, but it does not define all the features that the application must provide. The next step is to define the features as high-level use cases. A **use case** is a possible use of the application from the user's perspective.

NOTE: The terms "use case" and "scenario" are often used interchangeably. However, there is a key difference between the two. A **use case** defines a possible use of the application. A **scenario** is the set of steps involved in a use case.

Normally, there is one use case for each primary task a user must perform. To define these tasks, you need further interviews with the users, domain experts, and management.

To collect information from the users, you could follow a **user-centered** approach whereby you ask the users what they need and define those needs as the application requirements. The primary problem with this approach is that most of the time the users don't really know what they need. They may know what they do and have some idea of how the computer can make their job easier or more productive. But frequently, they don't really know how an application can help them.

Sometimes users do not even know the primary business goal being met by the tasks they are performing. They do the task this way because it has always been done this way, so they think the application should do it this way as well. However, the current process may not make sense in an automated system.

A better way to define project requirements is to take a **goal-centered** approach. This approach requires that you investigate further with the users and domain experts to establish the true goals behind the defined needs. These goals are then used to morph the defined needs into project requirements. The primary difference between this approach and the user-centered approach is that with this approach *you* have to dig deeper to the real goals instead of just asking the users.

A simple example can illustrate this point. Say your users are the salespeople who make calls to customers. As you are defining the requirements for a Purchase Tracker application, the users state the requirement: "We currently e-mail the accounting department if a customer's contact name has changed. It would be nice if the system sent this e-mail automatically." By digging further into this need, you find that the true goal is to ensure that the contact name is updated in the accounting database. The goal-centered requirement can then be stated: "Keep the accounting data current with customer data." This allows more efficient solutions, such as automatically creating a transaction to update the accounting data when a contact name is changed. This saves the company time and money both in the sales department, since they no longer need to send an e-mail, and in the accounting department, since they no longer need to receive the e-mail and manually adjust their records.

Several types of users may use the application. In the Purchase Tracker example, support staff enters customer and product information; external customers can maintain and view their own information; salespeople view desired purchase data; management gets reports; and another internal system is a user of product data. Including each of these different types of users, sometimes called **actors**, in this step helps ensure that you define all the appropriate use cases for the application.

NOTE: In the book *About Face*, Alan Cooper recommends giving each user profile a name: Vic the VP who has trouble with computers or Sal the busy salesperson. (See the "Additional Reading" section for information on Cooper's book.) This approach helps you think about the system's users and provides a context for the usage scenarios without getting personal by using real people's names and information.

For the Purchase Tracker example, the use cases are defined as follows:

- Support staff maintains customer information.
- Customers maintain their information.
- Support staff maintains product information.
- The inventory system obtains product information.
- Salespeople view purchases for their customers.
- Management receives reports on customer purchases and product statistics.
- Customers view their past purchases.

How many use cases you define depends on what your application must do. You can have anywhere from a few dozen to hundreds of use cases.

Be sure to write down the use cases so that you can easily refer to them throughout the project life cycle. Some designers indicate which specific user(s) provided input into each use case for tracking purposes.

Breaking the Application into Feature Sets

The days when software development projects included a year for analysis and design are all but gone. In today's fast-paced world, the business would change too much before the design were complete. And with the video game generation entering the workplace, the expectation is that new software is available *now*, not a year from now.

One of the best ways to create great software quickly is to break it into smaller pieces, with each piece defined as a separately scheduled project. The resulting smaller project is easier to manage, has less risk, and has a greater chance of success. It is easier to get that second project approved when the first project was a success!

NOTE: To prevent confusion between the word "project" used here to mean a unit of work and the word "project" meaning a separately compiled set of Visual Studio files, the term **unit of work** is used from this point forward to refer to the set of features included in one scheduled project.

Take the set of use cases defined in the prior step and define a unit of work. You can organize (group) *all* the use cases into appropriate logical units of work. Or you can just focus on the *first* unit of work and select the use cases to be done first, reevaluating the remaining use cases after the first unit of work is complete. Waiting to define the later units of work until you are ready to work on them gives you more flexibility to adjust priorities based on current corporate or user needs.

You then design only the use cases defined in the first unit of work. By designing a smaller piece of the application, you can more easily get focused information from the domain experts. It is easier to ask for details on one feature than for all of them at once. (You get better answers to "What customer information do you need to maintain?" than to "What do you want the new system to do?")

By designing and then developing smaller pieces, you can show more frequent progress. And, depending on the application and feature set, you may be able to provide interim deliverables. **Interim deliverables** are completed pieces of the application that can be delivered even though the entire application is not complete.

NOTE: Some project managers think that interim deliverables require too much work and are not worth the trouble. However, interim deliverables help with one of the most misunderstood words in software development—"done." Does "done" mean that you've finished the code entry? The syntax checking? You got it to compile? Or have you really finished every detail, from the tab order to the technical documentation to the lowest-level algorithms? Having interim deliverables provides a method of determining how "done" everything is at multiple points in the development cycle for the complete application.

Each unit of work does *not* have to be delivered *to the users*. If the set of features cannot be deployed without features from other units of work, you can complete the unit of work without delivering it to the users. For example, you could define a first unit of work to build the user interface for making purchases and a second unit of work to process payments. In this example, it does not make sense to deliver the first unit of work to the users, because it cannot be used without the second unit of work. You instead deploy both after completing the second unit of work.

Even though you may not deliver a unit of work to the users, defining the units of work still provides the benefits of an easier design process and getting to "done" on features of the application. It also allows you to deliver the features for testing and user documentation (if required) so that those tasks don't need to wait until just before deployment.

Although it sounds easy, selecting the appropriate set of use cases for a unit of work can be a challenging process. It is often not enough to prioritize and start with the highest-priority features, because the highest-priority features may depend on lesser-priority items.

In the Purchase Tracker application, for example, the highest-priority item is a customer's purchase history. But you can't produce the purchase history without first having customers, products, and purchases.

It would make more sense to deliver product tracking first. This would allow the users to start managing the set of products. A second unit of work could be the customer tracking, allowing users to start tracking customers. And so on.

You also need to consider the size of the pieces and the size of your team. The product tracking and customer tracking features may be too small to specify as two separate units of work. Combine scenarios to define units of work that are of a reasonable size. Depending on your team and corporate environment, a reasonable size may be anywhere from one to three weeks of work.

In evaluating the Purchase Tracker sample application scenarios, the first unit of work includes product maintenance, customer maintenance, and view of purchases. It does not include features for the customers to maintain or view their information, interfaces with other systems (such as inventory or accounting), or management reports. These are reserved for later units of work.

By organizing the use cases into manageable units, you can tackle smaller pieces. This allows you to get better information during the design and more quickly show results during development.

Detailing the Scenarios

Once you've picked a set of use cases that describe a cohesive subset of application features defined as a unit of work, you are ready to collect more design detail. It is time to flesh out each selected use case and detail it as scenarios. Scenarios provide the level of detail required to turn the use cases into a user interface and define the associated business logic.

A single use case can have one or more scenarios (sets of steps) associated with it. In the Purchase Tracker example, the "Support staff maintains customer information" use case may have a scenario for creating a new customer, updating an existing customer, and deleting a customer.

Each step in a scenario is normally of the form subject + verb + object. The subject defines who performs the step, the verb defines what is done, and the object defines what is affected. Notice that this defines *what* is done but not necessarily *how* the application will do it.

Also, a scenario defines what is done to perform the task within the context of the new application, not how the task is currently performed. This distinction is important because you don't want to get bogged down in "It's always been that way." There may be a better way.

Using the Purchase Tracker example, the "Support staff updates an existing customer" scenario is detailed as follows:

1. Support staff selects a customer to update.
2. The system retrieves the data for the selected customer and displays it.
3. The support staff can update any of the following data:
   - First Name
   - Last Name (required)
   - Address
   - City
   - State (a two-letter abbreviation)
   - Zip Code (required; a required minimum of five characters, plus four optional characters): Changing the zip code may reassign the customer's sales representative. The user should be notified of this.
   - Phone (an empty or valid phone number, entered with or without the parentheses and hyphens)
4. The support staff selects to save the changes.
5. The system saves the changes.

6. If the zip code was modified and the assigned sales representative changes due to this modification, the system notifies the sales representative associated with the original zip code and the sales representative associated with the new zip code.

Notice that step 1 does not define how this step happens. Will there be a search feature? A combo box with a list of customers? A grid with all customer data? These decisions are ignored at this point, allowing the conversation with the domain experts to focus on the *what* without concern for the *how*. (The user interface design, discussed in the next section, answers these *how* questions.)

Step 3 defines the data that must be managed for a customer. This includes validation requirements for that data and any business rules that the data must follow. Notice that the scenario assumes that the customer is an individual and not a company, since no company affiliation information is collected. It is important to clarify assumptions and collect as much detail as possible on the data requirements as part of the scenario process.

NOTE: It is best not to duplicate the definition of data for similar scenarios in the design documentation. Duplication can cause the definitions to become inconsistent. Instead, other scenarios can reference the scenario that describes the data. For example, the "Support staff creates a new customer" scenario would refer to the update scenario for the definition of the data to be created for a customer.

You may have noticed that step 6 identifies a new use case for managing the set of salespeople and their associated territories defined by zip code. The process of detailing your scenarios often leads to identification of new use cases. You then need to decide whether the new use case fits in with the current set of features you are designing or whether it will be added to the list for a future unit of work.

If you are familiar with the Unified Modeling Language (UML), you can model these use cases and scenarios visually. For more information on UML, see the "Additional Reading" section.

When you are finished detailing and documenting the scenarios for each use case in the current unit of work, you have the specifications you need to understand the application features you will be building. Validate this design by reviewing the scenarios with the domain experts. It should be easy for the domain experts to review the design, because the scenarios are written in terms of the business, not in technical terms.

Identifying the Business Objects

Business objects define the things involved with the application. Since the development process technically involves building classes and creating objects from those classes and not building scenarios, it is helpful at this point to use the scenarios to identify the business objects, define their properties and methods, and look at how they interact. This can help you further understand how the pieces of the application will fit together.

NOTE: Some methodologies require that you detail the objects before defining the scenarios. The order of these two steps is less important than ensuring that you do both steps. And in most cases, you may find that you go back and forth between the two steps as you detail scenarios and identify objects.

To identify the business objects, start with the basic things, or **objects**, with which the application must work. The easiest way to select these objects is to evaluate the nouns from the scenarios. If the noun describes an important thing in the application, it is a potential object.

NOTE: Technically, you are defining business *classes* at this point. But by convention these are called business *objects*.

As you identify each object, define what it is. This may seem obvious, but you may find that the definition of something as simple as a customer is not consistent for all users. For example, the sales department may consider anyone who *could* buy something to be a customer, whereas the accounting department considers only people who *have* bought something to be customers.

In the Purchase Tracker example, the objects are customer, product, and purchase. These are the nouns from the scenarios included in the first unit of work (assuming that the sales representative is handled in a later unit of work). A customer is defined as an individual who has purchased one or more of our products. A product is any item we sell. Each purchase is a single customer buying any quantity of one of our products. If a customer purchases more than one product, more than one purchase is defined.

For each object, define the data elements for which the object is responsible. These are called the **properties** of the object. Use the scenarios to review the data required by each object.

For the Purchase Tracker example, the customer object requires data to track the customer's first and last name, full address, and phone number.

Then define the business logic for which the object is responsible. This can include operations the object performs, data manipulation the object requires, support functions the object provides, or interactions the object allows. These are called the **methods** of the object. Start with the verbs in the scenarios to define possible methods.

For the Purchase Tracker example, the customer object must be retrieved and saved.

If desired, you can document each object on an index card, as shown in Figure 2.1. On each card, write the object name, its purpose or role, its properties, and its methods. This provides an effective method of documenting the objects, especially if this process is done as a group. Or you can just add this information to the design document in textual form.

NOTE: The idea of using index cards for object-oriented design was originally proposed by Kent Beck and Ward Cunningham (see the "Additional Reading" section). They call them Class-Responsibility-Collaboration (CRC) cards. These cards contained the class name, responsibilities of an instance of the class, and a list of the classes that collaborate with this class.

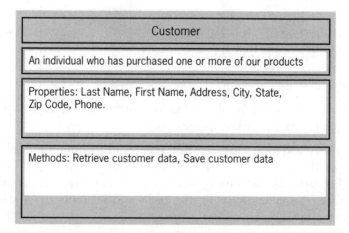

Figure 2.1 The customer object card for the Purchase Tracker application describes the object and lists its properties and methods.

You can draw the resulting objects as a domain model. A **domain model** is a visual representation of the business area (domain) described by the application. It depicts the associated objects and their relationships. At this point, the domain model may represent only part of the application, because it includes only the objects defined for the current unit of work. You can add to the model as you work through later units of work.

To build a domain model, draw each object as a box divided into three sections. Indicate the name of the object at the top of the box, the list of properties in the middle, and the methods at the bottom.

Draw lines between the boxes to represent the relationships between the objects. For example, a customer makes a purchase and a product is purchased. Figure 2.2 shows these relationships.

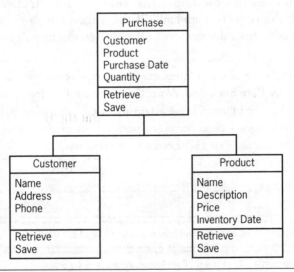

Figure 2.2   This simplified domain model visually summarizes the objects in the current unit of work for the Purchase Tracker application.

There are tools that can help you build a domain model, such as Visio. The model in Figure 2.2 was created using Microsoft PowerPoint. Visual Studio also provides a tool you can use to create this model called the Class Designer. See Chapter 6, "Class Tools and Techniques," for more information on the Class Designer.

Defining the set of objects along with their properties and methods helps clarify the things involved in the application. Validate the objects by walking through the scenarios. Ensure that each entity referenced by the scenarios is defined as an object, that every data element is a property of one of the objects, and that every action is defined as a method of one of the objects. After the objects are validated against the scenarios, add this information to your design documentation.

Summary

The goal-centered design phase steps you through the process of analyzing the application requirements. You define those requirements as a set of use cases, scenarios, and objects.

The first step is to define the application's purpose or goal. That gives you information on the needs that the application fills and the business processes it must perform. Then, focusing on that goal, define the usage scenarios to describe the application's features and how the users use those features to achieve the application objectives.

Organize the use cases into logical units of work that you can design and develop quickly. For the current unit of work, detail each use case as a set of scenarios or steps that the user must perform to complete the usage objective. Finally, identify the business objects involved in the scenarios. The business objects provide a first look at the things you need to build in your application.

When you complete this process, you have a design document that states the application's goal, lists the use cases, and details the scenarios and objects for the first unit of work.

User Interface Design

If users use your application during the majority of their work time, they could be spending more time with your application than with their families. So anything you can do to make that time more enjoyable....

Usability is one of the key factors of a good user interface design. Fitness for purpose is other key factor: the user interface must accomplish its objective. It must provide the user with a way to complete the tasks identified in the scenarios, which you defined in the prior phase of the design.

The scenarios summarize the tasks that the application (or unit of work) must perform. They define the *what*. The next step is to define the *how* from the user's perspective. How will the user search for a customer

2. DESIGNING SOFTWARE

or display the list of purchases? (The *how* from the developer's perspective is covered in the next phase.)

The purpose of the user interface design ("U") phase of the GUIDS Methodology is to help you convert the scenarios into a visual design. It details steps for defining the look and feel, navigation, and layout of the visual elements of your application.

The "U" phase is composed of the following steps:

- Define the conceptual user interface design.
- Define the navigation techniques.
- Design the form layouts.
- Optionally, build a prototype.

NOTE: It is sometimes tempting to skip the "G" phase and go right to creating the user interface prototype. Developing the visual part of the application is often the most fun and elicits the most excitement from the user community. It may even have been what you were asked to do: "This is the list of features we want; create a prototype." But you cannot design a good user interface without first understanding the true application requirements. So take a few hours and create the scenarios as defined in the preceding section before you move on to the user interface.

The remainder of this section details these steps. When these steps are complete, you have the design of the application's visual elements.

The result of the "U" phase is a design document that describes the application's visual design. Create this document using screen shots and a written description of the behavior of the form elements. You can lay out the designs using any number of tools. You can use Visual Studio and actually build the forms. Some user interface designers prefer to use graphic design tools such as Adobe Photoshop or Paint Shop Pro for this design process. Other designers prefer products such as Microsoft PowerPoint or just paper and pencil. The tool does not matter as long as the design provides the details needed to build the user interface.

With this document (and optional prototype), the users and domain experts can better visualize the application (or unit of work) and provide feedback on any missing features or incorrect scenarios.

Defining the Conceptual User Interface Design

An application is significantly easier to use if it has a standard and consistent look and feel. A conceptual user interface design defines that look and feel. The conceptual design describes the basic look of the forms, how they interact, and how basic user functions are performed.

It is the job of the user interface designer (which may be you) to define the application's basic look and feel. Do not ask the users what they want the application to look like. Instead, provide them with a conceptual design following basic Windows or Web standards.

When you go to buy a car, for example, you don't want the salesperson to ask you what you want the car to look like. It would be hard and very time-consuming to define all aspects of what you want the car to look and feel like. And what would happen if you defined something that just wasn't possible?

By taking on the task of designing the user interface, you also prevent design by consensus. When the design is done with too many people involved, it can end up inconsistent, with too many concessions required to get everyone's buy-in. With consistency being one of the key factors in usability, it is much better to have one or two people involved with the conceptual user interface design and to have all the other users and domain experts limited to providing feedback.

As you develop the conceptual design, consider these factors:

- **Windows or Web or both?** The standards used for Windows user interfaces are not the same as those used for Web UIs. So it is important to consider which portions of your user interface will be Windows and which will be Web. If you will provide both, you need two conceptual models.
- **What kinds of forms are needed?** Most applications have some type of data entry forms, some summary forms, and possibly some search or select forms. Be sure to include one of each kind in the conceptual design.
- **What common elements are needed?** For each type of form, define any common elements that the form needs and how those elements behave. For example, a data entry form needs elements to allow for operations such as new, save, or delete. How are these operations shown? Should they be on a menu, toolbar, or both? Should the save operation clear the form for entry/selection of

another entity? Should it close the form after every save? Or should it keep the contents of the form as is? Should there be a status message when a save is complete? Defining the common elements and their behavior as part of the conceptual design standardizes the look and feel of these common operations.

- **How should validation be handled?** Most applications are too restrictive with regard to validation. In many cases, an application can be more forgiving. If the user does not fill in all the data entry fields, it should still be an acceptable entry, and the user should be able to save. If there is a problem, provide a way for the user to see the error and have an easy way to correct it. For example, validation errors can be displayed with an error icon or in a panel on the screen without interrupting the user's flow.

- **What should the entities be called?** Consistency and familiarity with terminology used on the forms can have a large impact on your application's usability. Use terms familiar to the business, and use consistent terms throughout. For example, don't use *customer* on one screen and *buyer* on another when they both refer to the same entity.

- **Keep it simple.** Keep the primary features as easy as possible to access and use. Secondary features that are not used as often can be more out of the way, but it should be obvious how to find these features.

- **Make it flexible.** Define the conceptual design so that it can support the different ways in which users work over time. Forms with tab controls and modal forms can make the application less flexible, because the user cannot simultaneously view the data on both tabs or on multiple modal forms. The workday is full of interruptions and unanticipated requests. The software should give users the flexibility to move between tasks and between steps within a task without frustration.

- **Provide answers, not questions.** This is easiest to explain with an example. A programmer I worked with started her network-based executive information system by asking the executive what drive letter to attach to. I suggested that the application could figure this out, display it in the status bar, and allow the user to change it (if the user even knew what it was). She looked at me with a horrified expression and said, "But they need to set it specifically for their system so they don't use one intended for something else." Think about the user, not the computer; provide answers, not questions.

- **Make the design visually appealing.** Just because a form is used only for data entry or a report does not mean that it should be boring. How many data entry forms have you seen that are black and white, use the system font, and have a tedious vertical layout? You can add color, icons, and some style to make all the forms of your application look interesting. You can use simple colored lines to provide detail and separate different parts of the form.

As an example, the first unit of work for the Purchase Tracker application consists primarily of data entry forms. The conceptual design for these forms includes a combo box at the top for selection of the specific item to work with, such as a customer or product. After the user selects the item, the data for that item appears below the combo box. Figure 2.3 shows a sample data entry form for the Purchase Tracker application.

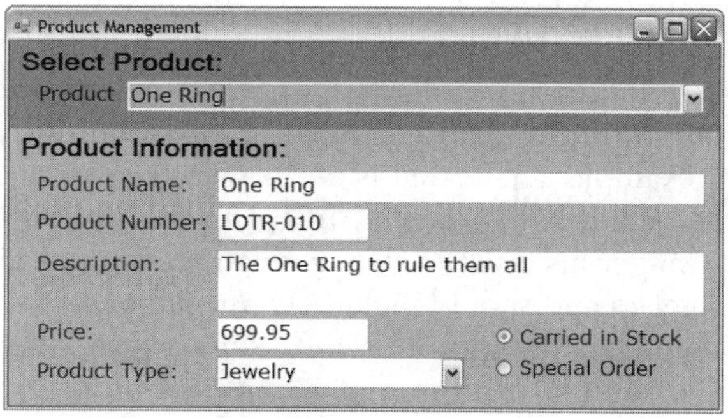

Figure 2.3   Sample data entry form for the conceptual design of the Purchase Tracker application.

The result of the conceptual user interface design is a layout of the basic form types (data entry form, summary form, search form, and so on). This includes a description of the common elements on the form and how they behave. This conceptual design is the basis for designing the individual forms of the application.

To validate the conceptual user interface design, build a realistic example of each of the basic form types, either with a design tool or with Visual Studio. Limit this to one form for each of the form types. Present these examples to the users for their review.

Reuse this conceptual user interface design in the design of the other units of work for the application to ensure a consistent look and feel between all parts of the application.

Defining the Navigation Techniques

A single application is composed of many forms, and the user needs a way to navigate to those forms. You need to define a standard set of navigation techniques so that the users can easily find the forms that they need to perform a particular task.

The most common navigational technique in Windows is a menu. A menu lists key features or tasks. When the user clicks the feature or task, a drop-down menu appears, allowing the user to select the specific task to perform.

Another common technique is to use a list or tree that provides a set of options or tasks. The user then picks a task from the list to open the appropriate forms to complete the selected task.

Regardless of the mechanism used to display options (menu, list, tree), be sure to name the features based on the tasks that the user performs, not on the computer's tasks. For example, "Receive Goods" is a better option name than "Create Inventory Transactions."

When defining the application's navigational requirements, be sure to think about both the relative importance of each task and how often it is used. For example, a task that is performed frequently should have a toolbar button or hot key to quickly bring up the form required to complete the task. Dangerous tasks, such as a delete all feature, should be somewhat harder to get to and should include confirmation of the operation.

Defining standards for how the user navigates between the forms in your application makes your application easier to learn and use. For more details on Windows Forms navigation techniques, see Chapter 4, "Building the User Interface Layer."

Designing the Form Layouts

After you have defined the standard conceptual design and navigation techniques, you are ready to design the layout for each of the forms in the application (or unit of work). The layout defines the placement of the visual elements on each form, along with how they behave.

The visual layout of each form is important at this point in the design process to ensure that the users understand what the application will do. The visual layouts help the users picture the scenarios. They also help the users define whatever other tasks, steps, or data they may have missed during the prior design phase.

Here are several guidelines to help you define the visual form layouts:

- **Lay out for maximum productivity.** The layout should optimize the user's productivity when completing the tasks defined in the scenarios. It is often tempting when using object-oriented techniques to define the user interface as one form per object. It is much better to design the forms based on the scenarios—the steps required to perform a task—even if that means pulling in information and processing from many different objects. For example, the form that displays purchase information such as date and quantity is much more useful if it includes details on the customer and the product that was purchased.
- **Be consistent.** The forms should provide a consistent look and feel as defined in the conceptual design. For example, if one data entry form uses a button called Save and another uses a button called Submit for the same purpose, the user may be confused.
- **Put the most important elements first.** The parts of the form the user interacts with the most should be readily available and at the beginning of the tab order. This helps the user quickly find what is needed and ignore what is less critical.
- **Visually group content.** If a form contains many data entry elements, it is easier for the user to find the desired element if they are grouped logically on the form.

As you complete the layout of each form, validate it by comparing it with its associated scenarios. Can the user easily perform the necessary task with the minimum number of steps? Are the tasks that the user performs more often the most easily accessible? By comparing the results of the user interface design with the scenarios, you ensure that every requirement is considered.

When you complete this step, you have the layout of the forms required for this application (or unit of work). If you developed the forms in Visual Studio, you can capture each form as a screen shot and paste it into a design document, along with a written description of the form's elements and how they behave. This can be readily reviewed with the users and domain experts.

Building a Prototype

Users often want to try out the user interface instead of just looking at it in pictures. That is the purpose of a prototype. A **prototype** is a working example of the forms of your application.

A prototype normally is composed of the primary forms in the application (or unit of work), along with the navigation features to move between them. Data displayed in each form is hard-coded into the form to minimize the amount of programming needed to display the form, yet give the user a good idea of how the form works.

Developing a prototype has many pros and cons, which is why this is an optional step.

The benefit of creating a prototype is that it allows the users to visualize the application and its navigation. This gives the users a better feel for how the application works. You can see how well your conceptual design works and how well it translates to the users' tasks. It helps you verify that the application does not feel different as the user moves from form to form. And the users can identify problem areas early enough to change them.

In some cases, however, the users can mistake the prototype for the completed application. This can cause difficulty if the application is complex and requires a significant amount of time to finish. This is the downside of building a prototype.

If you want to build a prototype, the easiest way is to use Visual Studio. See Chapter 3, "Building Projects," for details on starting an application and Chapter 4 for details on building forms.

Summary

The user interface design phase steps you through the process of detailing the user interface for your application.

The first step is to define the overall design of the user interface. This includes the conceptual design, defining the standard look and feel, and the navigational design, identifying how the user moves between the forms in the application.

You then use the scenarios and the conceptual design to define the layout of each form in the application. The layouts should be optimized to allow the user to readily perform the steps defined in each scenario.

When you complete this process, you have a design document that describes the conceptual and navigational design. It also contains screen shots of each primary form in the application, along with a description of its user interface elements.

Implementation-Centered Design

In Visual Studio, it is easy to build an application by creating some forms and putting a little code here and a little code there. This is fine if you are creating a simple demo application, but if you are building something of any significant size, or if others will be working with you, you need a more formal plan.

Imagine that you decide to build a house. You buy some wood and start nailing boards together. You may complete the house (or you may not), and it may keep out the rain (or it may not), and it may look okay (or it may not), but without a strong internal structure, you would be worried about that first windstorm! What the house is missing is the architecture. With a well-defined architecture and an implementation plan, you can be confident that what you build will reliably and resiliently fulfill its requirements. This is just as true with software as it is with houses and office buildings.

The purpose of the implementation-centered design ("I") phase of the GUIDS Methodology is to help you define an architecture and implementation plan for your application. It walks you through a set of steps to help you consider all the implementation details.

The "I" phase is composed of the following steps:

- Define the architecture.
- Design the application framework.
- Define implementation requirements.
- Convert the design into an implementation model.

The remainder of this section details these steps. When these steps are complete, you will have a better understanding of how to build the application.

As you build more applications, the first three steps may only require deciding that your corporate standard architecture, framework, and implementation requirements will be used again. There may be no need to revisit all these steps for every application.

The result of the "I" phase can be documented in an architectural specification document. Consider doing this as a Microsoft PowerPoint presentation or Word document that defines the basic application architecture and framework and lists the implementation requirements. This documentation could define a corporate standard, with all applications following the same basic architecture and framework. The implementation model describing the classes for a particular application and where they reside can be defined in a separate, application-unique document.

By defining the architecture and implementation plan and using it as a blueprint for the construction, you minimize your risk of building something that is too difficult to complete, that lacks a basic structure, or that does not meet the intended requirements.

Defining the Architecture

An architecture defines how an application is structured. It defines where code should reside and how that code communicates with other code in the application.

The most common type of architecture for .NET applications is a **three-tiered** or **N-tiered architecture**, where N means "any number." This architectural style involves breaking the application into three or more independent layers.

NOTE: The word "tier" in this context refers to a **logical tier**, sometimes called a **layer**. This means that there is a logical separation of responsibility in the application and that each layer may or may not reside on the same computer. In some literature, the word "tier" implies separate hardware; each tier of the application resides on a different computer. In this book, these are called **physical tiers**.

A classic three-tiered architecture is composed of a **presentation** (or user interface) **layer**, **business logic layer**, and **data access layer**, as shown in Figure 2.4. Each layer is independent and encapsulated and communicates only with the layers directly next to it.

NOTE: This architecture is sometimes depicted sideways, with the top layer being the UI and the other layers shown under it.

Each of these layers is described in the following sections.

Building your application as three (or more) logical layers has many advantages. It makes it clear where each piece of your code resides. It makes it easier to modify one piece without affecting other pieces of the application. You can more easily enhance it, adding the code for future units of work. You can independently test each piece. And it makes it easier to reuse functionality.

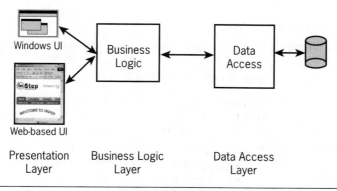

Figure 2.4   A classic three-tiered architecture defines a presentation layer, business logic layer, and data access layer.

Presentation Layer

The presentation layer is responsible for the user interface of the application. This includes Windows forms, Web pages, or a combination of both. All interaction with the user occurs in the presentation layer.

The code in the presentation layer includes only the functions necessary to manage the user interface, such as enabling/disabling controls. All the other logic resides in the business logic layer.

If your user interface is complex, you can divide the presentation layer into two separate layers: presentation user interface layer and presentation logic layer. The presentation user interface layer contains the basic look of the user interface. The presentation logic layer manages the logic of that user interface.

The presentation layer never accesses the database. It always uses the business logic layer to access any information it needs.

For example, in the Purchase Tracker application, all the forms required by the application are created in the presentation layer. Chapter 4 builds a Windows-based presentation layer as a separately compiled project.

By keeping all business logic out of the presentation layer, you can more easily change the user interface without affecting the application's basic logic. Remember when every manager suddenly wanted every business application to have a Web-based user interface? It was a relatively painless process for all the developers who had built their applications with an independent presentation layer.

Business Logic Layer

The business logic layer is responsible for the business logic of the application. It contains all of the business classes.

The business logic layer includes code for the business rules, defined as methods, and for management of business data, defined as properties. It does *not* include user interface elements, such as message boxes.

You can divide the business logic layer into two layers if you want to further separate the business logic itself from the code that creates and populates the business object. The separate code that creates a business object is sometimes called an object factory.

NOTE: If you have read any of my older *Doing Objects* books, I called these classes business object data transfer (BODT) classes.

The business logic layer never directly accesses the database. Instead, it accesses the data layer to obtain the data it needs.

For example, in the Purchase Tracker application, the `Customer`, `Product`, and `Purchase` classes are created in the business logic layer. Chapter 5, "Building the Business Logic Layer," demonstrates building a business logic layer as a separately compiled project.

By encapsulating all the business logic and business rules in logically organized classes in the business logic layer, you can more easily develop, enhance, and extend the application's logic with minimal impact on the other layers.

Data Access Layer

The data access layer is responsible for accessing the application data, whether that data resides in a file or in a database. It knows where to find the data, how to retrieve it, and how to update it.

The data access layer includes the code required to retrieve and save the application data. The data access layer does not include business logic. Instead, that logic resides in the business logic layer.

NOTE: There are some exceptions to this. For example, there are cases in which efficiency is gained from having some business logic in stored procedures in the database, especially if the logic is database-intensive.

For example, in the Purchase Tracker application, the majority of the application data is stored in a database, so a generalized data access class is built in the data access layer. This class retrieves and saves the application data in the database. Chapter 8, "Building the Data Access Layer," builds a simple data access class as a separately compiled project.

By using a data access class, you can more easily modify how the data is stored or accessed without impacting the remaining layers of the application. And if you make this class generalized, you can reuse it in every application that accesses a database.

Service-Oriented Architecture (SOA)

A section on architecture would not be complete without mentioning a Service-Oriented Architecture (SOA). **SOA** is an architectural style whereby loosely coupled applications provide services to each other. A **service** is a task performed by a service provider for a service consumer.

The easiest example is a payment processing service to handle credit cards or other types of payments. If you write an application that needs to accept payment, you most likely won't process that payment yourself. Instead, you make arrangements to use a payment processing service that can provide secure credit card processing.

Some designers like to think about SOA on a micro level whereby every application is a system of services. The data access layer provides a service to the business logic layer, the business logic layer provides a service to the user interface layer, and so on. You can think of your application in this manner. However, you most likely would not want to develop it this way.

Because of its requirement for loose coupling, the communication between the service provider and service consumer is much more complex than just calling a method on an object. You have to assume that the service provider and service consumer could be on different machines and possibly written in different languages on different operating systems. That is why SOA is frequently implemented as Web Services.

It is best to think about SOA on a macro level. Instead of thinking about your application as a set of services it provides to itself, think about what services the application needs to provide to or receive from other applications.

In the Purchase Tracker application, a later unit of work requires that the Purchase Tracker system keep customer information in synchronization with the accounting system. This is where SOA makes sense. If the accounting system provides a service to update customer information, the Purchase Tracker could use this service to ensure that any customer updates it manages are reflected in the accounting system. Alternatively, the Purchase Tracker application could provide a service that allowed retrieval of customer data by any other corporate application if the accounting system would prefer to pull the data.

To provide an SOA interface into your application, think of the service as another piece of code in the presentation layer. This type of design follows a standard Façade design pattern. The code then fits into your three-tiered architecture and can reuse any business logic in the business logic layer. (See the "Additional Reading" section of Chapter 1 for more information on design patterns such as the Façade pattern.)

Consider using SOA whenever your application is a piece of a larger puzzle. SOA defines a standard mechanism for applications within your organization or applications between your organization and related organizations (such as suppliers) to provide services to one another.

Designing the Application Framework

An **application framework** is a set of libraries and classes that implement the architecture of specific types of applications. Some frameworks include tools to assist developers in using the framework. By bundling reusable code into a framework, developers can focus more on the goal and the specific requirements of the application, and less on the details of the architecture.

.NET itself is a framework, providing a set of libraries and tools for the development of .NET applications. Although the .NET Framework is extensive, it does not include details that are unique to the types of applications you create.

For example, your application may require that the background color be changed for the control that has focus. The .NET Framework does not automatically do this, so you need to write your own code. By using an application framework that provides additional functionality common to your applications, you can minimize the time spent implementing this common code. Plus, if you are responsible for more than one application, you can use the same framework for every application, making them all easier to build and maintain.

An application framework normally includes reusable classes such as base form classes and code libraries, tools such as data designers and code generators, and reusable code pieces such as code snippets.

You can build your own application framework or select one from the many application frameworks available for .NET. The advantage of building your own is that you can tailor it to how your team works and how your applications normally function, but building it takes time. The advantage of selecting an existing framework is that you save the time of building it, but you must add the time to learn how to use it.

If you decide to use an existing framework, consider building a prototype application (an expanded "hello world," for example) using the framework so that you are familiar with the tools and features provided by the framework before beginning work on your real application.

If you select to build your own framework, whether you build a prototype depends on the approach you select to build it. There are two primary approaches for building your own framework:

- **Build it first.** Think through what you need in a framework, and build it before you begin developing the application. Use a prototype application to test the framework.
- **Build it as you go.** Build the application and define framework pieces as you go.

Both approaches have pros and cons.

The problem with building the entire framework first is that, if you don't already use an application framework, you may not know all the things a framework can do for you. Also, if you are new to .NET, you may not know what the .NET Framework does versus what you need your application framework to do. So how could you know what to build into your framework before you begin the application? Plus, building a framework first means a delay in producing results.

It is often easier to build the application and add code to the framework as necessary. For example, you find that a grid no longer sorts automatically if bound to a business object, so you write a sort routine in the business object base class portion of your framework so that all grids can sort with no further code. This approach, however, may lead to some refactoring as you move code into the framework. And if you are working in a team, you need to keep everyone apprised of every change to the framework for the framework to be truly beneficial.

This book takes the approach of building the application framework as you need it. This works well in this case because it provides a logical order to describe the concepts included in that portion of the framework.

Figure 2.5 shows the classes in the application framework built in this book and used by the Purchase Tracker application.

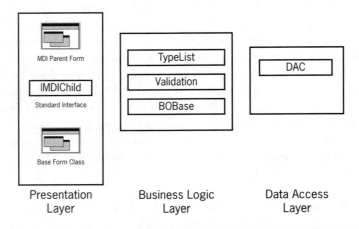

Figure 2.5 An application framework provides standard, reusable code in each layer of your architecture.

The application framework classes that support the presentation layer are built in Chapter 4. They include the following:

- The **MDI parent form** is a standard Multiple Document Interface (MDI) parent form that is part of the .NET Framework, tailored to the specific needs of a basic data management application such as the Purchase Tracker application.
- The `IMDIChild` **interface** ensures that all the MDI child forms implement a standard set of methods for performing create and save operations.
- The **base form class** contains the common user interface code that is needed by all forms.

The business logic layer classes of the application framework are built in Chapter 5. They include the following:

- The `TypeList` class supports types used in drop-down lists, such as customer types and product types.
- The `Validation` class contains general validation logic, such as required field checking and string length checking.
- The `BOBase` class is the base class for all the business objects. It tracks record status (insert, update, delete) and validation summary information.

The data access layer of the application framework contains one class, a data access class (DAC). This class, which is built in Chapter 8, includes all the code needed to perform queries for retrieving and saving data.

By using an application framework such as this, you won't need to write code for any of these features again. And if you build your own framework, you can add to it as you find other reusable code. See the "Additional Reading" section for more information on building frameworks.

Defining Implementation Requirements

In addition to the application requirements you defined during the earlier design phases, consider implementation requirements. These are requirements that the user may take for granted, such as security and quality, or that affect the development team, such as flexibility and maintenance.

The most common implementation requirements include the following:

- **Security:** How will the application data be secured? How will the application itself be secured? How will the application code be secured?
- **Concurrency:** How will the system handle multiple users? Where are transactions required?
- **Performance:** What are the performance requirements for the application? Where is that performance most critical? Application startup? Displaying each dialog? Does some of the data need to be cached for performance?

- **Flexibility:** Which features will require frequent changes? How can you implement those features to minimize the work to support those changes? For example, a tax application requires new tax calculations each year, so design it in a way that can easily be changed.
- **Scalability:** How many users does the application need to support? Will that number grow over time?
- **Quality:** What quality standards are required for the application?
- **Other systems:** Will other systems need to communicate with this system? If so, how will that communication be accomplished? Web services? Files?
- **Support:** What tools will be provided to assist with application support? Should there be a logging feature for the application to report its problems?
- **Physical implementation:** Where will the application reside? All on the user's system? Will there be a database server? An application server?
- **Deployment:** How will the application be deployed? Is an XCopy deployment required?

Consider these common requirements and include any applicable items in the requirements for your application. Keep these requirements in mind as you finish the design process and move into the development phase.

Converting the Design into an Implementation Model

The purpose of this step is to collect everything you have designed so far and convert it into a model that you can use to build the code. This may sound like a big step, but you already have most of what you need.

Back in the goal-centered design phase, you defined the set of business objects that your application needs. Each of these objects becomes a class in the business object layer. Recall that the class is the implementation of the object, including the code for the properties and methods.

In the user interface design phase, you defined the set of forms that your application needs. Each of these forms becomes a class in the user interface layer.

Earlier in this phase you identified that you need a data access layer. Since the data access code itself is part of your framework, the only other items you need in your data access layer are the database scripts.

To complete the model, consider the following:

- **Layer:** Ensure that each class is defined in the appropriate architectural layer. Forms belong in the presentation layer, business logic in the business logic layer, and data access in the data access layer.
- **Framework:** Don't include classes from your framework in the implementation model. They don't need to be implemented (or they need to be separately implemented if you are building the framework as you go), so do not include them in the model. (You can combine the framework with the implementation model if you want an overall view of the application for documentation purposes, but make it clear which parts the developers do not need to implement.)
- **Design patterns:** Are any existing design patterns applicable to your implementation? (See the "Additional Reading" section in Chapter 1 for information on design patterns.)
- **Lists:** In addition to managing one object at a time, the application may need to manage lists of objects. For the Purchase Tracker example, the user interface requires the display of a list of products and a list of customers. Add classes to the business object layer to manage these lists.

Document the results. Depending on the application's size, this can be done with a picture or in textual form. Figure 2.6 shows the implementation model for the Purchase Tracker application (the current unit of work).

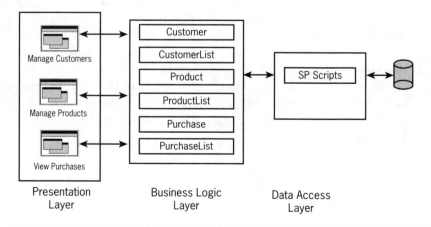

Figure 2.6 The Purchase Tracker application implementation architecture does not need to include any classes already defined in the framework (see Figure 2.5).

The presentation layer contains all the forms. The business logic layer contains the business objects. The data access layer does not include any classes, because the only class it needs is already provided by the framework. All that is needed are the stored procedure (or query) scripts. The remaining chapters of this book detail how to build this application.

Notice the list classes in the business logic layer. These manage lists or collections of objects. For example, the `CustomerList` class manages a list of customers. How would you know at this point that you needed list classes? The user interface design for Manage Customers defined a combo box that displays a list of all customers. So you know you need to manage that list of customers—hence, a `CustomerList` class. The same for products. And the user interface design for View Purchases displays a grid of all purchases made by the customer. So you know you need to manage a purchases list.

By defining an implementation model, you have the details you need to convert the model into code. Validate the implementation model against the original scenarios and against the defined implementation requirements to ensure that you have identified a class for every feature required by the application (or the current unit of work).

Summary

The implementation-centered design phase steps you through the process of defining the architecture and classes for your application.

You first define the architecture and application framework. This provides the basic structure of the application, detailing how your code should be organized. You can then define the implementation details in preparation for the development phase.

When you complete this process, you have a design document that describes your application's architecture and all its classes. Alternatively, you can create one document with your standard corporate application architecture and framework and then create a separate, application-unique document containing the design of the classes that are unique to a particular application.

Data Design

Every nontrivial application works with some data. It may be business-related information such as customer name, employee hours worked, or invoice amount. The application may need values supplied from another system, such as stock quotes or currency exchange rates. Some type of temporary data, such as object state information or intermediate calculations, may be required. The application may need configuration-related information, such as the last four files the user accessed or the last user-selected window locations.

Regardless of the type of information, the data needs to be designed in a logical manner so that it can be manipulated easily and efficiently. The application may add new data, review or edit existing data, or present the data in reports. A good data design makes accessing the data easier.

Visual Studio is a very powerful database application development tool. You can connect to most data stores, retrieve desired information, and then display it, modify it, and store it. With that power comes more choices: more options for data stores, more options for accessing the data stores, more options for mapping your objects to that data, and more options for passing that data between the layers of your application.

The purpose of the data design ("D") phase of the GUIDS Methodology is to help you logically organize the application data and to design how the application retrieves and works with that data.

The "D" phase is composed of the following steps:

- Define how to store the data.
- Define how the data access layer accesses that data.
- Define how the layers of the application provide that data to the other layers.

The remainder of this section details these steps. When these steps are complete, you will have a better understanding of how the application (or unit of work) stores and manages the data it requires.

The result of the "D" phase is the design of the data stores and the specification of how the data is accessed and passed throughout the application. The data design can be specified as a data document, as a data model, or both. The data access strategies can be included in the implementation design document. Documenting the design ensures that the data and data access mechanisms are well-defined for you and for anyone else working on the application, now and in the future.

Defining the Data Storage Mechanisms

Most business applications and many other types of applications store at least some of their data in a database, such as Microsoft Access, Microsoft SQL Server, or Oracle. Other data is stored in a file or other structure. Consider the data required by your application and where that data resides.

Some of the most common data storage mechanisms are

- Database
- XML data file
- Non-XML data file
- Configuration files

NOTE: Although historically the registry has been a common location for storing configuration information, it has fallen out of favor. Use a configuration file instead. One of the reasons for this shift is simplification of deployment.

Your application may use any combination of these data storage mechanisms. A complete discussion of designing data as appropriate for each selected data storage mechanism is beyond the scope of this book. But because a database is the most common data storage technique, this section includes some tips for designing a database. See Chapter 4 for a discussion of configuration files and how to access them in your application.

Database Terminology

Database design comes with its own set of terminology. This section provides an overview of key database terms.

A **relational database management system** (RDBMS) arranges data based on its relationship to other data in the database. It divides the data into logical homogeneous units called tables. A **table** is a logical grouping of related data elements that are stored in a row-and-column format, similar to a spreadsheet. In most cases, each business object defined for the application in the earlier phases of the design maps to one or more tables. The Purchase Tracker application has a Customer table, a Product table, and a Purchase table.

Each row in the table represents a **record**, which is a set of data for a particular object. For example, the Customer table may have 200 records, each containing the data for one customer.

Each column in the table represents a **field**, which is a particular data element. For example, a Customer table has LastName, FirstName, Address, City, State, Zip, and Phone fields associated with it. You may recognize these as the properties defined for the `Customer` class. If a property needs to be retained for the business object, it is often defined as a field in a table.

Designing a Relational Database

The first step in designing a relational database is to identify the entities required by the application and the data associated with those entities. An **entity** is an object that has associated data, such as customers and products. Using object-oriented techniques and the GUIDS Methodology, you've already identified the entities (objects) and their data (properties). So you have completed the first step.

The next steps of designing a relational database involve organizing the data as follows:

1. Define the tables.
2. Define the fields for each table.
3. Define the primary key for each table.
4. Normalize the data.
5. Optionally, build a data model.
6. Tune for performance.

Each of these steps is described in the following sections.

Defining the Tables

Start by defining a table for each of the application's objects that have data to be stored in a database. Although this often doesn't give you every table you need, it does provide an excellent starting point.

For example, the Purchase Tracker application has a Customer, Product, and Purchase table.

Add any other tables needed by the implementation. For example, you could add log tables to log changes to the data or login tables to track every login to the application.

Document the list of tables in a data design document. Many developers use Microsoft Excel for this, but you could use Microsoft Word or any other documentation tool.

Defining the Fields

For each table, define the fields appropriate for that table. A good starting point is the set of properties defined for the associated object during the earlier phases of the design. Any object property that must be retained has a field in one of the tables.

Add any other fields needed for the implementation. For example, you could add LastUpdateDate and LastUpdateUser to each table to track the most recent change to a record.

Document the list of fields in the data design document.

Defining the Primary Keys

In addition to the fields required for a table, define a primary key field. A **primary key** is a unique ID assigned to each record in a table. Use the primary key to uniquely identify each record. You can also use the primary key as a field in another table to connect related data in that table to this record. When you include the primary key in another table, the field is called a **foreign key**.

For example, each record in the Customer table has a unique CustomerID assigned as the key. Each Purchase record has a unique PurchaseID assigned as the key. Each Purchase record also includes a CustomerID foreign key field to associate the purchase with a particular customer. The CustomerID in the Purchase table can be used to find all purchases for a particular customer.

By convention, the ID field is named with the table name and suffixed with "ID." For the Purchase Tracker application, the Customer table has a CustomerID, the Product table has a ProductID, and the Purchase table has a PurchaseID as the unique primary key.

Ensure that the defined keys are meaningless. That is, don't use an existing field of the table for a key. For example, the customer's name should not be the primary key. If the name were used as the key, it would take up more space than a numeric key, and it would run the risk of needing correction. If there were 30 different purchases for Jessica Jones, and she changed her name to Jessica Elessar, every one of the 30 records would need to be updated to Jessica Elessar.

A story can better illustrate this point. A public utility company in the 1980s used the customer's phone number as the primary key in many of its critical databases. The thought was that each utility customer had one and only one phone number associated with a particular utility address, making it a good primary key. If a customer's phone number changed, however, the keys could not be changed, so a new set of rows had to be created. The technical staff had to develop many additional program features to allow the creation of these new rows and copying of historical information from one to another. Then came the age of multiple phone numbers per household and the advent of cellular phones, and the whole system fell apart. You can avoid this by using meaningless keys.

Normalizing the Data

After you have defined the tables and keys, you need to perform something called normalization. **Normalization** involves following a set of rules to remove redundancy and inconsistencies in the database. This results in a more flexible (and semantically correct) database structure.

Normalization involves the following:

- **Ensure that there is no repeating information.** For example, the Purchase Tracker application currently provides for one phone number per customer. If the users decide that a second phone number is needed, another column could be added for the second phone number. But now the database contains repeating information. And then the users find one customer who has three phone numbers, and you have to make coding changes again.

  A better answer is to put the phone numbers in a second table. The Customer table tracks each person, and the CustomerPhone table tracks each person's set of phone numbers. The CustomerPhone table includes the CustomerID as a foreign key to easily locate all the phone numbers for a customer.

- **Ensure that all data in a table is related to the table key.** For example, the Customer table has a key that uniquely identifies each customer record. That customer record would not include a field for the purchase price of the last purchased item, because that does not directly relate to the table's key. That field belongs in the Purchase table.

- **Ensure that all data in a table is independent and has no unnecessary relationships.** No data in the table should depend on other data in the table. Some data designers generalize this to mean no calculated fields, but actually this has a much broader implication for no redundancy. For example, the Purchase table contains the CustomerID field to define the customer making the purchase. The Purchase table does *not* need to include the address as a field because that field is already defined in the Customer table.

NOTE: From an academic perspective, normalization has three basic forms that map to the three points just listed:

- **First normal form:** A table is in first normal form if all the data elements are atomic. That is, the data elements are in a simple, tabular structure, and there are no repeating groups.
- **Second normal form:** A table is in second normal form if it is in first normal form and every data element in the record is dependent on the record's key.
- **Third normal form:** A table is in third normal form if it is in second normal form and all the fields in the table are mutually independent.

Other normal forms deal primarily with compound keys. In most cases, getting to the third normal form is sufficient. See the "Additional Reading" section of this chapter for references to database books for additional information on this topic.

One benefit of normalization is flexibility. For example, what if a customer record had repeating phone groups that allowed two phone numbers per customer and then the requirements define the need for a third? (As many times as the users tell you they will never need another one, you can be guaranteed there will be another one!) You would need to add the new name fields to the Customer table and modify the software to handle the new fields. If the phone numbers were in a separate table, adding another phone number would simply involve adding a new record to the table. No software changes would be required.

Building a Data Model

If desired, you can build a data model that illustrates your database design. A data model is a visual representation of the database needed by the application (or unit of work) that depicts the tables with their associated fields. It also shows the relationships between the tables.

The easiest way to build a data model is to use a data modeling tool. Visual Studio provides such a tool, as detailed in Chapter 8.

Figure 2.7 shows the resulting data model for the Purchase Tracker application (current unit of work).

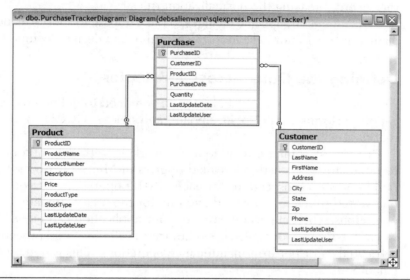

Figure 2.7 The data model for the Purchase Tracker database defines the tables and fields required by the Purchase Tracker application.

NOTE: The Customer table in the Purchase Tracker example contains an address with City, State, and Zip columns. Because the city and state depend on the zip code, you may consider this table to violate third normal form. However, it is left as is to simplify the coding examples later in this book.

Tuning for Performance

With normalized tables often comes the need to perform joins. A **join** is the combination of records based on a defined matching field, most often a key field. For example, the Customer and Purchase tables could be joined on the CustomerID to find all the purchases made by a specific customer. As you may guess, performing joins requires some processing time. Performing complex multijoins requires noticeable processing time. So you may need to tune your database for performance.

You may find that a particular frequently used join is too slow. To improve the performance, you can consider adding indexes or denormalizing the table. This may involve adding calculated or redundant fields in the record, breaking the normalization rules.

Document any specific changes to the database for performance, especially if it breaks normalization rules, in the data design document.

Defining the Data Access Strategies

After you know how the data is stored, you need to define how the application performs create, read, update, and delete (CRUD) operations on that data.

The most common technique for working with data in a database is to build stored procedures (called queries in Microsoft Access). You can build one stored procedure for each CRUD operation. Or you can build one stored procedure for read and one for the create, update, and delete operations. The data access layer of your application can use ADO.NET, the .NET Framework data access library, to call the stored procedures and retrieve data or perform maintenance operations. This is demonstrated in Chapter 8.

There are situations in which a stored procedure cannot be used to access data in a database. For example, if the data required by the application is too ad hoc, it may be difficult to write a stored procedure that is sufficiently generalized. In this case, you can write SQL statements directly in your application and use ADO.NET to execute them.

NOTE: Using SQL statements directly in your application is not recommended for performance and security reasons. Use stored procedures (QueryDefs in Microsoft Access) instead.

For data not stored in a database, such as configuration files, the .NET Framework provides classes to assist you in retrieving and updating data. The code to retrieve and update user configuration settings is presented in Chapter 4.

Defining How to Provide Data to Other Layers

To implement a three-tiered architecture, you can design your application to separate the user interface from the business logic from the data accessing. Your data access class retrieves the data. You are then faced with the question of how to transfer that data to the other layers. You need to define how the data access class provides the data to the business logic layer and how the business logic layer provides the data to the user interface layer.

You have many options for getting data from one part of your application to another. Here are several common options:

- **Pass a DataSet.** A **DataSet** is an ADO.NET data structure that contains the results of one or more queries accessible as rows and columns. For this option, the data access class retrieves data from the database directly into a DataSet and passes it to the business logic layer. The business logic layer reviews/modifies the DataSet to impose necessary logic. In some cases, this can be done with the DataSet's extended properties. The DataSet is then passed to the user interface layer, which gets the fields from the DataSet and displays them.

  The user interface code to populate a textbox would be something like this:

  ```
  LastNameTextBox.Text = CustomerDataSet.Tables(0). _
      Rows(0).Item("LastName").ToString
  ```

  To save the data, the user interface updates the DataSet and passes the DataSet back to the business logic layer for validation and to apply any business rules. The business logic layer then passes the DataSet to the data access class, which calls the update stored procedure to update the database.

- **Pass a DataTable.** The **DataTable** is an ADO.NET data structure similar to a DataSet, but it contains the results of only one query. This option is similar to the preceding option, but instead of a DataSet, it uses a DataTable.

  The user interface code to populate a textbox would be something like this:

  ```
  LastNameTextBox.Text = _
      CustomerDataTable.Rows(0).Item("LastName").ToString
  ```

- **Use object properties.** For this option, the data access class retrieves data from the database directly into a data structure such as a DataSet, DataTable, or DataReader and passes it to the business logic layer. The business logic layer uses the data to populate the associated business object properties. The user interface accesses the business object properties to populate the associated controls.

  The user interface code to populate a textbox would be something like this:

  ```
  LastNameTextBox.Text = aCustomer.LastName
  ```

  To save the data, the user interface updates the business object properties. The business logic layer then updates the DataSet or DataTable with its property values and passes it to the data access class. The data access class calls the update stored procedure to update the database.

  Or, after the user interface updates the business object properties, the business logic layer passes all the property values to the data access class, which calls the update stored procedure to update the database.

- **Use object binding. Object binding** lets you define at design time which object properties map to which user interface controls. For example, a textbox for the last name is bound to the `LastName` property of the customer business object. When the form loads, object binding automatically populates the textbox with the value of the `LastName` property. And if the user changes the value in that textbox, object binding updates the `LastName` property accordingly.

  For this option, the data access class retrieves data from the database directly into a data structure such as a DataSet, DataTable, or DataReader, and passes it to the business logic layer. The business logic layer uses the data to populate the associated business object properties. The business object properties are bound to user interface controls at design time, so the runtime automatically displays the data in the user interface from the object properties. No code is required.

  Because the object properties are bound to the user interface controls, updates to the data are automatically reflected in the object properties. No code is required. To save the data, the business logic layer passes the values of its properties to the data access class. The data access class calls the update stored procedure to update the database. (Or a DataSet or DataTable can be used, as in the preceding option.)

This book uses the object binding approach, as demonstrated in Chapter 7, "Binding the User Interface to the Business Objects." Object binding was selected because it requires significantly less code in the user interface. Each control in the user interface is bound to a specific property of the business object at design time. From that point forward, the .NET runtime ensures that the contents of the control and the business object properties are synchronized.

Summary

The data design phase steps you through the process of defining how your application will retrieve and store data.

The data required by the application was identified as object properties in the first phase of the design. The first step in this phase is to review the data associated with each object and define how to store that data. Then you can define how the application retrieves that data. As soon as the application has the data, it also needs a mechanism for providing that data to other parts of the application. For example, if you're using a three-tiered architecture, you need a way for the data access code that retrieved the data to pass that data to the business logic for processing and then to the user interface for display to the user.

When you complete this process, you have a design document that describes the data used by your application.

Strategies for Construction

There is more to developing software than just designing and coding. There is project management, scheduling, testing, documentation, testing, maintenance, testing, and version control. (Did I mention testing?) Defining strategies for these activities before beginning to build the application makes the entire application development process more efficient and easier to manage.

The purpose of the strategies for construction ("S") phase of the GUIDS Methodology is to help you define these strategies. This includes coding and naming conventions, source code control, documentation, and a development plan and schedule. And let's not forget a testing plan.

The "S" phase is composed of the following steps:

- Define the development plan.
- Define the standards.
- Select the construction tools/technologies.
- Define the development schedule.

By defining a standard set of tools, development conventions, and strategies, a team of developers can successfully work on the application. Even if it is just you, defining these strategies gives you a good starting point for the development. It allows you to develop source code that is easier to manage, maintain, and test.

The remainder of this section details these steps. When these steps are complete, you are ready to begin the construction phase and build the application!

The result of the "S" phase is the plan and tools you need to successfully build and deploy the application.

Defining the Development Plan

Planning the software development process involves defining who develops which code, when and how it is inspected, how often it is deployed, and how it is maintained.

The software development process, either formally or informally, includes the following basic steps:

- **Construction:** Writing code. This includes all construction activities including code commenting.
- **Inspection:** Testing code. This can include code walk-throughs, unit testing, functional testing, integration testing, load testing, and system testing.
- **Deployment:** Providing the application to the users.

- **Maintenance:** Modifying existing code. In this context, maintenance includes bug fixes and minor revisions. Follow the GUIDS Methodology for any large revisions. Ensure that the requirements for the modification are defined, designed, planned, scheduled, constructed, and tested.

There are several approaches to laying out the software development plan.

One Step at a Time

The One Step at a Time approach was historically quite common. It involved writing all the code, testing all the code, deploying the completed application, and then maintaining the application.

The upside of this approach is its clearly defined steps. The downside is the length of time from start to finish and the requirement to complete a step before moving on to the next step. Often, the construction gets delayed, so to meet the schedule the inspection is cut short. A shorter inspection results in increased maintenance and therefore significantly increased project life-cycle costs.

With the current need for more complex applications in a shorter amount of time, this approach is often abandoned for a more circuitous approach.

Rinse and Repeat

The Rinse and Repeat approach is the idea of doing each of the steps in a repetitive fashion. You develop the code for a logical unit of work, and that code is inspected and optionally deployed. The next logical unit of work then follows this process, and then another.

This approach has become quite popular, because it shows progress more quickly. It allows for the application to be done in logical pieces (the units of work discussed during the design). By giving (or at least showing) parts to the users early in the process, you can catch missing features or incorrect assumptions earlier in the process.

This is also an excellent opportunity to get the bug counts down to a reasonable level, thus preventing the bugs from delaying the final release. The project manager can provide additional motivation to the programmers by requiring that each programmer's critical bug count be zero before the programmer can move on to the next task.

Test-Driven

The Test-Driven approach involves defining the tests first, and then the application is developed to pass the tests.

The benefit of this approach is that the testing is brought to the front of the process instead of being left for the end. The downside of this approach is that the tests need to be exceptionally thorough. Any business rule or special case not covered by the tests is not developed. But on the other hand, is this better or worse than having the code for the special case never tested?

Writing Bug-Free Code

Writing bug-free code is a great goal during the software development process. If bugs are prevented by correctly developing the code the first time, no bug reports need to be submitted, tracked, or retested. The code is just right.

Here are some tips for writing bug-free code:

- **Complete the design process.** Many reported bugs are not really bugs at all but are open design issues peeking out of the code.
- **Follow the design.** If changes need to be made, make the changes to the design and then follow the design.
- **Develop exception handling.** Define a strategy for exception handling in your application and use it throughout the application.
- **Do unit testing.** Test your code as you go along to find and fix any problems right away. Taking a few minutes to test and debug each piece of the code now, when you are most familiar with it, minimizes the number of times you need to come back to this code, refamiliarize yourself with it, and change it.
- **Do code walk-throughs.** This involves discussing how the code works with another developer or group of developers. Although it's time-consuming, this process not only improves the code's quality, it also helps the less-senior developers improve their programming skills.
- **Don't leave parts unfinished.** These unfinished parts show up later as missing features and are defined as bugs. If you must leave something undone, mark it clearly. TODO comments (see Chapter 3) are great for this.

By following these suggestions, you can improve the quality of your code.

Defining the Standards

As much as we all hate them sometimes, standards are a very important part of software development. The better software standards and conventions you use, the easier it is for you to understand the code you have written. This is even more critical if your team has more than one developer.

Consider the following scenario. The software construction is well under way, and an experienced Visual Basic developer, Lee, is added to a three-person development team. Lee soon finds that the team has developed its own version of the corporate login screen instead of reusing the class developed for another project. Now the code that could have simply been reused must be completed, debugged, and tested.

Lee has spent much more time than anticipated getting up to speed on the rest of the code. There are few comments and little consistency in coding techniques. Lee is spending a lot of time just figuring out which modules perform which operations and which classes are used for what. Some simple headers on the classes and functions would have made the code so much easier to understand.

Lee also notices that in some code modules the number of contacts variable is `iNumContacts`, in others it is `_NumberOfContacts`, in others it is just `Contacts`, and in others it is just `i`. In some places, the `Contacts` variable is a string and is used for the contact description. In other places, the contact description is `_ContactDescription`, and in still other places, it is just `temp`. This confusion (and the possible bugs it could cause as Lee starts to modify this code) could have been avoided simply by defining some naming conventions.

Coding standards are guidelines for how the code for a project is written. They define things like program structure, variable scoping, syntax standards, exception handling, and commenting. Define coding standards before beginning to write code to ensure that the code is standardized between team members, simplifying the development and maintenance activities.

Here are some good reasons for coding standards:

- They help you manage the complexity of your application and keep your code organized so that it is easy to find things.
- They provide a consistent look to help you easily read and understand the code. Any developer familiar with the standards can pick up any piece of the code and understand the basic conventions used. This is helpful when you do code walk-throughs, when your testing team does code reviews, and for multiple-developer projects.

2. DESIGNING SOFTWARE

- They ensure a smooth transition to the maintenance activities, especially if someone else is providing those activities.

As with most things in life, define standards in moderation—not too little, not too much. It is very important to define standards that can be followed. Standards that are too restrictive or too lenient are ignored, defeating the purpose of establishing them in the first place.

Here are some categories to consider when defining your standards:

- **Commenting:** Ensure that comments provide clarity and answer *what* and *why*. They need to answer *how* only in cases where the code is not obvious. Some developers like to comment a method before they write the code, to clarify their thinking on the method's purpose. Commenting methods is easy using XML Comments (see Chapter 5).
- **Basic code structure:** Standards in this category include the use of Regions to provide an organized code structure (see Chapter 3).
- **Variable scope:** Scope defines the extent to which a variable is accessible in an application. For example, local scope implies that a variable can be accessed only from the local routine in which it was declared; global scope implies that a variable can be accessed from anywhere in the application. Scope variables as tightly as possible.
- **Naming conventions:** Visual Basic has several standard naming conventions. The suggestion here is to pick one and stick with it as part of your development standards. The latest commonly used conventions do away with prefixes and instead use suffixes to define object variables for controls and such. So instead of `txtLastName`, it is `LastNameTextBox`. This is the convention used in this book— but I am not fond of it. (I like being able to type `txt` and press Ctrl+Space to see the list of my `TextBox` controls.)
- **Syntax standards:** Syntax standards include the use of Option Strict and Option Explicit, using constants instead of hard-coded string or integer values, requiring use of a Case Else, when to use line-continuation characters, and so on. Using syntax standards makes the code easier to work with and helps prevent bugs.
- **Exception handling:** A standard mechanism for handling and reporting exceptions is crucial for developing a successful application. See Chapter 4 for details on exception handling with Visual Basic.

NOTE FOR VB6 DEVELOPERS: The standard for exception handling with Visual Basic 2005 is conceptually significantly different than with VB6. Please see Chapter 4 for more information.

See the "Additional Reading" section in this chapter for general recommendations on coding standards, conventions, and exception handling. For references to coding standards and conventions specifically for Visual Basic, see the "Additional Reading" section of Chapter 3.

Selecting the Construction Tools

The right tool for the right job, as they say. If you are reading this book, it is assumed that you plan to implement your application using .NET technologies. But that provides only part of the picture. You can save yourself time if you select any other tools and technologies that you plan to use before you start development.

Consider the following tools and technologies:

- Development environment, such as Visual Studio
- Development language, such as Visual Basic or C# (Although you can mix and match languages in an application, it is often best to stick with one language for consistency, standardization, and ease of maintenance.)
- Application framework, whether you build your own or use an existing one
- Database product, such as Microsoft Access, Microsoft SQL Server, or Oracle
- Third-party controls such as grids or charting tools
- Source code control, such as Visual Studio Team System or Visual SourceSafe
- Code analysis tools such as Visual Studio or FxCop
- Unit testing tools such as Visual Studio or NUnit
- Additional testing tools
- Third-party code security tools such as Dotfuscator
- Third-party deployment tools such as InstallShield
- Other developer productivity tools

When selecting tools and technologies, evaluate the tool's cost, including the time to learn to use it properly, against the productivity benefits to determine whether the tool is worth having. With Visual Studio's extensibility model, you can also build your own tools.

If you select technologies that you are not currently familiar with, you may want to develop a small test application using the technologies. This helps you become knowledgeable about the technology before attempting to implement it in your application. This is especially true if you are purchasing an application framework, because some are very complex and have a steep learning curve.

Defining the Schedule

As much as we would all like to skip this step, most projects require a schedule.

The project plan outlines how the project proceeds. It includes some basic decisions on how the project will be done, defines the tasks required to complete the project, and identifies the resource requirements for each task.

The schedule provides a time line for the plan. It defines milestones or checkpoints in the plan for the completion of tasks. Without a schedule, software gets the "soup syndrome." When is soup done? When you are hungry! Without a specified time for dinner, that soup will keep on cooking. Without a specific time frame for software, the application will keep changing, getting more and more features and tweaks.

Here are several key considerations when developing a schedule:

- **Scheduling means to plan for a certain amount of time.** This is a plan, not a commitment.
- **Estimates are not certain.** You can only estimate with certainty something you have already done, but then it takes zero time because you have already done it. If you haven't done it, you cannot estimate with certainty how long it will take.
- **Consider risk.** Some tasks are more risky than others because they may involve a new technology or technique. Add a risk factor to the estimates for risky tasks.
- **8 hours ≠ 1 day.** Most scheduling software takes the hour estimates, assumes an eight-hour day, and calculates the completion date based on this assumption. But most developers cannot code

for eight hours a day. They have meetings to attend, code reviews to perform, questions to answer, research to complete, maintenance activities on other applications, and so on.

By considering these factors and limiting the tasks to one unit of work, you can define a schedule that you can live with.

Summary

The strategies for construction phase steps you through the process of defining all the strategies for the development phase. This includes project management, programming standards, source code control, and so on.

With the design in hand, the tools and technologies selected, and the project plan and schedule in place, you are ready to start coding!

Conclusion

What Did This Chapter Cover?

This chapter introduced the GUIDS Methodology for software analysis and design.

This chapter covered the following key topics:

- The GUIDS Methodology provides a pragmatic, object-oriented approach to help you analyze and design an application. Using this methodology allows you to systematically work through the software design process. This design is critical to constructing solid software.
- The GUIDS Methodology provides guidelines for working through the analysis and design process. Adjust it as needed for your corporate environment and design style.
- **Goal-centered design** involves defining the basic goals of the application and how the user will use the application to perform tasks to meet those goals. Each task is defined as a use case. Select a subset of use cases for each unit of work. Then detail the steps required to perform the selected use cases with scenarios. From the

scenarios you can identify the real-world objects required for the application. Since each unit of work includes a limited number of use cases, the selected use cases can be swiftly designed and rapidly developed.

- **User interface design** involves defining the application's basic look and feel, including the navigation techniques. It also includes converting each scenario from the prior phase into a form or set of forms needed to perform the task. The focus is on defining a user interface centered on the user's goals.
- **Implementation-centered design** involves defining the architecture and framework that will be used for the application. It converts the real-world objects into classes that can be implemented.
- **Data design** involves defining the data that the application needs or uses and selecting the appropriate data stores to persist that data. If the application requires a database, this phase also defines the structure or required changes to that database. This phase includes defining how the application will access and pass that data through all the layers of the architecture.
- **Strategies for construction** involves defining the approach for the construction. This includes identifying the tools to be used, standards followed, and basic development approach. It also includes the definition of the development project plan and schedule.
- Document the design along the way. The design documentation is the blueprint for the development phase.

The next chapter begins the building process.

Building Along

The Purchase Tracker application was used as an example throughout this chapter to help you apply the design principles to a real application, albeit a simple one.

The next chapters detail each step of building the Purchase Tracker application with explanations, examples, and "building along" activities. Each "building along" activity provides step-by-step instructions for building a particular feature of the application or using a particular technique.

If you work through the entire book, you will have an operational Purchase Tracker application that you can use as a starting point for the other applications you build.

Additional Reading

Beck, Kent and Ward Cunningham. "A Laboratory for Teaching Object-Oriented Thinking." *SIGPLAN Notices*, Vol. 24, October 1989.

This article introduced the CRC cards that have become popular in object-oriented design.

Brooks, Frederick P., Jr. *The Mythical Man Month: Essays on Software Engineering*, 20th Anniversary Edition. Reading, MA: Addison-Wesley, 1995.

This is the classic book about considering the human element in project planning and scheduling.

Codd, E.F. *The Relational Model for Database Management, Version 2*. Reading, MA: Addison-Wesley Publishing Co., 1990.

E.F. Codd invented the relational database model. He describes it fully in this book.

Cooper, Alan. *About Face: The Essentials of User Interface Design*. Foster City, CA: IDG Books, 1995.

This is an insightful and entertaining book on user interface design concepts. Many of the examples are shown using Microsoft Windows applications.

Cooper, Alan. *The Inmates Are Running the Asylum*, Second Edition. Indianapolis, IN: Sams, 2004.

The focus of this book is on designing for people, not for engineers. The subtitle of this book, "Why High-Tech Products Drive Us Crazy and How to Restore the Sanity," sums it up.

Cooper, Alan. "The Perils of Prototyping." *Visual Basic Programmer's Journal*, Vol. 4, No. 6, August/September 1994.

This article provides a case for using paper and pencil instead of a programming tool for the high-level design of the user interface for an application.

Cwalina, Krzysztof, and Brad Abrams. *Framework Design Guidelines*. Upper Saddle River, NJ: Addison Wesley, 2006.

This is an *excellent* book if you are building your own framework. It provides general guidelines and many specific recommendations for handling everything from naming conventions to base classes to exceptions.

Fowler, Martin. *UML Distilled: Applying the Standard Object Modeling Language*. Reading, MA: Addison-Wesley, 1997.

This approachable book defines the basics of UML.

2. DESIGNING SOFTWARE

Hernandez, Michael. *Database Design for Mere Mortals: A Hands-On Guide to Relational Database Design*, Second Edition. Addison-Wesley, 2003.

This book provides an overview of relational database design that is not intimidating for those new to this concept.

Kurata, Deborah. *Doing Objects in Microsoft Visual Basic 6*. Indianapolis, IN: Sams, 1999.

Although this book has "Visual Basic 6" in the title, the first nine chapters cover the GUIDS Methodology in much greater detail that what is provided in this single chapter.

Kurata, Deborah. *Doing Web Development: Client-Side Techniques*. Berkeley, CA: Apress, 2002.

This book covers the design process for Web applications, including Web user interface design and architecture. It then goes through the process of building the application using HTML, CSS, JavaScript, XML, and XSL.

Kurata, Deborah. InStep Technologies Web site. Sept. 5, 2006. http://www.insteptech.com.

This Web site provides additional information on the GUIDS Methodology for application design.

Kurata, Deborah. "Ten Reasons to Go OO." *Visual Basic Programmer's Journal*, Vol. 6, No. 14, December 1996. http://www.ftponline.com/.

This is a Visual Basic 4 article, but it is still applicable to later versions of Visual Basic. It provides ten reasons to help sell you and your management team on making the move to OO. It includes such reasons as "No More Kevorkian Applications" and "Leverage Legacy Code."

Kurata, Deborah. "Why No Code?" InStep Technologies, Inc., 1998. http://www.insteptech.com/techlibrary/general/gen_oodesign.htm.

This white paper covers the reasons you can give your boss for why you are not coding. The responses range from serious reasons such as "Because I need to understand what I am building before I build it" to more tongue-in-cheek answers such as "I *am* coding."

Maguire, Steve. *Debugging the Development Process: Practical Strategies for Staying Focused, Hitting Ship Dates, and Building Solid Teams*. Redmond, WA: Microsoft Press, 1994.

If every developer could have only two books, I would recommend this one and *Code Complete*, listed shortly. This book focuses on what every member of the development team can do to make high-quality software ship on time. This book's anecdotal style, clear key points, and highlights section all make it easy and enjoyable to read.

McCarthy, Jim. *Dynamics of Software Development (Best Practices)*. Redmond, WA: Microsoft Press, 2006.

In this easy-to-read book, McCarthy provides a set of rules for software development, including such items as "Remember the triangle: features, resources, time" and "Don't trade a bad date for an equally bad date."

McConnell, Steve. *Code Complete*, Second Edition. Redmond, WA: Microsoft Press, 2004.

This book is highly recommended for every person writing any type of application. It provides details on topics such as variable naming, commenting, and good code construction techniques. This book contains chapters such as "The Power of Data Names," "Characteristics of High-Quality Routines," and "Managing Construction."

Microsoft Patterns & Practices. Microsoft. 27 Sept. 2006. http://msdn. microsoft.com/practices/.

This Web site provides a broad set of recommendations for designing, building, and deploying applications. It includes white papers, guides, articles, and prebuilt code. The most extensive set of prebuild code is the Enterprise Library. Check this out if you are looking for an existing framework for .NET development (although as of this writing it is only implemented in C#).

Norman, Donald A. *The Design of Everyday Things*. New York: Doubleday, 2002.

This book has great insights into the design of common things that you use. It does not specifically focus on software design, but it provides information applicable to designing in general.

Try It!

Here are a few suggestions for trying some of the techniques presented in this chapter:

1. Think about how the GUIDS Methodology is similar to how you have designed software in the past. How is it different?
2. Think about how the GUIDS Methodology could be applied when designing a real-world object. For example, if you were designing a new type of car, how would each of the following steps come into play?

- **Goal-centered design:** What objects does a car have? Engine, steering, air conditioning, radio, seats, and so on. What are the steps detailing the scenarios? Starting the car, driving the car, adjusting the temperature, setting the radio, and so on.
- **User interface design:** How should it look to the user? Placement of controls, color, texture, and so on.
- **Implementation-centered design:** How can it be built to meet the standards for emissions and miles per gallon defined during the requirements? Design the framework, define how the power gets to the wheels, and so on.
- **Data design:** How will it remember the last radio station or seat position?
- **Strategies for construction:** What quality control processes should be put in place? When should the first unit come off the assembly line?

3. Think about a prior application you have developed. Describe the objects for that application. Looking at the application from an object-oriented perspective, would you have done anything differently in designing and developing the application?

4. Think about your last software development effort. Did it have a formal or informal development process? What steps did you follow in developing the project? How well did it work?

5. Follow the GUIDS Methodology and add a feature to the design of the Purchase Tracker application to support tracking of salespeople and their territories, defined by zip code.

CHAPTER 3

BUILDING PROJECTS

The great successful men of the world have used their imagination...
they think ahead and create their mental picture in all its details,
filling in here, adding a little there, altering this a bit and that a bit,
but steadily building—steadily building.
—Robert J. Collier

Before you build any application, it is wise to think ahead and create a mental picture of the application. The GUIDS Methodology, detailed in Chapter 2, "Designing Software," provides the steps to help you think through your application design and architecture. But even if you are a "just do it" type of developer, you need to give some thought to the high-level design. Will it be a Windows application, Web application, or some of both? Will it include a data access component, business logic component, external libraries, or service components? What about a framework?

After you have the mental picture, you create the outline of the application by building a solution with a project for each component. Then you fill in here, add a little there by adding project items such as forms and classes, steadily building until the application is complete.

This chapter details how to create solutions, projects, and project items to implement your application using Visual Studio, the integrated development environment (IDE) for Visual Basic, and the other .NET languages. The chapter includes new Visual Studio 2005 features such as the Windows application framework, application events, global exception handling, solution folders, and building your own templates. Along the way, it provides some best practices for setting up new projects. It also begins the process of building the Purchase Tracker sample application, described in Chapter 2, which is the working example used throughout the book.

What Does This Chapter Cover?

This chapter demonstrates the following techniques:

- Creating a Visual Studio solution
- Defining multiple projects in a solution
- Creating solution folders
- Adding project items to a project
- Building project and project item templates
- Defining code regions
- Adding Task List comments
- Defining startup projects (yes, that is plural)
- Enabling the application framework
- Displaying a splash screen without writing code
- Implementing a global exception handler
- Setting references between projects in a solution
- Importing namespaces
- Defining Visual Studio settings
- Exporting Visual Studio settings

If you have been working with Visual Studio for a while, you already know how to create a solution, add projects to the solution, and add items to the projects, as described in the first few sections of this chapter. But if you want to "build along" as you read through the book, work through these first few sections before proceeding to the more advanced sections later in this chapter.

Creating a Solution

The first step to building any significant application is to create a solution. A **solution** is a set of related projects and other solution files that comprise your application. Working with a set of projects as a single solution allows you to easily edit, debug, and execute all parts of the application from within one Visual Studio session.

NOTE FOR VB6 DEVELOPERS: A Visual Studio solution is comparable to a project group in classic Visual Basic.

A **project** defines a separately compiled component in your application. It consists of a set of project items that work together to provide the functionality in the component. A project is usually compiled into an executable program (.exe) or class library (.dll). The number of projects that you add to a solution depends on how you layer your application. For most applications, you define a minimum of three projects: one for the user interface layer, one for the business logic layer, and one for the data access layer.

A **project item** is a Windows form, source code file, XML file, report, resource file, or any other type of item that you want to include in your project. You add project items to projects based on the project's purpose. For example, the project defined for the user interface layer includes a Windows Form project item for each form required in your application.

In working with .NET, another important term is assembly. An **assembly** is the set of files that comprise an installable component, including the code, resources, versioning, and so on. In most cases, an assembly maps to a single project.

And be careful about the word **application**. This book uses the term "application" from the user's perspective, which is basically everything that makes the particular software program function. This could be any number of executable programs and class libraries. Visual Studio often uses the term "application" synonymous with the term "assembly," so Visual Studio calls each project in your solution an application.

This section demonstrates how to create a solution, add projects to the solution, and add project items to the project to begin building an application.

Creating a Visual Studio Solution

The first step in creating an application is to create the solution for the application, although the process is somewhat hidden. In most cases, you don't create a solution separately. Instead, you define the solution when you create the first project for the application.

To create a solution:

1. Select **File | New | Project**. The New Project dialog is displayed (see Figure 3.1).

NOTE: If you see **File | New Project** instead of **File | New | Project**, your Visual Studio is set to use the Visual Basic Development settings. Many of your Visual Studio options and some of the dialogs will be different from those in this book. You can continue to use your settings and work with the differences, or you can change your settings.

To set your Visual Studio settings so that your environment matches the one used in this book, select **Tools | Import and Export Settings**. Select **Reset All Settings** and click **Next**. Choose whether to save your current settings, and click **Next**. Select **General Development Settings** and click **Finish**.

2. Define the type of project to create by selecting the desired project template.

Use the tree view on the left panel of the New Project dialog to select the project type and view the many different project templates for that project type in the right panel.

For example, to create a Visual Basic Windows application, select the **Visual Basic** node and then the **Windows** node from the Project types tree view on the left. Then select the **Windows Application** template from the list on the right.

3. Enter the project name.

Use standard naming conventions for your project name. One recommended standard is to use an abbreviation of the application name with a suffix defining the type of project. For example, you could name the Purchase Tracker Windows project PTWin.

Another standard, especially if you are building a product, is to use the *companyName.componentName* convention. For example, if you worked for a company named InStep, you could name the component InStep.PurchaseTracker.Windows or a shortened form of that, such as InStep.PTWin.

4. Select the desired file system location for the project.

5. Enter the name of the solution.

Use standard naming conventions for your solution name. One recommended standard is to use the full name of the application. For example, you could name the solution PurchaseTracker. Alternatively, you could use an abbreviation of the application name with "Solution" as the suffix, such as PTSolution.

6. Ensure that **Create directory for solution** is checked.
   If you create a directory for the solution, your solution is set up in a hierarchical structure in your file system, with each project defined in a directory under the solution directory. This makes it easy to keep the solution organized in your file system.
   The resulting New Project dialog is shown in Figure 3.1.

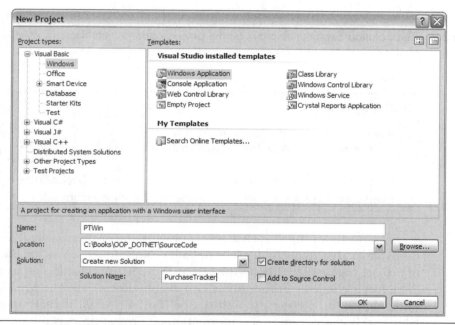

Figure 3.1   The New Project dialog allows you to create a solution for the project and select a project template for your preferred language and type of project.

NOTE: You may not see the same set of project types or templates in the New Project dialog as shown here due to differences in Visual Studio editions and variations in installed products.

7. Click **OK**.

Visual Studio creates the project and solution. The project appears in Solution Explorer, as shown in Figure 3.2.

Figure 3.2   The Solution Explorer displays all the projects and project items in your solution.

> **Building Along**
>
> For the Purchase Tracker sample application:
> - Create a new **Windows Application** project and an associated solution.
> - Name the project **PTWin**, and name the solution **PurchaseTracker**.
>
> The project appears in Solution Explorer, as shown in Figure 3.2.

When a new project is created, it contains one or more default project items and a My Project folder. The default project items depend on the type of project you created. For a Visual Basic Windows Application project, the default is a Windows Form project item named Form1.vb. The My Project folder holds the project properties. See "Setting Application Properties" later in this chapter for more information on project properties.

Notice that the solution you created is not shown in Figure 3.2. By default, the solution does not appear in Solution Explorer until you add a second project to the solution. If you prefer to always see the solution, you can change the default setting using **Tools** | **Options** | **Projects and Solutions**, as shown in Figure 3.3.

By checking the **Always show solution** checkbox and clicking **OK**, you set your Visual Studio default to show the solution, even if you have only one project. Solution Explorer then displays the solution, as shown in Figure 3.4.

It is also possible to create a blank solution without creating a project. This allows you to work with a set of solution items before defining a project and to fully control when and how projects are created.

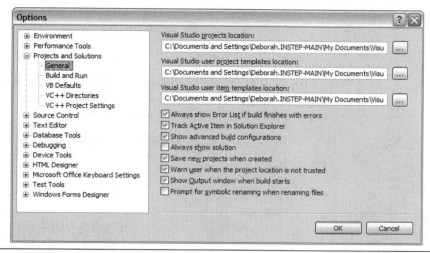

Figure 3.3 The Options dialog allows you to set (hundreds of) Visual Studio options. By default, the **Always show solution** checkbox is unchecked.

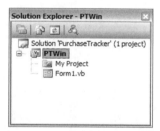

Figure 3.4 If you set the **Always show solution** option, or if you add a second project to the solution, the solution is displayed in Solution Explorer.

NOTE: In Visual Studio 2003, the recommended practice was to always start building an application by creating a blank solution. Visual Studio 2003 did not allow you to create a directory for the solution, so if you created the solution with the first project, it put the solution files in the same directory as the first project's files. Now that you can define a separate directory for the solution when creating the first project, as shown in Figure 3.1, you won't normally need to create a blank solution.

To create a blank solution:

1. Select **File** | **New** | **Project**.
   The New Project dialog appears.
2. Under Project types in the left panel of the New Project dialog, select **Other Project Types** | **Visual Studio Solutions**.
   The solution templates appear, as shown in Figure 3.5.

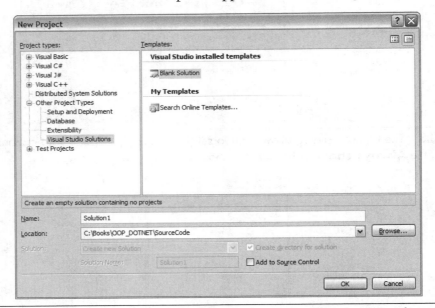

Figure 3.5　The Blank Solution template allows you to create a blank solution from the New Project dialog.

3. Select the **Blank Solution** template.
4. Enter a solution name and location, and click **OK**.

Visual Studio creates the empty solution. Even if you don't have the **Always show solution** option set, the empty solution appears in Solution Explorer.

Adding Projects to a Solution

After creating the solution, you can add projects to the solution to complete the basic outline of your application. This provides a high-level view of your entire application and its components.

To add a project to a solution:

1. Right-click the solution in Solution Explorer, and select **Add |
    New Project** from the context menu, *or* select **File | Add | New
    Project** from the main menu bar.
    The Add New Project dialog appears, similar to Figure 3.1, but
    without the option to create a solution.

NOTE: If you have only one project in the solution and you don't have the
Always show solution option set, you will not see the solution in Solution
Explorer.

---

2. Select the desired template.
3. Enter the project name.
    Use standard naming conventions for your project name. One
    recommended standard is to use an abbreviation of the application
    name with a suffix defining the type of project. For example, you
    could name the Purchase Tracker Business Object project PTBO.
    Another standard, especially if you are building products, is to use
    the *companyName.componentName* convention. For example, if
    you worked for a company named InStep, you could name the
    component InStep.PurchaseTracker.Business or a shortened form
    of that, such as InStep.PTBO.
4. Select the desired location for the project.
    This defaults to the appropriate directory based on the solution
    location.

NOTE: Visual Studio creates a directory in your computer's file system for each
project. If you created a directory for the solution, as shown in Figure 3.1, each
project directory is created under the solution directory. This establishes a directory hierarchy in your file system similar to the hierarchy depicted in Solution
Explorer.

---

5. Click **OK**.

Visual Studio creates the project, and it appears in Solution Explorer.

3. BUILDING PROJECTS

Building Along

For the Purchase Tracker sample application:

- Add a project to the solution for the business logic layer using the **Class Library** template.
  Name the project **PTBO**.
- Add a project to the solution for the data access layer using the **Class Library** template.
  Name the project **PTDAC**.

The solution and your three projects appear in Solution Explorer, as shown in Figure 3.6.

Figure 3.6 The basic outline of the application is represented in Solution Explorer.

Since this book is about Visual Basic, all the components in this book are Visual Basic projects. But they do not have to be. You can mix and match projects in different languages. For example, you could build a data access component in C# and other projects in VB and still include all of them in the same solution. However, you cannot mix project items within a project, meaning that a Visual Basic project can contain only Visual Basic code files, and C# projects can contain only C# code files.

If you are working on an application with many projects, another feature of a solution is the ability to define **solution folders**. Solution folders allow you to organize related projects into groups. This makes it easier to manage the projects in Solution Explorer.

To add a solution folder to a solution, right-click the solution in Solution Explorer and select **Add | New Solution Folder** from the context menu. The new folder appears in Solution Explorer. You can drag and drop projects into and out of solution folders to change the organization of your projects.

NOTE: Creating a solution folder in Solution Explorer does *not* create a directory in your computer's file system. So if you want the directory structure on your computer to match the folder hierarchy in Solution Explorer, you need to manually create directories on your computer for any solution folders you create in Solution Explorer.

When you are finished adding all the projects, and optionally solution folders, to the solution, you have a high-level view of all the components of your application. You can then add project items, as described in the next section, to steadily build your application until it is complete. Sounds easy, doesn't it?

Adding Project Items to a Project

If you have ever used any version of Visual Basic, you already know the simple steps for adding project items to a project. The only thing that has really changed is the large number of project item templates that are available.

Here are a few examples of project item templates:

- The About Box template creates an about box for your application. An **about box** is a form that displays details about your application, such as the application name, description, version, and copyright statement. It is frequently accessed by the user from an application's Help menu.
- The Login Form template creates a login form that you can use if you want to handle your own user authentication. See the "Authentication Mode" section later in this chapter for more information on authentication.
- The Splash Screen template adds a preconfigured splash screen to your application. A **splash screen** is a form that displays information about the application to a user while the application is loading. It appears when the application is launched and automatically disappears when the first form has completed loading.
- The Dialog template creates a form with OK and Cancel buttons. It includes the event handlers for those buttons. Use this template when you want to create a modal dialog that requests information from the user and then requires the user to click OK to accept that information or Cancel to cancel the operation.

You can select any existing project item template. You can also create your own custom project item templates, as discussed in the next section.

To add a project item to a project:

1. Right-click the project and select **Add | New Item** from the context menu, *or* select **Project | Add New Item** from the main menu bar.

   Instead of selecting New Item, you could select a specific type of item from the menu, such as Windows Form or Class.

   The Add New Item dialog is displayed as shown in Figure 3.7.

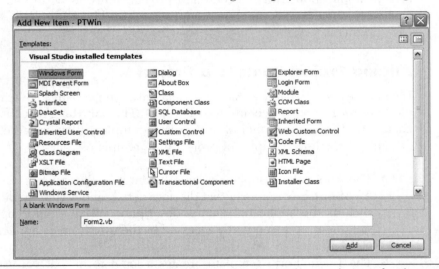

Figure 3.7   Use the Add New Item dialog to select a template and name for the item to add to your project.

NOTE: You may not see the same set of templates in the Add New Item dialog as shown here due to differences in Visual Studio editions and variations in installed products.

2. Select the desired template.
3. Enter the name for the project item.

   Use standard naming conventions for your project item name. One recommended standard is to use the entity name with a suffix defining the type of project item. For example, a Windows form for displaying product information would be named ProductWin.

See Chapter 4, "Building the User Interface Layer," for more information on building Windows forms.

For business logic classes, the recommended standard is to use the entity name alone. So the class providing the functionality for managing products would simply be named Product. See Chapter 5, "Building the Business Logic Layer," for more information on building classes.

4. Click **OK**.

After you click OK, Visual Studio creates the project item that is associated with the template. It copies any visual elements or code within the template to the new project item. The new project item then appears under the project in Solution Explorer. Double-click on the project item in Solution Explorer to open the project item in its default editor.

If you have a good idea of the items you need for your project, you can create them at this point. More commonly, however, you add items to your project as you build each feature of the application.

Building Along

For the Purchase Tracker sample application:

- Add a project item to the Windows Application project (**PTWin**) using the **Splash Screen** template.

  Name the project item **SplashScreen**.

Visual Studio adds a Windows Form project item to your project and copies all the visual elements and related code from the Splash Screen template to that Windows form.

If you attempt to run the application at this point, the application does not display the splash screen, because you have not yet defined your newly created form as the application's splash screen. This is done later in this chapter.

Leveraging Templates

In Visual Studio, a **template** is a predefined set of elements that Visual Studio can copy into your application. Visual Studio comes with a set of built-in templates, or you can build your own. The two primary types of templates used in Visual Studio are project templates and project item templates.

A **project template** defines a set of project properties and project items that Visual Studio can copy into a new project in your solution. Project templates appear in the New Project dialog (see Figure 3.1). The built-in project templates include common project types such as Windows Application and Class Library. For example, the Windows Application project template creates a new project, sets the Application Type application property to a Windows Application, and copies an empty Windows Form project item into your project. Although most of the built-in project templates add only one project item, a project template can add any number of project items.

A **project item template** defines a set of code or other elements that Visual Studio can copy into a new project item in your project. Project item templates appear in the Add New Item dialog (see Figure 3.7). The built-in project item templates include common project item types such as Windows Form and Class. They also include specialized types such as Splash Screen and About Box. For example, when you add a new Windows form using the Splash Screen project item template, Visual Studio creates the form and then copies all code and controls from the template.

When building and using templates, it is important to note that anything in the template is *copied* to the application when the template is used. For example, suppose you build a specialized template for a form project item and use it to create 50 forms. Then you find that you had a programming error or require a change in the template. You have to find all 50 forms and modify each copy of the code. If you are writing code that could change over time, you don't want to use a template and have copies of the code in multiple places. Instead, consider using other techniques, such as base classes, as discussed later in this book.

Creating Project Templates

Project templates allow you to copy the organizational structure and contents of a project to a new project. If you only ever work on just one project, there would be little value in building a project template. However, if you often need to build new but similar projects, defining a project template can make you more productive.

For example, if you frequently create Windows applications that need a splash screen, about box, first form, base form class (discussed in detail in Chapter 4), and other specific forms, you can build a project with these items and save it as a template. Every time you want to start a new Windows application, you can start by selecting your template. Visual

Studio copies all the defined forms and other code to your new application, saving you the time of including each item separately. You can also share your template with other members of your team, giving your team a common project starting point.

To create your own project template:

1. Create a new project in a new solution.

   This is the project that defines the project template. Name the project so that it is clearly defined as the project used as a project template.

   Select a solution directory different from the directory you are using for your application, since the template is not part of your application.

2. Set any desired project properties.

   See the "Setting Application Properties" section for more information on the available project properties.

3. Add any desired project items to the project.

4. Add any code or other elements to the project items.

5. Save the project.

6. Export the project as a template by selecting **File | Export Template**.

   The Export Template Wizard appears, as shown in Figure 3.8.

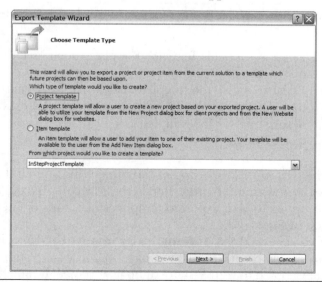

Figure 3.8   Use the Export Template Wizard to create either project or project item templates.

7. Select **Project template** to create a template from the project.
8. Select the project you would like to use to create the template.
9. Click **Next**.

    The second page of the wizard is displayed, as shown in Figure 3.9.

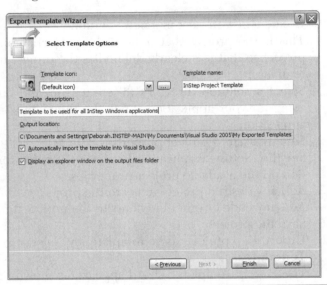

Figure 3.9 The second page of the Export Template Wizard allows you to set basic template properties.

10. Enter the details for your template, such as an icon, name, and description.

    Be sure to give the template a clear name, because that is the text that appears in the New Project dialog. Also provide a detailed description for the template.

11. Click **Finish**.

The wizard makes a copy of the project file and all the files for every project item within the project and creates a compressed (zip) file. It copies the zip file to your exported templates directory, defined as the Output location in Figure 3.9.

If you checked the **Automatically import the template into Visual Studio** checkbox on the second page of the wizard, the zip file is automatically copied to your Visual Studio user project templates location. This location is defined under **Tools | Options | Projects and Solutions** (see Figure 3.3). If you did not check that checkbox, you must manually copy the zip file from the exported templates directory to the Visual Studio user project templates location before you can use the template.

If you want your entire team to share your template, each member of the team can change the location of the Visual Studio user project templates location to a shared directory. Then "install" the template by copying the zip file to that shared directory. If your team cannot easily share a directory, the template can be copied to each developer's Visual Studio user project templates location.

Repeat this process to create any number of project templates.

To use your template, ensure that its zip file is in the directory defined as the Visual Studio user project templates location (see Figure 3.3). The template then appears in the Add New Project dialog, as shown in Figure 3.10.

All the project templates that have zip files in your Visual Studio user project templates location appear under My Templates in the New Project and Add New Project dialogs when you select Visual Basic as the project type.

NOTE: Your templates do *not* appear when you select any of the Visual Basic project subtypes, such as Windows or Office. Be sure that you click the Visual Basic node of the tree on the left to see your templates on the right.

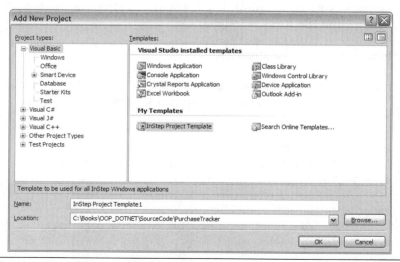

Figure 3.10 Your templates are displayed under the My Templates heading. The template is listed using the name you provided, and the text above the project item name is the template description you provided.

When you select the template and click **OK**, a new project is created. Any properties defined in the project template are set in the new project. Any project items contained in the project template are copied to the new project. You can then modify the project properties or project items as needed for your application.

Create project templates any time you find that you are creating projects with similar structure and content. Using custom project templates can save you time when creating a new project and can ensure that a common structure is used in new projects.

Creating Project Item Templates

Project item templates allow you to copy the contents of a project item. If you find that you are creating the same style of form or defining the same code constructs in each form or class, you may find that building a project item template can make you more productive. And if you are currently copying existing forms or classes when creating new forms or classes, these forms or classes can instead be defined as a template to automate that copying process.

For example, you could create your own form template and add basic controls that you use in all your forms, such as the `ErrorProvider` control. You can add any common code that you want in all your forms. For example, you may want to define a standard structure for the layout of the code within the form as follows:

```
Public Class InStepFormTemplate

#Region " Public Properties"
    'TODO: Add any public properties here
#End Region

#Region " Form Events"
    'TODO: Add event handlers for any form events here like Load
#End Region

#Region " Control Events"
    'TODO: Add event handlers for the controls here
#End Region

#Region " Private Methods"
```

```
    'TODO: Add a region for each method here
#End Region

End Class
```

Two coding techniques used in this code are regions and TODO comments.

The `#Region` directive allows you to organize your code into logical blocks. Regions provide a way to manage the source code in your code files without affecting the compiled application.

NOTE: The space in front of the region text is added so that the region text is easier to read when the region is collapsed.

You can collapse and expand regions using the plus (+) and minus (–) symbols in the far-left column of the Code Editor. This allows you to collapse all regions but the one you are working on, allowing you to focus on one set of routines at a time. You can also collapse all regions by right-clicking in the Code Editor and selecting **Outlining | Collapse to Definitions** from the context menu.

NOTE: To ensure that you can find text within collapsed regions when searching, be sure to check the **Search hidden text** checkbox under Find options in the Find and Replace dialog (**Edit | Find and Replace**) before searching. After you check this checkbox, it remains set for all future searches unless you uncheck it.

When you have many lines of code, using regions helps you hide the code you are not working with and view only the code that is relevant at any particular time. This helps you focus on the task at hand.

By defining regions in a template and using the template when adding forms to your project, you provide a standard code layout for all the forms of your application. This makes it easier for you, or any member of your team, to find code in any form, because they are all organized in the same manner. This simplifies both the development and the maintenance process, because the faster you can find the code, the faster you can work with it.

Although regions are demonstrated here in templates, you can use them anytime and anywhere in your code to better organize it.

The TODO token in a comment defines a Task List comment. A **Task List comment** is any comment in your code that you defined with a specialized token. You can use one of the built-in tokens, such as TODO, HACK, or UNDONE, or create your own tokens.

Use Task List comments to indicate work that is yet to be done, problems to be corrected, or other important design-time notes in your code. These are different from normal code comments in that all Task List comments appear in the Task List window (**View** | **Task List**), as shown in Figure 3.11.

NOTE: There are two different types of tasks, **User Tasks** and **Comments**. Be sure to select Comments from the drop-down list at the top of the Task List window to see the Task List comments.

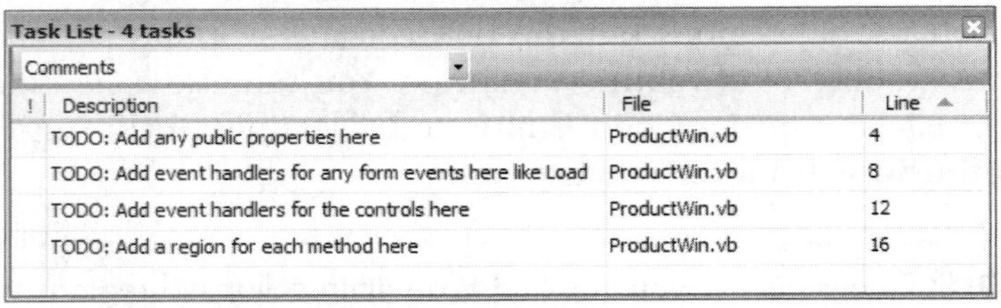

Task List - 4 tasks			
Comments			
!	Description	File	Line ▲
	TODO: Add any public properties here	ProductWin.vb	4
	TODO: Add event handlers for any form events here like Load	ProductWin.vb	8
	TODO: Add event handlers for the controls here	ProductWin.vb	12
	TODO: Add a region for each method here	ProductWin.vb	16

Figure 3.11 The Task List window displays all the Task List comments for your application. Double-click on any comment to jump to that comment in the Code Editor.

You can define your own tokens for your Task List comments using **Tools** | **Options** | **Environment** | **Task List**. So you could define tokens for TODAY or CRITICAL. If you work on a team, you could define tokens such as JOE and JESSICA. This would allow you to add Task List comments such as

```
'JOE: Please look at this code
```

and

```
'JESSICA: Please put these strings into a Resource File
```

Although Task List comments are demonstrated here in templates, you can use them anytime and anywhere in your code. Using Task List comments and the Task List window helps you quickly see the list of tasks and easily jump to the comment in the code to work on the task.

Incorporating Task List comments in your template provides information to the developer who uses the template. You can use Task List comments to identify the next steps that the developer should perform, warnings about any complexities in the template, or tips for using the template.

The project item template created in this example was for a form. You can build similar project item templates for classes and any other type of project item you use regularly in your application.

Once you have the project item content and code completed as you would like for your template, you need to export it as a template. The process for exporting a project item template is similar to creating a project template, as described in the preceding section. Select **File | Export Template** and then select **Item template** from the Export Template wizard, shown in Figure 3.8. Complete the rest of the wizard to finish the template. Your project item template is then listed in the Add New Item dialog whenever you add a new project item to your project.

By creating your own project and project item templates, you can save time when creating new projects and project items. By sharing the templates with your project team, you can promote consistency between all the projects and all the forms, classes, and other project items in your application.

Building and Running the Application

As you write the code for your application, you need to verify that the code is syntactically correct and that it operates as expected. This involves finding and fixing all syntax errors and then building and running the application.

How frequently you perform this verification depends on your coding standards and practices. Some recommendations define a time frame for this verification, such as never coding for more than one hour before verifying syntax and application execution. Other recommendations specify a particular checkpoint, such as the completion of a task or addition of a feature. In any case, frequently building and running the application from within Visual Studio as you make changes or enhancements ensures that the application continues to be operational. It helps you verify that any compile-time or obvious runtime errors are fixed soon after you code each feature, while the code is still fresh in your mind.

This section details how to build the application and set different startup configurations to run your application. After verifying that the code compiles and the feature executes, you are ready for unit testing. See Chapter 6, "Class Tools and Techniques," for more information on unit-testing your application.

Building the Solution

Earlier in this chapter, when the text mentioned "building the application," it was referring to the developer's process of writing the code for the application. But the word "build" has another meaning within Visual Studio in the context of projects and solutions.

The **build** process within Visual Studio compiles the application and displays any syntax errors. **Syntax errors** are errors that occur in your application due to incorrect use of the language or system libraries. This may be due to typographical errors, such as typing `Proprty` instead of `Property`, incorrect use of the language, incorrect use of a library, or missing keywords.

In most cases, Visual Studio immediately notifies you of a syntax error as you are typing code in the Code Editor by underlining the invalid syntax with a squiggly line. If you hover the mouse pointer over the squiggly line, a ToolTip appears, providing detailed information on the syntax error.

In addition, syntax errors are immediately displayed in the Error List window (**View** | **Error List**). You can double-click on an error in the Error List window to jump to the line of code that is causing the syntax error.

NOTE: Whenever possible, correct syntax errors as soon as you see them. Leaving syntax errors can adversely affect Visual Studio's ability to provide Intellisense.

When you have corrected all the syntax errors, you can build the project.

To build your project or all the projects in your solution:

1. Select the project or solution in Solution Explorer.
2. Right-click and select the desired build option from the context menu, *or* select the desired build option from the Build menu.

Visual Studio provides three different options for building your project(s):

- **Build** builds only the code files and components that have changed since the last build.
- **Rebuild** cleans the project and then builds all the code files and components.
- **Clean** deletes any intermediate and output files. It does not perform a build.

You can monitor the output of the build process using the Output window (**Debug** | **Windows** | **Output**). If any syntax errors are detected during the build process, they are displayed in the Error List window.

In most cases, you never need to build your project manually. Visual Studio builds it for you every time you run the application.

Setting Startup Projects

When you have multiple projects in a solution, Visual Studio needs to know which project it should execute when you run the application. You define the starting project by setting the solution's startup project.

The startup project defined for the solution is bold in Solution Explorer, as shown in Figure 3.6. By default, the first project that was added to your solution is defined as the startup project.

To change the startup project:

1. Select the project that is to be started.
2. Right-click the project and select **Set as StartUp Project** from the context menu, *or* select **Project** | **Set as StartUp Project** from the main menu bar.

Only executable projects, such as Windows Application and Console Application projects, can actually be used as startup projects. Even though you can specify a Class Library project as a startup project, if you try to start it, you receive a message: "A project with an Output Type of Class Library cannot be started directly."

One of the new features of Visual Studio 2005 is the ability to start multiple projects. This is useful when you have multiple executable projects in your solution. For example, in addition to the three projects created earlier in this chapter, you may have another Windows application that generates stored procedures (see Chapter 8, "Building the Data Access Layer," for more information on stored procedure generators). You then have a primary Windows application in your project, along with the stored procedure utility Windows application. You may want to run one or the other or both from within Visual Studio.

To set multiple startup projects:

1. Right-click the *solution* and select **Set StartUp Projects** from the context menu.

   The Solution Property Pages dialog is displayed, as shown in Figure 3.12.

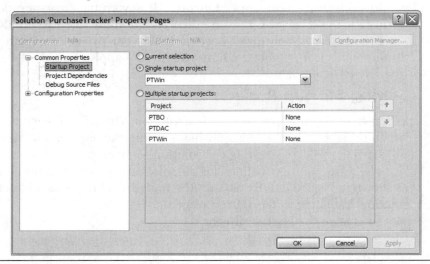

Figure 3.12   The Solution Property Pages dialog allows you to set solution properties such as startup projects.

2. Select the **Multiple startup projects** radio button.
3. Set the Action as desired for each project.

   An Action of **None** specifies that the project will not be started. An Action of **Start** or **Start without debugging** defines that the project is a startup project.
4. Use the up and down arrows to the right of the project grid to define the order in which the projects start.
5. Click **OK**.

When multiple projects are selected for startup, the solution is bold in Solution Explorer instead of one of the projects. When you run within Visual Studio, each project marked with a Start action is started based on the order of the project in the Solution Property Pages dialog.

There is also a **Current selection** radio button in the Solution Property Pages dialog. Selecting **Current selection** causes the currently selected project to be executed as the startup project. If you have multiple executable projects, but you want to run only one at a time, you can select this option.

If you select the **Current selection** radio button and then execute the application, the last project you selected is used as the startup project. You can see which project Visual Studio defines as the selected project, because it appears in bold in Solution Explorer. Try this. You will notice that as you work with files in one project or another that the bold changes to the project you are working on. Whichever project is shown in bold is the project that starts when you run the application.

By appropriately setting your startup project(s) for a solution, you can easily execute your application any time during your development process.

Starting the Application

When you have the startup project(s) selected, you are ready to run the application. There are many ways to start application execution.

To start application execution, use one of these techniques:

- Click the **Start Debugging** arrow on the Debug toolbar.
- Select **Debug | Start Debugging** from the main menu bar.
- Press the F5 key to start with debugging.
- Select **Debug | Start Without Debugging** from the main menu bar.
- Press Ctrl+F5 to start without debugging.

When you start with debugging, all the debugging tools are available to you. If you start without debugging (the last two bullets), the debugging tools are ignored. In most cases, you start with debugging.

Regardless of how you start the application, the first thing that Visual Studio does is build the solution. If the build completes successfully, Visual Studio executes the defined startup project(s).

NOTE: You cannot edit the application while it is running. You need to pause or stop the application before you can make any edits.

You can pause by clicking the **Break All** toolbar button, by selecting **Debug | Break All** from the main menu bar, or by hitting a break point. You can then make any desired edits and continue execution by clicking the **Continue** button, by selecting **Debug | Continue** from the main menu bar, or by using the stepping features (Step Into, Step Over, Step Out). The ability to pause, make edits, and continue is called **Edit and Continue**.

You can stop the application at any time by clicking the **Stop Debugging** toolbar button, by selecting **Debug | Stop Debugging** from the main menu bar, or by exiting the executing application.

Run the application often during the development process to ensure that it compiles and executes as expected.

Building Along

For the Purchase Tracker sample application:
- Set the Windows Application project (**PTWin**) as the startup project. By default, since it was the first project you created, it should already be set as the startup project.

Run the application. It displays the default Form1.

Setting Application Properties

As you add projects to your application, you can set project properties such as the user-friendly name and title. In Visual Studio, these are called **application properties** because Visual Studio views each individual project as a separate application.

After you set the application properties, they can be referenced within the application. For example, you can retrieve the user-friendly name and title to display in a splash screen or about box.

In Visual Basic 2005, additional properties allow you to set up application-level events, such as application start and termination events.

This section details how to set the application properties. It also describes the application events you can use to define startup or shutdown processing. The next section demonstrates how to use application events to create a global exception handler.

Setting Basic Application Properties

The application properties define the basic information about a project, including its name and description. By setting these properties, you provide additional documentation for your application.

To set the basic application properties for a project:

1. Select the project in Solution Explorer.

   From Visual Studio's point of view, every project is an application and has application properties.

   From your users' point of view, the application that they see is often only the Windows Application project, because that is the only project that provides a user interface. So it is most important to set the basic application properties for the primary Windows Application project.

   For the other projects in the solution, at a minimum set properties such as name, version, and copyright information for tracking and versioning purposes.

2. Open the Project Designer for the project by right-clicking the project and selecting **Properties** from the context menu, *or* select **Project | Properties** from the main menu bar, *or* double-click on the **My Project** folder under the project.

The Project Designer appears, as shown in Figure 3.13.

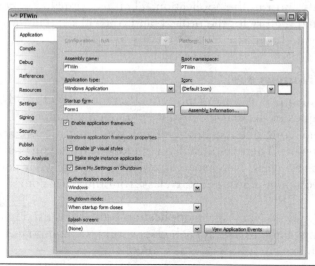

Figure 3.13   Use the Application tab of the Project Designer to set basic application properties.

The remainder of this section describes each of the application properties displayed in the Application tab of the Project Designer.

Assembly Name

The Assembly Name application property defines the name given to the compiled executable (.exe) or class library (.dll) file. This name defaults to the project name, but you can change it to any valid filename.

For the primary Windows Application project, consider setting the Assembly Name to the logical name of your application. The associated executable is then named with this logical name. For example, for the Purchase Tracker application, you can set the Assembly Name to PurchaseTracker. When you compile, the resulting executable is named PurchaseTracker.exe.

NOTE: Changing the Assembly Name does not change the project name.

You can access this name programmatically using the following line of code:

```
My.Application.Info.AssemblyName
```

To see the effect of setting the Assembly Name, change it for one of your projects and run the application. Then use your file system to navigate to the bin directory for the project, and you will see that the compiled file has the defined name.

Root Namespace

A **namespace** is an organizational naming structure that helps prevent the names of the classes in your components from conflicting with classes in other components. Imagine that you have a `Customer` class in your component. Then you install a component from your bank that also has a `Customer` class. Namespaces provide a way for your code to distinguish your component's `Customer` class from the bank component's `Customer` class.

The Root Namespace application property is used in conjunction with the class name to access each class within the component with the following syntax:

```
NamespaceName.ClassName
```

By default, the Root Namespace is set to the project name. So if you have a class named `Customer` in your PTBO Class Library component, by default you access the component using the following syntax:

```
PTBO.Customer
```

When you have a component that you use exclusively within your company, you can keep the default project name as the Root Namespace. In most cases, that provides for unique names.

However, if you are creating a public component, such as a product you sell, consider creating a namespace hierarchy for your application. The recommended namespace hierarchy for any public component has this form:

```
Company.(Product|Technology)[.Feature][.Subnamespace]
```

For example, Microsoft's library for Word tools is `Microsoft.Office.Tools.Word`. For the .NET Framework, Microsoft defined a root namespace called `System` for all the components relating to the .NET Framework. The specific features of the framework are then accessible through a hierarchy under `System`, such as `System.Windows.Forms` and `System.Data`. This identifies a component as part of the .NET Framework and makes the .NET Framework library component names unique. (Just be sure not to use `System` as the name of your application's Root Namespace!)

As another example, if the company InStep were to sell the Purchase Tracker application, it may want to set the root namespace for the Windows Application project to be `InStep.PurchaseTracker.UserInterface`. And if it were planning to sell an add-on component that provided an accounting system interface, it may want to give that project a root namespace of `InStep.PurchaseTracker.AccountingInterface`.

In addition to using the Root Namespace application property, you can define the namespace hierarchy using the `Namespace` keyword in your code. This allows you to define a Root Namespace for your project and different subnamespaces in different classes of that project. So you could set the Root Namespace application property to `InStep.PurchaseTracker` and then use the `Namespace` keyword as follows:

```
Namespace UserInterface
    Public Class CustomerWin
    End Class
End Namespace
```

And then for another form in the same project:

```
Namespace AccountingInterface
    Public Class AccountsWin
    End Class
End Namespace
```

The Root Namespace application property is appended to the beginning of any namespace defined in the code. So you reference the CustomerWin form as follows:

```
InStep.PurchaseTracker.UserInterface.CustomerWin
```

And you reference the AccountsWin form as follows:

```
InStep.PurchaseTracker.AccountingInterface.AccountsWin
```

Some developers prefer to define the entire namespace in the code so that it is more readily viewable instead of defining part of the namespace in the Root Namespace application property and part in the code. The code would then appear as follows:

```
Namespace InStep.PurchaseTracker.UserInterface
    Public Class CustomerWin
    End Class
End Namespace
```

and

```
Namespace InStep.PurchaseTracker.AccountingInterface
    Public Class AccountsWin
    End Class
End Namespace
```

This results in the same namespace hierarchies as in the prior code examples. Just don't forget to clear the default Root Namespace application property in this case.

Think about how your component will be used to determine the right Root Namespace for each project. For internal projects, you can use the project name, as defined by the default. When building products, consider defining a more complete namespace hierarchy.

Application Type

The Application Type application property identifies the type of the project, such as Windows Application or Class Library. By default, this is set to the type defined for the project template that you selected when you added the project to the solution. You can change the type at any time.

Icon

The Icon application property defines the graphic that is associated with your application. It appears any time an iconic view of your application is needed, such as on the Start menu or the desktop. Icons can be associated only with executable applications such as Windows and Console applications.

Startup Form/Object

The Startup Form/Startup Object application property allows you to define which code in the project starts when the component begins execution. The valid choices for this property depend on the selected Application Type. For Windows applications, this is most often a startup form. For Class Libraries, this is normally set to None.

NOTE: Prior to Visual Basic 2005, the recommendation was to always start your application with a `Sub Main` and not with a form in order to give you better control over the startup of your application. With the new Windows application framework, discussed in a moment, the current recommendation is to define your primary form as the startup form.

Assembly Information

Assembly information is additional information that you can enter to document the details of the assembly, such as title, description, copyright, and so on. This information is accessible in your application and is displayed in the file system when a user views the assembly file properties.

When you click the **Assembly Information** button, the Assembly Information dialog is displayed, as shown in Figure 3.14.

3. BUILDING PROJECTS

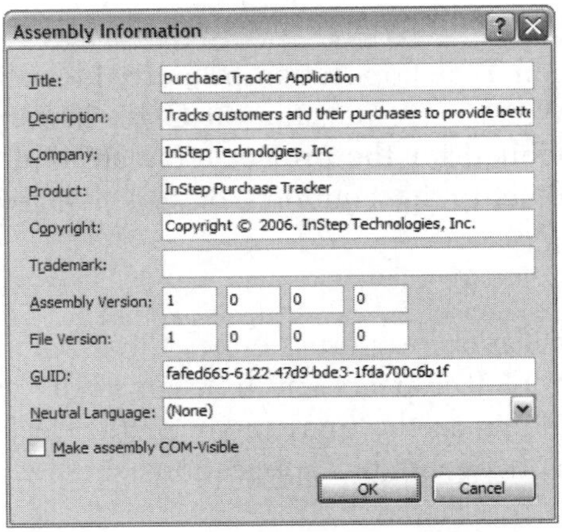

Figure 3.14 Fill in the Assembly Information dialog for your primary Windows Application project to ensure that the appropriate information is displayed in the splash screen and about box for your application.

Fill in all appropriate properties, and click **OK**. Note that the globally unique identifier (GUID) property is automatically set for you.

Building Along

For the Purchase Tracker sample application:
- Select the Windows Application project (**PTWin**) in Solution Explorer.
- Open the Project Designer and select the **Application** tab.
- Set the **Assembly Name** to the logical name of the application (**PurchaseTracker**).
- Set the Assembly Information properties *similar* to those shown in Figure 3.14.
  Leave the GUID as it was set for you.

These properties are used by the splash screen. They display when the splash screen is defined as the application's splash screen later in this chapter.

Once the properties are filled in, you can access each of these properties programmatically using the `My.Application.Info` object. For example, to obtain the description, use this line of code:

```
My.Application.Info.Description
```

Both the Splash Screen and About Box templates use these values to display information about the application.

Enable Application Framework

The **Enable application framework** checkbox in the Project Designer is for Visual Basic Windows applications only. It generates a standard set of startup code for your application and enables application events. It is a good idea to use this built-in application framework for all your Windows applications to provide a standard application pattern.

If you enable the application framework, you can then set Windows application framework properties as defined in the next sections.

Enable XP Visual Styles

Windows XP introduced a new Windows look and feel defined by Windows XP themes. When you enable XP visual styles, your Visual Basic Windows-based application automatically supports the Windows XP themes. When your application is run on a system that does not support Windows XP themes, the application is displayed with the traditional Windows look and feel.

Check this setting if you want Windows XP themes to be enabled if they are available on the user's system.

Make Single Instance Application

Most applications allow the user to run multiple instances. For example, you can launch Internet Explorer multiple times. Each time you launch it, a new Internet Explorer instance is displayed in a separate window. Other applications allow only a single instance. For example, if you launch Word a second time, another copy of Word is not started. A new document is created instead in the existing single instance.

You can make your Visual Basic Windows application single-instance by checking the **Make single instance application** checkbox. If you define your application to be single-instance, the users cannot launch a second copy of it.

Save My.Settings on Shutdown

Visual Studio 2005 supports application-defined end-user settings that you identify using the Settings tab of the Project Designer. For example, if the user moves a form to a specific location on the screen, you can retain the

3. BUILDING PROJECTS

location of form and return the form to that location the next time that the user accesses the form.

By checking the **Save My.Settings on Shutdown** checkbox, the .NET runtime ensures that the settings are saved when the user exits the application. For more details on defining and using application settings, see Chapter 4.

Authentication Mode

Authentication refers to the process of confirming the user's identity. The Authentication Mode property allows you to select Windows or Application-defined authentication.

In many cases, you can use the built-in Windows authentication within your application. Windows authentication determines whether the user has already logged in to a valid Windows account. It does not require any additional login to your application.

You can determine information about the user, such as the username and roles, using the `My.User` object. For example, the following line of code retrieves the user's username:

```
My.User.Name
```

If you need a custom login to track users separately from their Windows login, select Application-defined authentication. You must then build a login form and perform the necessary username and password authentication.

Shutdown Mode

The Shutdown Mode property defines when the application should be shut down. The application can be shut down when the startup form closes or when the last form closes. The choice you make depends on how the forms of your application interact with each other.

If your application has a main form that is defined as the startup form and that remains open the entire time the user is interacting with the application, select to shut down when that startup form closes.

If your application displays forms in a more ad hoc fashion, with no main form necessarily remaining open while the user is interacting with the application, select to shut down when the last form closes. This causes the application to shut down when the user closes the last open form. If you select this approach, be careful with hiding forms. If you hide a form instead of closing it, it could remain open but hidden, and it could prevent the application from shutting down.

Splash Screen

How many times have you written code that displays a splash screen? When you define a splash screen as one of the application properties, the display of the splash screen is handled automatically. You don't have to write any code.

To define a splash screen for your application:

1. Add a form to your Windows Application project for the splash screen.
   Use the **Splash Screen** template, as described earlier in this chapter, to automatically generate a standardized splash screen.
2. Select the splash screen from the **Splash screen** drop-down in the Project Designer (see Figure 3.13).
3. Set assembly information in the Assembly Information dialog, as described earlier. You need this step because the values displayed in the splash screen are the values set in this dialog.

If you run the application at this point, it displays your splash screen, similar to Figure 3.15. After a few seconds, the application hides the splash screen and shows your startup form.

Purchase Tracker
Application

Version 1.00

Copyright © 2006. InStep Technologies, Inc.

Figure 3.15   When you define a splash screen as one of the application properties, the application displays the splash screen automatically, without writing any code.

By default, your application displays the splash screen for a minimum of two seconds. If the application is still loading the startup form after two seconds, the splash screen remains visible until the startup form is loaded. If you want to increase the minimum time that your splash screen displays, you can set the application's `MinimumSplashScreenDisplayTime` property. See the Visual Studio help system for the exact syntax of this property and details on where it needs to be set in your code.

By building a splash screen and then setting application properties, you can build a standardized splash screen. All with no code!

Building Along

For the Purchase Tracker sample application:
- Select the Windows Application project (**PTWin**) in Solution Explorer.
- Open the Project Designer and select the **Application** tab.
- Select your splash screen (**SplashScreen**) in the **Splash screen** drop-down.
  You've already created a splash screen and populated the assembly properties, so this is the only step you need to do.

Run the application. It displays your splash screen for a few seconds. The application then hides the splash screen and shows your startup form (Form1). The splash screen presents several assembly information properties, such as the title and copyright, as shown in Figure 3.15.

View Application Events

Clicking the **View Application Events** button in the Project Designer generates an ApplicationEvents.vb code file that is added to your project. In this file, you can write code to handle application events such as `Startup`, `Shutdown`, and `UnhandledException`. See the next section for an example of writing code for an application event.

By setting the properties for each project in your application, you have documentation for the application and general application information that is accessible in your code.

Enabling the application framework provides additional built-in project features such as the display of a splash screen, enabling XP themes, and writing code for application-level events.

Implementing a Global Exception Handler

Application failures will occur. The user could perform a sequence of operations or enter a value that you don't expect, the connectivity to your database could be interrupted, the code could have a logic error, or many other possibilities. The .NET Framework provides structure exception handling (SEH) to help you manage application failures.

An **exception** is a failure that occurs in your application. Exceptions fall into two broad categories: expected and unexpected.

Expected exceptions are those that your application plans for and responds to. For example, you expect that a user-requested customer may not be found in the database. So you add code to check for this condition and respond with an appropriate message to the user.

Unexpected exceptions are those that you know may happen, but don't necessarily know when or where. These are more difficult to plan for. Logic errors are a good example of this type of exception. This is especially true in cases where the logic error corrupts some underlying data and the exception occurs later when that data is processed, possibly far from the actual logic error.

Structured exception handling allows you to define a code structure to handle both expected and unexpected exceptions generated in your application. This is the purpose of the `Try/Catch` blocks provided in the .NET Framework. See Chapter 4 for more information on creating `Try/Catch` blocks to implement structured exception handling in your application.

The goal of exception handling is to never allow the application to abort with a system error. Your application should handle all expected *and* unexpected exceptions. In the case of unexpected exceptions, handle the exception by logging exception details to a file or some other source so that you can more quickly determine the cause of the exception. Then you can display a user-friendly message to the user and terminate the application gracefully.

To catch every possible exception, you need to do one of the following:

- Ensure that every application entry point has a `Try/Catch` block to catch every possible exception.
  This is actually much harder than it sounds. Since your application is event-driven, every event is a possible entry point into your application code. So you would have to add a `Try/Catch` block to *every* event handler in your application.
- Write code for the `UnhandledException` application event.

With Visual Basic 2005, Windows applications provide application events. One of these application events is the `UnhandledException` event, which the application generates whenever an unhandled exception occurs. You can write code for this event to catch any exception not specifically handled by your application.

Implement a global exception handler as follows:

1. Select the Windows Application project in Solution Explorer.
2. Open the Project Designer for the project by right-clicking the project and selecting **Properties** from the context menu, *or* select **Project | Properties** from the main menu bar, *or* double-click on the **My Project** folder under the project.
   The Project Designer appears, as shown in Figure 3.13.
3. Select the **Application tab** of the Project Designer if it is not already selected.
4. Ensure that the **Enable application framework** checkbox is checked.
5. Click the **View Application Events** button.
   An ApplicationEvents.vb code file is added to your project, if it does not already exist, and is opened. The generated code is as follows:

```
Namespace My

    ' The following events are available for MyApplication:
    '
    ' Startup: Raised when the application starts, before
➥the startup form is created.
    ' Shutdown: Raised after all application forms are
➥closed.  This event is not raised if the application
➥terminates abnormally.
    ' UnhandledException: Raised if the application
➥encounters an unhandled exception.
    ' StartupNextInstance: Raised when launching a
➥single-instance application and the application is already
➥active.
    ' NetworkAvailabilityChanged: Raised when the network
➥connection is connected or disconnected.
    Partial Friend Class MyApplication

    End Class

End Namespace
```

6. Select (**My Application Events**) from the Class Name drop-down at the top left of the Code Editor.
7. Select **UnhandledException** from the Event drop-down at the top right of the Code Editor.

The following event handler code lines are generated:

```
Private Sub MyApplication_UnhandledException( _
   ByVal sender As Object, _
   ByVal e As Microsoft.VisualBasic. _
   ApplicationServices.UnhandledExceptionEventArgs) _
   Handles Me.UnhandledException

End Sub
```

NOTE: Chapter 4 provides detailed information on building event handlers.

8. Add code to handle the unhandled exception within the event handler.

Any exception that is not handled anywhere else in the application is handled by this code. Most commonly, this code should log the error and display a message to the user.

NOTE: The `UnhandledException` event *never* occurs when you are running within Visual Studio. To test the code in this event, you must run the application outside of Visual Studio by running the executable in the bin directory for the Windows Application project.

With the new `UnhandledException` application event, you can now ensure that your application catches any unexpected exception.

Referencing Projects in a Solution

Each project within a solution is an independent component. You cannot access code in one project from another project without first setting a reference from the one project to the other project. For example, you cannot call the business logic project from the user interface project unless the user interface project has a reference to the business logic project.

To add a reference to a project:

1. Select the project in Solution Explorer.
   This is the project that needs to reference another project. For example, if the user interface Windows Application project needs to access the business object Class Library project, select the Windows Application project.
2. Open the Project Designer for the project by right-clicking the project and selecting **Properties** from the context menu, *or* select **Project | Properties** from the main menu bar, *or* double-click on the **My Project** folder under the project.
3. Select the **References** tab.
   The References tab of the Project Designer appears, as shown in Figure 3.16.

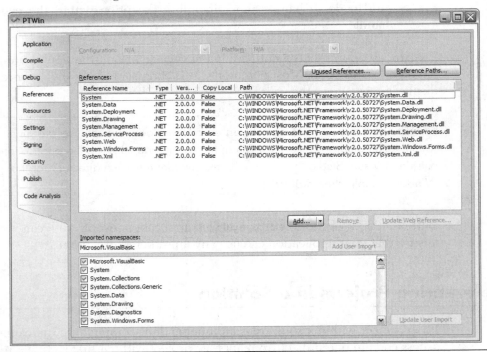

Figure 3.16   The References tab of the Project Designer allows you to define the project references and imports.

4. Click the **Add** button.

   The Add Reference dialog is displayed. This dialog allows you to set a reference to other .NET components, COM components, or other projects within your solution.

5. Click the **Projects** tab.

   The Add Reference dialog Projects tab is shown in Figure 3.17.

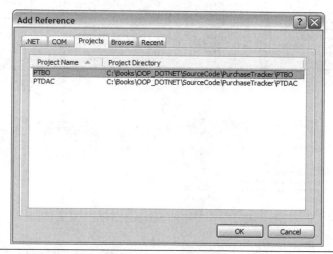

Figure 3.17   The Projects tab of the Add Reference dialog allows you to reference other projects within the solution.

6. Select one or more projects to reference, and click **OK**.

   The project you selected in step 1 can then access classes in the projects selected in this step. For example, select PTBO to allow the project selected in step 1 to access the classes in the business object component. At this point, you can access the classes in the PTBO component using the fully qualified namespace and class name.

   Normally, the user interface component accesses the business logic component, and the business logic component accesses the data access component. So you would set a reference from the user interface project to the business object project and from the business object project to the data access project.

   The selected project(s) are then added to the set of references and to the Imported namespaces list, as shown in Figure 3.18.

7. Optionally, select the project(s) in the **Imported namespaces** list to check them.

3. BUILDING PROJECTS

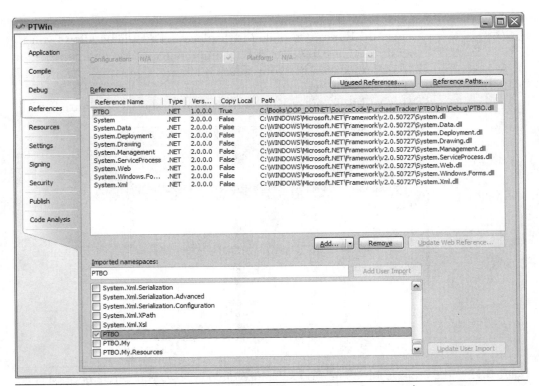

Figure 3.18   Check the projects in the Imported namespaces list to make it easier to access the classes within the project.

NOTE: A problem with Visual Studio sometimes requires that you click the checkbox twice to check the imported namespace.

If you import the namespace for a component, you can access the classes in that component without the fully qualified namespace.

When you set a reference to a component, as shown in step 6, you can access a class in the component by typing the namespace of the component and the name of the class, as follows:

```
PTBO.Customer
```

Visual Studio can find the class using this fully qualified name. But if you have a long namespace or an extensive namespace hierarchy, typing the fully qualified name can get tedious. (See the "Root Namespace" section for more information on namespaces and namespace hierarchies.) It would be much easier if you could just type the name of the class, like this:

```
Customer
```

This is possible if you import the namespace, as shown in step 7. When you import a namespace, Visual Studio can find any class in the namespace without requiring that you qualify the class name with the namespace.

When you type a class name into your code without the fully qualified namespace, Visual Studio resolves the class name by looking through the imported namespaces. If the class is found in one and only one namespace, all is well. If the class does not belong to one of the checked namespaces, or if the same class name is found in multiple namespaces, Visual Studio displays an error.

When you import a namespace using the Project Designer, as described in step 7, you import the namespace for all files in the project. It is also possible to import a namespace for specific project files by using the `Imports` keyword.

To import a namespace in one code file, type the `Imports` statement at the top of the code file before any other declarations. For example, to import the `InStep.PurchaseTracker.AccountingInterface` namespace, use the following `Imports` statement:

```
Imports InStep.PurchaseTracker.AccountingInterface
```

You can then use the name of any class in that namespace without fully qualifying the name, but only within the code file containing the `Imports` statement.

You can also use the Imported namespaces list to import .NET Framework namespaces for a project. Notice in Figure 3.16 that the `System.Diagnostics` namespace is checked by default. This allows you to access the `Debug` class by typing `Debug` instead of `System.Diagnostics.Debug`. You can check any other .NET Framework namespaces to import those as well.

3. BUILDING PROJECTS

> ### Building Along
>
> For the Purchase Tracker sample application:
> - Add a reference from the Windows Application project (**PTWin**) to the business object Class Library project (**PTBO**).
>   Be sure to check **PTBO** as an imported namespace.
> - Add a reference from the business object Class Library project (**PTBO**) to the data access Class Library project (**PTDAC**).
>   Be sure to check **PTDAC** as an imported namespace.
>
> By setting references, you can access the business logic component from the user interface component and the data access component from the business logic component of your application when they are coded in later chapters.

Defining Visual Studio Settings

There is one last thing to do before you start coding your application, and that is defining your desired Visual Studio settings. **Settings** is the general name for all the options you can define using **Tools | Options** or set in other dialogs, such as the Find and Replace dialog.

Visual Studio provides a huge number of settings. You can define settings for your Visual Studio environment, your projects, how you want your text editor to look, and so on.

One of the most important settings at this point is your Visual Basic defaults (**VB Defaults**) under the **Projects and Solutions** node, as shown in Figure 3.19.

Option Explicit identifies whether each variable in your application must be declared. If this is set to Off when you create your project, you don't need to declare a variable before using it. If it is set to On when you create your project, you must declare every variable. By default, this is set to On, and it is highly recommended that this remain on.

For example, if Option Explicit is off, you can write code as follows:

```
x = "This is a test"
```

If Option Explicit is on, you must change the code to declare the variable before using it:

```
Dim x As String
x = "This is a test"
```

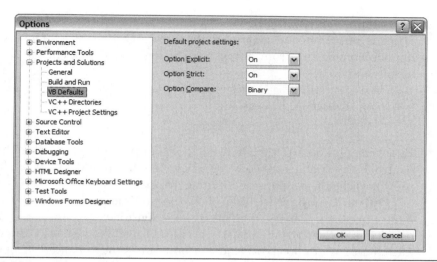

Figure 3.19 Any Visual Basic default settings that you set in the Options dialog apply only to new projects you create, not to existing projects.

Or you can declare it on the same line on which you assign it:

```
Dim x As String = "This is a test"
```

By setting Option Explicit to On in each of your projects, you ensure that every variable in your application is declared. This is highly beneficial, because it minimizes the number of coding mistakes due to mistyped variable names. If Option Explicit is on and you declare a variable called `LastName` and then mistype it as `LstName`, you get a compile-time error. If Option Explicit is off and you don't declare the variable, the system sees `LastName` and `LstName` as two different variables, causing no compile-time error but possible (and hard-to-find) runtime errors.

Option Strict identifies whether variables are automatically cast or converted between different data types. If it is set to Off when you create your project, you don't need to worry about the data types of your variables. If it is set to On when you create your project, you must explicitly cast or convert your variables. By default, this is set to Off. But it is highly recommended that this be set to On.

For example, if Option Strict is off, you can write code as follows:

```
Dim x As String
x = 17
```

3. BUILDING PROJECTS

The runtime automatically converts the number 17 to a string. If Option Strict is on, this code generates the error "Option Strict On disallows implicit conversions from 'Integer' to 'String'". You must change the code as follows:

```
Dim x As String
x = 17.ToString
```

By setting Option Strict to On in each of your projects, you ensure that you control how variables are converted between different data types. This can prevent difficult-to-find programming errors.

Option Compare identifies how the runtime compares string values: binary or string. Binary compare is case-sensitive, so `LastName` doesn't equal `lastname`. String compare is case-insensitive, so `LastName` equals `lastname`. Your choice depends on how you want to handle strings. The default is binary.

After your project is created, modifying these settings does not modify the values defined for the project. The modified settings affect the default only when creating new projects. To update the project values after creating the project, use the Compile tab of the Project Designer, as shown in Figure 3.20.

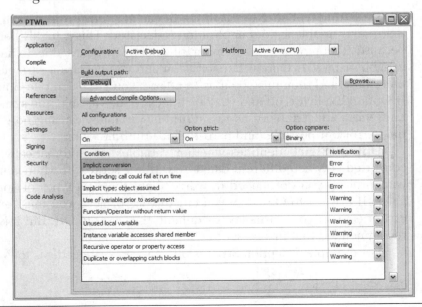

Figure 3.20 For existing projects, settings can be changed in the Compile tab of the Project Designer.

> **NOTE:** You can override any of these Option settings in a particular code file by adding an `Option` statement to the top of the code file using the Code Editor.

Notice the Condition/Notification grid on this tab. It allows you to define how you are notified when specific conditions are found in your code. For example, you can identify how an implicit conversion is handled. A Notification of **None** means that you won't be notified. Setting the Notification to **Warning** or **Error** causes a warning or error to appear in the Error List if the condition is found in your code. For example, you could set Option Strict to Off and then set the **Implicit conversion** notification to **Error** to have finer control over how conversions are handled in your code. Setting other condition notifications in this grid can assist you by preventing possible runtime errors.

Building Along

For the Purchase Tracker sample application:

- Set the **Option Strict** and **Option Explicit** properties for each of your projects to **On** using the **Compile** tab of the Project Designer. This ensures that both properties are set to On for all your *existing* projects.
- Set the **Option Strict** and **Option Explicit** properties to **On** in the **Options** dialog (**Tools | Options**). This ensures that both properties are set to On by default for any *new* projects you create.

After your VB Default settings are defined, you can use the Options dialog to set any other desired settings. You can also define settings on other dialogs, such as the Find and Replace dialog (**Edit | Find and Replace**).

As soon as you have all your settings exactly how you want them, you can export them to a file. This allows you to store a backup of your settings, copy your settings to another computer, or share them with your team.

To export your settings:

1. Select **Tools | Import and Export Settings**.
   The Import and Export Settings Wizard is displayed.

2. Select the **Export selected environment settings** button to export your settings, and click **Next**.

    The second page of the wizard is displayed, as shown in Figure 3.21.

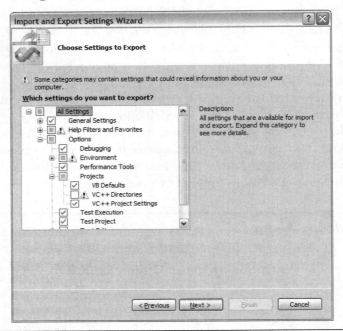

Figure 3.21   The Choose Settings to Export page of the Import and Export Settings Wizard gives you fine control over the settings you want to export.

3. Select which settings to export, and click **Next**.

    You can select to export all your settings, or only specific settings.

4. Define the desired name and location of the resulting settings file, and click **Finish**.

    By default, the settings file has a .vssettings extension. You can use the export option to export different sets of settings. For example, you could export all your settings to one file for your own personal backup and export just some of the settings you want to share with your team to a different file.

    The selected settings are then exported to the defined directory and filename.

To import the settings, select **Tools | Import and Export Settings**, select the **Import selected environment settings** button in the first page of the wizard, and specify which settings to import in the second page of the wizard.

Setting your desired settings before you begin coding ensures that your environment is set up to be as efficient and effective as possible. By exporting the settings to a file, you can keep a copy of them. You can use the copy to restore settings, import the settings on another computer, or share settings with your team.

Conclusion

What Did This Chapter Cover?

This chapter provided some basic information on building a solution, adding projects to the solution, and adding project items to the project to build the basic structure of your application. It then provided details on how to build project and project item templates, define startup projects, set application properties, implement a global exception handler, set references between projects in the solution, and set Visual Studio settings.

This chapter covered several productivity enhancers:

- Using a solution and defining each layer of the application as separate projects in that solution makes the code easier to build, debug, test, and maintain.
- By defining a project template, you can quickly start a new project with all the project items you normally include in a project.
- By defining a set of project item templates, you can copy the basic elements of your project items, such as forms and classes.
- Using the `Region` directive helps you organize your code so that you can find your routines more quickly. You can then expand or collapse regions so that you can focus on only the code you are working on.
- Taking advantage of Task List comments, you can easily mark problem or incomplete areas of your code and quickly return to that code using the Task List window.
- If your solution has multiple executable projects, setting the solution startup to **Current selection** makes it easy to execute any project by simply selecting it and then running the application.

- Defining a splash screen as part of the application framework properties saves you the time of building the splash screen and writing the code to display and then close it.
- Implementing a global exception handler using application events makes it easy to ensure that no exceptions are left unhandled.
- Setting condition notifications in the Compile tab of the Project Designer can help you identify possible programming errors at compile time instead of runtime, saving you debugging time.
- Setting Visual Studio settings and then exporting them to a file makes it easier to set up your Visual Studio environment on multiple computers or to ensure that your team uses the same settings.

The next chapter provides information on building Windows forms, including how to handle events and build a base form class.

Building Along

If you are "building along" with the Purchase Tracker sample application, this chapter built the basic structure, including a Windows Application project for your user interface component, a Class Library project for your business logic component, and a Class Library project for your data access component.

Although it does not yet do anything useful, you can run the Purchase Tracker application at this point. It displays the splash screen first and then the empty Form1.

When building production-level applications, you may want to consider enhancing this basic application structure as follows:

- Add library or utility projects to handle standard tasks such as validation and security.
- Build more extensive templates for your projects and project items to standardize commonly used project and project item elements.

The next chapter begins building the user interface layer of the Purchase Tracker sample application.

Additional Reading

DiMauro, Giuseppe and Francesco Balena. *Practical Guidelines and Best Practices for Microsoft Visual Basic and Visual C# Developers*. Microsoft Press, March 2005.

This book provides some excellent best practices for building applications.

Foxall, James. *Practical Standards for Microsoft Visual Basic*. Microsoft Press, February 2000.

Although it's a little older, this book provides dozens of useful hints for writing clearer, faster, and more maintainable code.

Parsons, Andrew and Nick Randolph. *Professional Visual Studio 2005*. WROX Press, 2005.

This book takes an IDE-centric approach to performing specific tasks, demonstrated in the context of building XML Web services.

Try It!

Here are a few suggestions for trying some of the techniques presented in this chapter:

1. Try the solution features by building a test solution and adding several projects to it. Then add several solution folders and reorganize the solution by dragging and dropping projects into the solution folders.

   Look at the directory structure that was created in your file system. Notice that if you built a directory for the solution, the project directories are created under the solution directory. However, no directories are created for the solution folders.

2. Create a project template that includes common project items you would want to copy in a project.

   For example, you could build a My Windows Application template that includes an about box, splash screen, and other standard project items.

3. Create a project item template that includes common code and/or visual elements.

   For example, you could build a My Windows Form template that includes standard visual elements such as a selection panel with a combo box at the top and a detail panel at the bottom. It could also include standard code such as Regions, Task List comments, and event handlers for the combo box.

4. Try out your new templates by starting a new solution, using your project template to add a new project, and then using your project item template to add some new project items to the project.

3. BUILDING PROJECTS

5. Add some code regions to the application.
   Try opening and closing the code regions and searching for text within the closed regions.

6. Add some Task List comments to the application.
   Try creating your own Task List token, use the token in your code, close the Code Editor, and then use the Task List window to jump back to the code.

7. Work with the startup project options by creating two Windows Application projects in one solution. Change the title bar text in the default form for each application so that you can see which one is running.
   Try setting one project as the startup, and execute the application. Try setting both projects as the startup, and execute the application. Try setting the current project as the startup, and execute the application.

8. To try out the application properties, create a Windows Application project, and add an about box to the project using the About Box template. Set the about box as the startup form, and set other assembly details. When you run the application, the assembly details appear in the about box.

9. Implement application events by adding a message box to the `Startup` and `Shutdown` events for one of your projects. The `Startup` message box appears when you start that project, and the `Shutdown` message box appears when you close the application.

10. Try some of the condition notifications in the Compile tab of the Project Designer. Then write a little code in your application to see the impact of the conditions.
    For example, set the **Use of variable prior to assignment** notification to **Error**, and then insert code such as this:

    ```
    Dim x As String
    If x = "yes" Then

    End If
    ```

    You get an error in the Error List window stating that the variable `x` is used before it is assigned.

11. Set some of your Visual Studio settings, and try the Export feature.

CHAPTER 4

BUILDING THE USER INTERFACE LAYER

Better keep yourself clean and bright; you are the window through which you must see the world.
—George Bernard Shaw

The user interface (UI) is the window through which your users must see and interact with your application. By keeping the user interface clean and bright on the outside, you present a nice look and feel to the user, making it easier to use your application. And keeping it clean and bright on the inside makes it easier for you to maintain it and to implement the many changes that are inevitably requested.

This chapter assumes that you know how to build the outside of your user interface—that you know how to add controls on forms to create a nice look for your application. The focus here is on building the inside—the code behind the user interface. This includes defining event handlers, building a base form class, and using standard programming interfaces to work with your forms in a consistent manner. The Purchase Tracker sample application begun in the preceding chapter is used to demonstrate these techniques.

What Does This Chapter Cover?

This chapter demonstrates the following techniques:

- Creating a form using a template
- Using smart tags
- Setting the tab order
- Understanding partial classes
- Documenting the form using XML comments
- Creating an event handler with the `Handles` clause

- Using `AddHandler` to add event handlers at runtime
- Iterating through all the controls on a form
- Building a base form class
- Using form instances
- Building an MDI user interface
- Defining a standard programmatic interface
- Saving user and application settings
- Drawing graphics
- Printing a form
- Using structured exception handling
- Defining strongly typed resource strings
- Using composite formatting

It also covers the following Visual Basic concepts:

- Understanding the purpose of the `Inherits` keyword
- Casting variables
- Creating a recursive method
- Using `OrElse` and `AndAlso` for short-circuiting
- Using `Me` to reference a derived class instance
- Using `MyBase` to reference a base class instance
- Understanding when to use the `Using` keyword

When building your application's UI, you have two primary choices. You can build a Windows-based UI or a Web-based UI. Some applications have both, using a Windows-based UI for internal users and a Web-based UI for external users. This chapter focuses on a Windows-based UI. If you are doing a Web-based UI, see the "Additional Reading" section of this chapter for reference material.

Creating a Form

In a Windows-based application, you create the user interface by building a set of forms. Each form is composed of a set of visual elements defined with controls, and the code behind those controls.

It is often the user interface that changes the most. The users provide you with some requirements, and you define a user interface to meet those requirements. But then the users see the user interface and have additional suggestions for improvements, enhancements, and new features.

So you can save time over the life of your application by building the user interface to be as easily changeable as possible.

It is straightforward to modify the form's layout, adding or moving controls, changing label text, and so on. With a little bit of forethought, you can build the code behind the controls so that it is also easy to modify. One technique for making the code behind your forms effortless to change is to have a standardized and logical structure for the code, as described in this section. Another technique is to build a base form class, which is described later in this chapter.

This section outlines the process of building both the visual elements and the code behind the form.

Building the Visual Elements of the Form

The first step in building a user interface is to build the outside—to add controls to the form to define its appearance. Anyone doing any Visual Basic or other visual programming language already knows how to do this, so only the high-level steps are described here.

To create the visual elements of a form:

1. Right-click the project and select **Add | New Item** from the context menu, *or* select **Project | Add New Item** from the main menu bar.

   Alternatively, you could select **Add | Windows Form** from the context menu, *or* select **Project | Add Windows Form** from the main menu bar.

2. Select the **Windows Form** template, name the form, and click the **Add** button.

   If you created your own form template using steps from the preceding chapter, you can use your form template here.

   Use standard naming conventions for your form name. One recommended standard uses the entity name with a suffix defining the type of project item. You could use a suffix of "Win" (ProductWin) or "Form" (ProductForm). Whichever you select, be consistent.

NOTE: If you are doing both Windows and Web development, you may want to use "Win" and "Web" as the suffixes instead of "Form" since there are both Windows forms and Web forms.

Visual Studio creates the form file with a .vb extension, adds it to Solution Explorer, and then displays the form in the Forms Designer.

3. Add `Panel`, `Label`, and other controls as desired to complete the visual design.

Use standard naming conventions for your control names. The old Visual Basic standard was to use a two- or three-letter abbreviation for the type of control as a prefix, such as `txtName` or `cmdOK`. The current standard is to use the full control type name as a suffix, such as `NameTextBox` or `OKButton`. (When Visual Studio creates controls for you, as shown in Chapter 7, "Binding the User Interface to the Business Objects," it uses this standard.) Whichever you select, be consistent.

The result could look something like Figure 4.1.

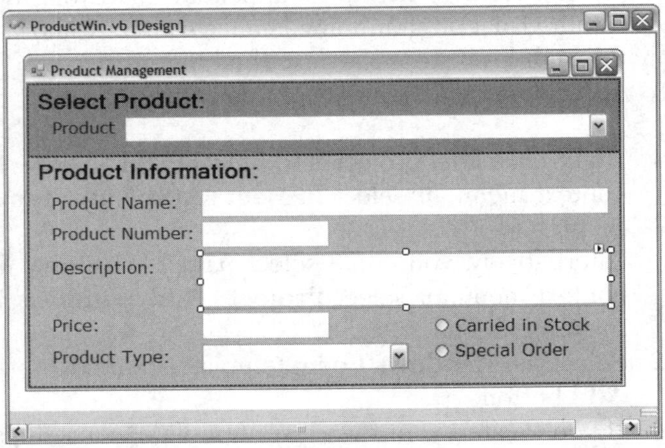

Figure 4.1   With Visual Studio, you can easily build the visual layout of the form.

NOTE: There is an easier way to create forms using the Data Sources window. See Chapter 7 for more information.

Notice the two `Panel` controls in Figure 4.1. `Panel` controls allow you to lay out the other controls in a visually interesting and end-user task-oriented manner. In this design, panels separate the form's visual elements.

The top panel defines a selection area where the user can select the item to edit, and the bottom panel contains an informational area to display the item information. Using the `Dock` property, you can dock a `Panel` control to the top of the form to provide the selection area and dock a `Panel` control to fill the remainder of the form to provide the informational area.

NOTE: Use the Document Outline window (**View | Other Windows | Document Outline**) to work with the controls on your form in outline view. With outline view, you can more readily see which controls are on other controls and move the controls between containers such as `Panel` or `TabControl` controls.

Building Along

For the Purchase Tracker sample application:

- Visual Studio created a default form for you when you created the Windows Application project (**PTWin**). In *Solution Explorer*, change the name of this default form from Form1 to **ProductWin**.
  When you change the name of a form in Solution Explorer, Visual Studio changes the form name in the Code Editor accordingly.

NOTE: In prior versions of Visual Studio, the recommendation was to always remove the default form from the project, because changing the name of the default form did not change the name of the form class. Visual Studio 2005 fixed that problem.

This form is a data entry form for products that can be purchased.

- Add two `Panel` controls to the form, and set their `Dock` property.
- Add a `Label` control to each of the panels to describe their contents to the user.
- Add a `Label` and `ComboBox` control to the selection area panel.
  Be sure to name the controls following your naming convention.
- Add `Label`, `TextBox`, and other controls to the informational area panel, as shown in Figure 4.1.
  Be sure to name the controls following your naming convention.

NOTE: Do not try to resize the Description `TextBox` control to allow for multiple lines at this point, as shown in the figure. This step is handled in the next "Building Along."

Run the application. It displays your splash screen and then shows the ProductWin form, but it doesn't do anything because there is no code behind it yet.

One of the new features in Visual Studio 2005 is the designer smart tag. A **smart tag** is a context-sensitive menu provided on controls in the designer that allows you to perform common design-time tasks.

To use the smart tag feature:

1. Select the control in the Forms Designer.
   A smart tag glyph in the shape of an arrow appears in the upper right of the control, as shown with the Description `TextBox` control in Figure 4.1.
2. Click the smart tag glyph.
   The options appropriate for the selected control are displayed for selection.

Use smart tags any time you want to view or edit the most common properties for a control without leaving the design surface.

NOTE: The options available in the smart tag for a control are not adjustable. However, if you build your own control, you can define custom smart tags. See the "Additional Reading" section for more information on building custom controls.

Building Along

For the Purchase Tracker sample application:
- Display the **ProductWin** form in the Forms Designer.
- Select the **Description** `TextBox` control on the **ProductWin** form. The smart tag glyph appears in the upper right of the control.
- In the smart tag context menu, check the **MultiLine** checkbox. When checked, the user can enter multiple lines of text at runtime.

> ■ Expand the height of the **Description** `TextBox` control.
>
> Run the application. It displays your splash screen and then shows the ProductWin form. Enter multiple lines of text into the Description textbox to try out the multiline feature.

A few other things you may want to do at this point are to give the form some style, prepare the form for resizing, and define the tab order, as described next.

Form Style

Define a basic color and font scheme for your application, and use it consistently throughout all your forms. To save time, you can set a default font for a form or panel. All the controls on that form or panel then use the default font unless you specify a different font for a control.

Resizing

Allowing the user to resize forms in your application gives the user some flexibility in working with the forms. The user can make a form bigger to see more information, or smaller to more easily see the form along with other information on the screen.

Set the form's `FormBorderStyle` property to `Sizable` to allow the user to size the form. Then use the `Anchor` and `Dock` properties of the controls on the form to define how they are resized as the form resizes.

Building Along

For the Purchase Tracker sample application:

- Display the **ProductWin** form in the Forms Designer.
- Set the form's **FormBorderStyle** property to **Sizable**.
- Use the **Anchor** and **Dock** properties of the controls on the form to define how each control resizes as the form is resized.

  You set the `Dock` property for both `Panel` controls in an earlier "Building Along." For the **Product** ComboBox and **Description** TextBox controls, set the `Anchor` to `Top, Left, Right`. This ensures that the widths of both controls grow and shrink as the form width changes. For the other controls, leave their `Anchor` property as the default.

> Run the application. It displays your splash screen and then shows the ProductWin form. Resize the form and see how the controls resize. If they don't resize as desired, adjust the Anchor and Dock properties. Repeat until you get the desired resizing results.

Tab Order

To make it easier for the user to move around on the form, set the tab order to a logical sequence. The **tab order** defines the order in which the controls are accessed if the user presses the Tab key. Normally, this is defined from left to right and from top to bottom.

Visual Studio provides a Tab Order feature in the Forms Designer for this purpose.

To set the tab order for a form:

1. Select **View | Tab Order** from the main menu bar to activate the Tab Order feature.

   The form appears with the tab order values displayed, as shown in Figure 4.2.

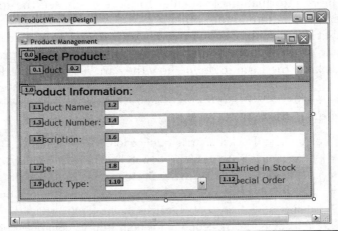

Figure 4.2   The Tab Order feature of the Forms Designer allows you to view and set the tab order for the controls on your forms.

2. Click the controls in the order in which they should be accessed. The tab order numbers change automatically.

If your controls are on a container control, such as a `Panel`, click the container first to set the container's tab order number, and then click each control in the container in order. The containers are given the base tab order numbers (0, 1, and so on). The controls in the container are given numbers within that container (0.0, 0.1, 1.0, 1.1, and so on).

If you make a mistake, turn off the Tab Order feature by selecting **View** | **Tab Order** again, and turn it back on to start over.

3. When you are finished with the tab order, select **View** | **Tab Order** again to turn off the feature.

Even though the user cannot set focus to a label, defining the tab order of each `Label` control is important if you plan to use mnemonics. In this context, a **mnemonic** is a character in the text of a label that appears underlined. When the user presses Alt plus the underlined character, the control that follows the `Label` control in the tab order receives focus. This provides keyboard navigation to controls on your form.

To set a mnemonic, insert an ampersand character (&) in front of the character you want to have underlined in the `Text` property of the `Label` control. For example, if you want the user to press Alt+D to jump to the Description textbox, set the `Text` property of the Description `Label` control to `&Description`. Then ensure that the `Label` control's `UseMnemonic` property is set to `True` and that the `Label` control immediately precedes the associated `TextBox` control in the tab order.

Use the Tab Order feature for every data entry form to set a logical tab order and allow the user to smoothly tab from control to control.

Building Along

For the Purchase Tracker sample application:

- Display the **ProductWin** form in the Forms Designer.
- Use the Tab Order feature to set the tab order of the controls on the form.

  Select the top `Panel` control first, and then select every control on that panel. Then select the bottom `Panel` control, and then select every control on that panel. The result appears in Figure 4.2.
- If desired, set up keyboard navigation to some of the controls on the form using mnemonics.

Run the application. It displays your splash screen and then shows the ProductWin form. Use the Tab key to move through the controls on the form. If you set the tab order correctly, you should move through the controls from left to right, starting at the top of the form and continuing to the bottom.

Use the techniques in this section to build the visual elements for all the forms in your application. Be sure that the overall design, including colors, fonts, and styles, is consistent in all the forms to make them appear to the user as a cohesive application.

Building the Code for the Form

After the form's visual elements are in place, you can focus on the code behind the form. Visual Studio automatically adds some of the code for you. You can then add whatever custom code is needed to implement the form's functional features.

Viewing Your Form Class

To view the code for a form in the Code Editor, select the form in Solution Explorer and click **View Code** on the Solution Explorer toolbar. You will see that Visual Studio automatically defined your form class. You build all your code for the form in this class:

```
Public Class ProductWin

End Class
```

If you worked with Visual Studio 2002 or 2003, you may notice that something is missing from this code. The automatically generated hidden region of code that programmatically defined all the controls on the form, along with their associated properties, is gone. Well, it is not really gone—just moved.

Viewing Visual Studio's Generated Code

The .NET 2.0 Framework introduced the concept of partial classes. A **partial class** allows you to divide a class into multiple physical code files. Partial classes are primarily used to split generated code segments from customizable code segments. This allows a code generator to rebuild its code segments without affecting the code you write. You may see some documentation refer to a partial class as a **partial type**.

For Windows forms, the customizable class (where you write your code) is shown in Solution Explorer with the form name and a .vb extension. The designer-generated class is named with the form name and a .designer.vb extension. By default, the designer-generated class is hidden in Solution Explorer.

To view the generated partial class:

1. Select the Windows Application project in Solution Explorer.
2. Click **Show All Files** on the Solution Explorer toolbar, *or* select **Project | Show All Files** from the main menu bar.

   All the files associated with the Windows Application project appear in Solution Explorer, as shown in Figure 4.3.

Figure 4.3   View all of the files in the project directory by selecting the project and clicking Show All Files on the Solution Explorer toolbar.

3. Open the node named with your Windows form in Solution Explorer.
4. Double-click on the designer-generated code file, which is named with the .designer.vb extension.

The designer-generated partial class is displayed in the Code Editor. The basic structure of the partial class, with all the detailed code removed for brevity, is as follows:

```
<Global.Microsoft.VisualBasic.CompilerServices.
➥DesignerGenerated()> _
Partial Class ProductWin
    Inherits Windows.Forms.Form


End Class
```

The `Partial` keyword in this code example defines that this is a part of the ProductWin class and that the rest of the code is in another code file. The `Inherits` keyword defines the class that this form inherits from. By default, Windows forms inherit from the `Form` class in the `System.Windows.Forms` .NET Framework library. This makes the class behave as a Windows form.

If you look at a designer-generated partial class, you will see that it includes the code to define all the controls on the form, along with all the properties that you set for the controls. Visual Studio uses the designer-generated class to retain all the form and control information. The .NET runtime uses the designer-generated class to build the form at runtime.

When you are finished looking at the partial class, you can hide all the extra files by unselecting **Show All Files** in the Solution Explorer toolbar or by unselecting the **Project** | **Show All Files** option from the main menu bar.

Since this partial class is for the designer-generated code, do *not* add any of your custom code to this class. Instead, use the customizable class (defined with the .vb extension) for your code.

You can create your own partial classes. However, best practices suggest that you not use partial classes unnecessarily. Use them only when you need to separate generated code from custom code or provide functionality in a class that you cannot extend in any other way.

As an example, suppose you have a VB6 component that you are calling that needs the Visual Basic 2005 code to pass it a scripting dictionary or some other structure that does not work well with Option Strict On. But you want to ensure that Option Strict is set On in your class, as defined in Chapter 3, "Building Projects." To allow the majority of your class to keep Option Strict On, you can create a partial class with Option Strict Off for the routines that require it to be off and still encapsulate all the functionality in one class.

Documenting the Form

The first code you should write is the documentation for the form. This ensures that the form's purpose is clear before you write any other code. Creating the documentation is easy with Visual Studio's XML comments feature.

To create documentation for the form:

1. Open the form in the Code Editor.
2. Move the insertion point immediately before the word `Public` in the `Public Class` statement.

3. Type three comment markers, defined in Visual Basic with apostrophes (' ' '), and press the Enter key.
   The XML comments feature automatically creates the structure of your form documentation, as follows:

```
'''  <summary>
'''
'''  </summary>
'''  <remarks></remarks>
Public Class ProductWin

End Class
```

NOTE: If you type the three comment markers in the empty line above the class definition instead of on the same line as the class definition, you don't need to press the Enter key to generate the documentation structure.

---

4. Type a summary of the form's purpose between the `summary` tags and any remarks between the `remark` tags.
   Your documentation may be similar to this:

```
'''  <summary>
'''  Displays the form for entry of Product information
'''  </summary>
'''  <remarks></remarks>
```

Use the `summary` tags to describe the form and the `remarks` tags to add supplemental information. The `summary` is the most important tag, because it is the one used by Visual Studio.

When you provide a summary of the form using XML comments, your form displays documentation about itself in appropriate places within Visual Studio. For example, the summary appears in the List Members box, shown in Figure 4.4. Open the List Members box by typing a part of the class name in the Code Editor and pressing Ctrl+Spacebar *or* by selecting **Edit | Intellisense | List Members** from the main menu bar *or* by clicking the **Display an Object Member List** icon on the Text Editor toolbar.

Using XML comments to document your classes, including your form classes, makes it easier for you and other developers to work with your classes.

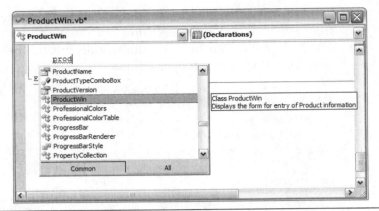

Figure 4.4   The documentation provided in the List Members box is the summary defined in the XML documentation for the class.

Building Along

For the Purchase Tracker sample application:
- Open the **ProductWin** form in the Code Editor.
- Add documentation for the **ProductWin** form using XML comments.

In the Code Editor, view the comments by typing prod and then pressing Ctrl+Spacebar to display the List Members box, as shown in Figure 4.4.

Organizing the Code Structure

Code that is organized is much easier to maintain, because you can quickly find the code that needs to be changed. When you standardize this organizational structure, any member of the team can quickly locate and modify any form code, because the layout of each form's code is the same.

A form is normally composed of a set of private properties, some form event handlers, many control event handlers, and some private methods. You define this organizational structure of a form using regions, as described in Chapter 3. If you built a form template using the information from Chapter 3 and then used that template when creating your form, these regions are already defined in your code. If not, you can create the regions as follows:

```
Public Class ProductWin

#Region " Private Properties"

#End Region

#Region " Form Events"

#End Region

#Region " Control Events"

#End Region

#Region " Private Methods"

#End Region

End Class
```

Add any other regions as needed to define the standard types of code for your forms. For example, if your form exposes properties, you can add a Public Properties region.

NOTE: Once you define the standard set of regions to use in your forms, define a custom form template, as described in Chapter 3. Provide this template to all the members of your team. This ensures that all the forms of your application follow your standard structure.

As you develop the code for the application, private properties are added to the Private Properties region, form event handlers are added to the Form Events region, and so on. To further aid in the organization, you can insert the routines within each region in alphabetical order.

NOTE: If you don't use a region, delete it. For example, if your form has no private properties, delete the Private Properties region. This makes it clear that the form has no private properties without opening the Private Properties region to see that it has no private properties.

Use regions to organize the structure of your code. By defining a standard set of regions, you can more easily work with code written by any member of your coding team. And by expanding and collapsing regions, you can more easily focus on one set of code at a time.

Building Along

For the Purchase Tracker sample application:
- Open the **ProductWin** form in the Code Editor.
- Add the regions as defined in this section.

In the Code Editor, open and close the regions to see how they hide and show their contents.

Creating Event Handlers

Building Windows applications has always been about responding to events: a form loading, a button clicked, a combo box entry selected. Visual Basic has always made it easy to place controls on forms and respond to each control's events. The basic technique for putting controls on forms has not changed much since the first versions of Visual Basic, but there are now more techniques for responding to the events from those controls using event handlers.

An **event handler** is a method that is executed in response to an event. For example, a Windows form generates a `Load` event when the form is loaded. You can write an event handler to handle the `Load` event and execute specific code when the form loads. If you have ever double-clicked on a control on a form and then written code in the generated method, you have created an event handler.

This section details how to create an event handler for one control or for a set of controls at design time. It also describes how to define event handlers at runtime.

Creating an Event Handler for One Control

If you want to respond to a specific event from one control, you can create an event handler for that one control's event. For example, if you want to respond to a click on a specific button, you can create an event handler for the `Click` event on that button.

The technique for creating an event handler for one event from one control has not changed. Just double-click on the control, and Visual Studio generates the event handler for the most common event for that control.

If you need to create an event handler for an event that is not the most common event for the control, there are a few more steps. The specific steps depend on whether you generate the event handler when in the Code Editor or in the Forms Designer.

To write an event handler for an event generated by a single control using the Code Editor:

1. Open the form in the Code Editor.
2. Select the control name from the Class Name drop-down at the top left of the Code Editor.
3. Select the event name from the Event drop-down at the top right of the Code Editor.

Visual Studio then generates the event handler method signature and displays it in the Code Editor.

To write an event handler for an event generated by a single control from the Forms Designer:

1. Open the form in the Forms Designer.
2. Select the control on the form.
3. View the Properties window (**View** | **Properties Window**).
4. Click **Events** in the Properties window toolbar.
5. Double-click on the desired event.

Visual Studio generates the event handler method signature and displays it in the Code Editor.

For example, you could write an event handler for the `Enter` event to change the background color of a `TextBox` control when the user enters the control. Select a `TextBox` control on a form, view the events in the Properties window, and double-click on the `Enter` event. The resulting event handler generated in the Code Editor looks similar to the following:

```
Private Sub NameTextBox_Enter(ByVal sender As Object, _
    ByVal e As System.EventArgs) Handles NameTextBox.Enter

End Sub
```

Notice that the generated name of the event handler is similar to the name given to event procedures in classic versions of Visual Basic. However, the event handler name no longer has any intrinsic meaning. It is just the method (subroutine) name. You could modify the preceding event handler as follows:

```
Private Sub ProcessEnter(ByVal sender As Object, _
        ByVal e As System.EventArgs) Handles NameTextBox.Enter

End Sub
```

It is the `Handles` keyword that defines the control and event that the handler processes. The `ProcessEnter` method handles the `Enter` event for the textbox named `NameTextBox` because that is the control and event that are defined in the `Handles` clause.

Once you create the event handler with the correct signature, the event handler appears in the Events view of the Properties window for the control, as shown in Figure 4.5.

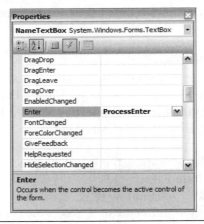

Figure 4.5 The Events view of the Properties window lists all the events that are implemented for the control, along with the name of the method defined as the event handler.

NOTE: If you add the event handler using `AddHandler`, as described later in this section, it is *not* listed for the event in the Properties window.

The parameters for all control event handlers are similar. The first parameter defines the object, usually the control, that generated the event:

```
ByVal sender As Object
```

The parameter is declared `As Object` to define a general `sender` object. This allows the same event handler to be used for many different types of controls.

To access the `sender` object's properties or methods, you need to cast the `sender` variable from the general `Object` data type to a specific control type. **Casting** is translating a variable that is defined to be of one type to another type.

Visual Basic and the .NET Framework provide several different ways to cast variables from one type to another. You can use the Visual Basic conversion functions such as `CStr`, `CInt`, and `CType`. If you are converting to a string, you can use the .NET Framework `ToString` method. If you are converting from a generalized type to a more specific type, you can use the `DirectCast` or `TryCast` keywords.

NOTE: `DirectCast` and `TryCast` provide somewhat better performance than `CType` when you're converting from the `Object` data type to a more specific data type.

`DirectCast` casts a variable from a defined type to a more specialized type in the same object hierarchy. `TryCast` is similar to `DirectCast`, but it doesn't fail if the operation is unsuccessful. Instead, it returns `Nothing`.

You can use the `DirectCast` and `TryCast` keywords only when casting from a general type to a more specific type, such as from type `Object` to type `Control` or, even more specifically, to type `TextBox`. The cast type *must* be in the same object hierarchy as the original type. So you can use these keywords to cast from a variable declared as a general `Object` data type to a `Control` data type, because a control *is* an object, but you cannot use them to cast from a `String` data type to an `Integer` data type, because an integer *is not* a string.

Cast a variable from an object type to a more specific type as follows:

```
Private Sub ProcessEnter(ByVal sender As Object, _
    ByVal e As System.EventArgs) Handles NameTextBox.Enter
```

```
      Dim tb As TextBox
      tb = DirectCast(sender, TextBox)
End Sub
```

This code casts the `sender` object variable from a general `Object` data type to the more specific `TextBox` type. The `DirectCast` method is used here instead of the `TryCast` method because this is an event handler for the `TextBox` control, so there is little possibility that the cast could fail.

The second parameter of the event handler defines the event arguments. It normally has this form:

```
ByVal e As System.EventArgs
```

This parameter provides access to any arguments associated with the event. For example, the event arguments for the `FormClosing` event allow you to cancel the event and stop the form from closing.

A frequent user interface requirement is to highlight the control on the form that has input focus. The user can then easily glance at the form and see which control is active. To implement this requirement, you need to respond to the `Enter` event and change the control's background color when the user enters the control. You also need to respond to the `Leave` event to change the background color back to the default color when the user leaves the control.

NOTE: `Enter` and `Leave` events are designed for this type of operation and should be used instead of `LostFocus` and `GotFocus`.

To complete the control highlighting example, the `Enter` event handler sets the background color of the `TextBox` control to a specific color as the user enters the control:

```
Private Sub ProcessEnter(ByVal sender As Object, _
   ByVal e As System.EventArgs) Handles NameTextBox.Enter
   Dim tb As TextBox
   tb = DirectCast(sender, TextBox)
   tb.BackColor = Color.BurlyWood
End Sub
```

Casting is required in this example because the `sender` variable is declared to be of type `Object`, and an `Object` does not have a `BackColor` property. Casting the variable to a `TextBox` provides access to the `BackColor` property.

Notice that this code works only for `TextBox` controls because of the casting. If you want to reuse this code for other types of controls, you may want to cast to the more general `Control` type, which also has a `BackColor` property:

```
Private Sub ProcessEnter(ByVal sender As Object, _
    ByVal e As System.EventArgs) Handles NameTextBox.Enter
    DirectCast(sender, Control).BackColor = Color.BurlyWood
End Sub
```

The `Leave` event handler sets the background color back to its original color:

```
Private Sub ProcessLeave(ByVal sender As Object, _
    ByVal e As System.EventArgs) Handles NameTextBox.Leave
    DirectCast(sender, Control).BackColor = _
                    Color.FromKnownColor(KnownColor.Window)
End Sub
```

NOTE: The `FromKnownColor` method of the `Color` object allows you to specify a system color—in this case, the standard Window color.

The `ProcessEnter` event handler sets the background color of the `NameTextBox` control when the user enters the control and `ProcessLeave` sets the background color back to its normal color when the user leaves the control.

But the original requirement was to have *each* control change its background color when it gets focus, and change the color back when it loses focus. One way to accomplish this requirement is to create `Enter` and `Leave` event handlers for each control on the form. But there is an easier way to assign multiple controls to an event handler as described in the next sections.

Defining a specific event handler for a specific control and event is most useful when unique code is required for that control and event. For example, when implementing the `Click` event on a `Button` control or `SelectedValueChanged` event on a `ComboBox` control, you have code in the event handler unique to the control and event.

Building Along

For the Purchase Tracker sample application:
- Display the **ProductWin** form in the Forms Designer.
- Select the **Product Name** TextBox control.
- Double-click on the **Enter** event in the Properties window for the control.
  Visual Studio generates the appropriate event handler for the control and displays it in the Code Editor.
- In the Code Editor, change the name of the event handler method to **ProcessEnter**.
- Add code to the event handler to change the **BackColor** property of the TextBox control.
- Follow similar steps for the **Leave** event.
  Name the event handler **ProcessLeave**.

Run the application. It displays your splash screen and then shows the ProductWin form. Use the Tab key to move through the controls on the form. When you move into the Product Name textbox, the control's background color changes to the defined color. When you tab out of the control, the background color changes back.

Creating an Event Handler for Several Controls

To provide consistency in your user interface, you often want a set of controls to have the same behavior. For example, suppose your application needs to change the background color of the control that has focus. To implement this requirement, you need to define Enter and Leave event handlers for each control on the form.

A set of controls can share an event handler by simply adding another control and event name to the Handles clause like this:

```
Private Sub ProcessEnter(ByVal sender As Object, _
    ByVal e As System.EventArgs) _
    Handles NameTextBox.Enter, DescriptionTextBox.Enter
    DirectCast(sender, Control).BackColor = Color.BurlyWood
End Sub
```

Instead of typing each of these, you can have Visual Studio automatically add the Handles clause for the other controls by using the Events view of the Properties window (see Figure 4.5).

To associate an event handler with additional controls and events from the Forms Designer:

1. Open the form in the Forms Designer.
2. On the form, select the control to add to the event handler.
3. View the Properties window (**View | Properties Window**).
4. Client Events in the Properties window toolbar.
5. In the Properties window, locate the control's event to add to the event handler and select the event handler name from the drop-down list.

   Only methods defined with appropriate event handler parameters are listed for selection.

When you have completed these steps for each control, you will see that Visual Studio added the control's event to the `Handles` clause.

The `ProcessEnter` event handler then handles the `Enter` events for each control defined in the `Handles` clause. You can add any number of controls to the `Handles` clause to use the same event handler for those controls. Since the `sender` variable in this example is cast to a general `Control` object, you can even add controls of other types to the `Handles` clause, such `ComboBox` or `MaskedEdit` controls.

NOTE FOR VB6 DEVELOPERS: This is definitely an advantage over the Visual Basic classic control arrays that could only share events for controls of the same type.

If the event handler needs to perform differently based on the control that generated the event, the event handler can reference the control's `Name` property. For example:

```
Private Sub ProcessEnter(ByVal sender As Object, _
   ByVal e As System.EventArgs) _
   Handles NameTextBox.Enter, DescriptionTextBox.Enter
   If DirectCast(sender, Control).Name = "NameTextBox" Then
       ' Use one color for name
      DirectCast(sender, Control).BackColor = Color.LightYellow
   Else
       ' Use a different color for other fields
```

```
        DirectCast(sender, Control).BackColor = Color.BurlyWood
    End If
End Sub
```

This code sets the control's background color to one color if it is the `NameTextBox` control and to a different color for any other control, based on the control name.

NOTE: Care must be taken when using the control's `Name` property in this manner. If the control name is changed at a later time, this code needs to be adjusted as well.

You could use `NameTextBox.Name` instead of the quoted string. The code then generates a compile error if the `TextBox` control's name is changed.

NOTE: If you find you are using extensive `If` or `Select` statements in your event handlers, the code may not be general enough to use one event handler. Consider using separate event handlers instead.

Adding controls to the `Handles` clause to accomplish this objective has one major downside. Each time you add a control to the form, you need to remember to add the control to both the `Enter` and `Leave` event handlers. It would be much better if the event handlers were assigned to the controls automatically at runtime, as described in the next section.

Supporting events from multiple controls with one event handler using the `Handles` clause is most useful if the event handler supports only a few well-defined controls and events. For example, a Print button on a toolbar and a Print option on a menu could use the same event handler by adding both to the `Handles` clause.

Building Along

For the Purchase Tracker sample application:
- Display the **ProductWin** form in the Forms Designer.
- Select the **Description** `TextBox` control.
- Select **ProcessEnter** from the drop-down for the **Enter** event in the Properties window for the control.

Visual Studio adds the second `Handles` clause to the event.

■ Select **ProcessLeave** from the drop-down for the **Leave** event in the Properties window for the control.

Visual Studio adds the second `Handles` clause to the event.

Run the application. It displays your splash screen and then shows the ProductWin form. Use the Tab key to move through the controls on the form. When you move into the Product Name or Description textbox, the control's background color changes to the defined color. When you tab out of the control, the background color changes back.

Creating an Event Handler for Controls at Runtime

Any time you need to associate an event handler with a set of controls that could change over time, consider assigning the control events to the event handler at runtime. As the form loads, you can iterate through all the controls on the form and associate the control's event with a particular event handler. As you add controls to the form, the new controls are automatically associated with the defined event handler.

You associate a control and event with an event handler using the `AddHandler` statement. The `AddHandler` statement associates a control's event with an event handler at runtime. There is also a `RemoveHandler` statement if you want to remove the event handler at runtime.

To use the `AddHandler` statement:

1. Create the event handler method *without* the `Handles` clause:

```
Private Sub ProcessEnter(ByVal sender As Object, _
    ByVal e As System.EventArgs)
    DirectCast(sender, Control).BackColor = _
                            Color.BurlyWood
End Sub
```

For code organization, an event handler without a `Handles` clause is normally implemented in the Private Methods region instead of the Control Events region.

2. In the form's `Load` event, insert an `AddHandler` statement, referencing the control, event, and event handler:

```
AddHandler NameTextBox.Enter, AddressOf ProcessEnter
```

The first parameter of the **AddHandler** statement defines the control's name and the event to handle. The second parameter defines the event handler. The **AddressOf** operator allows you to define the method that is executed when the event occurs for the specific instance of the control. More specifically, the **AddressOf** operator creates a delegate that references the specified event handler method. A **delegate** is an object you can use to call the methods of other objects.

The **AddHandler** statement must execute before the event can occur. So, for this example, the **AddHandler** statement is in the **Load** event for the form:

```
Private Sub ProductWin_Load(ByVal sender As Object, _
    ByVal e As System.EventArgs) Handles Me.Load
    AddHandler NameTextBox.Enter, AddressOf ProcessEnter
    AddHandler NameTextBox.Leave, AddressOf ProcessLeave
    AddHandler DescriptionTextBox.Enter, AddressOf ProcessEnter
    AddHandler DescriptionTextBox.Leave, AddressOf ProcessLeave
End Sub
```

But this still requires that the **AddHandler** statement be defined for every control. A better approach is to loop through all the controls on the form and assign the event handler.

In classic versions of Visual Basic, all the controls on a form were accessible through a controls collection. Now the controls collection for the form contains only the actual controls *on* the form. In the example shown in Figure 4.1, the form has only two controls *on* the form: the selection **Panel** control and the information **Panel** control. All the other controls are on one of the **Panel** controls and are considered to be *children* of the **Panel** control on which they reside. So where the classic Visual Basic controls collection was flat, the current controls collection is hierarchical.

To iterate through all the controls on the form, you need to create a method that is recursive. **Recursive** means that the method calls itself. This allows the code to be run for every level of the hierarchy.

The code required to recursively iterate through all the controls on a form and set their event handlers is as follows:

```
Private Sub AddEventHandlers(ByVal ctrlContainer As Control)
    For Each ctrl As Control In ctrlContainer.Controls
        If TypeOf ctrl Is TextBox Then
            AddHandler ctrl.Enter, AddressOf ProcessEnter
            AddHandler ctrl.Leave, AddressOf ProcessLeave
        End If
```

```
      ' If the control has children,
      ' recursively call this function
      If ctrl.HasChildren Then
          AddEventHandlers(ctrl)
      End If
   Next
End Sub
```

The `For` loop processes each control that is physically on the form. If the control has children, this method then calls itself passing in the control. This causes the method to process any controls that are physically on the container control. This repeats until all controls and all children of all controls are processed.

The code in this example sets only the handler for `TextBox` controls. You can modify it to handle other controls by changing the `TypeOf` line as follows:

```
If TypeOf ctrl Is TextBox OrElse TypeOf ctrl Is ComboBox Then
```

This line of code sets the handler for `TextBox` and `ComboBox` controls. You can add other control types as well by adding additional `OrElse` clauses.

NOTE: If you have not been using the `OrElse` and `AndAlso` operators, it is highly recommended that you use them instead of `Or` and `And` for your conditional expressions. Using `OrElse` and `AndAlso` can improve your application's performance, because they allow short-circuiting. **Short-circuiting** is the process whereby if the first expression defines the resulting condition of the statement, the second expression is not evaluated.

For example, in the preceding line of code, if the type of the control is a `TextBox`, the condition is true, and the code within the `If` statement is executed without evaluating the second expression.

Because these event handlers should be set up before the `Enter` events could occur, call the `AddEventHandlers` method in the `Load` event handler for the form, and pass in the form as the control to process.

```
Private Sub ProductWin_Load(ByVal sender As Object, _
    ByVal e As System.EventArgs) Handles Me.Load
    AddEventHandlers(Me)
End Sub
```

Here, Me refers to the currently running instance, which is the instance of the form that is being loaded. The AddEventHandlers method starts with the controls on the form and adds event handlers for all the appropriate controls and all the children of all the controls.

The only thing left to do before this code is finished is documentation. Add XML comments for each method (ProcessEnter, ProcessLeave, and AddEventHandlers) by inserting three comment markers (''') immediately in front of the Private keyword for the method. For example, the ProcessEnter XML comments are as follows:

```
''' <summary>
''' Sets the background color when the user enters the control
''' </summary>
''' <param name="sender">Control generating the event</param>
''' <param name="e">Event arguments</param>
''' <remarks></remarks>
Private Sub ProcessEnter(ByVal sender As Object, _
    ByVal e As System.EventArgs)
    DirectCast(sender, Control).BackColor = Color.BurlyWood
End Sub
```

Notice how the XML comments automatically create the appropriate param tags based on the method's parameters. See Chapter 5, "Building the Business Logic Layer," for more information on documenting your methods using XML comments.

Use the AddHandler statement instead of the Handles clause on the event handler any time you want to add event handlers for a control and event at runtime. The AddHandler statement is also required if you are adding the control at runtime.

Building Along

For the Purchase Tracker sample application:

- Open the **ProductWin** form in the Code Editor.
- Remove the Handles clause from the **ProcessEnter** and **ProcessLeave** event handlers.
  Add XML comments for the methods.
- Add the **AddEventHandlers** method to the form's Private Methods region using the code defined in this section.
  Be sure to define XML comments for the method.

- Create an event handler for the form's **Load** event, and call the **AddEventHandlers** method, passing Me as the parameter.

Run the application. It displays your splash screen and then shows the ProductWin form. Use the Tab key to move through the controls on the form. The background color of each control changes to the defined color as you tab through it. When you tab out of the control, the background color changes back.

If you are not seeing the background color change in the ComboBox control, check your AddEventHandlers method, and ensure that the TypeOf checks for both TextBox and ComboBox controls.

Coding Event Handlers

The type of code that you add to an event handler depends on what you need your application to do when the event occurs. A combo box selection event may need to look up data for the selection and display it. An OK button click event may need to perform user-entry validation, save the data, and then close the form.

Regardless of the specific code needed in your event handler, here are some common guidelines and best practices when coding your event handlers:

- An event handler should have a maximum of four or five lines of code.

  If your event handler requires more than a few lines of code, consider writing the code in a separate private method (subroutine or function) within the form. The event handler can then call the method.

  Keeping your event handlers small makes them easier to manage and test.
- Code in the event handler (or associated method) should contain only user interface code.

  The purpose of the user interface component of your application is to manage the user interface. The user interface should include only code to respond to the form and control events and perform any other user interface manipulation, such as disabling controls and displaying messages.

Any code that validates business rules or performs any business processing should reside in the business object classes, detailed in Chapter 5. The user interface code can then call code in the business object classes to perform the necessary validation and processing.

■ If the code in the event handler or any code that the event handler calls could generate an exception that the event handler can handle, include an exception handler.

See the "Handling Exceptions" section later in this chapter for more information on exception handlers.

As you build each form of your application, you need to write event handlers to handle the events raised by the form and its controls. When writing an event handler for one control and one event, create the event handler and assign the single control's event in the `Handles` clause.

If you want to define an event handler to handle an event from several controls, create the event handler and assign each control's event in the `Handles` clause.

When you have a large set of controls that use the same event handler, such as the `Enter` and `Leave` events described in this section, create the event handler without the `Handles` clause and assign the control and event to the event handler using the `AddHandler` statement.

In all cases, be sure to document your event handler methods and follow the common guidelines for coding event handlers presented in this section to construct the best possible user interface component.

Building a Base Form Class

An important consideration in building your application's user interface is to construct the code for the forms so that the forms behave similarly. As the user learns the techniques for working with one form in the application, those techniques can be leveraged in working with other forms in the application. This minimizes the requirements for end-user training and support and maximizes end-user satisfaction.

One technique for achieving consistent behavior in all the forms of your application is to use inheritance. **Inheritance** is a way to reuse code by defining a class, called a **base class**, and using that class as the basis for the creation of any new class, called a **derived class**. The derived class then reuses all the code from the base class, gleaning its attributes and behaviors.

NOTE: Using inheritance is different from using a template. When you use a template, the code from the template is copied into your code. You can then modify that copied code as needed. If you later find an error in that copied code, you need to find everywhere it was copied and make the correction.

When you use inheritance, the code is reused at runtime. So any change made to the base class is recognized by all the derived classes when the application is executed.

You can take advantage of inheritance in a Windows Application project by building a form that is your **base form class**. The code in this form defines the standard behavior to reuse in other forms. You then inherit from that base form class when you create the other forms for the application. These forms are called **derived form classes**. The new forms then inherit all the attributes and behaviors of the base form class. You can even put controls on the base form class to display them on every derived form, providing **visual inheritance**.

This section details how to build a base form class. It then demonstrates how to create a derived form class by inheriting from the base form class. By using inheritance with your form classes, you can achieve a consistent behavior across all the forms of your application.

Creating the Base Form Class

Defining a set of event handlers and hooking them up by iterating through all the controls on the form, as demonstrated in the preceding section, ensures that each control on a form behaves consistently. But an application normally has many forms.

To provide consistent functionality in all the forms in your application, you could add the event handler code to a form template, as described in Chapter 3. The code would then be copied into each form that uses the template. But what if the user wants to change the behavior, like setting the background color to a different color? You would then need to modify the copied code in every form.

Another option is to build a separate utility class to contain the common event handler code. Each form would then call this utility class to hook up the controls. But this requires that each form correctly call the utility class methods.

A much better option is to build a base form class. A base form class is a normal Windows form that contains any visual elements you would like to have on all your forms. It also contains all the code that defines the common behavior for your forms. Any other form in your application can then inherit from this base form class to leverage the common controls and code.

The technique used to create a base form class is no different from creating any other form: add a new form to the project, and then add visual elements and code as needed. The only thing that makes a particular form a base form class is that other forms in the application inherit from this form.

To build a base form class:

1. Add a project item to your Windows Application project using the Windows Form template.
   If you created your own form template, you can use it here.
   Use a clear name for the base form class. This helps you (and your project team) keep track of the base form class.
2. Optionally add controls as desired.
   If common user interface elements appear on many of the forms of your application, such as a particular icon or set of buttons, adding these to the base form class may be useful. Any controls on the base form class appear on every form that inherits from the base form class, providing visual inheritance. Frequently, however, forms need to be tailored for a particular scenario so you won't add controls to the base form class.
3. Add code as desired.
   Add any code that is common to the forms of your application to the base form class.

Event handlers that provide a consistent response to form or control events are one of the most common types of code added to a base form class. Adding event handlers to the base form class ensures that specified events are handled consistently on any form that inherits from the base form class. It also minimizes the amount of repetitive code in the forms. Following the example from the prior sections, to implement the `Enter` and `Leave` event code in all forms, it makes sense to move all the code from the preceding section to a base form class.

When working with a base form class, you may need to refer to the instance of the derived form that inherits from this base form class. For example, the code in the base form class that calls the `AddEventHandlers` method for the current form is as follows:

```
Private Sub PTBaseWin_Load(ByVal sender As Object, _
    ByVal e As System.EventArgs) Handles Me.Load
    AddEventHandlers(Me)
End Sub
```

Here Me refers to the currently running instance, which is the instance of the derived form that inherits from this base form class.

NOTE: When the runtime loads a derived form class, it also loads the base form class automatically. You don't have to call the base form class to load it. Add any code to the Load event for the base form class that needs to execute when every derived form is loaded.

If other events need consistent processing throughout your application, you can add event handlers for these events in the base form class. Once you have your base form class in place, and your forms inherit from it, you have an application that has a very consistent feel. As the application changes over time and forms are added to the project, any new form inherits the same feel with very little work.

You may find that you need more than one set of standard form behaviors. For example, you may have one set of standard processing for your primary maintenance forms and another set of standard processing for your modal dialogs. Or you may have one set of processing for editable forms and one set for read-only forms. To achieve this requirement, you can define multiple base form classes.

NOTE: .NET does not support multiple inheritance. Any class can inherit from only one base class. So, in this example, any one form can inherit from only one base form class. But different forms can inherit from different base form classes.

You can define a hierarchy of base form classes. For example, a PTBaseWin class has code that is used by all forms. A PTEditBaseWin class inherits from PTBaseWin and adds functionality to support editable forms. A PTReadOnlyBaseWin class also inherits from PTBaseWin but provides functionality to support read-only forms. Any form in your application can then inherit directly from PTBaseWin or from one of the derived forms: PTEditBaseWin or PTReadOnlyBaseWin.

> ### Building Along
>
> For the Purchase Tracker sample application:
> - Add a form project item to the Windows Application project (**PTWin**) using the **Windows Form** template.
>   If you created your own form template using steps from the preceding chapter, you can use your form template here.
>   Name the form **PTBaseWin**.
>   If not already added by the selected template, add the standard set of regions to the form as described earlier in this chapter.
> - Cut the **ProcessEnter** and **ProcessLeave** methods from the **ProductWin** form and paste them into the **PTBaseWin** form.
>   Paste them into the Private Methods region.
> - Cut the **AddEventHandlers** method from the **ProductWin** form and paste it into the **PTBaseWin** form.
>   Paste it into the Private Methods region.
> - Cut the line of code from the **Load** event of the **ProductWin** form that called the **AddEventHandlers** method and paste it into the **Load** event of the **PTBaseWin** form.
>
> You now have an operational base form class that ensures the controls on all derived forms consistently process the Enter and Leave events. But at this point, the base form class does not actually do anything. To make use of the base form class, you need to inherit from it, as described in the next section.

Inheriting from the Base Form Class

People may say that you have your father's eyes or your mother's nose or your grandfather's temper. You inherit many common attributes and behaviors from the hierarchy that is your family tree. In software development, inheritance basically means the same thing. The parent (base class) has particular attributes and behaviors. Any child from that parent (derived class) inherits all the parent's attributes and behaviors.

NOTE: Unlike your family tree, however, the .NET Framework supports only single inheritance, meaning that each child can have only one parent. But it does support a hierarchy so that the child can have a parent, grandparent, great-grandparent, and so on. Each generation inherits every attribute and behavior of every prior generation.

The technique you use to inherit from the base form class depends on whether you are adding the inheritance to an existing form or adding a new form to the project. For existing forms, you need to change the `Inherits` statement in the hidden designer-generated code.

To define the inheritance for an existing form:

1. Select the Windows Application project in Solution Explorer.
2. Click **Show All Files** on the Solution Explorer toolbar, or select **Project | Show All Files** from the main menu bar.
   All the files associated with the Windows Application project appear in Solution Explorer in a tree view structure as shown in Figure 4.3.
3. In Solution Explorer, open the node for the form for which you want to set the inheritance.
4. Double-click on the designer-generated code file, which is named with the .designer.vb extension.
   The designer-generated partial class is then opened in the Code Editor.
5. Change the `Inherits` statement to inherit from your base form class instead of `Windows.Forms.Form`.

The resulting code looks similar to the following:

```
<Global.Microsoft.VisualBasic.CompilerServices.
➥DesignerGenerated()> _
Partial Class ProductWin
    Inherits PTBaseWin
```

The form, ProductWin in this case, now inherits from the base form class, `PTBaseWin`. Since the base form class inherits from `Windows.Forms.Form`, the ProductWin form still behaves like a Windows form, but it also has all the attributes and behaviors of the base form class.

As you add forms to your application, you want them to inherit from the base form class as well. The new forms then support the attributes and behaviors of the base form class, in this case consistently handling the `Enter` and `Leave` events.

To define the inheritance for a new form:

1. Select the Windows Application project in Solution Explorer.
2. Right-click the project and select **Build** from the context menu, *or* select **Build | Build PTWin** from the main menu bar.

The project containing the base form class must be compiled for it to be found by Visual Studio.

3. Add a project item to your Windows Application project selecting the **Inherited Form** template.

4. Enter the form name and click **Add**.

The Inheritance Picker dialog is displayed, as shown in Figure 4.6. Notice that all the forms in your Windows Application project are displayed because nothing distinguishes a form as a base form class other than your naming convention.

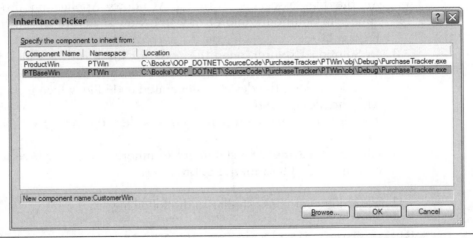

Figure 4.6 The Inheritance Picker dialog allows you to select the base form class. The form you are adding inherits from this class.

5. Select the base form class and click **OK**.

Visual Studio adds the new form to your project. If you look at the designer-generated partial class for the new form, you will see that the `Inherits` statement was set to the base form class you selected in the Inheritance Picker.

Repeat this process for each form you add to your application. If you forget to use the Inherited Form template when you add the form, you can use the steps to define the inheritance for an existing form, which was detailed earlier in this section.

Every form that inherits from the base form class has all the attributes and behaviors of the base form class. You don't have to write or modify any code.

> ### Building Along
>
> For the Purchase Tracker sample application:
> - Select the Windows Application project (**PTWin**) in Solution Explorer.
> - Click **Show All Files** on the Solution Explorer toolbar.
> - Open the **ProductWin.vb** node in Solution Explorer.
> - Double-click on the **ProductWin.designer.vb** file to open it in the Code Editor.
> - Change the `Inherits` statement to inherit from your base form class (**PTBaseWin**).
>
> Run the application. It displays your splash screen and then shows the ProductWin form. Use the Tab key to move through the controls on the form. The background color of each control changes to the defined color as you tab through it, just like it did before. You won't fully see the benefits of inheritance until you add more forms to your application.

Calling Code in the Base Form Class

In addition to event handlers, you may want to add other standard code to the base form class. You can then call this code from any of the derived forms.

For example, suppose you have a requirement to display a title on each of the forms of your application with a standard look. The title lists the logical name of the form along with the name of the particular item that was selected on the form, as shown in Figure 4.7.

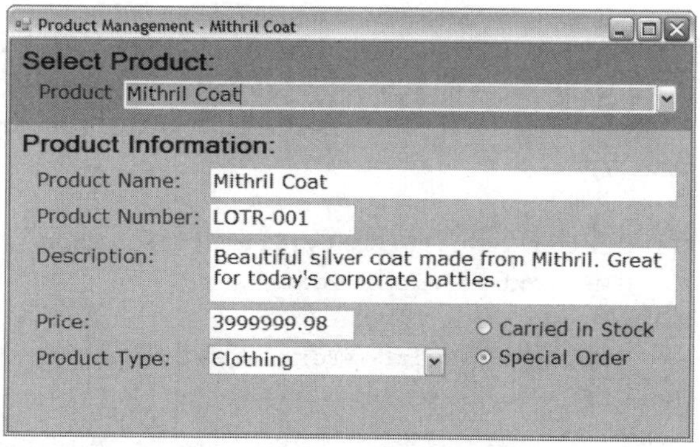

Figure 4.7   The title bar text for the ProductWin form displays the name of the form, along with the name of the particular product that was selected for edit.

NOTE: If you are not a *Lord of the Rings* fan, you may not know that Mithril is a fictional silver-like substance that can be used to make very strong chain mail garments. The Mithril Coat is the "small shirt of mail" given to Frodo by Bilbo, his uncle.

You could add code in each form to display the title bar text. But inevitably the user will decide that the title should be formatted differently, such as with a colon (Product Management: Mithril Coat) or with parentheses (Product Management (Mithril Coat)). You would then need to modify every form.

By putting the code in the base form class, you can modify the format of the title bar text in one place and have it appear consistently with that format in every form that inherits from the base form class.

For example, a method in the base form class that formats the title bar text is as follows:

```
#Region " SetFormTitle"
    ''' <summary>
    ''' Formats the text in the window's title bar
    ''' </summary>
    ''' <param name="ItemTitle">Name of the selected item</param>
    ''' <remarks>The current window text may already have an item
    ''' displayed with it — if so remove it</remarks>
    Protected Sub SetFormTitle(ByVal itemTitle As String)
        Dim separator As String = " - "
        Dim windowText As String = Me.Text

        If Me.Text.Contains(separator) Then
            windowText = windowText.Remove( _
                            Me.Text.IndexOf(separator))
        End If

        If String.IsNullOrEmpty(itemTitle) Then
            Me.Text = windowText
        Else
            Me.Text = windowText & separator & itemTitle
        End If
    End Sub
#End Region
```

Notice that this method is declared with the `Protected` keyword. `Protected` defines that only this form and forms that inherit from this base form can call this method. The reference to `Me` in this method refers to the currently running instance, which is the instance of the derived form that inherits from this base form class.

NOTE: The `IsNullOrEmpty` method is new in the .NET 2.0 Framework.

This method cannot be called automatically like the `Enter` and `Leave` events because the event that signals a change to this text may not be consistent in all the derived forms. In this example, you would call it from the `SelectedValueChanged` event for the Product `ComboBox` control and when the user created a new product. Add this line of code in each form whenever you need to change the title bar text:

```
MyBase.SetFormTitle(newItemText)
```

`MyBase` refers to the base form class. At runtime, the system looks for the `SetFormTitle` method in the base form class. If it is not found, it looks for it in the next class up the inheritance hierarchy until the method is found.

If you later need to change the format of the title, you can change it in the base form class and the modification is reflected at runtime in all forms that inherit from this base form class.

By building a base form class and inheriting from it for every form in your application, you attain consistent user interface behavior throughout your application. As you later need to change the behavior of the user interface, you can change it in one place and have the change reflected in every form that inherits from the base form class.

Navigating to Forms

As soon as you have more than one form in your application, you need a way to navigate between the forms. There are several common approaches for defining how your forms work together in the user interface for your application.

This section looks at the most common Windows user interface conceptual designs and several techniques for implementing the code for the user interface. It then details the code required to navigate between the forms of your application.

The next section details the MDI approach. Even if you are not using the MDI approach for your user interface, you may want to use some of the techniques presented in that section. Specifically, you may want to implement a programmatic interface as described in the "Calling a Custom Method in the Active Form" section.

Selecting a User Interface Approach

One of the key tenets of user interface design is consistency. Once the users know how to access one feature of the application, they should be able to directly leverage that knowledge to access the other features of the application. To promote consistency, select one primary user interface conceptual design approach for your application and use that approach throughout the application.

The following is an overview of the most common Windows user interface approaches.

Single Document Interface

The Single Document Interface (SDI) approach defines a single primary form in the application, with secondary forms used only for supplemental tasks. Notepad is an example of an SDI application.

If you are building a text editor application, for example, you can define one single primary form that is the text editor. Your secondary forms provide for supplemental tasks such as selecting fonts or colors. These secondary forms are most often modal, allowing the user to make a selection and then immediately dismiss the form before continuing.

Other types of applications that benefit from an SDI approach include point of sale applications and management console applications.

Having one primary form in your application reduces confusion and distractions for the user. SDI is great for situations where you want the user to focus on one key form.

Controller Form

The controller form approach defines a primary form in the application and all the other forms are accessed from this form. This is similar to the SDI approach but allows for extended functionality and modeless secondary forms.

If you are building a simple management application, such as Customer Management, you may have a grid form that lists all your customers. This is the primary form in the application. Double-clicking on one of the entries in the grid form displays the customer information details for review or edit. Right-clicking a grid entry provides a menu to access the customer's credit information, purchase history, and so on. So the primary form controls access to all the other forms in the application.

This approach works best in single purpose applications that don't have a large number of forms. The downside of this approach is that it is easy to lose track of all the forms of the application because they are not constrained by a single workspace or container.

Multiple Document Interface

The Multiple Document Interface (MDI) approach defines a container within which all the other features of the application are accessed. The container normally includes a menu, toolbar(s), and a status bar. Options on the menu and toolbar provide access to all the other forms that are displayed as independent windows within the client area of the MDI form. Microsoft Excel is an example of an MDI application. You can easily work with multiple spreadsheets within the Excel workspace.

MDI allows the user to view many different types of information as separate forms within the MDI container. The user can lay out the forms, or use the MDI options to arrange the forms in a cascading fashion or tiled vertically or horizontally. And minimizing the MDI container minimizes all the forms within the container, making it easy to keep track of all the forms.

NOTE: Visual Studio itself can be set to use the MDI approach (**Tools** | **Options** | **Environment** | **General** | **Window Layout**). When you set the Window Layout to **Multiple documents** the editors and designers each appear as separate forms within the Visual Studio container.

A built-in MDI Parent Form template is provided in Visual Studio to assist you with building an MDI user interface. It includes the standard set of menu and toolbar options to save you the time of defining them all manually.

Use the MDI approach when you have different types of information to display and you want the user to be able to view multiple types simultaneously. MDI is great for multifeatured business applications, such as Purchase Tracker.

Multi-Pane Interface

The multi-pane interface approach defines a container similar to the MDI container and, like MDI, normally includes a menu, toolbar(s), and a status bar. Options on the menu and toolbar provide access to all the application's features. However, instead of independently displaying a form within the container, the multi-pane interface approach displays the information within a specific pane of the container form. Microsoft Outlook is an example of a multi-pane interface application.

NOTE: This approach is sometimes called a **shell** approach because the main form is basically the shell of the application.

Although they're much more full-featured than an application such as Notepad, multipane applications are often considered to be SDI applications because they are developed with one primary form.

If you are building a management application, such as Customer Management, you may want to use a multi-pane interface to provide all the management information on one form that is visually separated with panes. You could define your panes similar to Outlook with a navigation pane on the left that allows the user to quickly navigate to a customer, a summary pane in the middle that provides summary information about the customer, and a detail pane on the right that provides detail based on the selected summary information.

NOTE: Visual Studio itself, by default, uses a tab-based multi-pane approach. Each open editor and designer window appears as a tab on the primary pane. Toolboxes and support windows can be attached in secondary panes around the primary pane.

New built-in container controls, including `SplitContainer` and `ToolStripContainer` controls, are provided in Visual Studio to assist you with building a multi-pane interface.

This approach is great when there is only one basic type of information to manage, like in the Customer Management example, or there are only a few types of information to manage and they are each managed independently, like Outlook's mail, contacts, and calendar features.

Summary

The user interface approach you select for your application depends on several factors. First consider the features of the application. Some applications lend themselves more to one approach over another. For example, Outlook displays only one type of information at a time. If your application needs to provide the user with more flexibility in concurrently viewing many types of information, such as customers *and* products *and* inventory, an Outlook-like approach may not be your best choice.

You may also consider what types of user interfaces your users are comfortable with. For example, if the users are very familiar with Microsoft Excel, you may want to select an approach that is Excel-like. If they really like Microsoft Outlook, you may want to select an Outlook-like approach.

Be sure to think about maintenance and enhancements as well. Normally, it is the user interface that changes the most over the life of the application. Selecting a user interface approach that is too difficult to maintain or enhance may add large amounts of time, and therefore money, to your project over its lifetime. For example, if you build a simple SDI Notepad-like interface for your application, it may be difficult to add more complex features to the application over time.

Selecting an Implementation Approach

Whereas the user interface approach defined how the user interacts with the application, you also need to select an approach for building the user interface layer. Consistency is also important here to leverage code reuse, maximize developer productivity, and simplify maintenance and enhancements.

The following is an overview of the most common user interface implementation approaches.

Form Approach

The form approach is the most common approach for building Windows applications. This approach involves adding a Windows Form project item to the project for each form to display to the user.

This approach is great in its simplicity. It provides for leveraging code from a base form class. In addition, it provides the utmost in flexibility with regard to how each form looks. You can easily modify the contents of each form to uniquely tailor it to the specific user scenario.

Form Approach with Wrapped Controls

This approach is a variant of the basic form approach. It involves creating user controls from existing controls and using the user controls to build your forms.

User controls are controls you create in Visual Studio that you can then use on your forms. You can create your own controls from scratch (using the Custom Control project item), create your own control from an existing control (using the User Control project item), or build a user control by combining existing built-in controls (using the User Control project item). See the "Additional Reading" section for more information on creating user controls.

NOTE FOR VB6 DEVELOPERS: User controls were called ActiveX controls in VB6.

A user control you build from existing built-in controls is called a **wrapped control** because you are basically wrapping the existing controls with your own code. This technique makes it easy to add functionality to an existing control or to reuse a set of controls as a unit.

For example, you could wrap the built-in `TextBox` control and add properties and methods, such as a `SelectOnEnter` property. You can also add events. This allows you to have your own specialized control that you can use on any form.

Some developers are strong proponents of wrapping *every* built-in control used in an application. By wrapping every control, you can change how controls behave at any time in the life of the application without having to change every form that contains the control. For example, you would build your own textbox, label, and button controls based on the built-in `TextBox`, `Label`, and `Button` controls. You then use the wrapped controls instead of the built-in controls to build the forms. This book favors implementing common functionality in a base form class over using wrapped controls because it does not depend on the specifics of the controls, which seem to change with each new version of Visual Studio.

A good use of wrapping controls is when you have a set of controls that you need to reuse as a unit. Assume that a requirement of your application is a find feature on each grid-based form. The find feature has a standard user interface with a `Label` control, `TextBox` control, and `Button` control. The user types a value into the textbox and clicks the button to find the value in the grid. You can build a user control that contains the `Label`,

`TextBox`, and `Button` controls along with the code that implements the find functionality. This can then be easily added to any grid-based form, saving time and ensuring consistent operation of the find feature. This type of user control is often referred to as a **composite control** because it is composed of other controls.

Wrap sets of controls that are used together to more easily reuse the controls as a single unit. Wrap individual controls only as needed to add your own properties, methods, or events.

User Control Approach

The user control approach involves adding a User Control project item to the project for each set of information to be displayed to the user instead of adding a form. This is different from the prior approach in that this approach requires only one form. All the different types of functionality needed by your application are provided within the user controls themselves.

The user control approach is recommended if you are planning to use the multi-pane approach. You define the possible contents of each pane within a user control and then display the appropriate user control in the pane based on the user's actions.

You can break down the user interface further, with common sets of user interface functionality implemented in user controls that are then combined to build more complex user controls.

However, it is possible to go overboard with this approach. If the application is built by combining user controls that are made up of more user controls that are in turn made up of more user controls, it becomes very difficult to modify the application. For example, you could use this approach to create the form shown in Figure 4.7. You could create a user control with a panel and label. Then create a second user control with a label and combo box. Then create a third user control with a label and textbox. Then create a fourth user control containing four instances of the third user control and one instance of the second user control and put it all on one instance of the first user control. If this sounds confusing, it is!

If the user just wants one visual element changed, you have to drill down through each level of the user controls to find where you need to make the change. As you make the change, you then worry about the impact of the change everywhere else the user control is used. This becomes even more complex if the user controls are combined at runtime.

NOTE: One of my clients had a Web application done in which the developers overused this approach. When the client took over maintenance of the application, they wanted to make changes such as correcting spelling in labels. They could not find where to make these simplest of modifications because there were so many controls within controls within controls, all built at runtime. So they asked my company to completely rewrite the user interface so that they could maintain the application. So keep maintenance in mind, especially if you don't plan on maintaining the application for the rest of its (and your) life.

Use the user control approach whenever you are implementing a multi-pane user interface. Define the set of information to be displayed in a pane within each user control. Just don't overdo it with user controls within user controls within user controls, making it difficult to maintain and enhance the application.

Model-View-Controller Approach

The Model-View-Controller (MVC) pattern is a classic design pattern for building an application with a user interface. It involves breaking the application into three types of classes: the model, the view, and the controller.

The view handles the display of information. It includes the basic code that defines the controls displayed to the user.

The controller catches the user actions and maps them into predefined commands. For example, the controller would catch a click on a toolbar Save button or the selection of the Save option on the File menu and map them both to a `ProcessSave` command.

The model manages the behavior and data. It provides the data to the view when requested and updates its data based on requests from the controller. The model is most often implemented as a set of business object classes.

For proper separation of duties, the model is independent of the view and controller. The view and controller must depend on the model for application logic and data.

In most Windows applications, the view and the controller are combined. The code behind the form handles both the view of the data and handling of the events. In Web-based applications the view and the controller are more clearly separated. The view is defined by the HTML displayed in the browser and the controller is defined with the code behind the page that runs on the server.

However, you can more formally define the MVC pattern in a Windows application. You can build a controller class that wires up the controls on the form and then converts the events to specific model commands, such as `ProcessSave`, and view commands, such as `RefreshDisplay`.

Microsoft's Patterns and Practices group provides user interface application blocks that are based on the MVC pattern. Use these blocks as a starting point if you want to use the MVC pattern. (See the "Additional Reading" section for a link to the Microsoft Patterns and Practices.)

The MVC pattern is frequently used when implementing the multi-pane user interface approach because it provides facilities to keep all the information in all the panes in synchronization. If the user changes information in one pane, the MVC pattern ensures all the other panes are updated appropriately.

Summary

The implementation approach you select for the user interface of your application may be obvious due to corporate standards or your personal style. But looking at other available choices may lead you to incorporate additional techniques.

You may also find that you use a combination of these choices. For example, you may have one multi-pane form in your application that uses the MVC pattern and user controls. Other forms may be implemented as simple forms. Still other forms make use of wrapped controls.

Displaying a Form

The .NET runtime automatically displays your first form for you. So you don't need to write any code. If you select an implementation approach that uses more than one form, you need to know how to access the other forms so you can display them.

When you create a form at design time, you are creating a form class. To access any of the properties or methods of the form, such as the `Show` method, you need to work with an instance of the class. This instance is an object created from the form class. You can create your own form instances or use the built-in default form instance.

This section provides the steps for using form instances to display a form.

Using Default Form Instances

Visual Basic 2005 reintroduced the concept of default form instances, which were available in classic versions of Visual Basic but not Visual Basic 2002 and 2003. A **default form instance** is an instance of a form that is automatically provided at runtime. You don't need to declare or instantiate it.

To access a default form instance, use the `My.Forms` object. This object maintains a collection of default instances for every form class that exists in your project.

NOTE: My is new in Visual Basic 2005. My is a speed dial into the .NET Framework to provide easy access to commonly used features. Type My. to list the set of types accessible from the My keyword.

For example, say you have a Comment button on a ProductWin form that opens a CommentWin form for review and entry of comments relating to a particular product. The code in the Comment button `Click` event in the ProductWin form would look like this:

```
#Region " Control Events"
    Private Sub CommentsButton_Click(ByVal sender As Object, _
        ByVal e As System.EventArgs) Handles CommentsButton.Click
        My.Forms.CommentWin.ShowDialog()
    End Sub
#End Region
```

The `My.Forms` object Intellisense provides the list of all the forms in the project so you can easily select the form to show. You use the `ShowDialog` method to show the form as a **modal dialog**, which is a dialog that must be dismissed before returning to the prior form. Alternatively, you can use the `Show` method to show the form as a **modeless** form.

NOTE: Be careful not to overuse modal forms in your application. Modal forms can be very frustrating for the user. Imagine working with a modal form that requires you to enter 50 fields. Halfway through entering the data, you need to look up something for one of the fields. Because the form is modal, you can only click OK or Cancel. You don't want to cancel and lose your work, but you can't click OK either, because it validates the fields and doesn't permit saving half the fields as empty. (Having too many required fields is also frustrating for the user, but that's another story.) Modeless forms are often more practical, because they match the ad hoc way in which information is accessed in the real world.

As a shortcut, you can also access the default instance without the `My.Forms` object as follows:

```
CommentWin.ShowDialog()
```

Using default form instances can be confusing, because it appears that you are working with a shared (static) class and not an instance. (The `Shared` keyword is discussed further in Chapter 5.) You also don't have as much control over these instances. What if you want to define a second instance of the form?

In general, using default form instances is *not* considered to be a best practice. Instead, create your own form instances as described next.

Creating Your Own Form Instances

Because of the possible confusion and limitations with the built-in default form instances, in most cases you create and manage your own form instances. To create a form instance, declare an object variable for the form instance, instantiate an object, and assign the instantiated object to the object variable. The technique you use to do this is exactly the same as declaring and instantiating any other object.

You declare the object variable using the `Dim` or `Private` keywords. You instantiate the object using the `New` keyword.

Using the same CommentWin form example from the preceding section, the code in the Comment button `Click` event looks like this when you create your own instance:

```
#Region " Control Events"
    Private Sub CommentsButton_Click(ByVal sender As Object, _
        ByVal e As System.EventArgs) Handles CommentsButton.Click
        Dim frmCommentWin As New CommentWin
        frmCommentWin.ShowDialog()
    End Sub
#End Region
```

This code declares `frmCommentWin` as the object variable. The `New` keyword creates an instance of the `CommentWin` class and assigns it to the `frmCommentWin` object variable. The object variable is then used to call the `ShowDialog` method and show the form.

You can see that you need only one more line of code in this case, so using the default form instance does not save you much.

Closing a Form

A discussion of accessing forms would not be complete without also discussing how to close the forms. The technique you use to close a form depends on how the form was shown (modal or modeless).

There are several ways a form can be closed at runtime:

- The user clicks the close box in the upper-right corner of the form. The .NET runtime closes the form automatically.
- Code in your application calls the `Close` method of the form. This code often resides in the event handler for an OK, Cancel, or Close button.

If the form is opened modally, a form can also be closed at runtime as follows:

- You define a button on the form that has its `DialogResult` property set to a value other than `None` (such as `OK` or `Cancel`) and the user clicks that button. The .NET runtime closes the form automatically and returns the `DialogResult` property value as the return value of the `ShowDialog` method.

When a *modeless* form is closed, all the resources on the form are released and the form is disposed. You can no longer display the form without creating a new instance (or using the default instance).

When a *modal* form is closed, it is not disposed. This allows you to close the form yet still access data on the form. When you are finished with the form, you can call the `Dispose` method directly to dispose of the form and then set the form instance to `Nothing` as follows:

```
#Region " Control Events"
    Private Sub CommentsButton_Click(ByVal sender As Object, _
        ByVal e As System.EventArgs) Handles CommentsButton.Click
        Dim frmCommentWin As New CommentWin
        frmCommentWin.ShowDialog()

        frmCommentWin.Dispose()
        frmCommentWin = Nothing
    End Sub
#End Region
```

You can prevent the closing of a form at run time by handling the `FormClosing` event and setting the `Cancel` property of the `CancelEventArgs` passed as a parameter to your event handler. This gives you an opportunity to check for unsaved changes or perform other processing and optionally cancel the closing of the form.

Building an MDI User Interface

A **Multiple Document Interface** (MDI) application allows the user to display multiple forms (referred to as documents in this context) at the same time, all within a visual container. The container is called an **MDI parent form** and the forms displayed within the container are called **MDI child forms**. The MDI parent form often has a menu bar and toolbar at the top and a status bar at the bottom. All the MDI child forms are displayed within the body of the MDI parent form. Microsoft Excel is an example of an MDI application.

Using MDI as the technique for navigation between the forms in your application has many benefits. The menu bar and optional toolbar at the top provide guidance to the user about the available application features. The user can go directly to the desired option without having to navigate through a set of forms. Since MDI supports display of multiple forms, it also makes it easy for the user to view multiple items at the same time, such as displaying information about two customers or displaying customer information and purchase information for that customer.

Using MDI requires two basic steps. First, you define one form as the MDI parent form in your application. This is the form that is the container for all the other forms of the application. Second, you define each form displayed within the MDI parent container as an MDI child form.

Creating an MDI Parent Form

The first step in building an MDI user interface is to create the MDI parent form. The MDI parent form normally includes a menu bar, one or more toolbars, a status bar, and a client area where the MDI child forms are displayed.

To add an MDI parent form to your application:

1. Add a project item to your Windows Application project using the **MDI Parent Form** template.

   The MDI Parent Form template provides a Windows form that is defined as an MDI parent form and provides the appropriate default controls, such as the menu bar, toolbar, and status bar as shown in Figure 4.8. It also generates code to implement many of the menu bar and toolbar items. This code is generated in your form class and not in the designer-generated partial class. You can edit, expand, or delete this code as needed.

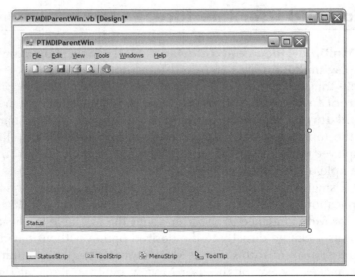

Figure 4.8   The MDI Parent Form template provides the basics for your MDI parent form.

2. Use the Project Designer to set the MDI Parent Form as the startup form for the application.

   See Chapter 3 for information on defining a startup form as part of the application properties.

If you already have a form that you want to make the MDI parent form or if you want to create the MDI parent form yourself, you can define the MDI parent without the template.

To create an MDI parent form without using the template:

1. Add a project item to your Windows Application project using any Windows template, *or* open an existing Windows form to use as your MDI parent form.
2. Set the **IsMdiContainer** property for the form to **True** in the Properties window.
3. Add `MenuStrip`, `ToolStrip`, `StatusStrip`, or other controls to the form.

NOTE: If you want to prepopulate the menu or toolbar with the most common options, use the smart tag on the `MenuStrip` or `ToolStrip` and select Insert Standard Items. The most commonly used options are added to your menu or toolbar. You can then edit or remove them as desired.

If you used the MDI Parent Form template or selected Insert Standard Items for the menu strip, your MDI parent form contains operational code so you can try it out at this point. Notice that the options in the menu and toolbar may or may not be applicable to your application.

Building Along

For the Purchase Tracker sample application:
- Add a project item to the Windows Application project (**PTWin**) using the **MDI Parent Form** template.
  Name the form **PTMDIParentWin**.
- Add XML comments to document the form.
- Use the Project Designer to set **PTMDIWin** as the startup form for the application.

Run the application. It displays your splash screen and then shows the MDI parent form. The MDI Parent Form template includes code for some of the menu and toolbar options, so try them out. Select the **File | New** option from the MDI parent menu bar to create several blank forms. Then use the options in the **Windows** menu to lay out those forms within the container.

Don't be constrained by the pre-built options and code; tailor the MDI parent form to your application. The standard menu items include File, Edit, and Tools menus, but these items may not make sense for your application. You could change the name of the File menu to the name of your application. You could remove the Edit menu entirely. You could add menus for Products, Customers, and so on. As you add features to your application, add appropriate menu options to the MDI parent form.

NOTE FOR VB6 DEVELOPERS: Visual Studio provides for in-place editing of the menu. Simply display the MDI parent form in the designer, click the `MenuStrip` control and add menus or menu options by typing where it displays "Type Here." You can move the menus and menu options using drag and drop.

You can also tailor the toolbar to contain only those tools that make sense for your application. Or, you could remove it entirely. You could instead put the toolbar on the base form class and inherit from the base form class when creating the MDI child forms to display the toolbar on each child form.

NOTE: Visual Studio comes with an image library under Program Files\ Microsoft Visual Studio 8\Common7\VS2005ImageLibrary that has many useful bitmaps. However, the library is a compressed (zip) file. You must unzip the file before you can use the icons and bitmaps from the library.

Some of these images include a transparent color that appears as Fuchsia. To display the image as transparent, set the `ImageTransparentColor` property of the color to Fuchsia.

Be sure to remove any excess code from the MDI parent form as well. For example, the prebuilt save code saves to a file. In most business applications, your code saves data to a database. So the prebuilt save code can be deleted.

Using an MDI parent form gives your users a consistent working space from which they can access all the features of your application. If you are not using the MDI approach for your application, you can still use the `MenuStrip`, `ToolStrip`, and `StatusStrip` controls to provide a standard look and feel to your user interface.

Building Along

For the Purchase Tracker sample application:

- Display the **PTMDIParentWin** form in the Forms Designer.
- Modify the File menu for the Purchase Tracker application.
  Change the **File** menu name to **Purchase Tracker**, remove the **New**, **Open**, and **Save As** menu options and add a **View Purchases** option.
- Delete the entire **Edit** menu.
- Delete the **New Window** option from the **Windows** menu.
- Add a **Products** menu with a **Manage Products** option.
- Add a **Customers** menu with a **Manage Customers** option.
- Modify the **toolbar** by replacing the **Open** button on the toolbar with a **Delete** button.
- Add a user-friendly form caption by setting the **Text** property of the form in the **Properties** window.
- Open the **PTMDIParentWin** form in the Code Editor.
- Delete any extraneous code, and reorganize the remaining code with regions as desired.
  Remove the code for the deleted New, Open, and Save As menu options. (This includes the `ShowNewForm`, `OpenFile`, and `SaveAsToolStripMenuItem_Click` methods.)
  Remove the code for all the deleted Edit menu options.

Run the application. It displays your splash screen and then shows the MDI parent form. View your menu changes.

Creating an MDI Child Form

After creating the MDI parent form, create all the forms that appear within it. These MDI child forms provide the user interface for all the features of your application.

You create an MDI child form just like you create any other form. The form becomes an MDI child form by setting its `MdiParent` property at runtime.

To add an MDI child form to your application:

1. Create a form.
   Any form can be an MDI child form.

2. Ensure that there is a menu option and/or toolbar option on the MDI parent form that the user can use to display the child form.
3. Add code in the `Click` event for the menu or toolbar option to create a form instance and set the MDI parent of the form to the instance of the MDI parent form.

```
Dim frmProductWin as New ProductWin
frmProductWin.MdiParent = Me
```

This last line of code defines the form as an MDI child form.
4. Add code in the `Click` event for the menu or toolbar option to display the form.
You normally show the form as a modeless window. Your MDI child forms should not be modal.

The `Click` event handler code in the MDI parent form is similar to the following:

```
Private Sub ProductMenuItem_Click(ByVal sender As Object, _
    ByVal e As System.EventArgs) Handles ProductMenuItem.Click
    Dim frmProductWin As New ProductWin
    frmProductWin.MdiParent = Me
    frmProductWin.Show()
End Sub
```

This code creates an instance of the ProductWin form. It then sets the `MdiParent` property of the ProductWin form instance to the instance of the MDI parent form, defined with `Me` in this case. Finally, it shows the form as a modeless window.

Repeat these steps for every MDI child form that you want to display from the MDI parent form.

Building Along

For the Purchase Tracker sample application:
- Display the **PTMDIParentWin** form in the Forms Designer.
- Double-click on the **Manage Products** option in the **Products** menu.
  Visual Studio generates the event handler for the menu item's **Click** event and displays it in the Code Editor.

> - Add code to the **Click** event handler to create an instance of the product form (**ProductWin**), set the **MdiParent** property, and display the form.
>
> Run the application. It displays your splash screen and then shows the MDI parent form. Select **Products** | **Manage Products** to display the ProductWin form.
>
> Notice how the MDI child form stays within the bounds of the MDI parent form. If your MDI child form appears on top of the MDI parent form, you may have forgotten to set the `MdiParent` property.

Accessing MDI Child Forms

An MDI parent form provides a working space for the users of your application. From the MDI parent form, the user can select a task to perform and the MDI parent carries out the desired operation, such as displaying the appropriate MDI child form or acting on the active MDI child form. To accomplish these operations, the MDI parent form must access the MDI child forms.

The technique you use to access an MDI child form from an MDI parent form depends on the type of operation. The most common types of operations are

- Displaying the MDI child form
- Acting on the active MDI child form
- Looping through all MDI child forms
- Calling a custom method in the active MDI child form

This section covers the techniques required to perform each of these types of operations.

Displaying the MDI Child Form

Many of the user tasks provided by an MDI application require that an MDI child form be displayed to perform the task. For example, if the user wants to maintain product information, the user would pick the Manage Products option from the MDI parent Product menu. The code would then display an MDI child form that allows the user to view or modify product information.

The code required to display an MDI child form was presented in the preceding section. Use that code whenever you need to display an MDI child form.

Acting on the Active MDI Child Form

Some operations performed by the MDI parent form need to act on an MDI child form that is already displayed. For example, a Print menu option prints the contents of the currently active MDI child form.

To reference the currently active MDI child form, use this line of code:

```
Me.ActiveMdiChild
```

The `ActiveMdiChild` property provides access to the currently active MDI child form, which is the form that the user is currently working with.

For a complete example of implementing a Print feature, see the "Additional User Interface Techniques" section later in this chapter.

Looping Through All MDI Child Forms

The MDI parent form may need to perform operations on all the displayed MDI child forms. For example, the Close All option in the Windows menu needs to call the `Close` method on each of the displayed MDI child forms.

To loop through all the open MDI child forms, use the `MdiChildren` collection of the MDI parent form as follows:

```
For Each childForm As Form In Me.MdiChildren
    childForm.Close()
Next
```

This particular code loops through all the child forms and closes them. If you use the MDI Parent Form template to create your MDI parent form, your code already includes this loop in the event procedure for the Close All option in the Windows menu.

NOTE FOR VB6 DEVELOPERS: Notice that you can now declare the iterator variable directly in the `For` statement. In the preceding example, the `childForm` variable is declared `As Form` within the `For` statement.

Use a similar technique when you need to loop through all the child forms and perform other operations.

Calling a Custom Method in the Active Form

The MDI parent may need to perform some operations on the active MDI child form by calling a custom method in the active MDI child form. For example, to implement the Save menu and toolbar options, the MDI parent form could call a custom `ProcessSave` method on the active MDI child form.

This task may seem easy to do by simply referencing the active MDI child form using code like this:

```
Me.ActiveMdiChild.ProcessSave    'Syntax error
```

But this code does not work. The `ActiveMdiChild` property is of type `Form`, and there is no `ProcessSave` method on a `Form` object.

For the MDI parent form to call a custom method on an MDI child form, you have to define some other data type that you can use that has access to the custom method. The easiest way to define this other data type is to create a standard programmatic interface for your MDI child forms. You can then reference any custom method defined in the standard programmatic interface by using the interface data type.

To define a standard programmatic interface for MDI child forms:

1. Add a project item to your Windows Application project using the **Interface** template.

   Use standard naming conventions for your interface name. The standard is to prefix the interface name with an "I" and use the basic purpose of the interface as the remainder of the name.

2. Add the definition for any properties or methods you will add to the MDI child forms that you want to access from the MDI parent form.

   The programmatic interface defines the list of properties and methods, but does not implement them. The interface assumes that the properties and methods are implemented in the MDI child forms.

The resulting code appears similar to the following:

```
''' <summary>
''' Standard programmatic interface for MDI child forms
''' </summary>
''' <remarks></remarks>
Public Interface IMDIChild
    Function ProcessDelete() As Boolean
    Function ProcessNew() As Boolean
    Function ProcessSave() As Boolean
End Interface
```

NOTE: This example demonstrates use of a programmatic interface with MDI child forms. However, you can use interfaces anywhere in your application. For example, if your application needs to provide three different costing components, you could define one standard interface on all three so you can access any of the three components using one set of code.

This interface must then be applied to any MDI child form that needs to provide these methods. This is done by **implementing** the interface in the MDI child form. The MDI parent form can then access the defined methods through this interface.

To implement the interface:

1. Open the MDI child form in the Code Editor.
2. Add the `Implements` statement to the class definition for the MDI child form.

   The code to implement an interface is:

   ```
   Public Class ProductWin
       Implements IMDIChild
   ```

   Although the `Implements` statement could technically be added to the designer-generated partial class, it is highly recommended that the `Implements` statement be inserted into your custom code. This is because the `Implements` statement generates the signatures for your custom code, as shown in the next step.
3. Press the Enter key after the name of the interface.

   The signatures for all the properties and methods defined in the interface are automatically added to the MDI child form. For example, the code for the `ProcessSave` method signature is as follows:

```
Public Function ProcessSave() As Boolean _
    Implements IMDIChild.ProcessSave

End Function
```

4. Add code to implement the properties and methods.
   Add whatever code is needed to perform the operation defined by
   the signature.

When the interface is in place and the appropriate properties and
methods are implemented in the MDI child forms, you can call the method in the MDI child form from the MDI parent form. Cast the active MDI
child form to the interface using `DirectCast` as described earlier in this
chapter. The interface methods are then available in Intellisense, and you
can call them as follows:

```
Private Sub SaveToolStripMenuItem_Click(ByVal sender As Object, _
    ByVal e As System.EventArgs) _
    Handles SaveToolStripMenuItem.Click, SaveToolStripButton.Click
    DirectCast(Me.ActiveMdiChild, IMDIChild).ProcessSave()
End Sub
```

This code handles both the Save menu option and the Save toolbar button. It calls the `ProcessSave` method on the active MDI child form if the
active MDI child form implements the `IMDIChild` interface. Because it is
possible that the active MDI child form does not implement the interface,
use a `TryCast` here to make the code more solid:

```
Private Sub SaveToolStripMenuItem_Click(ByVal sender As Object, _
    ByVal e As System.EventArgs) _
    Handles SaveToolStripMenuItem.Click, SaveToolStripButton.Click
    Dim frmMDIChild As IMDIChild
    frmMDIChild = TryCast(Me.ActiveMdiChild, IMDIChild)
    If frmMDIChild Is Nothing Then
        MessageBox.Show("You must open a window that supports " _
            & " a save before you can save an entry")
    Else
        frmMDIChild.ProcessSave()
    End If
End Sub
```

This code uses `TryCast` to attempt a cast from the active MDI child form to the defined programmatic interface. If the form does not support the defined interface, the cast sets the form variable to `Nothing` and an error message is displayed. If the cast is successful, the code calls the `ProcessSave` method in the MDI child form.

The MDI parent has many techniques available to it for accessing MDI child forms. Create an instance to show an MDI child form, use the `ActiveMdiChild` property to access an active MDI child form, or loop through the MDI child forms using the `MdiChildren` collection to access each open MDI child form. If you need to call a custom method on an MDI child form, create a programmatic interface using the `Interface` statement and then implement that interface in the MDI child forms. The MDI parent can then call the custom method using the interface.

Building Along

For the Purchase Tracker sample application:

- Add a project item to the Windows Application project (**PTWin**) using the **Interface** template.
  Name the interface **IMDIChild**.
- Add XML comments to document the interface.
- Add **ProcessDelete**, **ProcessNew**, and **ProcessSave** methods to the interface as shown in this section.
- Open the **ProductWin** form in the Code Editor.
- Use the `Implements` statement to implement the **IMDIChild** interface in the **ProductWin** form.
  Be sure to press the Enter key after the `Implements` statement to generate the interface method signatures.
- Add code to perform the operation defined by each signature.
  For a simple test at this point, display message boxes such as the following:
  ```
  MessageBox.Show("Saving")
  ```
- Open the **PTMDIParentWin** form in the Code Editor.
- Add code to the Save menu option and Save toolbar button `Click` events to call the **ProcessSave** method.
  Make your code solid by using the `TryCast` keyword as shown in the prior code example.
- Add similar code for the New and Delete toolbar button `Click` events.

Run the application. It displays your splash screen and then shows the MDI parent form. Select **Products** | **Manage Products** to display the ProductWin form. Then select **Purchase Tracker** | **Save** to see your "Saving" message box. Repeat for the Save, New, and Delete toolbar buttons to see appropriate messages. Close the ProductWin form and try the menu options and toolbar buttons again to see your error messages.

Additional User Interface Techniques

In addition to the concepts covered so far in this chapter, you may want to incorporate other techniques into your user interface.

For example, you may want to save end-user settings, draw graphics on your forms, or allow the user to print the contents of a form.

This section provides details on each of these techniques.

Saving User and Application Settings

A common user request is for your application to remember its state so the application can be returned to that state when the user runs the application again. For example, if the user positioned the forms of the application in a specific manner and then closed the forms, the user expects that the forms are returned to their last defined locations with their last defined sizes when they are reopened.

Visual Studio 2005 provides a Settings tab in the Project Designer to help you manage application settings. **Application settings** allow you to store and retrieve property settings and other information for your application. You can use application settings to maintain custom application settings and end-user preferences.

You can use this feature for application settings that you don't want hard-coded into the application, such as the connection string (see Chapter 8, "Building the Data Access Layer," for more information on connection strings). You can also use this feature to store end-user preferences such as form size and location and color choices. In either case, application settings are available within the code of your application using the `My.Settings` object.

To define an application setting:

1. Determine which application and user settings you want to retain. For example, you may want to save the form size and location.
2. Open the Project Designer for the **Windows Application** project. Right-click the project in Solution Explorer and select **Properties** from the context menu, *or* select **Project** | **Properties** from the main menu bar, *or* double-click on the **My Project** folder under the project to open the Project Designer.
3. Select the **Settings** tab.
4. In the **Name** column of the grid, type the name of the setting. Each setting must have a unique name. For example, use FormLocation to define a setting for the location of the form and FormSize for the size.
5. In the **Type** column of the grid, select the appropriate data type for the setting.
   You can select any data type that can be converted to a string.
   For example, a form's location is of type `System.Drawing.Point`, and size is of type `System.Drawing.Size`.
6. In the **Scope** column of the grid, define the scope: User or Application.
   Select **User** scope to define a setting that is saved for each user at runtime. Select **Application** scope to define a setting that is saved for the application. The code cannot change application-scoped settings at runtime.
7. Define any default value in the **Value** column.

The result is shown in Figure 4.9.

For user preferences that are application-wide, you can set the setting in the application's `Shutdown` event (see Chapter 3 for more information on the `Shutdown` event). But for form-specific user preferences, you normally set the value of the setting before the form is closed. For the form size example, set the `FormSize` setting before closing the form:

```
Private Sub ProductWin_FormClosing(ByVal sender As Object, _
    ByVal e As System.Windows.Forms.FormClosingEventArgs) _
    Handles Me.FormClosing
    If Me.WindowState = FormWindowState.Normal Then
        My.Settings.FormSize = Me.Size
    Else
```

```
      ' If the form was maximized or minimized,
      ' return to the restore state
        My.Settings.FormSize = Me.RestoreBounds.Size
    End If
End Sub
```

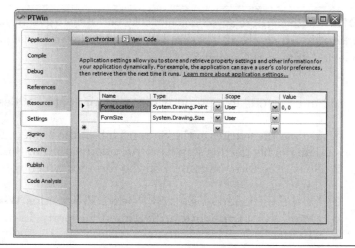

Figure 4.9 The Settings tab of the Project Designer allows you to define user preference and application settings.

Notice how this code first checks the form state. If the `WindowState` is normal, you can simply store the form size. But if the `WindowState` is any other state, such as minimized or maximized, you must use the `RestoreBounds` size. Additionally, you could define a setting for `WindowState` so you can return the form to its original state.

You then restore the setting when the form or application is opened. For application-wide user preferences, you can restore the settings in the application's `Startup` event (see Chapter 3). For form-specific user preferences, restore the settings when opening the form:

```
Private Sub ProductWin_Load(ByVal sender As Object, _
    ByVal e As System.EventArgs) _
    Handles Me.Load
    If My.Settings.FormSize <> System.Drawing.Size.Empty Then
        Me.Size = My.Settings.FormSize
    End If
End Sub
```

Some application settings, such as form location, can be bound directly to a property of a form or control at design time. When you bind a setting, you don't need to set or restore it. The setting is automatically set before the form is closed and automatically restored when it is opened again.

NOTE: The settings are saved automatically only if the **Save My.Settings on Shutdown** checkbox is checked as described in the "Setting Application Properties" section of Chapter 3.

To bind a setting to a property of a form or control at design time:

1. Define the setting in the Settings tab of the Project Designer. The details for this step were provided earlier in this section.
2. Select the form or control on the form for which you want to bind a setting.
3. View the Properties window (**View** | **Properties Window**).
4. Open the **(Application Settings)** property in the Properties window.
5. Map the desired property to the defined setting.

The result is shown in Figure 4.10.

In this example, the form's `Location` property is bound to the `FormLocation` setting. No code is needed to set or restore this setting.

Figure 4.10   The ApplicationSettings properties allow you to bind a setting to a specific form or control property.

NOTE: The form size cannot be bound directly, because it requires additional code to handle the maximized and minimized case.

The settings are stored in two XML files: an app.config file, which is created at design time when you create the first application setting, and a user.config file, which is created at runtime when the user changes the value of any user setting. The .NET runtime saves the user.config settings when the application is closed and retrieves the settings when the application is opened again. The user.config file is stored under C:\Documents and Settings*your username*\Local Settings\Application Data (called the local user profile) or in C:\Documents and Settings*your username*\Application Data (called the roaming user profile) under a directory named with the company name and a subdirectory with the application name. (See Chapter 3 for details on setting the company name as part of the Assembly information.)

NOTE: If you use ClickOnce deployment, the settings are saved in the ClickOnce data directory and not in the local user configuration file.

The `userSettings` section of the user.config XML file for the two settings defined here looks like this:

```
<userSettings>
    <PTWin.My.MySettings>
        <setting name="FormLocation" serializeAs="String">
            <value>57, 11</value>
        </setting>
        <setting name="FormSize" serializeAs="String">
            <value>566, 362</value>
        </setting>
    </PTWin.My.MySettings>
</userSettings>
```

Use settings whenever you have application data that you don't want to hard-code into the application and when you want to store and retrieve user preferences.

Building Along

For the Purchase Tracker sample application:
- Use the Project Designer for the Windows Application project (**PTWin**) to add the **FormSize** and **FormLocation** settings as shown in Figure 4.9.
- Open the **ProductWin** form in the Code Editor.
- Add an event handler for the **FormClosing** event and add the code to set the **FormSize** setting as detailed in this section.
- Add code to the event handler for the **Load** event to restore the **FormSize** setting as detailed in this section.
- Display the **ProductWin** form in the Forms Designer and bind the form's **(ApplicationSettings) Location** property to the **FormLocation** setting as shown in Figure 4.10.

Run the application. It displays your splash screen and then shows the MDI parent form. Select **Products | Manage Products** to display the ProductWin form. Size and position the form as desired. Close the form and re-open it. It appears with the same size and position you had set.

If desired, find the associated user.config XML file, and take a look at its contents.

Using a Settings Key to Define Settings per Form

The preceding section demonstrated how to use the basic settings features in Visual Studio to define both application-scoped and user-scoped settings. But the `FormLocation` and `FormSize` sample settings work for only one form. For a consistent user interface, you would want the settings retained for all the forms.

One way to define settings for each of your forms is to define a unique set of settings for each form. You could then use the techniques defined in the preceding section. But that would be a significant amount of work, especially if your application has a large number of forms.

A better approach is to create your own `MySettings` object and use the `SettingsKey` property of that object to define a key for each form. To minimize the amount of repeated code required for this, add the code to the base form class defined earlier in this chapter.

To define settings for each form, begin by creating your own `MySettings` object. Insert a property into your base form class that creates and retains your specialized `MySettings` object as follows:

```
Private _settings As My.MySettings
Private ReadOnly Property Settings() As _
    System.Configuration.ApplicationSettingsBase
    Get
        If _settings Is Nothing Then
            _settings = New My.MySettings
        End If
        Return _settings
    End Get
End Property
```

This code declares a private member variable to retain your custom **MySettings** object. It defines a private read-only property that initially creates an instance of your custom setting. It then returns the custom setting for use within the base form class. See Chapter 5 for more information on **Property** statements.

The next step is to create a method in your base form class to apply the settings from your custom **MySettings** object. This method is called when the form is loaded to apply the settings to your form, basically resetting the form size and location to the saved settings.

```
''' <summary>
''' Apply the settings for every form
''' </summary>
''' <remarks></remarks>
Private Sub ApplySettings()
    Settings.SettingsKey = Me.Name
    Dim theSettings As My.MySettings
    theSettings = DirectCast(Settings, My.MySettings)

    If theSettings.FormSize <> Drawing.Size.Empty Then
        Me.Size = theSettings.FormSize
    End If
    If theSettings.FormLocation <> Drawing.Point.Empty Then
        Me.Location = theSettings.FormLocation
    End If
End Sub
```

The first line of this method sets the **SettingsKey** to the name of the form. This ensures that the settings are associated with the particular form. The next two lines cast your **Settings** property to the **MySettings** class.

This maps the appropriate settings to the `MySettings` property, so the `SettingsKey` *must* be set before performing this cast

The casting is required because the `Settings` property is of the base type `System.Configuration.ApplicationSettingsBase`. To access your specific properties, you need to cast it to the `MySettings` class.

NOTE: Visual Studio generates the `MySettings` class. It can be found in the My Project subdirectory for the project in the Settings.Designer.vb file.

The remainder of this method is similar to the code in the preceding section for applying the settings. When defining your own settings, you cannot use binding with the Properties window. You instead need to manually create the code to set the properties.

You also need to create a method in your base form class to set the settings in your custom `MySettings` object. This method is called when the form is closed to save the settings.

```
''' <summary>
''' Sets the settings for every form
''' </summary>
''' <remarks></remarks>
Private Sub SetSettings()
    Settings.SettingsKey = Me.Name
    Dim theSettings As My.MySettings
    theSettings = DirectCast(Settings, My.MySettings)

    If Me.WindowState = FormWindowState.Normal Then
        theSettings.FormSize = Me.Size
    Else
        ' If the form was maximized or minimized,
        ' return to the restore state
        theSettings.FormSize = Me.RestoreBounds.Size
    End If
    theSettings.FormLocation = Me.Location

    Settings.Save()
End Sub
```

The first line of this method sets the `SettingsKey` to the name of the form. This ensures that the settings are associated with the particular form.

The next two lines cast your `Settings` property to the `MySettings` class. This maps the appropriate settings to the `MySettings` property, so the `SettingsKey` *must* be set before performing this cast.

The middle set of code is similar to the code in the prior section for setting the `FormSize` setting. The code to manually set the `FormLocation` is also defined because it was no longer set automatically using binding.

The last line of code saves your settings. This is no longer done automatically, because you are saving your particular settings.

After the two methods are in place, modify the form `Load` and `FormClosing` events in the base form class to call these two methods.

The form `Load` event handler is as follows:

```
Private Sub PTBaseWin_Load(ByVal sender As Object, _
    ByVal e As System.EventArgs) Handles Me.Load
    AddEventHandlers(Me)

    ' Ensure the form is set appropriately as per the settings
    ApplySettings()
End Sub
```

The form `FormClosing` event handler is as follows:

```
Private Sub PTBaseWin_FormClosing(ByVal sender As Object, _
    ByVal e As System.Windows.Forms.FormClosingEventArgs) _
    Handles Me.FormClosed
    SetSettings()
End Sub
```

If you had two forms called ProductWin and CommentWin, the resulting user.config file would look similar to this:

```
<userSettings>
    <PTWin.My.MySettings.ProductWin>
        <setting name="FormLocation" serializeAs="String">
            <value>189, 2</value>
        </setting>
        <setting name="FormSize" serializeAs="String">
            <value>434, 359</value>
        </setting>
    </PTWin.My.MySettings.ProductWin>
    <PTWin.My.MySettings.CommentWin>
```

```
        <setting name="FormLocation" serializeAs="String">
            <value>50, 140</value>
        </setting>
        <setting name="FormSize" serializeAs="String">
            <value>184, 190</value>
        </setting>
    </PTWin.My.MySettings.CommentWin>
</userSettings>
```

Notice that there are now specialized versions of the `PTWin.My.MySettings` tags for ProductWin and CommentWin. Any form that inherits from the base form class gets a section in this user.config file to define its settings.

NOTE: You may still have the old `PTWin.My.MySettings` tag in your user.config file. You can clear your user.config files at any time by clicking the Synchronize button on the Settings tab of the Project Designer as shown in Figure 4.9. This deletes the user.config files. They are recreated the next time you run the application.

If you want to retain properties for each form or for some other specialized keys, use the `SettingsKey` property. Settings you defined can then be applied to each key, as shown with the `FormLocation` and `FormSize` settings in this example.

Building Along

For the Purchase Tracker sample application:

- Open the **ProductWin** form in the Code Editor and remove the code that manages the **FormLocation** and **FormSize** settings that you created in the prior "Building Along."
- Display the **ProductWin** form in the Forms Designer and remove the **(ApplicationSettings) Location** property binding that you set in the prior "Building Along."
- Open the base form class (**PTBaseWin**) in the Code Editor and add the **Settings** property and **ApplySettings** and **SetSettings** methods as defined in this section.

- Modify the **Load** event of the base form class (**PTBaseWin**) to call the **ApplySettings** method.
- Add a **FormClosing** event handler to the base form class (**PTBaseWin**) to call the **SetSettings** method.
- Use the Project Designer for the Windows Application project (**PTWin**) to clear your prior settings by clicking the **Synchronize** button in the **Settings** tab, as shown in Figure 4.9.

Run the application. It displays your splash screen and then shows the MDI parent form. Select **Products | Manage Products** to display the ProductWin form. Size and position the form as desired. Close the form and reopen it. It appears with the same size and position you had set.

If desired, find the associated user.config XML file, and take a look at its contents. It now includes a key value with the settings tag.

Drawing Graphics

Drawing graphics was easy in the classic versions of Visual Basic. You could use the circle, line, rectangle, or polygon controls to draw just about anything. These controls are not available in Visual Studio. Instead, you have to write code to perform your drawing.

To draw graphics on a form:

1. Determine the control on which you would like to draw the graphics.

   You can draw graphics directly on the form or on any control on the form. If you draw directly on the form but have other controls, such as panels, that are displayed on the form, the other controls may cover the drawn graphics.

2. In the `Paint` event for the control you are drawing on, create a `Pen` or `Brush` object to use for the drawing.

   Use a `Pen` to draw an object and a `Brush` to fill an object.

3. Include code to set the properties of the `Pen` or `Brush` such as a width, style, and so on.

4. Also in the `Paint` event, draw using the `PaintEventArgs` parameter of the `Paint` event.

NOTE: Care must be taken when using `Pen` and `Brush` objects because they are **unmanaged resources**. That means that the .NET Framework does not manage them. Specifically, it does not automatically handle the dispose of the objects. You must be careful and ensure that you dispose of any unmanaged objects when you are finished with them.

The following code draws a red rectangle within the borders of a `TableLayoutPanel` control on the splash screen form.

```
Private Sub DetailsLayoutPanel_Paint(ByVal sender As Object, _
    ByVal e As System.Windows.Forms.PaintEventArgs) _
    Handles DetailsLayoutPanel.Paint
    Using redPen As New Pen(Color.Firebrick)

        redPen.Width = 4.0F
        redPen.LineJoin = Drawing2D.LineJoin.Bevel
        e.Graphics.DrawRectangle(redPen, _
            New Rectangle(2, 2, DetailsLayoutPanel.Width - 4, _
                            DetailsLayoutPanel.Height - 4))
    End Using
End Sub
```

The first line of code uses the `Using` statement, which marks the beginning of a `Using` block. A `Using` block provides assistance in managing object instances, particularly those containing unmanaged resources such as file handles, COM wrappers, SQL connections, and drawing objects. The first line of the `Using` block acquires the resource, basically creating a variable and initializing it to the appropriate system resource. The code within the `Using` block then uses the resource as needed. The `End Using` statement automatically disposes of the resources defined in the `Using` statement. The `Using` block is similar to a `Try/Finally` construct in that the `End Using` statement always executes, even if an unhandled exception occurs. The benefit of using a `Using` block is that unmanaged resources are appropriately acquired, used, and disposed.

NOTE: To use the `Using` statement with object instances from your classes, you must implement `IDisposable` in your class. See Chapter 5 for more information on `IDisposable`.

In this sample code, the `Using` block acquires a reddish `Pen` object. Code within the `Using` block sets the `Pen`'s attributes. In this case, the code sets the `Width` and `LineJoin` properties. The `LineJoin` property defines the style for the areas in which the lines are connected.

The `PaintEventArgs Graphics` object is used to draw the graphic—in this case, a rectangle. Parameters of the `DrawRectangle` method allow you to define the rectangle's top-left corner, width, and height. The `End Using` statement then disposes of the `Pen` object.

NOTE: The `Paint` event is raised many times during the execution of your application. So ensure any code in the `Paint` event performs well.

Since the graphics are drawn with code, they do not appear on the form until you run the application. The result is shown in Figure 4.11.

Figure 4.11 The rectangle around the Version and Copyright information was drawn using the code described in this section.

Draw graphics anywhere on your forms where you want to add some visual effects or draw the user's attention.

Printing

Tools provided with Visual Studio and third-party products can help you build and print reports. But what if the users just want to print the contents of their forms? A new method in the .NET Framework makes printing forms relatively easy.

If you implemented your MDI parent form using the MDI Parent Form template, you already have Print, Print Preview, and Print Setup options on the File menu and Print and Print Preview icons on the toolbar. You can either remove the options and icons or write code to support them. This section provides the code you need to implement them.

Implementing Printing

There may be times when a user wants a quick printed copy of a form. Implementing a Print feature in your application could be very useful.

To implement printing:

1. Ensure that there is a way for the user to select to print a form.
   If you used the MDI Parent Form template, a menu option and toolbar icon for printing already exist. Otherwise, you can add a menu option, toolbar icon, or button to provide for printing.
2. Add the `PrintDocument` control to the form from which the user initiates the printing process.
   If you have an MDI parent form, add the `PrintDocument` control to the MDI parent. Otherwise, add it to whichever form controls the printing.
   The `PrintDocument` control is a component that you use to print text or graphics within a Windows application. Give the control a logical name, such as PTPrintDocument.
3. In the event handler for the control that initiates printing, write the line of code required to begin the printing process.
   Printing occurs by calling the `Print` method of the `PrintDocument` control, as follows:

   ```
   PTPrintDocument.Print()
   ```

   This generates the `PrintPage` event for the `PrintDocument` control.
4. Add code to the `PrintPage` event handler for the `PrintDocument` control to define what to print.

It is this last step that is a bit more work. Printing the current form requires that you first define a rectangle that is the size of the form, and then define a bitmap that is the size of the form, and finally draw the form as a bitmap using the rectangle to define the amount of the form to draw.

Once you have the bitmap, you can print it using the `DrawImage` method of the `PrintPageEventArgs Graphics` object.

When you look at your results, you will see that the bitmap is the size of the form, which may not fit nicely on the printer page. To scale the bitmap to match the size of the paper, you need a little more code.

The complete code for printing a form is presented next and is described in the following text.

```
Private Sub PTPrintDocument_PrintPage(ByVal sender As Object, _
   ByVal e As System.Drawing.Printing.PrintPageEventArgs) _
   Handles PTPrintDocument.PrintPage
   Dim r As Rectangle
   Dim frmToPrint As Form = Me.ActiveMdiChild

   ' Define a (0,0) based rectangle for the image
   r = New Rectangle(0, 0, frmToPrint.Width, frmToPrint.Height)

   ' Create the bitmap of the image
   Dim b As New Bitmap(frmToPrint.Width, frmToPrint.Height)
   frmToPrint.DrawToBitmap(b, r)

   ' Draw the bitmap to the printdocument scaled
   ' to the printer's margins, but keeping the
   ' same aspect ratio
   Dim iNewHeight As Integer, iNewWidth As Integer
   Dim dPrinterAspectRatio As Double = _
           e.MarginBounds.Height / e.MarginBounds.Width
   Dim dFormAspectRatio As Double = _
           frmToPrint.Height / frmToPrint.Width

   If dFormAspectRatio > dPrinterAspectRatio Then
       ' Form has bigger height, set the height to max and scale
       iNewHeight = e.MarginBounds.Height
       iNewWidth = _
         CType(e.MarginBounds.Height / dFormAspectRatio, Integer)
   Else
       ' Form has a bigger width, set the width to max and scale
       iNewHeight = _
         CType(e.MarginBounds.Width * dFormAspectRatio, Integer)
       iNewWidth = e.MarginBounds.Width
   End If
```

```
' Define a new rectangle for the scaled image
r = New Rectangle(e.MarginBounds.X, e.MarginBounds.Y, _
                    iNewWidth, iNewHeight)
e.Graphics.DrawImage(b, r)
End Sub
```

NOTE: Based on the recommended practices for coding event handlers presented earlier in this chapter, the code in this event handler is too long and should be defined within a new method. That new method is then called from this event handler.

This example assumes that the user wants to print the currently active form, so a variable is declared to retain a reference to the currently active MDI child form.

A rectangle is then defined. This rectangle identifies the portion of the form to be printed. In this example, the entire form is printed so the rectangle begins at (0, 0) and is the size of the form.

The next step is to define the bitmap that contains a drawn image of the form. The size of the bitmap is set to the full size of the form.

The `DrawToBitmap` method is a new **Form** method. It draws the portion of the form defined by the rectangle to a bitmap. In this case, the rectangle is the size of the form so the entire form is drawn to the bitmap. At this point, the bitmap is available to be printed, but it is not scaled to the size of the printer page.

The printer's aspect ratio is calculated by dividing the margin-bound size of the printer page height by its width. The form's aspect ratio is calculated by dividing the form's height by its width.

If the form's aspect ratio is larger than the printer's aspect ratio, the form has a larger height so the height is set to the printer page's height and the width is scaled with the appropriate aspect ratio.

If the form's aspect ratio is smaller than the printer's aspect ratio, the form has a bigger width than the printer's page so the width is set to the printer page's width and the height is scaled with the appropriate aspect ratio.

The new rectangle is created and sized to the scaled image. The `DrawImage` method of the `PrintPageEventArgs` Graphic object is called to draw the bitmap on the printed page scaled to the appropriate size. The page then prints using the default printer.

When the form prints, what you see is what you get. So if you have other controls on tabs or controls on the form that are out of view, they are not included on the printed copy of the form.

Building Along

Because a large amount of code is required for printing, you can skip this "Building Along" without impacting any "Building Along" activities in later chapters. Just remove the Print menu and toolbar options from the MDI parent form.

If you want to implement form printing, for the Purchase Tracker sample application:

- Display the MDI parent form (**PTMDIParentWin**) in the Forms Designer and add the **PrintDocument** control.
  Name it **PTPrintDocument**.
- Add an event handler that handles the **Click** event for both the Print menu option and Print toolbar button. In this event handler, call the **PTPrintDocument.Print** method to perform the printing.
- Add an event handler for the **PTPrintDocument PrintPage** event. Add code to this event as defined in this section.

Run the application. It displays your splash screen and then shows the MDI parent form. Select **Products | Manage Products** to display the ProductWin form. Then select **Purchase Tracker | Print** and the ProductWin form is printed to your default printer. Click the Print button in the toolbar, and the form is printed again.

NOTE: If you access the Print menu option when no active MDI child form is displayed, the application generates an error. Handling exceptions is covered later in this chapter.

Implementing Print Preview

Print preview allows the user to view what a printout looks like before actually printing it. It uses the same `PrintDocument` control and associated code required to implement the Print feature. So once you have the Print feature implemented, adding a print preview feature is easy.

To implement a Print Preview feature:

1. Ensure that there is a way for the user to select a Print Preview. This is most logically defined near the Print option.
2. Add the `PrintPreviewDialog` control to the form from which the user initiates the Print Preview process.
   This is normally the same form containing the `PrintDocument` control. Give the `PrintPreviewDialog` control a logical name, such as PTPrintPreview.
3. In the event handler for the control that initiates the Print Preview, write the code required to display the Print Preview dialog.
   The code requires two simple steps: associate the appropriate `PrintDocument` control with the Print Preview dialog and then show the dialog as follows:

```
PTPrintPreview.Document = PTPrintDocument
PTPrintPreview.ShowDialog()
```

If you don't like the appearance of the built-in Print Preview dialog and would like to create your own, you can create a form to be used as your Print Preview dialog. Add the `PrintPreviewControl` control to the form along with any other controls you would like. Then add the code to associate the `PrintDocument` control with the `PrintPreviewControl` control and call `ShowDialog`.

Building Along

If you skipped the prior "Building Along," you can skip this one as well without impacting any "Building Along" activities in later chapters.

If you want to implement form print preview, for the Purchase Tracker sample application:

- Display the MDI parent form (**PTMDIParentWin**) in the Forms Designer and add the **PrintPreviewDialog** control.
  Name it **PTPrintPreview**.
- Add an event handler that handles the **Click** event for the **Print Preview** menu option. Add the code defined in this section to associate the **PrintDocument** control with the Print Preview dialog and then show the dialog.

Run the application. It displays your splash screen and then shows the MDI parent form. Select **Products | Manage Products** to display the ProductWin form. Then select **Purchase Tracker | Print Preview** to display the Print Preview dialog.

NOTE: If you access the Print Preview menu option when no active MDI child form is displayed, the application generates an error. Handling exceptions is covered later in this chapter.

Implementing Print Setup

Print setup allows the user to define the printer and other print settings before printing. In some applications, the Print menu option provides this feature and the user must view this dialog every time printing is required. In this example, the features are separated to give the user an easy way to print to the default printer without accessing the setup dialog. Either way you prefer, this feature is easy to implement because it uses the same `PrintDocument` control and associated code required to implement the Print feature.

To implement a Print Setup feature:

1. Ensure that there is a way for the user to select a Print Setup.
   This is most logically defined near the Print option. In some cases, the setup is handled in the Print option, and a separate Print Setup option is not desired.
2. Add the `PrintDialog` control to the form from which the user initiates the Print Setup process.
   This is normally the same form containing the `PrintDocument` control. Give the control a logical name, such as PTPrintDialog.
3. In the event handler for the control that initiates the Print Setup, write the code required to display the Print dialog.
   The code involves associating the appropriate `PrintDocument` control with the Print dialog, displaying the Print dialog, and then, if the user clicked OK, printing the document as follows:

```
PTPrintDialog.Document = PTPrintDocument
Dim oResult As DialogResult = PTPrintDialog.ShowDialog
If oResult = Windows.Forms.DialogResult.OK Then
     PTPrintDocument.Print()
End If
```

Building Along

If you skipped the prior "Building Along," you can skip this one as well without impacting any "Building Along" activities in later chapters.

If you want to implement print setup, for the Purchase Tracker sample application:

■ Display the MDI parent form (**PTMDIParentWin**) in the Forms Designer and add the **PrintDialog** control.
Name it **PTPrintDialog**.

■ Add an event handler that handles the **Click** event for the **Print Setup** menu option. Add the code defined in this section to associate the **PrintDocument** control with the Print dialog, show the dialog, and then print.

Run the application. It displays your splash screen and then shows the MDI parent form. Select **Products | Manage Products** to display the ProductWin form. Select **Purchase Tracker | Print Setup** to display the Print dialog. If you click the OK button, the ProductWin form is printed. If you click the Cancel button, nothing is printed.

NOTE: If you access the Print Setup menu option when no active MDI child form is displayed, the application generates an error. Handling exceptions is covered later in this chapter.

The topics in this section detailed how to print a form, including print preview and print setup features. You can use these techniques to print the forms in your applications. With some tailoring of the code in the `PrintPage` event handler, you can also use these techniques to print any information.

Handling Exceptions

Stuff happens. Network connections fail. Users do the unexpected. Things just don't always go as you had planned. A production-quality application needs to anticipate the unexpected, the unknown possibilities, and the exceptional cases and react accordingly. This is the purpose of exception prevention and handling in your application.

This section first looks at some defensive development techniques. It then details how to throw and catch exceptions and how to use a resource file for error text.

Defensive Development

Defensive development is a technique whereby you develop your application with a focus on defending each of your methods from harm. This means that you tenaciously validate each incoming parameter, verify any required preconditions, and do whatever it takes to ensure proper execution of the method. By spending the time implementing defensive development techniques while you are building the application, you may find that you spend much less time on debugging and support of the application after it is deployed.

As an example, code in the event handler for the PrintPage event in the prior section generates an unhandled exception if the user does not open an MDI child form before selecting to print. There are several ways you can defensively handle this situation:

- Modify the code that displays the menu so that the Print options are grayed out or hidden if no active MDI child form exists.
  This approach is used often, but it has one key drawback. When the options are grayed out, the user has no indication as to why, which could then prompt a support call.
- Modify the code that handles the `Click` event for each of the Print options to check for an active MDI child form and display a message to the user if there is none.
  This is a good approach because it defensively prevents a potential problem and allows the user to easily discover how to correct the problem.
- Modify the code in the `PrintPage` event (or the method called by the `PrintPage` event) to check for an active MDI child form.

This approach is also good. Some would say it is better than the preceding option, because the check is in the method itself.

Implementing the second option is easy. In the print option event handler, add code similar to this:

```
If Me.ActiveMdiChild Is Nothing Then
    MessageBox.Show("Please open a form to print before " _
            & "selecting this option")
Else
    PTPrintDocument.Print()
End If
```

Implementing the third option is similar. In the `PrintPage` event (or the method called by the `PrintPage` event), add the code to check for an active MDI child form.

Immediately following this line:

```
Dim frmToPrint As Form = Me.ActiveMdiChild
```

add the following code:

```
If frmToPrint Is Nothing Then
    e.Cancel = True
    MessageBox.Show("Please open a form to print before " _
            & "selecting this option")
Else
    ...
End If
```

Because the `PrintPage` event was already generated, the runtime continues to attempt to print. So if there is no active MDI child form to print, the first thing the code needs to do is cancel the `PrintPage` event. It then displays an appropriate message to the user. The `Else` clause contains all the other code for the `PrintPage` event processing shown in the prior section.

You can also combine the second and third options to perform the check in both the Print menu options and in the `PrintPage` event. By performing the check first in the Print menu options, you prevent the Print dialog from displaying when there is no active MDI child form. By performing the check also in the `PrintPage` event, you ensure that the event code handles the problem in case the Print menu options don't. This defensive coding technique protects your code from changes to other code in the application.

Using Resource Files for Message Text

Message text is another one of those things that seem to change frequently. Maybe you have a boss that likes to interject ideas for improving the messages. Maybe you have a marketing department that wants the wording "just so." Maybe you have helpful testers or usability experts that want to provide feedback. Or maybe you have to support localization. Whatever the situation, you can make your life much easier if you separate message text from your code.

Visual Basic provides resource files to aid you in managing your text strings external from your code. Visual Basic 2005 makes the task of defining and referencing text strings even easier with its improved Resource File editor and strongly typed resource file entries.

To add a text string to a resource file:

1. Open the Project Designer for the **Windows Application** project.
   Right-click the project in Solution Explorer and select **Properties** from the context menu, *or* select **Project | Properties** from the main menu bar, *or* double-click on the **My Project** folder under the project to open the Project Designer.
2. Select the **Resources** tab.
3. In the **Name** column of the grid, type the name of the string.
   Use good naming conventions so that you can more easily manage your strings. This is important because you may have many strings. Since you can sort the strings by name, you may want to define a naming convention so that all strings begin with the name of the entity or feature (or an abbreviation thereof), such as "Product" or "Print."
   For example, for the print error message in the prior section, the resource string name is PrintErrActiveForm.
4. In the **Value** column of the grid, type the actual text.
   For example, for the print error message in the prior section the resource string value is "Please open a form to print before selecting this option".
5. Enter any comments in the **Comment** column.

You can then use the text string anywhere in the project by referencing its name as follows:

```
My.Resources.PrintErrActiveForm
```

Using the code example from the preceding section, replace the hard-coded message text string with the string from the resource file:

```
If Me.ActiveMdiChild Is Nothing Then
    e.Cancel = True
    MessageBox.Show(My.Resources.PrintErrActiveForm)
Else
    PTPrintDocument.Print()
End If
```

In addition to message strings, you can use this technique to put any strings from your application into the application resource file.

You can make the resource strings more general by using composite formatting. **Composite formatting** enables you to define a text string that contains indexed placeholders, defined with {0}, {1} and so on. When you use that string, you then define the ordered values for those placeholders. The result is a string consisting of the original text intermixed with the formatted values. You can use composite formatting with .NET Framework methods such as `String.Format`, `Console.WriteLine`, and `Debug.Print`.

For example, say you want to validate that several of the fields on the form are required. You could create a string resource to say "Product Name is required, please enter a valid string" and another that says "Product Number is required, please enter a valid number" and so on. It may be more efficient to add one generalized string to the resource file that says "{0} is required, please enter a valid {1}".

To use the generalized resource file string, call the String.Format method and define the string and the ordered values to fill the placeholders:

```
MessageBox.Show(String.Format(My.Resources.ValidationRequired, _
                    "Product Name", "string"))
```

The first parameter to the Format method is the string, in this case the resource file string name. The second parameter is the replacement for the {0} placeholder, the third parameter is the replacement for the {1} placeholder, and so on in an ordered fashion. The resulting string appears as "Product Name is required, please enter a valid string".

NOTE: Take care when using this technique with resource files that are localized, because any replacement strings hard-coded in your application also need to be localized.

Using a resource file for your strings makes it easier to maintain and manage the strings separate from your application. And leveraging the new My.Resources object makes it easy to reference the strings using strongly typed names.

Building Along

For the Purchase Tracker sample application:
- Select the Windows Application project (**PTWin**) in Solution Explorer.
- Open the Project Designer and select the **Resources** tab.
- Add a **ValidationRequired** resource string to the Resources tab.
- Set the text to "{0} is required, please enter a valid value".
- Optionally, add code to the **Load** event of the ProductWin form to display a message containing the **ValidationRequired** resource string:

```
MessageBox.Show(String.Format(_
    My.Resources.ValidationRequired, "Product Name"))
```

- If you implemented printing in the Purchase Tracker application, also add the **PrintErrActiveForm** resource string as defined in this section. It will be used in the next "Building Along" activity.

Run the application. It displays your splash screen and then shows the MDI parent form. Select **Products | Manage Products** to display the ProductWin form. If you added a message box, it appears before the ProductWin form is displayed.

After trying this, remove the message box. The resource string is used for validation in Chapter 7.

Throwing Exceptions

Using defensive development techniques and displaying a message to the user when there is a problem is a great way to handle expected exceptions, especially when the user can do something to correct the problem. But in many cases it is not appropriate to display a message to the user. In these cases, throwing exceptions may be a better option.

As an example, look again at the code defined earlier in this chapter to support printing. This is not code that you want to write for every application you build. Instead, you write it once and put it into a class library that you can then reuse in every application. But code in a class library should never display messages to the user. The code instead needs to notify the calling code if it has a problem and allow the calling code to define how to respond to the problem.

When a problem exists, there are several ways a method can notify the code that called it:

- Return an error code.
  A common C programming language convention was to always return an error code from every method. The calling code could then check the return code to determine if an error occurred.
  The problem with this technique is that it requires that the calling code always remember to check the return value. This was a common programming mistake in many C applications. Another problem is that it then prevented returning a more logical object from the method and instead required passing the return values as parameters. This technique is not used much anymore because of these drawbacks.
- Throw an exception.
  Throwing an exception is the ".NET way" for a method to notify its calling code of any problems.

You can throw one of the many predefined exceptions available in the .NET Framework, or you can create your own exception classes. See Chapter 5 for more information on creating your own exception classes.

To throw a .NET Framework exception:

1. Use defensive development techniques to determine which code should throw an exception.

2. Examine the .NET Framework exceptions to determine which exception makes sense in that situation.
3. Throw the exception using the `Throw` statement.

For example, instead of displaying a message box when there is no active MDI child form, add code that throws an exception:

```
If frmToPrint Is Nothing Then
    e.Cancel = True
    Throw New InvalidOperationException( _
                My.Resources.PrintErrActiveForm)
End If
```

The `If` no longer needs an `Else` statement. Throwing an exception can simplify your method's structure because when the exception is thrown, processing immediately flows to the calling code (after executing any `Finally` clause, as described in the next section). If there is no error, flow continues in the method.

The message text defined for the exception can be any descriptive text, since it is not displayed to the user. However, you can still put these text strings in the resource file, as described in the preceding section. Be sure to make the message text descriptive, because it can help you debug the code if a problem occurs.

Here are some of the most common .NET Framework exceptions you can throw:

- `ArgumentException` specifies a general error with one of the parameters passed into the method.
- `ArgumentNullException` specifies that one of the parameters passed into the method is null (`Nothing`).
- `ArgumentOutOfRangeException` specifies that one of the parameters passed into the method has a value that is out of the valid range of values.
- `InvalidOperationException` specifies a general error in the operation of the method.

NOTE: Always throw the most specific exception that is feasible for your condition. For example, throw `ArgumentNullException` instead of the more general `ArgumentException` if the argument is null (`Nothing`). *Never* throw `Exception` or `ApplicationException`.

Throw an exception from a method any time the method parameters, method state, or method operations are invalid. The code that called the method can then catch the exception and proceed accordingly.

Building Along

This "Building Along" has two different sets of steps: one to use if you implemented printing and want to add exception handling to the printing code, and one to use if you did not implement printing but still want to try some exception handling.

If you want to implement exception handling in your printing, for the Purchase Tracker sample application:

- Open the MDI parent form (**PTMDIParentWin**) in the Code Editor.
- Cut the code from the **PrintPage** event handler and copy it to a new **ProcessPrintPage** method. Then call the new method from the **PrintPage** event handler.

    The **ProcessPrintPage** method signature is as follows:

    ```
    Private Sub ProcessPrintPage(ByVal e As _
        System.Drawing.Printing.PrintPageEventArgs)
    ```

- Modify the code in the **ProcessPrintPage** method to throw an exception, as shown in this section.

Don't run the code yet, because there is no code at this point to catch the exception.

If you want to try exception handling without implementing printing, for the Purchase Tracker sample application:

- Open the **ProductWin** form in the Code Editor.
- Throw an exception in the **ProcessDelete** method as follows:

    ```
    Public Function ProcessDelete() As Boolean _
        Implements IMDIChild.ProcessDelete
      MessageBox.Show("Deleting")
      Throw New InvalidOperationException("Cannot delete")
    End Function
    ```

Don't run the code yet, because there is no code at this point to catch the exception.

Catching Exceptions

Exceptions can be thrown by your code, as described in the preceding section, or thrown by the runtime if there is a problem with the operation of your code. You can catch both expected and unexpected exceptions.

Using good defensive coding techniques, your methods throw exceptions when they find a problem with their parameters, state, or operations. And since that is where the majority of your code is, your methods will most likely be the source of any unexpected runtime exceptions as well. So it may seem that you want to catch exceptions in every method, but that is not the recommended practice.

NOTE FOR VB6 DEVELOPERS: The recommended practice for error handling in classic Visual Basic applications was to put an `On Error` statement in every method. That practice is no longer recommended with the new exception handling features provided in the .NET Framework.

The recommended practice is to catch exceptions as follows:

- Catch an exception where it will be handled.
  For example, if you have a method that accesses external hardware, and that hardware is not found, catch the exception in that method and handle it.
  If you won't handle the exception within the method, don't catch it. Allow the error to propagate up to the code that called the method. If the exception is not handled by that code, don't catch it. It again propagates to the method that called it. This propagation continues up the call stack until the exception reaches the event handler code that presumably is at the top of the call stack.
- Catch an exception in the event handler that called the method to display a specific message.
  If an exception is not handled in any method in the call stack, it propagates to the event handler at the top of the call stack. Most frequently, the event handler is in a Windows form, making it feasible to catch the exception, display a message to the user about the error, and proceed appropriately.
  If you don't need to display a specific message, don't catch the error. Allow it to propagate to the global exception handler and display a general message.

- Catch an exception in the global exception handler.
  If the application has an unhandled error, the global exception handler, defined in Chapter 3, can catch the exception. This prevents any unhandled exception from being displayed to the user.

NOTE: If you allow the global exception handler to handle the message, the application cannot easily continue, because the global exception handler has no context as to where or how the error occurred. If you want to continue from an exception, handle the exception in the event handler that called the method.

Handle an exception with a `Try/Catch` block. Insert a `Try/Catch` block in each method or event handler that catches and handles an exception. The `Try` part of the `Try/Catch` block contains the code that could potentially generate an exception. The `Catch` block defines the code to catch and handle the exception. An optional `Finally` block identifies code that executes when the method or event handler is finished executing, whether or not it caught an exception.

The following example demonstrates the use of a `Try/Catch` block from within an event handler:

```
Private Sub PTPrintDocument_PrintPage(ByVal sender As Object, _
    ByVal e As System.Drawing.Printing.PrintPageEventArgs) _
    Handles PTPrintDocument.PrintPage
  Try
      ProcessPrintPage(e)

  Catch ex As InvalidOperationException
      MessageBox.Show(My.Resources.PrintErrActiveForm)

  End Try
End Sub
```

In many cases, all the code in the event procedure is within the `Try` block. You identify one `Catch` block for every error that you want to catch and handle. In this example, only the `InvalidOperationException` is handled. All other exceptions are propagated to the global exception handler.

Once a `Catch` block is executed, none of the other `Catch` blocks below it are evaluated. For example, the following code never executes the `Catch` block for the `InvalidOperationException`:

```
Catch ex As Exception
    MessageBox.Show("Unhandled exception")
Catch ex As InvalidOperationException
    MessageBox.Show(My.Resources.PrintErrActiveForm)
```

The first `Catch` block catches any exception and handles it, preventing the second `Catch` block from executing. If you want to define a specific event handler and also have one that can catch any other exception, put the specific exception first:

```
Catch ex As InvalidOperationException
    MessageBox.Show(My.Resources.PrintErrActiveForm)
Catch ex As Exception
    MessageBox.Show("Unhandled exception")
```

> **NOTE:** Although they are used in this example for demonstration purposes, do not catch exceptions of type `Exception` or `ApplicationException` in your code unless that code specifically plans to handle those exceptions. Instead, allow the global exception handler to catch these unexpected errors, log the problem, and terminate gracefully.

Building Along

This "Building Along" has two different sets of steps: one to use if you implemented printing and want to add exception handling to the printing code, and one to use if you did not implement printing but still want to try some exception handling.

If you do want to implement exception handling in your printing, for the Purchase Tracker sample application:

- Open the MDI parent form (**PTMDIParentWin**) in the Code Editor.
- Add a `Try/Catch` block to the **PrintPage** event handler, as shown in this section.

Run the application. It displays your splash screen and then shows the MDI parent form. Without opening any child forms, select **Purchase Tracker | Print** to see your message.

If you want to try exception handling without implementing printing, for the Purchase Tracker sample application:

- Open the MDI parent form (**PTMDIParentWin**) in the Code Editor.
- Add a `Try/Catch` block to the **Click** event for the **Delete** toolbar button as follows:

```
Private Sub DeleteToolStripButton_Click(_
        ByVal sender As Object, _
        ByVal e As System.EventArgs) _
        Handles DeleteToolStripButton.Click
    Try
        Dim frmMDIChild As IMDIChild
        frmMDIChild = TryCast(Me.ActiveMdiChild, _
                                    IMDIChild)
        frmMDIChild.ProcessDelete()
    Catch ex As InvalidOperationException
        MessageBox.Show(ex.Message)
    End Try
End Sub
```

Run the application. It displays your splash screen and then shows the MDI parent form. Select **Products | Manage Products** to display the ProductWin form. Click the Delete button on the MDI parent form toolbar to see your error message.

Inserting strategically placed `Try/Catch` blocks within your application can help ensure that your application is robust and does not display unhandled exception errors to your users.

Conclusion

What Did This Chapter Cover?

This chapter described how to build the user interface layer for your application. It demonstrated techniques for implementing event handlers, building a base form class, using form instances, creating an MDI application, implementing a standard programmatic interface, and handling exceptions. It also provided information on using smart tags, using XML comments and regions, saving user and application settings, drawing graphics, printing, and adding strings to the resource file.

This chapter covered several real productivity enhancers:

- Using smart tags provides a quick way to access the most common properties of controls in the Forms Designer.
- Using the Tab Order view of the Forms Designer can make it a breeze to check or set the tab order for your form.
- Writing generalized event handlers allows you to use the same event handler for multiple controls on a form.
- Building a base form class provides standardized processing for all the forms of your application and significantly reduces the amount of code required in each form.
- Using the MDI Parent Form template automatically generates much of the standardized MDI parent code for you.
- Saving user and application settings using the Settings feature of Visual Studio minimizes the amount of code that you need to write to manage these settings.
- Using a resource file provides quick programmatic access to the strings in your application while making it easy to modify those strings.
- Making use of the `Using` keyword ensures that unmanaged resources are correctly disposed without the need to write any extra code.

The next chapter provides information on building your application's business logic layer, including how to create high-quality methods and build a base business object class.

Building Along

If you are "building along" with the Purchase Tracker application, this chapter added a base form class that you can inherit from as you create every other form in the application. It also added an MDI parent form to the application and implemented some of its functionality, such as form printing, print preview, and print setup. Exception throwing and handling were also put into place to enhance the application's robustness.

You can run the Purchase Tracker application and view the Product form. You can also use the Save, New, and Delete buttons, but they only display a message at this point.

When building production-level applications, you may want to consider enhancing the basic user interface layer as follows:

- **Status messages**
  A status bar at the bottom of the MDI parent form displays status messages. You can add code in the forms to display appropriate messages to the user, such as "update complete."
- **Enabling/disabling panels**
  When the user first opens a form, if you want the user to select an entry from the list and not type anything else into the form, you can disable the information panel at the bottom of the form. After the user selects an entry, you can enable the information panel to allow edits. Alternatively, you could leave the information panel enabled. If the user types information into the panel, assume you need to create a new entry.
- **Handling changes to values in the combo box**
  If the user changes data that is displayed in the combo box, modify the combo box contents accordingly. For example, if the user updates the product name, the product name drop-down should recognize the change. To implement this, add code to the `ProcessSave` method in the form to repopulate the combo box list if the field displayed in the combo box (the product name in this example) is changed.
- **Handling a delete**
  First, it is a good idea to request confirmation of a delete. That way, the user won't inadvertently delete something. If the delete is confirmed, clear the data from the user interface and remove the item from the combo box. To implement this, add code in the `ProcessDelete` method to display a message box for confirmation. After the delete (which would be handled in the business object), clear the form contents and repopulate the combo box list.
- **Handling an insert**
  When the user performs an insert, clear any existing data in the user interface to allow entry of the new data. After the data is saved, add the item to the list in the combo box. To implement this, add code in the `ProcessNew` method to clear the form contents. Then add code to the `ProcessSave` method to repopulate the combo box list when the user saves a new entry.

4. BUILDING THE USER INTERFACE LAYER

- **Enabling/disabling features based on role**

  You may have features in the application that are not available to all the users of the application. For example, you may have some administrative features for modifying the standard set of type codes for product types, customer types, and so on.

  One way to limit these features to people with administrative rights is to write a separate application for these features and provide that application to the administrators.

  A more common technique is to add the features to the primary application and then enable and disable the features based on the user's role. The user interface (the MDI form in the Purchase Tracker example) would then determine which menu options were enabled for the user by writing code similar to the following:

```
Private Sub PurchaseMenu_DropDownOpening(ByVal sender _
    As Object, ByVal e As System.EventArgs) _
    Handles PurchaseMenu.DropDownOpening
    If My.User.IsInRole(_
        ApplicationServices.BuiltInRole.Administrator) Then
            ManageTypesMenuItem.Enabled = True
    Else
            ManageTypesMenuItem.Enabled = False
    End If
End Sub
```

  Instead of hard-coding the roles in the UI, you could consider building a `Security` class in the business logic layer that would identify which roles could access which features. This `Security` class could optionally access a database to retrieve this information. The UI would then call the `Security` class to determine the roles that can access a feature and then use the `IsInRole` method to determine if the current user has one of the defined roles.

- **Enabling/disabling controls based on role**

  Some applications limit which users can update values in the user interface. So you may need to display some values as read-only based on the user's role. You can use the techniques described in the preceding bullet point to enable/disable controls based on the user's role.

The next chapter implements the business logic layer of the Purchase Tracker sample application.

Additional Reading

Esposito, Dino. *Programming Microsoft ASP.NET 2.0 Core Reference.* Microsoft Press, November 2005.

This book covers all the core components of ASP.NET 2.0, including Web controls, master pages, data access, data binding, state management, and security services. If you are doing Web development, this book provides information on how to build the user interface component of your application.

Kurata, Deborah. "Give Your Forms a Base." *CoDe* magazine, March/April 2004.

This article describes how to create a base form class. The techniques presented in this article show ways that you can minimize the amount of repetitive code you need to write to manage the user's interaction with your forms.

Kurata, Deborah. "Inheritance 101." *CoDe* magazine, May/June 2005.

Extend your knowledge of inheritance to more easily extend your applications. This article provides an overview of inheritance and shows how you can leverage inheritance to more effectively reuse code in your applications.

Kurata, Deborah. "Life Without Control Arrays in Visual Basic .NET." MSDN Library, July 11, 2003.

This article is for VB6 developers who are moving to .NET and who want to understand how .NET provides all the features of control arrays without having control arrays.

Kurata, Deborah. "Retaining Multiple Sets of User Settings." *CoDe* magazine, July/August 2006.

You can find more information on user settings in this article.

MacDonald, Matthew. *Pro .NET 2.0 Windows Forms and Custom Controls in C#.* Microsoft Press, December 2005.

If you are planning to build your own user controls, this is a great book. However, all the examples are in C#, so you would need to convert them to VB yourself.

Microsoft Patterns and Practices. *Enterprise Solution Patterns Using Microsoft .Net: Version 2.0: Patterns & Practices.* Microsoft Press, September 2003.

This book provides a wealth of information on implementing patterns with .NET. Specifically, it includes detailed information on the MVC pattern, albeit for ASP.NET. (Much of the information in this book is also available on the Web at http://msdn.microsoft.com/library/default. asp?url=/library/en-us/dnpatterns/html/ESP.asp.)

Microsoft Patterns and Practices. *Smart Client—Composite UI Application Block.* December 2005. http://msdn.microsoft.com/practices/apptype/ smartclient/default.aspx?pull=/library/en-us/dnpag2/html/cab.asp.

This set of Web pages provides detailed information on using the Composite UI application block for smart client development. It also provides links for downloading this reusable component.

Microsoft Patterns and Practices. *User Interface Process (UIP) Application Block.* April 2004. http://msdn.microsoft.com/library/default.asp?url=/ library/en-us/dnpag/html/uipab.asp.

This set of Web pages provides detailed information on using the User Interface Process application block, which implements the MVC pattern. It also provides links for downloading this reusable component.

Petzold, Charles. *Programming Microsoft Windows Forms.* Microsoft Press, November 2005.

Although it is written with C# code examples, this book provides a detailed look at many of the details of efficiently building effective Windows applications.

Try It!

Here are a few suggestions for trying some of the techniques presented in this chapter:

1. Add a Sales Rep form to the Windows Application project.
   Ensure that the form inherits from your base form class. Add controls as appropriate for name, e-mail address, and so on. Set the tab order appropriately.
   Define this form as the startup form, and run the application. Notice how the controls automatically support the `Enter` and `Leave` events.
2. Add a menu option to the MDI parent form to display the Sales Rep form.

If you have not created an MDI parent form, add one to a Windows Application project. Reset the startup form to the MDI parent form.

Try positioning the Sales Rep form and then closing it. When you open it, the size and location are reset to the prior values. This should just work, with no code changes or additions.

Try printing the Sales Rep form. If you implemented the Print features as described in this chapter, it should print, with no code changes or additions.

3. Modify the code in the Sales Rep form to implement the IMDIChild interface.

4. Add an about box using the About Box form template, and connect it to the correct menu option in the MDI parent form.

5. Draw graphics on the about box using the techniques presented in this chapter.

CHAPTER 5

BUILDING THE BUSINESS LOGIC LAYER

If you have class, you've got it made. If you don't have class, no matter what else you have, it won't make up for it.
—**Ann Landers**

If you have classes in your application, you've got it made. If you don't have classes, no matter what else you have, it won't make up for it. Classes are central to development in .NET.

In fact, it is difficult to build a .NET application without using classes. If you added a form to your project, you have already created a class. A form is just a class that inherits from the .NET Framework `System.Windows.Forms.Form` class, which gives the class the attributes and behaviors of a form.

In the preceding chapter, you saw how to use classes to build the user interface layer. This chapter shows you how to build classes for the business logic layer.

This chapter covers the fundamentals of creating classes and defining properties and methods. It also details more advanced topics such as using generics and building a base business object class. The Purchase Tracker sample application is used to demonstrate these techniques.

What Does This Chapter Cover?

This chapter demonstrates the following techniques:

- Creating a class
- Documenting the class with XML comments
- Adding exception classes to your class file
- Defining properties

- Defining property accessibility
- Understanding generics
- Handling `Nullable` types
- Defining methods
- Passing parameters `ByVal` or `ByRef`
- Overloading methods
- Marking methods as obsolete
- Creating a base business object class
- Overriding base class members

This chapter covers the basics of how to create a class and then builds on those basics to detail some of the new Visual Basic 2005 features such as XML comments and generics. If you have already been doing object-oriented programming in Visual Basic, you already know the basics. But if you want to "build along" as you read through this book, work through the basics before moving on to the more advanced features later in this chapter.

Creating a Class

A **class** describes the things in your application, such as customers or products. Each piece of data associated with the class is defined as a **property** of the class. Each set of functionality associated with the class is defined as a **method** of the class.

For example, the Purchase Tracker sample application works with products. The products are described by a `Product` class. Each attribute of the products, such as name, number, description, price, and so on, is represented in the class as a property. Each process that must be performed for the products, such as retrieving, saving, and so on, is defined in the class as a method.

A single item, such as an individual product (a ring or sword, for example), is represented by an **object** created from the class. Because an object is an instance of a class, the act of creating an object from the class is called **instantiation**.

A common metaphor is to think of the class as the blueprint, and the object as the building constructed from the blueprint. Any number of buildings can be created from the same blueprint. Another metaphor is a cookie cutter. The class is the cookie cutter, and the objects are all the cookies created from the cookie cutter.

> **NOTE:** The terms **class** and **object** are sometimes used interchangeably. Technically, however, the class is the data and logic that you define at design time. The objects are instances of the class created at runtime.
>
> The phrase "business objects" is really a misnomer, because they are really "business classes." In this book, the term "business object classes" is sometimes used to distinguish the difference.

If you are building a nontrivial application, build it as a set of layers, as described in Chapter 2, "Designing Software." Implement each layer as a separate project in a solution, as described in Chapter 3, "Building Projects." This gives you separately compiled components, one for each layer.

You build each layer as a set of classes. The user interface layer is comprised of a set of form classes (as shown in Chapter 4, "Building the User Interface Layer") following the user interface design. The business logic layer (as described in this chapter) includes the set of classes you build following the implementation design. The data layer (detailed in Chapter 8, "Building the Data Access Layer") contains classes that provide the interaction between the database and the business logic layer.

When you construct the business logic layer, it is important to define the pertinent set of classes. For each class, you define the appropriate properties and methods. This ensures that the correct set of information and logic is encapsulated in each class, making it easier to work with and maintain the class.

> **NOTE:** Even if you don't go through the design phase, you need to think through the application to identify the appropriate set of classes for your business logic layer.

You normally define one class for each key thing involved with the application. For example, the Purchase Tracker sample application has products, customers, and purchases. The products map to a `Product` class, with properties to manage product information and methods to retrieve, save, and perform any other required processing on product information. The customers map to a `Customer` class, and so on. For more information on defining classes for your application, see Chapter 2.

You can also define classes for other implementation logic. For example, you could create a class to manage application logging or security. These implementation-based classes were also discussed in Chapter 2.

This section details the process of creating a class. You can use these techniques to create each class needed by your application.

Adding a Class to a Project

There are many ways to add a class to a project. As discussed in the preceding chapter, adding a form project item actually adds two class files to the project. It adds a class in one file with a .vb extension and a partial class in another file with a .designer.vb extension.

When building the business logic layer, you normally add one class project item for each business object class (such as Product and Customer) and one for each implementation class (such as Logging and Security).

NOTE: You may want to define standard implementation classes in a separate utility component instead of in the business object component. That way, it can more readily become a part of your reusable framework, as discussed in Chapter 2.

To add a class to a project:

1. Right-click the project in Solution Explorer and select **Add** | **New Item** from the context menu, *or* select **Project** | **Add New Item** from the main menu bar.
   Alternatively, you could select **Add** | **Class** from the context menu, *or* select **Project** | **Add Class** from the main menu bar.
2. Select the **Class** template, name the class, and click the **Add** button.
   If you created your own class template using the steps in Chapter 3, you can use your template here.
   Use standard naming conventions for your class name. The most common standard is to name the class using the singular name of the business entity or implementation feature represented by the class. For products the class name would be Product, for logging the class name would be Logging, and so on.
   Visual Studio creates the class file with a .vb extension, adds it to Solution Explorer, and then displays the class in the Code Editor.

When Visual Studio creates the class file, it automatically generates the class declaration as follows:

```
Public Class Product

End Class
```

You can add any number of classes to your projects as needed by your application. Regardless of the class's purpose or location, the basic process of building a class is the same.

NOTE: Throughout this chapter, classes are created in the business object Class Library project. You can use these same techniques to add classes to other parts of your application. For example, your Windows Application project may require classes to manage user interface features such as standard grid processing. Or you may create a utility or general library component that requires classes.

Building Along

For the Purchase Tracker sample application:

- Visual Studio created a default class for you when you created the business object Class Library project (**PTBO**). In *Solution Explorer*, change the name of this default class from Class1 to **Product**. When you change the name of a class in Solution Explorer, Visual Studio changes the class name in the Code Editor accordingly.

NOTE: When you change the class name in Solution Explorer, Visual Studio modifies the class name in your code only if the class name matched the name defined in Solution Explorer. For example, say you don't modify the class name in Solution Explorer, but you instead change the name directly in the class file. If you later change the name in Solution Explorer, it does not change the name you entered in the class file.

Documenting the Class

It is always a good idea to add documentation for a class immediately after adding the class. By adding the documentation right away, you focus on the class's purpose, which helps you keep the class encapsulated. It is also much easier to document each class as you go along instead of facing the large task of going back later and documenting all the classes.

To document the class:

1. Open the class in the Code Editor.
2. Move the insertion point immediately before the word `Public` in the `Public Class` statement.
3. Type three comment markers, defined in Visual Basic as apostrophes (`'''`), and press the Enter key.
   The XML comments feature automatically creates the structure of your class documentation as follows:

```
'''  <summary>
'''
'''  </summary>
'''  <remarks></remarks>
Public Class Product

End Class
```

NOTE: If you type the three comment markers in the empty line above the class definition instead of on the same line as the class definition, you don't need to press the Enter key to generate the documentation structure.

---

4. Type a summary of the class's purpose between the **summary** tags and any remarks between the **remark** tags.
   Your documentation may be similar to this:

```
'''  <summary>
'''  Provides product management features such as
'''  retrieving product data and saving product changes
'''  </summary>
'''  <remarks>Use this class to work with products
'''  </remarks>
```

Use the `summary` tags to describe the class and the `remarks` tags to add supplemental information. The `summary` is the most important tag because it is the one used by Visual Studio.

When you provide a summary of the class using XML comments, your class displays documentation about itself in appropriate places within Visual Studio, such as in the List Members box, shown in Figure 5.1. Open the List Members box by typing a part of the class name in the Code Editor and pressing Ctrl+Spacebar *or* by selecting **Edit** | **Intellisense** | **List Members** from the main menu bar *or* by clicking the **Display an Object Member List** icon on the Text Editor toolbar.

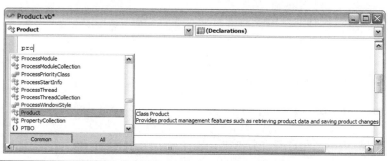

Figure 5.1   The documentation provided in the List Members box is the summary defined in the XML documentation for the class.

Using XML comments to document your classes makes it easier for you and other developers to work with your classes.

Building Along

For the Purchase Tracker sample application:
- Open the **Product** class in the Code Editor.
- Add documentation for the **Product** class using XML comments.

In the Code Editor, view the comments by typing `pro` and then pressing Ctrl+Spacebar to display the List Members box, as shown in Figure 5.1.

Organizing the Code Structure

Code that is organized is much easier to maintain, because you can quickly find the code that needs to be changed. When you standardize this organizational structure, any member of the team can quickly locate and modify any class code, because the code structure of each class is the same.

A class is normally composed of a set of properties and public and private methods. Public methods are methods that can be called from outside of the class, and private methods are those used only within the class.

You define the organizational structure of a class using regions, as described in Chapter 3. If you built a class template using the information in Chapter 3 and then used that template when creating your class, these regions are already defined in your code. If not, you can create the regions as follows:

```
Public Class Product

#Region " Properties"

#End Region

#Region " Public Methods"

#End Region

#Region " Private Methods"

#End Region

End Class
```

Add any other regions as needed to define the standard code structure for your classes. For example, if your class has a constructor, you can add a Constructor region as defined later in this section.

NOTE: Once you define the standard set of regions to use in your classes, define a custom class template, as described in Chapter 3. Provide this template to all the members of your team. This ensures that all the classes of your application follow your standard structure.

As you develop the code for the application, properties are added to the Properties region, public methods are added to the Public Methods region, and so on. To further aid in the organization, you can insert the properties and methods within each region in alphabetical order.

NOTE: If you don't use a region, delete it. For example, if your class has no private methods, delete the Private Methods region. This makes it clear that the class has no private methods without opening the region to see that it has no private methods.

You can also put regions within regions. So, you can put each method in its own region within the Private Methods or Public Methods region. This makes it easier to focus on the code, because you can close all methods except for the one you are working with.

Building Along

For the Purchase Tracker sample application:
- Open the **Product** class in the Code Editor.
- Add the regions as defined in this section.

In the Code Editor, open and close the regions to see how they hide and show their contents.

Instantiating an Object

Once a class is defined, you can create objects from the class. This is called object instantiation. You then use the object to access the properties and methods defined in the class.

To create an object from a class:

1. Declare an object variable.
   For example:

   ```
   Dim prod as Product
   ```

2. Create a new instance of the class, and assign the object variable to reference that new instance.
   For example:

   ```
   prod = New Product
   ```

NOTE FOR VB6 DEVELOPERS: The Set statement is no longer required when assigning an object reference to an object variable.

---

3. Access the properties and methods for the object by using the object variable and a period (.).
For example:

```
prod.ProductName
```

Alternatively, you can accomplish the first two steps in one code line as follows:

```
Dim prod as New Product
```

This line declares the object variable and assigns it to reference a new object from the Product class.

NOTE FOR VB6 DEVELOPERS: In classic versions of Visual Basic, it was highly recommended that you not put the New keyword on the declaration because of how instances were created. This is no longer the case, so the preceding syntax is generally recommended.

Defining the Constructor

A **constructor** is a built-in method in a class that the .NET runtime executes when an object is first instantiated (created). You add code in the constructor to perform any initialization operations for a new object.

You define a constructor by creating a New method in the class as follows:

```
#Region " Constructors"
    Public Sub New()

    End Sub
#End Region
```

The constructor executes when you create an object from the class. For example:

```
Dim prod as New Product
```

When the .NET runtime executes this line of code, it calls the New method in the Product class and runs any code in your constructor.

NOTE FOR VB6 DEVELOPERS: There is no longer an `Initialize` event for a class. Any code you would have put into the `Initialize` event can go into the constructor.

You can pass data into the constructor by defining parameters. The constructor is then called a **parameterized constructor**. For example, this constructor defines a `productID` as a parameter:

```
#Region " Constructors"
    Public Sub New(ByVal productID as Integer)

    End Sub
#End Region
```

You pass the parameter to the constructor when creating the instance of the object:

```
Dim prod as New Product(1)
```

or

```
Dim prod as Product
prod = New Product(1)
```

Multiple constructors can be defined for a class. For example, you could define a constructor with no parameters and one with a parameter. The .NET runtime knows which constructor to call based on the parameters passed to the constructor. Defining one method (in this case, `New`) with two different signatures is called **overloading** and is described in detail later in this chapter.

In many cases, you don't need any specialized code to be executed when the object is instantiated, so you don't need to create a constructor. If you don't create one, the runtime executes an empty constructor for you.

In other cases, you may want a more formal object creation pattern. The most common formal pattern for object creation is called the Factory pattern. A **pattern** is a reusable solution for a recurring problem. The **Factory pattern** defines a standard solution for creating objects. Instead of creating an instance of a class using the `New` keyword, the Factory pattern defines a method that creates and returns an instance of the class.

5. BUILDING THE BUSINESS LOGIC LAYER

This makes the process of creating object instances more explicit. See the "Additional Reading" section at the end of Chapter 1, "Introduction to OO in .NET," for more information on patterns.

NOTE: The Factory pattern has two implementations: one using a factor *class* and the other using a factory *method*. This example uses a factory method.

If you elect to apply the Factory method, you no longer use this style of code to create an object:

```
Dim prod as Product
prod = New Product
```

You instead use code like this:

```
Dim prod as Product
prod = Product.Create()
```

The `Create` method, and the syntax used to call it, are defined in detail later in this chapter.

NOTE: If you select to use a Factory method pattern, other code in the application should use the Factory method and not directly instantiate an object using the `New` keyword. To prevent any code from creating an instance of your object without using the Factory method, define an empty constructor and use the `Private` keyword. For example:

```
#Region " Constructors"
    Private Sub New()

    End Sub
#End Region
```

Use constructors or a Factory pattern method to define any code that must be executed when first creating an object from the class. Don't bother creating a constructor if you have no initialization code.

Building Along

For the Purchase Tracker sample application:

- Open the **Product** class in the Code Editor.
- Add a region for a constructor.
- Add a **private** constructor with no code in the constructor.
  This ensures that code outside of the class cannot create objects from the class. Instead, a Factory pattern method is added in a later "Building Along" activity.
- Open the **ProductWin** form in the Code Editor.
- In the **Load** event for the **ProductWin** form, add code to create an object from the **Product** class:

```
Dim prod As Product
prod = New Product
```

  Visual Studio underlines part of the second code line and displays an error: "'PTBO.Product.Private Sub New()' is not accessible in this context because it is 'Private'".

NOTE: If Visual Studio displays an error on the first line stating "Type 'Product' is not defined," either you did not set a reference from the Windows Application project (PTWin) to the business object Class Library project (PTBO), or you did not import the PTBO namespace. See the "Referencing Projects in a Solution" section in Chapter 3 for details.

- In the **Product** class, comment out the private constructor by inserting comment markers before each of the two code lines of the constructor. The lines of code added in the preceding step are now syntactically correct.

Leave the private constructor commented out for now. This allows you to try out some of the upcoming features. The private constructor will be uncommented when the Factory pattern method is added in a later "Building Along" activity.

Defining the Destructor

A **destructor** is a built-in method in a class that the .NET runtime executes when an object is destroyed. You define a destructor by creating a `Finalize` method in the class. But using a destructor is not recommended, because it does not necessarily execute when you expect it to, and it may not execute at all.

It may seem that the destructor should execute when you specify that you no longer need the object. For example, the following code defines that you no longer need the specified object reference:

```
prod = Nothing
```

But this code does not destroy the object. It just releases the object, making it available for destruction.

Your code does not define when an object is destroyed—the .NET garbage collector does. The **garbage collector** is a memory manager that manages the allocation and release of memory for all .NET applications. The garbage collector performs garbage collection when it needs to. It then releases the memory allocated to a managed object and destroys the object if that object is no longer used. But because you cannot predict when the garbage collector will perform garbage collection, you don't know exactly when your object will be destroyed. Therefore, you cannot know when your destructor will be executed. (See the "Additional Reading" section for more information on the garbage collector.)

In most cases, you don't need to write any cleanup code that executes when an object is destroyed, so you don't need to care about this. You can just allow the garbage collector to destroy your object when it gets around to it.

But if your object works with unmanaged resources, you do need to write some cleanup code. **Unmanaged resources** are system resources that are not directly managed by the .NET runtime, such as database connections, window handles, open files, network connections, and graphic resources. You need to explicitly release unmanaged resources when your object is released.

Because the execution of the `Finalize` method is unpredictable, do not put the code to release unmanaged resources in the destructor. Create a `Dispose` method instead, and explicitly call `Dispose` when you release the object. Add code in the `Dispose` method to perform any cleanup activities required for your object—primarily, releasing any unmanaged resources used by your object. And since you are explicitly calling `Dispose`, you control when the unmanaged resources are released.

NOTE FOR VB6 DEVELOPERS: There is no longer a `Terminate` event for a class. Any code you would have put into the `Terminate` event can go in the `Dispose` method.

Define a `Dispose` method by implementing the .NET Framework `IDisposable` interface. Using the `IDisposable` interface to define your `Dispose` method ensures that you have a standardized programmatic interface for disposing of your objects.

To implement a `Dispose` method, do the following:

1. Open the class in the Code Editor.
2. Add the `Implements` statement to the class definition to implement the `IDisposable` interface:

```
Public Class Product
      Implements IDisposable
```

3. Press the Enter key after the name of the interface.
   The Code Editor automatically adds the signatures for all the properties and methods defined in the interface and related code to the class. This generated code uses the recommended design pattern for proper cleanup of any unmanaged resources that your application uses.

Visual Studio adds two sets of generated code as part of the `IDisposable` interface implementation, defining two `Dispose` methods. The first part of the generated code provides a `Dispose` method that you can customize to your requirements:

```
Private disposedValue As Boolean = False   ' To detect redundant
➥calls


' IDisposable
Protected Overridable Sub Dispose(ByVal disposing As Boolean)
    If Not Me.disposedValue Then
        If disposing Then
            ' TODO: free unmanaged resources when explicitly called
        End If
```

5. BUILDING THE BUSINESS LOGIC LAYER

```
            ' TODO: free shared unmanaged resources
        End If
        Me.disposedValue = True
    End Sub
```

The `disposedValue` variable keeps track of whether the object has already been disposed so that it won't dispose it again.

The parameter passed to this customizable `Dispose` method defines whether `Dispose` is called from the `IDisposable` interface `Dispose` method (shown next). If so, the code should free any unmanaged resources, so put your cleanup code here, by the first TODO Task List comment. If you have shared resources (those defined without a specific instance), put that cleanup code by the second TODO Task List comment.

When all the unmanaged resources are freed, this code sets the `disposedValue` property so that it won't dispose again.

The second part of the generated code defines the implemented interface:

```
#Region " IDisposable Support "
    ' This code added by Visual Basic to correctly implement the
    ' disposable pattern.
    Public Sub Dispose() Implements IDisposable.Dispose
        ' Do not change this code.  Put cleanup code in
        ' Dispose(ByVal disposing As Boolean) above.
        Dispose(True)
        GC.SuppressFinalize(Me)
    End Sub
#End Region
```

This code is meant to be left unchanged. This interface `Dispose` method first calls the customizable `Dispose` method to perform the cleanup. It then calls the `SuppressFinalize` method on the garbage collector. `SuppressFinalize` tells the garbage collector that it does not need to perform further cleanup on the object because the object was already cleaned up by the customized `Dispose` method.

NOTE: Some dispose patterns suggest that you also override the `Finalize` method. In the `Finalize` method, you call the customizable `Dispose` method and pass in `False`. Overriding the `Finalize` method is not recommended due to the performance and complexity costs of using a finalizer. See the *Framework Design Guidelines* book, listed in the "Additional Reading" section, for more information.

Unlike the `Finalize` destructor, the `Dispose` method is *not* called automatically. The code that created the object must manually call `Dispose` explicitly when destroying the object as follows:

```
prod.Dispose()
prod = Nothing
```

If your code creates an object using the `Using` statement, as defined in the preceding chapter, the .NET runtime automatically calls the `Dispose` method at the end of the `Using` block, so you don't need to explicitly call `Dispose`. The `Using` statement also ensures that `Dispose` is called even if an error occurs within the `Using` block.

In this example, the `Using` statement is as follows:

```
Using prod As Product = New Product
    ' Code to work with the object here
End Using
```

Or, if you are using a `Create` Factory pattern method:

```
Using prod As Product = Product.Create()
    ' Code to work with the object here
End Using
```

NOTE: You can use the `Using` statement only if the class (`Product` in this case) implements the `IDisposable` interface.

If your class does not have or use any unmanaged resources, it can leave it up to the garbage collector to clean things up, and no `Dispose` method is needed. If your class does use unmanaged resources, implement a `Dispose` method using the `IDisposable` interface, as described in this section. Any code that creates an object from your class must then correctly destroy it when it is finished with it by calling the object's `Dispose` method or by using the `Using` statement.

> **Building Along**
>
> For the Purchase Tracker sample application, do not implement the `IDisposable` interface in the `Product` class. The `Product` class does not access any unmanaged resources, so it does not need to have any special dispose processing.

Using Partial Classes

By convention, each business object class resides in a single class file. The `Product` class is in the Product.vb file, the `Customer` class is in the Customer.vb file, and so on. But that is not a requirement. A class can be divided between any number of class files.

You can break a class into two or more files by defining **partial classes**. Partial classes are used primarily in situations where you have a code generator that generates part of the class and custom code for the remainder of the class. By placing the generated code in a file separate from the custom code, you can more easily regenerate the generated code without affecting the custom code. Every time you add a form to a project, Visual Studio creates a partial class and generates the code defining the controls on your user interface in that class, as described in Chapter 4.

To define a partial class for your class:

1. Right-click the project in Solution Explorer and select **Add | New Item** from the context menu, *or* select **Project | Add New Item** from the main menu bar.
   Alternatively, you could select **Add | Class** from the context menu, *or* select **Project | Add Class** from the main menu bar.
2. Select the **Class** template, name the class, and click the **Add** button.
   You cannot have two code files with the same filename, so name the partial class with a unique name.
   Visual Studio creates the class file with a .vb extension, adds it to Solution Explorer, and then displays the class in the Code Editor.
3. In the Code Editor, add the `Partial` keyword to the class definition, and modify the class name to match the original class name.

For example, the class definition of a partial class for the `Product` class is as follows:

```
Partial Public Class Product

End Class
```

When the application is built, the code in the file for the class and the files for any partial classes are combined into one logical class. So the runtime behaves as if there is only one class.

One other benefit of partial classes is the ability to separately define Option Strict. Your primary class can have Option Strict set to On, and your partial class can have Option Strict set to Off. This is useful if you have code that needs to work with objects without concern for conversion of their types, such as when calling components written in VB6 or other Component Object Model (COM)-based technologies.

Don't use partial classes unnecessarily. Dividing a class into multiple class files for no particular purpose makes it more difficult to maintain the class. It is more difficult to find where code resides and see how it interacts with other code in the class.

Use partial classes for the defined purpose—separating generated code from custom code. If you are not writing your own code generators, you may never need to create a partial class. If you use third-party code generators, you may notice the partial classes that they create.

Adding Multiple Classes to a Class File

A single class file can contain any number of classes. Although you normally define a class within its own class file, you can add support classes for that class directly in the same class file.

For example, say you define a `ProductOutOfStockException` class that is used only by the `Product` class. You can define this exception class in the same code file as the `Product` class:

```
End Class ' End of the Product Class

<Serializable()> _
Public Class ProductOutOfStockException
    Inherits ApplicationException

    Public Sub New(ByVal message As String)
        MyBase.New(message)
    End Sub
```

```
    Public Sub New(ByVal message As String, _
        ByVal inner As Exception)
        MyBase.New(message, inner)
    End Sub

    Public Sub New( _
        ByVal info As _
        System.Runtime.Serialization.SerializationInfo, _
        ByVal context As _
        System.Runtime.Serialization.StreamingContext)
        MyBase.New(info, context)
    End Sub
End Class
```

NOTE: This class was created with the Exception snippet. See the next chapter for details on using snippets.

NOTE: The `Serializable` attribute on this class defines that the exception class can be serialized. **Serialization** is the process of converting an object into a sequence of bytes for either storage or transmission to another location. For example, you could serialize an object to a file to save the value of all the object's properties.

This attribute is added to the exception class to support remoting. **Remoting** is the process of passing an object to another computer by serializing the object. If an exception occurs on the remote computer, the exception is serialized and remoted back to the original application.

For more information on remoting, see the Lhotka book in the "Additional Reading" section. See the `System.Runtime.Serialization` .NET Framework class documentation for more information on serialization. See the later section "Obsolescing Methods" for more information on attributes.

This class inherits from `ApplicationException` to ensure that it behaves as an exception. It contains three methods, each of which calls the associated base class method. Using the same named methods with different parameters is described later, in the section "Overloading Methods." You can create your own exceptions any time using this style of exception class.

> **NOTE:** Although the exception snippet inherits from `ApplicationException`, best practices define that you should inherit from `Exception` instead. `ApplicationException` was originally set up for your use, as defined in the preceding example. However, it was misused within the .NET Framework, so the Framework developers recommend that you do not use `ApplicationException` in your code. (See the "Additional Reading" section for the reference to the *Framework Design Guidelines* book containing this recommendation.)

Don't put multiple *business object* classes in a single class file. Reserve this feature for adding support classes or exception classes only. For example, business object-unique exceptions are an excellent type of class to add to a business object class file.

Defining Properties

The **properties** of a class define the data associated with the class. For example, a `Product` class has ProductName, ProductID, and InventoryDate properties. Each object created from the class can have a different set of values for these properties.

This section details the process of creating a property. It then covers some additional techniques for working with properties.

Creating the Property

Create a property in a class for each data attribute identified for the class during the design phase. Following best practices, defining properties requires two steps.

First you create a private variable to retain the property value. This private variable is called a **backing variable** or **backing field** and retains the property's value. You make the variable private so that it cannot be directly accessed by any code outside of the class.

Next you create a `Property` statement. The `Property` statement defines the property and the accessors used to get and set the property. The `Set` accessor, sometimes called the **setter**, sets the property's value, and the `Get` accessor, sometimes called the **getter**, returns the property's value.

This technique encapsulates the property by providing access to it only through the accessors. You can write code in the accessors to validate data, perform formatting, or any other business logic.

To define a property:

1. Open the class in the Code Editor.
2. Declare a private variable for the property.
   For example:

   ```
   Private _ProductName As String
   ```

   By making the variable private, you ensure that code outside of this class can not access the property directly. All code must access the variable value through the **Property** statement.

   Use good naming conventions for your private variable. There are several common conventions, such as prefixing the property name with m or m_ to define the variable as member-level. The convention that is currently gaining popularity is to prefix the property name with an underscore to indicate that the variable should not be used anywhere in the code except in the **Property** statement.

3. Create the **Property** statement for the property.
   For example:

   ```
   Public Property ProductName() As String
   ```

   Use good naming conventions for your property name. The recommended convention is to use the property's human-readable name, concatenating the words and using Pascal case, whereby each word in the name is capitalized.

4. Press the Enter key to automatically generate the remaining structure of the **Property** statement:

   ```
   Public Property ProductName() As String
       Get

       End Get
       Set(ByVal value As String)

       End Set
   End Property
   ```

5. Add code within the **Get** and **Set** blocks.

The minimum code in the getter returns the value of the private variable:

```
Get
     Return _ProductName
End Get
```

NOTE FOR VB6 DEVELOPERS: Use the `Return` statement instead of using the property's name to return a value.

Add any other code to the getter, such as formatting or data conversions. For example, for a product number, the getter could add hyphens or other characters used by the human reader that are not necessarily stored with the actual data.

The minimum code in the setter sets the value of the private variable:

```
Set(ByVal value As String)
     _ProductName = value
End Set
```

Add any other code to the setter, such as validation or data conversion. For example, code could validate that the product name is not empty before it is assigned to its private variable.

NOTE FOR VB6 DEVELOPERS: The `Property` statement is similar to the VB6 property procedures. However, there is no separate `Let` and `Set`. The `Set` statement is no longer needed to assign object variables. Object variables can now be assigned with a simple equals sign, as with any other variable (remember from Chapter 1 that *everything* in .NET is basically an object).

Repeat these steps to define each property of your class. Alternatively, you can use code snippets or the Class Designer, as described in the next chapter, to assist you in defining the properties of your class.

Use properties to define the data managed by your business object. Use `Property` statements to provide access to the properties from other parts of the application.

Building Along

For the Purchase Tracker sample application:

- Open the **Product** class in the Code Editor.
- Add the **ProductName** property, as defined in this section.
- Open the **ProductWin** form in the Code Editor.
- In the **Load** event for the **ProductWin** form, add code to set and then display the **ProductName** property:

```
Dim prod as Product
prod = New Product
prod.ProductName = "shoes"
Debug.WriteLine(prod.ProductName) ' Displays shoes
```

Run the application. It displays your splash screen and then shows the MDI parent form. Select **Products | Manage Products** to display the ProductWin form. The debug message appears in the Immediate window (**Debug | Windows | Immediate**) or in the Output window (**Debug | Windows | Output**), depending on your settings.

Property Statements Versus Public Variables

The example in the preceding section seemed like much more code than simply adding a public variable. Why bother with `Property` statements?

Using a private variable and public `Property` statements has several advantages over just using public variables:

- You can add code that is executed before a property is assigned. This code can perform validation, such as to ensure that no invalid values are assigned to the property.
- You can add code that is executed before a property is retrieved. This code can format or convert the value. For example, it could add dashes to the product number for the human reader even though the dashes are not stored with the data.
- Without a `Property` statement, any code that references the class can manipulate or destroy the property value at will.
- Some of the Visual Studio tools, such as object binding, recognize only properties defined with `Property` statements. (See Chapter 7, "Binding the User Interface to the Business Objects," for more information on object binding.)

For these reasons, always use private variables and public `Property` statements to define the properties for your classes.

Documenting the Property

It is always a good idea to add documentation for a property immediately after defining the property. By adding the documentation right away, you have it in place so that you can use the documentation as you build the remainder of the application.

To document the property:

1. Open the class in the Code Editor.
2. Move the insertion point immediately before the word `Public` in the `Public Property` statement.
3. Type three comment markers, defined in Visual Basic as apostrophes (`'''`), and press the Enter key.
   The XML comments feature automatically creates the structure of your property documentation as follows:

```
''' <summary>
'''
''' </summary>
''' <value></value>
''' <returns></returns>
''' <remarks></remarks>
```

NOTE: If you type the three comment markers in the empty line above the property definition instead of on the same line as the property definition, you don't need to press the Enter key to generate the documentation structure.

---

4. Type a summary of the property between the `summary` tags, the value of the property between the `value` tags, and so on.
   Your documentation may be similar to this:

```
''' <summary>
''' Gets or sets the product name
''' </summary>
''' <value>Product Name</value>
''' <returns>Product Name</returns>
''' <remarks></remarks>
```

Use the `summary` tags to describe the purpose of the `Property` statement. By convention, a `Property` statement summary begins with the text "Gets or sets the..." for a read-and-write property, "Gets the..." for read-only properties, and "Sets the..." for write-only properties.

In this example, the `value` and `returns` tags don't provide very useful information, because the product name is self-explanatory. These two tags could be deleted in this case. However, in other cases the property may not be as obvious, so the documentation defined in the XML tags is more useful. For example, a `Status` property is not as obvious, and the XML documentation could provide further information, such as what the status value means and what it actually returns.

When you provide a summary of a property using XML comments, the summary appears in appropriate places within Visual Studio. For example, the summary appears in the Intellisense List Members box when you type the object variable name and a period (`.`).

Using XML comments to document your properties makes it easier for you and other developers to work with your properties.

Building Along

For the Purchase Tracker sample application:
- Open the **Product** class in the Code Editor.
- Add documentation for the **ProductName** property using XML comments.

In the Code Editor, view the comment by typing `prod.` in the **Load** event in the **ProductWin** form.

When you type the period (`.`), Visual Studio displays the Intellisense List Members box, showing all the properties and methods for the class. Click the `ProductName` property to see the XML comments. Be sure to remove this code; otherwise, the project will have a syntax error.

Defining Property Accessibility

In most cases, properties are public. The primary purpose of properties is to provide public access to the data relating to a particular object. But in some cases, you may want the property to be read-only and, in rare cases, write-only. You can define a property's accessibility using additional keywords in the `Property` statement.

Some fields should be changed only by code in the class, not by any code outside the class. For example, a `ProductID` should not be changed by code outside the class, because the ID is the key property used to identify the product. It should be set only when the product is created and then never changed. (See Chapter 8 for more information on primary key fields.)

You can define a property to be read-only using the `ReadOnly` keyword. If you need to define a property as write-only, you can use the `WriteOnly` keyword.

```
Public ReadOnly Property ProductID() As Integer
    Get

    End Get
End Property
```

When you make the property read-only or write-only using the keyword, the code in the class cannot access the property either. If the property is read-only, the code in the class must access the private backing variable to update the value. It would be better to define the accessibility on the accessors so that the getter could be public but the setter could be private. This would allow the code in the class to set the property but make it appear read-only outside this class.

To define separate accessibility on the accessors, add an accessibility keyword to either the getter or setter:

```
Public Property ProductID() As Integer
    Get

    End Get
    Private Set(ByVal value As Integer)

    End Set
End Property
```

Notice the `Private` keyword on the setter. This allows the getter to be public but restricts the setter to be private. The code within the class can then get or set the property, and code outside the class can only get the property.

Some restrictions and rules apply when you use accessibility on the accessors:

- The accessibility on the `Property` statement must be less restrictive than the accessibility on the accessor.
  For example, you cannot define the `Property` statement to be private and then make the getter public.
- You can add accessibility to the getter or setter, but not both.
  If the getter needs to be friend and the setter needs to be private, for example, make the `Property` statement friend (the least restrictive), and make the setter private.
- If you use the `ReadOnly` or `WriteOnly` keywords, you cannot add accessibility on the accessor.

Define accessibility appropriately to ensure that your properties are accessed only as they should be. Most properties are public, but for some properties, such as IDs, define private setters to allow reading but not setting of the property.

Building Along

For the Purchase Tracker sample application:
- Open the **Product** class in the Code Editor.
- Add a **ProductID** property with a private setter, as defined in this section.
- Add code to declare a backing variable, and get and set its value in the property.
- Add documentation for the **ProductID** property using XML comments.

This new property is used later in this chapter.

Handling Nulls

A data type is said to be **nullable** if it can be assigned a value *or* a null reference. **Reference types**, such as strings and class types, are nullable; they can be set to a null reference, and the result is a null value. **Value types**, such as integers, Booleans, and dates, are *not* nullable. If you set a value type to a null reference, the result is a default value, such as 0 or false. A value type can express only the values appropriate to its type; there is no easy way for a value type to understand that it is null.

The .NET Framework 2.0 introduces a `Nullable` class and an associated `Nullable` structure. The `Nullable` structure includes the value type itself and a field identifying whether the value is null. A variable of a `Nullable` type can represent all the values of the underlying type, plus an additional null value. The `Nullable` structure supports only value types because reference types are nullable by design.

For example, say you have a `Product` class with a `ProductID` property defined as an integer, a `ProductName` property defined as a string, and an `InventoryDate` property defined as a date. The following code sets each property to `Nothing` to assign a null reference:

```
Dim prod as Product
prod = New Product
prod.ProductID = Nothing
prod.ProductName = Nothing
prod.InventoryDate = Nothing

Debug.WriteLine(prod.ProductID)     ' Displays 0
Debug.WriteLine(prod.ProductName) ' Displays (Nothing)
Debug.WriteLine(prod.InventoryDate)
                                    ' Displays 1/1/0001 12:00:00 AM
```

If you view these values, they are 0, `Nothing`, and 1/1/0001 12:00:00 AM, respectively. The `ProductID` and `InventoryDate` properties are value types and therefore cannot store a null. Instead, they store a default value when they are assigned a null reference.

There may be cases, however, when you need your code to really handle a null as a null and not as a default value. It would be odd, for example, to handle a null date by hard-coding a check for the 1/1/0001 date.

To make a value type property nullable, you need to declare it using the `Nullable` structure. However, you still want your property to be strongly typed as an integer, date, Boolean, or the appropriate underlying type. The ability to use a class or structure for only a specific type of data is the purpose of generics.

Generics allow you to tailor a class, structure, method, or interface to a specific data type. So you can create a class, structure, method, or interface with generalized code. When you use it, you define that it can work only on a particular data type. This gives you greater code reusability and type safety.

> **NOTE:** A number of generic collection classes are also provided in the .NET Framework. These are great for creating collections of objects in which only a particular type of object can be in the collection. (See the next chapter for more information on generic collections.) You can use the generic types defined in the .NET Framework or create your own.

The .NET Framework built-in `Nullable` structure is generic. When you use the structure, you define the particular data type to use.

As a specific example, an `InventoryDate` property that allows the date to be a date or a null value uses the generic `Nullable` structure as follows:

```
Private _InventoryDate As Nullable(Of Date)
Public Property InventoryDate() As Nullable(Of Date)
    Get
        Return _InventoryDate
    End Get
    Set(ByVal value As Nullable(Of Date))
        _InventoryDate = value
    End Set
End Property
```

Notice the syntax of the `Nullable` structure. Since it supports generics, it has the standard `(Of T)` syntax, where `T` is the specific data type you want it to accept. In this case, the `Nullable` structure supports dates, so the `(Of Date)` syntax is used. This ensures that the `Nullable` structure contains only a date or a null value.

You can then use this property in your application as needed. For example:

```
Dim prod as Product
prod = New Product
If prod.InventoryDate.HasValue Then
    If prod.InventoryDate.Value < Now.Date.AddDays(-10) Then
        MessageBox.Show("Need to do an inventory")
    End If
Else
    MessageBox.Show("Need to do an inventory - never been done")
End If
```

The `HasValue` property of the `Nullable` class defines whether the value type has a value—in other words, whether it is null. If it does have a value, you can retrieve the value using the `Value` property of the `Nullable` class.

NOTE: The `Nullable` type does not support the compare (=) operator. So you cannot use code such as:

```
If prod.InventoryDate = Nothing Then
```

You must instead use the `HasValue` and `Value` properties, as shown in the preceding code example.

The `Nullable` structure is exceptionally useful when you're working with databases, because empty fields in a database are often null. Assuming that you have an `InventoryDate` field in a table, you could write code as follows:

```
If dt.Rows(0).Item("InventoryDate") Is DBNull.Value Then
    prod.InventoryDate = Nothing
Else
    prod.InventoryDate = _
            CType(dt.Rows(0).Item("InventoryDate"), Date)
End If
```

The `If` statement is required here because you cannot convert a `DBNull` to a date using `CType`. So you first need to ensure that it is not a null.

Use the `Nullable` structure any time you need to support nulls in a value type, such as an integer, Boolean, or date.

Building Along

For the Purchase Tracker sample application:

- Open the **Product** class in the Code Editor.
- Add the **InventoryDate** property, as defined in this section.
- Add code to declare a backing variable, and get and set its value in the property, as defined in this section.
- Add documentation for the **InventoryDate** property using XML comments.
- Open the **ProductWin** form in the Code Editor.

- In the **Load** event for the **ProductWin** form, add code to set and then display the **InventoryDate** property:

```
Dim prod as Product
prod = New Product
prod.InventoryDate = Now()
Debug.WriteLine(prod.InventoryDate)
                    ' Displays 9/25/2006 1:45:53 PM
```

Run the application. It displays your splash screen and then shows the MDI parent form. Select **Products | Manage Products** to display the ProductWin form. The debug message appears in the Immediate window (**Debug | Windows | Immediate**) or in the Output window (**Debug | Windows | Output**), depending on your settings.

By adding properties to your classes, you provide your application with easy access to object data. This allows the user interface, for example, to display and update the data.

Stateful Versus Stateless Classes

For some developers, myself included, it may seem unnatural at first to have properties defined for your business objects. Until recently, the best practice for Web applications and large-scale systems was to keep your business objects stateless so that they did not retain any property values between calls. The business objects consisted of only methods. Any data needed by those methods was passed in as parameters.

Stateful classes were deemed inappropriate for Web applications because there was no efficient way to maintain the values of the properties between calls to a page.

Stateful classes were deemed inefficient for large-scale systems with application servers because each time the user interface requested a property from the business object, a network hit was required to retrieve the data from the application server and pass it down. These were called "chatty" calls.

With the simplicity of deployment, all application components are now often deployed to the user's system, reducing the need for application servers. And many features have been added to simplify Web state management.

With many of the new features of .NET and today's architectural practices, it now makes sense to build stateful business objects. This opens the door for building objects that can easily support object binding.

Defining Methods

The **methods** of a class define the behavior and functionality associated with the class. Methods are implemented as subroutines and functions. For example, a `Product` class has `Create` and `Save` methods.

This section details the process of creating a method. It then covers some additional techniques for defining methods.

Creating a Method

Methods define the logic in your application. Create a method in a class for each set of business logic identified for the class during the design phase.

Implement a method using a subroutine when the method does not need to return a value, or a function if the method *does* need to return a value.

To define a method:

1. Open the class in the Code Editor.
2. Create the subroutine or function for the method.
   For example:

   ```
   Public Function Create
   ```

   Use good naming conventions for your method name. The recommended convention is to use the method's human-readable name, concatenating the words and using Pascal case, whereby each word in the name is capitalized.

   The purpose of this particular method is to create an instance of the business object class using the Factory pattern, so it was named `Create`. Some developers don't like to use that name because it could imply that a new item, such as a new product, is being created when instead an instance is created for an existing item. Alternatively, you could name this method `CreateInstance` or `GetProduct` or simply `Retrieve`.
3. Add the parameters appropriate for the method.
   For example:

   ```
   Public Function Create(ByVal prodID As Integer)
   ```

   Parameters define the data that is passed into or out of the function or subroutine. The number, name, and type of the parameters depend on the data that needs to be passed. In this example, the product ID is passed in to create an object populated with data for the defined ID.

Use good naming conventions for your parameter names. The recommended standard is to use a logical parameter name, concatenating the words and using camel case, whereby the first letter is lowercase and the beginning of every other word is capitalized. Be sure that the parameter names do not conflict with any of your property names.

4. If you are defining a function, define the method's return type. For example:

```
Public Function Create(ByVal prodID As Integer) _
                                 As Product
```

The return type depends on the data that needs to be passed back from the function. In this example, the return type is an instance of the **Product** class.

5. Press the Enter key to automatically generate the method's remaining structure:

```
Public Function Create(ByVal prodID As Integer) _
                                 As Product


End Function
```

6. Add code within the method to perform the desired operation.
7. If you're implementing a **Function**, use the **Return** statement to return the value.

NOTE FOR VB6 DEVELOPERS: Use the **Return** statement instead of using the method's name to return a value.

The purpose of this particular **Create** method is to create an instance of the class. As discussed earlier in this chapter, objects are often created from a class using the Factory pattern. The **Create** method is then used, instead of the constructor, to create instances of the class.

A **Create** method used to create an instance of a class would look similar to this:

```
Public Function Create(ByVal prodID As Integer) As Product
    Dim prod As Product
```

```
' Create a new instance
prod = New Product()

' Populate the object
If prodID = 1 Then
    prod.ProductID = 1
    prod.ProductName = "Mithril Coat"
    prod.InventoryDate = #4/1/2006#
End If

Return prod
End Function
```

The first line of this function declares an object variable. The `New` keyword is then used to create a new instance of the `Product` class. The object properties are then populated. Notice that these are hard-coded in this case. The property values will be assigned from data in a database in Chapter 8. For now, the values are hard-coded so that the `Create` method works at this point without needing the data access layer in place just yet. The last line of the function returns the instantiated and populated `Product` object.

Although these steps demonstrate a `Create` method, you can create any type of method using these steps. Alternatively, you can use the Class Designer, as described in the next chapter, to assist you in defining the methods of your class.

Use methods to perform all of the processing required by your application. To create good methods, ensure that each method has a single purpose and that the method is no longer than about one page. If a method is long, break it into multiple methods. This makes each method much easier to build and maintain.

Building Along

For the Purchase Tracker sample application:
- Open the **Product** class in the Code Editor.
- Add the **Create** method, as defined in this section.
- Open the **ProductWin** form in the Code Editor.
- In the **Load** event for the **ProductWin** form, modify the code to call the **Create** method and display the resulting values:

```
Dim prod as Product
prod = New Product
prod = prod.Create(1)
Debug.WriteLine(prod.ProductID)    ' Displays 1
Debug.WriteLine(prod.ProductName)
                        ' Displays Mithril Coat
Debug.WriteLine(prod.InventoryDate)
                        ' Displays 4/1/2006 12:00:00 AM
```

Run the application. It displays your splash screen and then shows the MDI parent form. Select **Products | Manage Products** to display the ProductWin form. The debug messages appear in the Immediate window (**Debug | Windows | Immediate**) or in the Output window (**Debug | Windows | Output**), depending on your settings.

Passing Parameters

Parameters to methods are passed either `ByVal` or `ByRef`. `ByVal` is short for "by value" and means that the parameter value is evaluated and then its value is passed to the method. `ByRef` is short for "by reference" and means that a reference to the parameter is passed to the method.

If you don't specify the passing mechanism, the default is `ByVal`. In most cases, you want to pass your parameters by value.

NOTE FOR VB6 DEVELOPERS: The default in the classic versions of Visual Basic was `ByRef`, so watch for this when converting from VB6 to Visual Basic 2005.

The only time you need to use `ByRef` is when you want to modify the parameter within the method and allow the calling code to receive the modified value upon return from the method call. `ByRef` can also be used to return parameters from the method if you need more than one return value.

For example, a `ProcessRequest` method needs to return the number of items processed and a response string to the calling code. The method signature uses the `ByRef` keyword as follows:

```
Private Function ProcessRequest(ByVal requestType As String, _
    ByRef requestResponse As String) As Integer
    Dim itemsProcessed As Integer = 0

    ' Code that performs the request

    requestResponse = "Test Reply"
    Return itemsProcessed
End Function
```

This function is called as follows:

```
Dim requestCount As Integer
Dim response As String
requestCount = ProcessRequest("Test", response)
Debug.WriteLine(requestCount.toString & " " & response)
                                        ' Displays 0 Test Reply
```

If the `requestResponse` parameter was declared using the `ByVal` keyword, the `response` variable would always return `Nothing`, because it would not pass back the changed value from the function. By using the `ByRef` keyword, the `response` variable is set to the changed value.

Documenting the Method

It is always a good idea to add documentation for a method immediately after creating the method. You may even want to add the documentation just after defining the method signature and before you write the code within the method. By adding the documentation right away, you focus on the method's purpose, which helps you keep the method encapsulated. It is also much easier to document each method as you go along instead of facing the large task of going back later and documenting all the methods.

To document the method:

1. Open the class in the Code Editor.
2. Move the insertion point immediately before the word `Public` in the `Public Function` or `Public Sub` statement.
3. Type three comment markers, defined in Visual Basic as apostrophes (`' ' '`), and press the Enter key.

The XML comments feature automatically creates the structure of your method documentation as follows:

```
'''   <summary>
'''
'''   </summary>
'''   <param name="prodID"></param>
'''   <returns></returns>
'''   <remarks></remarks>
```

Notice how this automatically generates a `param` tag with the name of each method parameter.

NOTE: If you type the three comment markers in the empty line above the method definition instead of on the same line as the method definition, you don't need to press the Enter key to generate the documentation structure.

---

4. Type a summary of the method between the `summary` tags, the parameter descriptions between the `param` tags, and so on. Your documentation may be similar to this:

```
'''   <summary>
'''   Creates a populated instance of this class
'''   </summary>
'''   <param name="prodID">ID of the product to
'''   create</param>
'''   <returns>Instance of the Product class</returns>
'''   <remarks></remarks>
```

Use the `summary` tags to describe the method's purpose and the `param` tags to define each parameter. The `summary` and `param` are the most important tags because they are used by Visual Studio.

When you provide method documentation using XML comments, your method displays documentation about itself in appropriate places within Visual Studio. For example, the documentation appears in the Intellisense List Members box when you type the object variable name and a period (`.`).

Using XML comments to document your methods makes it easier for you and other developers to work with your methods.

Building Along

For the Purchase Tracker sample application:
- Open the **Product** class in the Code Editor.
- Add documentation for the **Create** method using XML comments.

In the Code Editor, view the comment by typing `prod.` in the **Load** event in the **ProductWin** form. When you type the period (`.`), Visual Studio displays the Intellisense List Members box, showing all the properties and methods for the class. Click the `Create` method to see the XML comments. Be sure to remove this code; otherwise, the project will have a syntax error.

Overloading Methods

There may be times when you want to have different sets of parameters for a method. For example, you may want your `Create` method to accept an ID or string name. Or you may want a `Retrieve` method to work with no parameters to retrieve all the data or an ID to retrieve data for a particular ID.

You could define different method names to support different signatures, but a better way is to use overloaded methods. An **overloaded method** is a method that has the same name as another method but different parameters.

For example, the `Create` method defined in this section has a parameter for a product ID. If you want to allow creating objects by name as well, you could define an overloaded `Create` method as follows:

```
Public Function Create(ByVal prodName As String) As Product
    Dim prod As Product

    ' Create a new instance
    prod = New Product()

    ' Populate the object
    '...

    Return prod
End Function
```

A method can have any number of overloads, each with different sets of parameters. The parameters are evaluated based on the number and type of parameters, not the parameter names. So if you defined a `Create` method with a product name string parameter, you could not add a `Create` method with a description string parameter. This is because when you call the function and pass a string, the .NET runtime would not be able to tell which `Create` method you want to execute. Each overload must have a unique set of parameters.

Overloading is also great for enhancing your methods. For example, suppose you originally created a `Create` method with one parameter. You then need to add a `withComments` parameter to define whether to populate comment information. If code in your application calls the original `Create` method you don't want to break that code by adding a new parameter. Instead, you can create an overload for the `Create` method with the new parameter without needing to modify any existing code that calls the original method:

```
Public Function Create(ByVal prodName As String, _
    ByVal withComments As Boolean) As Product
    Dim prod As Product

    ' Create a new instance
    prod = New Product()

    ' Populate the object
    '...

    If withComments Then
        ' also populate the comments
    End If

    Return prod
End Function
```

In many cases, the code you need to execute in each of the overloaded methods is similar. So a common technique is to have one overload call the other. So the `Create` method from the prior code example could be changed to the following:

```
Public Function Create(ByVal prodName As String) As Product
    Return Create(prodName, False)
End Function
```

The overload with one parameter simply calls the other overload, passing a default value for the `withComments` flag. In most cases, the majority of the code is in the overload with the most parameters.

Each overload appears in the Intellisense Parameter Info, as shown in Figure 5.2.

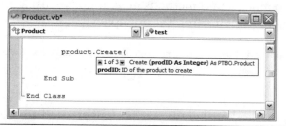

Figure 5.2 The 1 of 3 advises you that this method has three overloads. Use the up and down arrows to show the Parameter Info for each overloaded method.

Use overloading any time you want to define methods with the same name but different method signatures. Be sure that the signatures differ in the number or type of parameters.

> **Building Along**
>
> You can skip this "Building Along" without impacting any "Building Along" activities in later chapters. However, these overloads do appear in future screen shots to demonstrate how overloaded functions appear.
>
> If you want to try out overloading, for the Purchase Tracker sample application:
>
> - Open the **Product** class in the Code Editor.
> - Add the two **Create** method overloaded functions as described in this section.
>
> In the Code Editor, view the overloads in Intellisense as shown in Figure 5.2.

Defining Shared Methods

Shared methods, sometimes called **static methods**, are methods that are shared between all the instances of a class. They do not require that you create an object before calling the method.

For example, if you want to display something to the debug window, you don't first create an instance of the `Debug` class and then use an object variable to call the `WriteLine` method. Instead, you call the `WriteLine` method directly for the class itself. The `WriteLine` method is a shared method.

You define shared methods in your classes using the `Shared` keyword on the method signature. For example:

```
Public Shared Function Create(ByVal prodID As Integer) As Product
   ...
End Function
```

When a method is shared, you no longer need to create an object from the class before using the method. So instead of using code that looks like this:

```
Dim prod as Product
prod = New Product
prod = prod.Create(1)
```

the code instead looks like this:

```
Dim prod as Product
prod = Product.Create(1)
```

Notice that the code does not create an instance and uses the class name (`Product` in this example) instead of the object variable name (`prod`) to call the method. This is because a shared method cannot be accessed using an instance.

NOTE: If you do try to call a shared method using an object variable instead of the class name, you get a warning stating that you cannot access a shared member through an instance.

The most common use of shared methods is for Factory pattern methods, as shown in the `Create` method example, and for function libraries. The .NET Framework makes extensive use of shared methods in its function libraries, such as the `WriteLine` method in the `Debug` class.

You can also use the `Shared` keyword on properties to share a property across all instances. This is useful for properties such as a count that needs to be aware of all instances.

When defining a shared property or method, keep the following in mind:

- A shared property or method cannot reference nonshared properties.

  In the `Create` method example, the shared method created an instance of the class and used that instance to reference the properties. It cannot access the properties without an instance, because those properties are not shared. The properties are unique for each instance.

- A shared property or method cannot reference a nonshared method of the class.

  If you need to call a nonshared property or method of the class within the shared property or method, you can create an instance of the class and use that instance to call the nonshared property or method.

- `Me` is not valid within a shared property or method.

  `Me` references the current running instance, and a shared property or method does not have an instance.

Use the `Shared` keyword any time you want to define a property or method that is shared across all instances of your class. Access shared properties and methods using the class name instead of an instance variable.

Building Along

For the Purchase Tracker sample application:
- Open the **Product** class in the Code Editor.
- Add the `Shared` keyword to the **Create** method, as defined in this section.
- Uncomment the private constructor.

  The Factory pattern method is now in place, so your code should no longer create an instance of the class using the `New` keyword.
- Open the **ProductWin** form in the Code Editor.

- In the **Load** event for the **ProductWin** form, modify the code to call the **Create** method and display the resulting values:

```
Dim prod as Product
prod = Product.Create(1)
Debug.WriteLine(prod.ProductID)    ' Displays 1
Debug.WriteLine(prod.ProductName)
                        ' Displays Mithril Coat
Debug.WriteLine(prod.InventoryDate)
                        ' Displays 4/1/2006 12:00:00 AM
```

Run the application. It displays your splash screen and then shows the MDI parent form. Select **Products | Manage Products** to display the ProductWin form. The debug messages appear in the Immediate window (**Debug | Windows | Immediate**) or in the Output window (**Debug | Windows | Output**), depending on your settings.

Obsolescing Methods

Code changes over time. Methods that you created today may no longer be needed tomorrow. But if you delete them, every piece of code that calls the method needs to be changed. Depending on the features you are implementing, this may be necessary. But in many cases, you can define a smoother obsolescence plan.

Obsolescence is the concept in which methods become obsolete over time. Instead of changing a method for a new feature, you add a method overload to support the new feature, essentially making the original method obsolete. That way, you need to change only the code required for the new feature, not every piece of code that calls the original method. You can then obsolete the original method so that you don't forget to remove it at a later point in time.

In looking at the `Create` method example from earlier in this chapter, you defined the method with a product name parameter. Suppose you later find that you need to sometimes manage comment information. So you add an overloaded method with a flag defining whether to handle comment information. You want every call to the method to ultimately call the new method signature. But in the interim, by having the original method remain in place, any unchanged code still works.

To identify a method as obsolete, use the `Obsolete` attribute. An **attribute** is metadata that you can associate with programming elements such as classes, properties, and methods. Attributes are defined in Visual Basic using less-than (<) and greater-than (>) signs. Attributes must be defined on the same line as the declaration of the class, property, or method to which the attribute is assigned. Use the line-continuation character (_) to separate the attribute from the declaration so that they are easier to read.

For example, to define one overload of the `Create` method as obsolete, add the `Obsolete` attribute to the method:

```
<ObsoleteAttribute( _
    "Use the Create(prodName, withComments) instead", False)> _
Public Shared Function Create(ByVal prodName) As Product
        Return Create(prodID, False)
End Function
```

The attribute's name can be defined with or without the "Attribute" suffix; either `Obsolete` or `ObsoleteAttribute` can be used. Your coding standards may define that the suffix is included for clarity or not included for brevity. Either way, be consistent with all attributes.

Some attributes, such as the `Obsolete` attribute, have parameters. The first parameter in this case is a message to any developer using your obsolete method, and the second parameter is an error flag. This message appears in the Error List window (see Figure 5.3) as a warning if the second parameter is `False`, or as an error if the second parameter is `True`. This gives the developer using the method a warning or error, depending on your standard method obsolescence path.

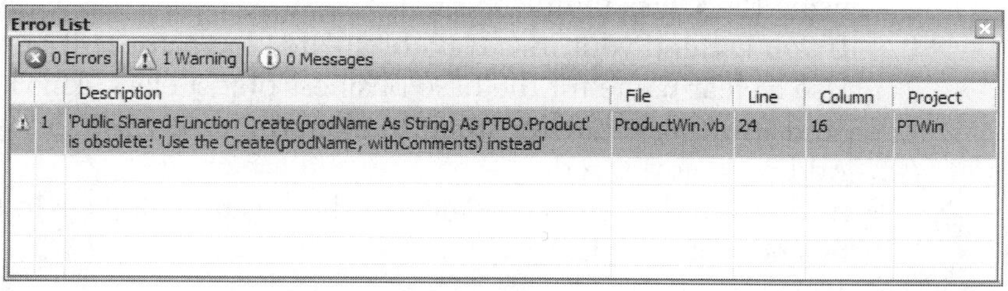

Figure 5.3   When you define a property or method as obsolete, any developer using the method knows that the property or method is on the obsolescence path.

Define a standard obsolescence plan for your application. This plan defines when properties and methods are made obsolete, how long they should be obsolete in a warning mode, and at what point they should be marked with a compile-time error. This provides a phased approach to modifying your application.

Building a Base Business Object Class

Business objects have standard housekeeping tasks that they must perform. For example, they must keep track of their state (unchanged, added, modified, deleted). The purpose of a base business object class is to define a standard set of operations that are applicable to all business objects. This keeps the housekeeping code out of the business objects themselves.

Creating base classes was covered in detail in Chapter 4, which demonstrated how to build a base form class. This section provides information on building a base business object class. For all the definitions, benefits, and techniques of building a base class, see Chapter 4.

Creating the Base Business Object Class

The primary code in a business object base class is housekeeping code—code that manages the object state, whether it is "dirty" (meaning changed), and whether it is valid. The base business object class performs any task that is common for all the business objects.

To create a base business object class:

1. Add a project item to your business object Class Library project using the **Class** template.
   If you created your own class template, you can use it here.
   Use a clear name for the base business object class. This helps you (and your project team) keep track of the base class.
2. Add code as desired.
   Add any code that is common to the business objects to the base business object class.

As an example, the base business object class can keep track of the object state. The code required for this has three parts. First, the set of valid business object states must be defined. Then one or more properties must be created to expose the state. Finally, a method is needed to manage the state.

The set of valid business object states can be implemented using an enumeration, defined with the `Enum` keyword. An **enumeration** defines a set of named constants whose underlying type is an integer. You can define the integer assigned to each constant; otherwise, the enumeration sets each constant to a sequential integer value starting with 0.

For example, the business object state values are defined in an enumerated type as follows:

```
Public Enum EntityStateEnum
    Unchanged
    Added
    Deleted
    Modified
End Enum
```

In this example, the value of `Unchanged` is 0, `Added` is 1, and so on. Any variable declared to be of this enumeration type can be assigned to one of these defined constants.

A business object's state is exposed by defining a property that gets and sets the object's state. For example, an `EntityState` property could be defined as follows:

```
Private _EntityState As EntityStateEnum
''' <summary>
''' Gets the business object state
''' </summary>
''' <value>Unchanged, Added, Deleted, or Modified</value>
''' <returns>Value identifying the entity's state</returns>
''' <remarks></remarks>
Protected Property EntityState() As EntityStateEnum
    Get
        Return _EntityState
    End Get
    Private Set(ByVal value As EntityStateEnum)
        _EntityState = value
    End Set
End Property
```

Notice that the property uses the `Protected` keyword to ensure that it can be accessed only by classes that inherit from this base class. The setter uses the `Private` keyword to ensure that code outside of the class cannot modify the entity's state.

You may want to define other properties that expose the object state in different ways. For example, it is common for a business object to have a Boolean `IsDirty` property that identifies whether an entity has been changed. Although the `EntityStateEnum` could be used to determine this, adding an `IsDirty` property provides a shortcut:

```
''' <summary>
''' Gets whether the business object has changes
''' </summary>
''' <value>True or False</value>
''' <returns>True if there are unsaved changes;
''' False if not</returns>
''' <remarks></remarks>
Protected ReadOnly Property IsDirty() As Boolean
    Get
        Return Me.EntityState <> EntityStateEnum.Unchanged
    End Get
End Property
```

This property does not have its own private backing variable. Instead, it uses the value of the `EntityState` property.

You also need code that manages the state. This is normally implemented as a method:

```
''' <summary>
''' Changes the state of the entity
''' </summary>
''' <param name="dataState">New entity state</param>
''' <remarks></remarks>
Protected Sub DataStateChanged(ByVal dataState As EntityStateEnum)
    ' If the state is deleted, mark it as deleted
    If dataState = EntityStateEnum.Deleted Then
        Me.EntityState = dataState
    End If

    ' Only set data states if the existing state is unchanged
    If Me.EntityState = EntityStateEnum.Unchanged _
       OrElse dataState = EntityStateEnum.Unchanged Then
        Me.EntityState = dataState
    End If
End Sub
```

This code sets the state appropriately. This is not as simple as just assigning the state to the value passed in to the method, because some states cannot be changed. For example, if the state is already defined to be `Added`, further changes to the object leave the state as `Added`. And if the state is `Deleted`, it does not matter which other state it was; it needs to be deleted.

In your code, call `DataStateChanged` with a state of `Added` when the user creates a new item. Call `DataStateChanged` with a state of `Deleted` when the user deletes an item. Call `DataStateChanged` with a state of `Modified` whenever the user changes any of the data associated with an object. Because you defined all your object data with properties, you can add the call to `DataStateChanged` to the setter for each property, as described in the next section.

Building a base business object class keeps the majority of the house-keeping code out of the business object class itself and lets you focus on the unique business rules and business processing code required for the specific business object.

Building Along

For the Purchase Tracker sample application:

- Add a class project item to the business object Class Library project (**PTBO**) using the **Class** template.
  If you created your own class template using steps from Chapter 3, you can use your class template here.
  Name the class **PTBOBase**.
  If not already added by the selected template, add the standard set of regions to the class as described earlier in this chapter.
- Add documentation to the class using XML comments.
- Add the code defined in this section.

You now have an operational base business object class that ensures the business objects from all derived classes consistently handle their state. But at this point, the base class does not actually do anything. To make use of the base class, you need to inherit from it, as described in the next section.

Inheriting from the Base Business Object Class

After you create a base business object class, you use it by inheriting from it. Each business object class that needs to manage its state can inherit from the base business object class. The business object then has access to the properties and methods from the base business object class.

The `Inherits` keyword specifies that a class inherits from another class. Add the `Inherits` keyword to any business object class as follows:

```
Public Class Product
    Inherits PTBOBase
```

The class, in this case `Product`, then has all the properties and methods from the base business object class. You can easily see this by typing `Me.` somewhere within a property or method of the `Product` class. The Intellisense List Members box displays properties and methods of both the base class (`PTBOBase`) and the derived class (`Product` in this case).

To take advantage of the code in the base business object class, the derived classes can use the properties and methods of the base class. For example, when a property in the business object is changed, the code calls the `DataStateChanged` method in the base business object class to correctly set the business object state.

The code in the `ProductName` property provides an example:

```
Public Property ProductName() As String
    Get
        Return _ProductName
    End Get
    Set(ByVal value As String)
        If _ProductName <> value Then
            Dim propertyName As String = "ProductName"
            Me.DataStateChanged(EntityStateEnum.Modified)
            _ProductName = value
        End If
    End Set
End Property
```

NOTE: This code does not currently use the `propertyName` variable. It is used later when validation code is added in Chapter 7.

The `Dim` statement declaring the `propertyName` variable could be a `Const` statement instead since the property name does not change within the property.

The setter code first determines whether the value is the same as it was. If so, it does not reset it. If the value is indeed changed, the setter sets a variable for the property's name. The `DataStateChanged` method in the base business object class is then called and passed a state of `Modified`. Finally, the property value is changed to the passed-in value.

In every derived class, modify each updatable property to include similar code. When any property value changes, the object is marked as modified. This ensures that each object is aware of its state so that it can react accordingly.

Building Along

For the Purchase Tracker sample application:

- Open the **Product** class in the Code Editor.
- Modify the **Product** class to inherit from the base business object class (**PTBOBase**), as demonstrated in this section.
- Modify the setter for each *updatable* property defined in the **Product** class, to include a call to `DataStateChanged` as shown in this section.

NOTE: `ProductID` is not updatable because its setter is private. So it should not call the `DataStateChanged` method.

NOTE: Recall that the `InventoryDate` is a `Nullable` type. `Nullable` types do not support the not-equal (`<>`) operator. So to check the value of the `InventoryDate` property against the value passed in, you need to use some additional code:

```
If (_InventoryDate.HasValue<>value.HasValue) OrElse _
    (_InventoryDate.HasValue AndAlso _
    value.HasValue AndAlso _
    InventoryDate.Value <> value.Value) Then
  Dim propertyName As String = "InventoryDate"
```

```
        Me.DataStateChanged(EntityStateEnum.Modified)
        _InventoryDate = value
End If
```

This code first determines if the property has a value. The code changes the value only if the HasValue changes or if it has a current value and that value has changed.

■   Modify the **Create** method to reset the object's entity state to Unchanged after it sets the property values. This ensures that the entity state tracks the user's changes, not changes made to the properties when they are first populated.
Add the following code as the last line of the Create method:
```
        prod.DataStateChanged(EntityStateEnum.Unchanged)
```

Overriding Base Class Members

Sometimes the derived class needs to modify the functionality of one of the base class members. When this is required, you can **override** the base class member by implementing the property or method in the derived class. When the property or method is called, the implementation in the derived class overrides the implementation from the base class.

For example, say that one business object requires some additional processing in the base class DataStateChanged method. To override this method, implement the method in the business object using the exact same method signature:

```
''' <summary>
''' Changes the state of the entity
''' </summary>
''' <param name="dataState">New entity state</param>
''' <remarks></remarks>
Protected Sub DataStateChanged(ByVal dataState As EntityStateEnum)
    MyBase.DataStateChange(dataState) ' Performs base processing

    ' Do unique code
    ...
End Sub
```

Notice that this code calls the base business object class to perform its processing and then performs its unique processing. It could instead perform its processing first and then call the base business object class. Or it can do all of its own processing.

Use overriding whenever the derived class needs its own implementation of a property or method in the base class.

Conclusion

What Did This Chapter Cover?

This chapter described how to build code in the business logic layer for your application. It provided information on defining properties, coding methods, using generics, and building a base business object class.

This chapter covered several real productivity enhancers:

- Writing class documentation using the XML documentation feature makes it easy to create the class's documentation. That documentation is then available in many places within Visual Studio, making it easier for you or your team to work with the class's properties and methods.
- Defining regions helps you focus on the code you are working on.
- Using partial classes for generated code makes it easier to regenerate the generated code without impacting the custom code.
- Handling nulls using the generic `Nullable` structure simplifies working with value types and null values.
- Defining a Factory pattern method or class library method with the `Shared` keyword makes it easy to call the method, because you don't need to create an instance of the class.
- Building a base business object class provides standardized processing for all your application's business objects and significantly reduces the amount of housekeeping code required in each business object class.

The next chapter provides additional tools and techniques for working with classes.

Building Along

If you are "building along" with the Purchase Tracker sample application, this chapter added the basic code you need for your business object component.

Since the user interface from the preceding chapter does not yet reference any information in the business object component, running the application provides the same results as at the end of the preceding chapter.

The next chapter adds functionality and unit testing to the business object component of the Purchase Tracker sample application using some of the new Visual Studio 2005 tools and techniques.

Additional Reading

Cwalina, Krzysztof, and Brad Abrams. *Framework Design Guidelines*. Upper Saddle River, NJ: Addison Wesley, 2006.

This is an *excellent* book for any .NET developer. It provides general guidelines and many specific recommendations for handling everything from naming conventions to base classes to exceptions.

Lhotka, Rockford. *Expert VB 2005 Business Objects*, Second Edition. APress, 2006.

This book demonstrates how to build a framework for business objects that handles all the complex issues of .NET. It then shows you how to build Windows Forms, Web Forms, and Web Services interfaces on top of the objects, using all the data binding and other productivity features built into .NET 2.0 and Visual Studio 2005.

Richter, Jeffrey. "Garbage Collection: Automatic Memory Management in the Microsoft .NET Framework." *MSDN* magazine, November 2000.

This article provides details on the .NET garbage collector.

Try It!

Here are a few suggestions for trying some of the techniques presented in this chapter:

1. Add a `SalesRep` business object class to the business object Class Library project.
   Ensure that the class inherits from the base business object class. Add properties for name, employee number, and so on. Add a `Create` method using the same Factory pattern defined in this chapter. Add other methods as appropriate.
2. Add an exception handler class, such as `SalesRepNotFound-Exception`, to the `SalesRep` class code file using an exception class.
   Throw the exception in the `Create` method if the ID passed into the method is not the ID you hard-coded data for.
3. Add several overloads for the `Create` method in the `SalesRep` class.
4. Make one of the overloads obsolete using the techniques presented in this chapter.

CHAPTER 6

CLASS TOOLS AND TECHNIQUES

The right tool for the right job.
—**Anonymous**

Some aspects of building classes can be tedious, such as the process of defining all the properties and signatures for all the methods. But with the right tool, you can relieve the tedium and become more productive.

This chapter details some of the cool tools in Visual Studio, such as Class Designer, code snippets, and unit testing tools. It also covers more advanced techniques, such as managing master/detail object relationships. The Purchase Tracker sample application is used to demonstrate these techniques.

What Does This Chapter Cover?

This chapter demonstrates the following techniques:

- Using Class Designer
- Using Object Test Bench
- Inserting code snippets
- Creating your own code snippets
- Writing and running unit tests
- Implementing master/detail classes
- Using generic collections

Everything in this chapter involves new features of Visual Studio 2005 or Visual Basic 2005. However, not every feature is in every edition of Visual Studio. If a specific feature presented in this chapter is not available in some editions, this is noted in the appropriate section.

Using Class Designer

A picture is worth a thousand words, as the saying goes. Class Designer provides a visual design environment that allows you to visualize and manipulate your classes. You can create diagrams of your classes, visually create new classes, and edit existing classes.

Using Class Designer, you can quickly create the basic structure of each class, including all its properties and methods. The resulting class diagrams communicate your application's design. You can print them, you can save them as an image and post them on your developer Web page, or you can include them in a presentation.

Class Designer is also a great tool for visualizing an application you did not build. Use it when working with existing code to view the class structure. This gives you a good picture of each layer of the application.

This section details the steps for creating a class diagram. It then describes how to create and edit classes using the diagram. It also introduces Object Test Bench.

NOTE: Class Designer/Object Test Bench is not available in the Express Editions of Visual Studio. If you are using an Express Edition and are "building along" with the Purchase Tracker sample application, you need to create the class defined in this section using the techniques presented in the preceding chapter.

Creating a Class Diagram

A class diagram is just another Visual Studio project item. You can use the same technique to add an empty class diagram to your project as with any other type of project item. Or you can create a class diagram for all the classes in an existing project, for any set of classes, or for a single class.

To create a class diagram from scratch:

1. Right-click the project containing the classes to diagram in Solution Explorer and select **Add | New Item** from the context menu, *or* select **Project | Add New Item** from the main menu bar.

2. Select the **Class Diagram** template, name the diagram, and click the **Add** button.

   Use standard naming conventions for your class diagram. Since you could have more than one diagram for a project, give the diagram a descriptive name. For example, if you plan to create a class diagram that contains your primary business object entities, you could name it MainEntitiesDiagram.

   Visual Studio creates the diagram file with a .cd extension, adds it to Solution Explorer, and then displays the empty diagram in Class Designer.

To create a class diagram for all the existing classes in a project:

1. Right-click the project containing the classes to diagram in Solution Explorer and select **View Class Diagram** from the context menu.

   Visual Studio creates a diagram file with a default name and .cd extension and adds it to Solution Explorer. It then adds all of the classes in the project to the diagram and displays the result in Class Designer. The diagram contains a box for each class defined in your project.

NOTE: If you build a class diagram for all the classes in the project, you may get more than you expect. Any classes that Visual Studio creates, such as settings and resource classes, are also included in the diagram. You can either remove any undesired classes from the diagram or use the next procedure instead to build the diagram for classes you select.

To create a class diagram for one or more classes in your project:

1. Right-click a class or selected set of classes in Solution Explorer, and select **View Class Diagram** from the context menu.

   Visual Studio creates a diagram file with a default name and .cd extension and adds it to Solution Explorer. It then adds the selected classes to the diagram and displays the result in Class Designer, as shown in Figure 6.1.

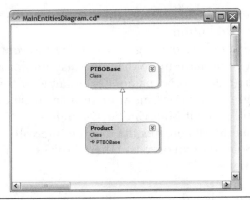

Figure 6.1 Class Designer provides a visual view of your classes.

Building Along

For the Purchase Tracker sample application:
- Create a class diagram for the **Product** class and base business object class (**PTBOBase**) in the business object Class Library project (**PTBO**).

Name the diagram **MainEntitiesDiagram**.

The result appears similar to Figure 6.1.

Adding Items to the Designer

Once you have a class diagram, you can add existing classes or new items to the diagram.

To add an existing class to the diagram:

1. Open the diagram in Class Designer.
2. Drag the class from Solution Explorer, and drop it onto the design surface.

Visual Studio adds the class to the diagram.

When a diagram is open in Class Designer, the Class Designer toolbox displays the types of items you can add to the diagram, as shown in Figure 6.2. You can add a class, structure, interface, and enumeration. You can also add relationships and comments.

Figure 6.2   The Class Designer toolbox provides the items you can use to build your class diagram. Double-click on or drag an item from the toolbox to the design surface to add the item to the diagram.

To add a new item to the diagram:

1. Open the diagram in Class Designer.
2. Double-click on the item icon in the Class Designer toolbox, *or* drag the icon from the toolbox and drop it onto the design surface, *or* select **Class Diagram | Add** from the main menu bar.
3. Depending on the item you added, a dialog may appear. Enter the requested detail information, and click **OK**.
   For example, if you select the Class item to add a new class to your diagram, the New Class dialog is displayed, as shown in Figure 6.3. Enter information for the class in the dialog, and click **OK**.

Figure 6.3   The New Class dialog allows you to define a new class.

Class Designer displays the new item in the diagram and generates the associated code. For example, if you add a new class to the diagram, Class Designer creates a class file, adds it to Solution Explorer, and builds the class as you had specified in the New Class dialog.

You can create all your classes and other structures using Class Designer if you prefer the visual view.

Building Along

For the Purchase Tracker sample application:
- Open the **MainEntitiesDiagram** diagram in Class Designer.
- Add a new class to the diagram.
  Name the class **Customer**, and select to create a new file for the class named **Customer.vb**.

Class Designer adds the new class to the diagram and to Solution Explorer.

Defining Inheritance

If you defined a base class for your business objects, as described in the preceding chapter, each of your business objects can inherit from that class. In Class Designer, you define an inheritance relationship using the Inheritance tool in the Class Designer toolbox.

To define an inheritance relationship:

1. Select the **Inheritance** tool from the Class Designer toolbox (see Figure 6.2).
   The cursor changes to an inheritance icon.
2. Click the class that is to use inheritance.
   This defines the beginning point of the inheritance relationship line.
3. Click the base class that the class inherits from.
   This defines the endpoint of the inheritance relationship line.

Open the Code Editor for the class, and you will see that Class Designer generated the `Inherits` statement for you:

```
Public Class Customer
    Inherits PTBOBase
```

Use the Inheritance tool any time you want to define an inheritance relationship from within Class Designer.

Building Along

For the Purchase Tracker sample application:
- Open the **MainEntitiesDiagram** diagram in Class Designer.
- Add an inheritance relationship between the **Customer** class and the base business object class (**PTBOBase**).

Class Designer adds the inheritance relationship to the diagram and adds the `Inherits` statement to the class.

Defining Properties and Methods

From Class Designer, you can view, add, or edit class properties and methods.

To view the properties and methods for a class:

1. Select the class in Class Designer by clicking it.
2. Open the Class Details window for the selected class by selecting **View** | **Other Windows** | **Class Details** from the main menu bar *or* by right-clicking the class in Class Designer and selecting **Class Details** from the context menu.

The Class Details window appears, as shown in Figure 6.4.

The Class Details window provides a wealth of information, including the summary XML comments you created for your properties and methods. You can change any of the property or method details by editing the values in this window. The change is then immediately reflected in the associated code.

For example, you can add summary XML comments for the `InventoryDate` property by typing directly into the Summary column for the `InventoryDate` row in the Class Details window. If you then open the Code Editor for the `Product` class, you will see that the summary XML comments were added to the `Property` statement.

6. CLASS TOOLS AND TECHNIQUES

Class Details				
Name	Type	Modifier	Summary	Hide
⊟ Methods				☐
⊞ Create	Product	Public	Creates a populated instance of this class	☐
⊞ Create	Product	Public	Creates a populated instance of this class	☐
⊟ Create	Product	Public	Creates a populated instance of this class	☐
(prodID	Integer	ByVal	ID of the product to create	
) <add parameter>				
⊞ New		Private		☐
<add method>				
⊟ Properties				☐
⊞ InventoryDate	Nullable(Of Date)	Public		☐
⊞ ProductID	Integer	Public	Gets the ID of the product	☐
⊞ ProductName	String	Public	Gets or sets the name of the product	☐
<add property>				
⊟ Fields				☐
_InventoryDate	Nullable(Of Date)	Private		☐
_ProductID	Integer	Private		☐
_ProductName	String	Private		☐
<add field>				
⊟ Events				
<add event>				

Figure 6.4 The Class Details window displays all the properties and methods for a class and allows you to add or edit properties and methods.

You can add properties, methods, fields, or events to the class from this window or from Class Designer directly. There are many ways to add these class members.

For example, use one of the following techniques to add a property to a class:

- Right-click the class in Class Designer and select **Add | Property** from the context menu.
- Right-click the **Properties** node for the class in Class Designer, and select **Add | Property** from the context menu.
- Select the class in Class Designer, and then select **Class Diagram | Add | Property** from the main menu bar.
- Type in the Class Details window in the **Properties** node containing the text **<add property>**.
- Select **New Property** from the New Member drop-down list on the Class Details toolbar shown to the left of the Class Details window.

NOTE: Although these techniques specifically describe how to add properties, you use the same general techniques to add other types of items, such as methods and fields.

Regardless of how you created the property, the property then appears in Class Designer, in the Class Details window, and in the Code Editor for the class. This makes it easy for you to go back and forth between the designer view and the code view.

In the past, most visual tools performed a round trip to keep your diagrams in sync with your code. The tool would perform one trip to convert a diagram into code. If changes were made to the code, the tool would require a return trip to convert the code back to a diagram—hence the term *round trip*. But these conversions often resulted in loss of detail as the tool converted back and forth between code and the diagram.

Class Designer does not perform a round trip. It does not actually "trip" at all. It is simply another view of the same data. This means that you don't lose any detail as you go from code to designer and back to code.

To move from the designer view to the Code Editor, double-click on the item in Class Designer, *or* right-click Class Designer and select **View Code** from the context menu.

Use Class Designer if you prefer to build your properties and methods using a visual tool instead of typing the code.

Building Along

For the Purchase Tracker sample application:

- Open the **MainEntitiesDiagram** diagram in Class Designer.
- Add a property to the **Customer** class.
  Name the property **LastName**, and give it a **string** data type.
- Add appropriate XML comments for the property in the **Summary** column of the Class Details window.
- Add a method to the **Customer** class.
  Name the method **Create**, and give it a return type of **Customer**. Define a **custID** parameter of type **integer**.
- Add appropriate XML comments for the method in the **Summary** column of the Class Details window.
- View the generated code in the Code Editor.
  Class Designer generates the `Property` statement, the method, and associated XML comments.
- In the Code Editor, declare a private backing variable for the `LastName` property, as defined in the preceding chapter.

- Add code to the **LastName** Property statement to get and set the backing variable. Be sure to include the code that calls the DataStateChanged method from the base class, as shown in the preceding chapter.
- Add code to the **Create** method similar to the first Create method defined for the Product class in the preceding chapter. Be sure to add the Shared keyword to the declaration.
- Modify the **Create** method to reset the object's entity state back to Unchanged after it sets the property values.
  This ensures that the entity state tracks the user's changes, not changes made to the properties when they are first populated.
  ```
  cust.DataStateChanged(EntityStateEnum.Unchanged)
  ```
- Add a **private constructor**, as shown in the preceding chapter, to ensure that all other code must use the Create method to create an instance of the class.

You now have the beginnings of a Customer class.

Using Object Test Bench

As you are building your classes and implementing your methods, you may want a quick test of a method to confirm its results. Object Test Bench (OTB) provides simple object-level testing. You can use OTB to create an instance of your class, invoke methods, and evaluate the results. Since this section focuses on Class Designer, it covers how to use OTB from Class Designer, but you can also access these features from the Class View window (**View | Class View**).

NOTE: OTB does not take the place of good unit testing. See "Performing Unit Testing" later in this chapter for more information.

The technique you use to test a method depends on the type of method. For static methods (those defined with the Shared keyword), you can simply call the method. For nonshared methods, you need to create an instance of the class before you can call the method.

To test a static method with OTB:

1. Ensure that the project containing the method you want to test is set as the startup project.

> **NOTE:** The OTB features do not appear unless the project is defined as the startup project. See Chapter 3, "Building Projects," for information on defining a startup project.

2. Build the project.
3. Right-click the class containing the method you want to test in Class Designer, and select **Invoke Static Method** from the context menu.

   Any static methods you defined in that class using the `Shared` keyword are listed for selection.
4. Select the static method to execute.

   The Invoke Method dialog appears, as shown in Figure 6.5.

Figure 6.5   The Invoke Method dialog provides the opportunity to enter the parameters for your method.

> **NOTE:** Your XML documentation may not appear correctly in the Documentation Comments section of the Invoke Method dialog. At the time of this writing, there was an error in the evaluation of the XML in this dialog.

5. Enter the required parameter value(s) and click **OK**.

> **NOTE:** When entering string parameters, you need to include quotes around the string value. For example, to enter a name for a string parameter, type `"Jessica"`.

The Method Call Result dialog, shown in Figure 6.6, displays the result of your method call.

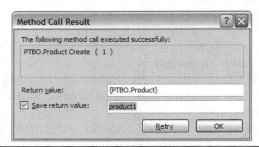

Figure 6.6   The Method Call Result dialog displays the result of your method call.

From this dialog, you can view the return value. If you check the **Save return value** checkbox, you can save the return value. If you click the **Retry** button, you are returned to the Invoke Method dialog so that you can execute the method again with different parameters.

To test an instance method with OTB:

1. Ensure that the project containing the method you want to test is set as the startup project.

NOTE: The OTB features do not appear unless the project is defined as the startup project. See Chapter 3 for information on defining a startup project.

2. Build the project.
3. Right-click the class containing the method you want to test in Class Designer, and select **Create Instance** from the context menu.
   Any constructors you have defined in your class are listed for selection. If you have no constructors, a default constructor is listed.
4. Select the desired constructor.
   The Create Instance dialog appears, as shown in Figure 6.7.
   The instance (named `TestProductInstance` in this example) appears in the Object Test Bench window, as shown in Figure 6.8.
5. Enter the desired instance name, and click **OK**.
6. Right-click the instance in the Object Test Bench window, and select **Invoke Method** from the context menu.
   The methods, both instance and static (shared), are listed.

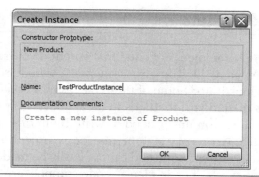

Figure 6.7 The Create Instance dialog allows you to define the details for the instance.

Figure 6.8 The Object Test Bench window provides access to object instances so that you can execute instance methods.

7. Select the method to invoke.
   The Invoke Method dialog is displayed (similar to Figure 6.5).
8. Enter the required parameter value(s), and click **OK**.

NOTE: When entering string parameters, you need to include quotes around the string value. For example, to enter a name for a string parameter, type `"Jessica"`.

The Method Call Result dialog (see Figure 6.6) displays the result of your method call.

If you save the return value, it is added to the Object Test Bench window (see Figure 6.8). From the Object Test Bench window, you can hover the mouse pointer over the value to view the data associated with the return value.

Using the Object Test Bench features, you can perform a quick test of any methods in your classes.

6. CLASS TOOLS AND TECHNIQUES

Using Code Snippets

Are there some pieces of code that you find yourself writing over and over and over again? Do you ever use a piece of code so seldom that you always need to look it up? Some of these pieces may make sense as standard components or standard methods in an application framework, like logging or validation, so you never need to write them or look them up again. Other pieces, like `Property` statements, loops, exception handlers, or file input/output, are more unique and cannot easily be made into standard methods. For these types of code pieces, code snippets are a perfect answer.

A **code snippet** is a prebuilt intelligent piece of code, sometimes referred to as an expansion template, that you can easily insert into the Code Editor. Visual Studio comes with a large library of built-in code snippets for Visual Basic. You can also build your own code snippets.

Using code snippets makes it quick to add predefined code pieces to your application. Creating your own code snippets allows you to create a library of custom code pieces and share them with other developers.

This section demonstrates how you can insert existing code snippets into your application, how to build your own code snippets, and how to use the open-source Snippet Editor.

Inserting Code Snippets

Code snippets include standard programming constructs, such as loops and `Property` statements, to help you quickly build common code blocks. They include common programming tasks, such as creating an MDI child form, to help you quickly insert commonly used code. They also include many lesser-used programming techniques, such as drawing a filled rectangle, to provide assistance with tasks that you don't use as often and would otherwise need to look up. With all of this functionality available at your fingertips, code snippets can greatly enhance your productivity.

To insert a code snippet into the Code Editor:

1. In the Code Editor, place the insertion point where the snippet is to be inserted.
2. Right-click and select **Insert Snippet** from the context menu, *or* type a question mark (`?`) and press the Tab key.
   The Code Snippet Picker appears, as shown in Figure 6.9.

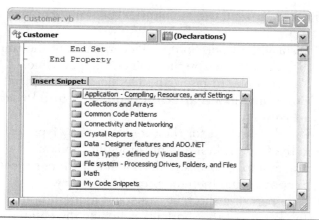

Figure 6.9 The Code Snippet Picker presents the code snippets you have available depending on the language associated with the Code Editor you are working in.

3. Double-click *or* press the Tab key on the snippet folders to navigate the hierarchy and find the desired snippet.
   To back up in the hierarchy, press the Backspace key *or* press Alt+Tab. To cancel the Code Snippet Picker, press the Esc key.
4. Double-click on the desired snippet.
   Visual Studio inserts the code associated with the selected snippet into the Code Editor at the current insertion point.

Snippets also have shortcuts to minimize the steps required to access a snippet. The shortcut associated with a snippet is displayed in the ToolTip of the Code Snippet Picker entry.

To insert a code snippet using the shortcut:

1. In the Code Editor, place the insertion point where the snippet is to be inserted.
2. Type the shortcut and press the Tab key.
   Visual Studio inserts the code associated with the selected snippet into the Code Editor at the current insertion point.

For example, when you're building classes, one of the more tedious tasks is defining all the properties. You have to create a private backing variable and a property getter and setter for every property. A more efficient way to create your properties is to use the Define a Property code snippet.

6. CLASS TOOLS AND TECHNIQUES

There are several ways to insert a code snippet:

- Display the Code Snippet Picker, navigate the snippet folders and then double-click on the defined snippet name.
  For example, to insert the Define a Property code snippet, select **Common Code Patterns** | **Properties and Procedures** | **Define a Property**.
- Use the shortcut for the code snippet by typing the shortcut name in the Code Editor and pressing the Tab key.
  For example, to insert the Define a Property code snippet, type `property` and then the press the Tab key.
- Type part of a shortcut name and a question mark, then press the Tab key to list the shortcuts matching the entered value.
  For example, to insert the Define a Property code snippet, type `pro?`, and then press the Tab key to display the list of shortcuts that begin with "pro."

When the Define a Property snippet is inserted into the Code Editor, the following code is generated:

```
Private newPropertyValue As Integer
Public Property NewProperty() As Integer
    Get
        Return newPropertyValue
    End Get
    Set(ByVal value As Integer)
        newPropertyValue = value
    End Set
End Property
```

Many snippets contain highlighted text, called replacements. A **replacement** is a variable or other text in the snippet that you can replace with a unique value when you insert the snippet. Modifications to a replacement cascade through the snippet, so changing any replacement automatically changes all other replacements with the same text.

Visual Studio makes it easy to modify the replacements. When Visual Studio inserts the snippet, it sets focus to the first replacement. You type the desired value for the replacement and press the Tab key. Visual Studio cascades your replacement value through the snippet and moves the focus to the next replacement. This process is repeated until all replacement values are entered or until you leave the snippet. The replacement highlights remain on for further editing until the Code Editor is closed.

For example, to define a `FirstName` property, type `_FirstName` in the first replacement (`newPropertyValue`) and press the Tab key. Notice how the value is cascaded to the getter and setter. Type `String` in the second replacement and press the Tab key. `Integer` is then replaced with `String` throughout the snippet. Finally, type `FirstName` in the next replacement (`NewProperty`) and press the Tab key, and you are done. The result is as follows:

```
Private _FirstName As String
Public Property FirstName() As String
    Get
        Return _FirstName
    End Get
    Set(ByVal value As String)
        _FirstName = value
    End Set
End Property
```

If the snippet you insert requires a reference or import that you don't currently have set, Visual Studio automatically adds the reference and associated import when you insert the snippet.

Inserting snippets into your code is quick and easy and saves you from all that typing. Using snippets can also save you time, because they provide prebuilt code for tasks that you may not perform very often.

Building Along

For the Purchase Tracker sample application:

- Open the **Customer** class in the Code Editor.
- Use the Define a Property code snippet to insert string properties for **FirstName**, **Address**, **City**, **State**, **Zip**, and **Phone**.
- Add code to each `Property` statement to call the `DataStateChanged` method from the base class, as shown in the preceding chapter.
- Use the Define a Property code snippet to add a **CustomerID** property.
  The `CustomerID` property in the `Customer` class is implemented like the `ProductID` in the `Product` class:

```
Private _CustomerID As Integer
Public Property CustomerID() As Integer
    Get
        Return _CustomerID
    End Get
    Private Set(ByVal value As Integer)
        _CustomerID = value
    End Set
End Property
```

- Add documentation for each property using XML comments.
- Modify the **Create** method to set default values for each of the new properties.

You now have the majority of your Customer class.

Managing Code Snippets

Visual Studio comes with a large library of code snippets, many more are available online, and you can develop your own. So you need a way to manage these code snippets. That is the purpose of the Code Snippets Manager.

The Code Snippets Manager, available from the Tools menu (**Tools | Code Snippets Manager**), provides a summary of each snippet, its shortcut, type, author, and location, as shown in Figure 6.10.

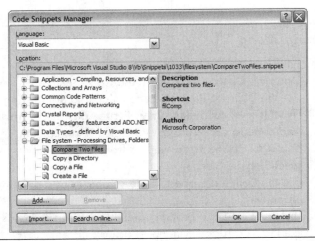

Figure 6.10   The Code Snippets Manager helps you organize your snippets.

For each language (Visual Basic, Visual C#, Visual J#, and XML), the Code Snippets Manager lists every snippet using the same hierarchy as the Code Snippet Picker. Select a snippet from within the hierarchy to see its details, including its shortcut, in the pane on the right.

To add a new folder to the hierarchy, use the Add button. To remove a folder and its contents from the hierarchy, use the Remove button. This allows you to reorganize your snippet folders as you desire.

To add a new snippet to a folder, select the folder and use the Import button. This assumes that you already have a new snippet and just want to import it into Visual Studio. Creating your own snippet is described in the next section. Use the Search Online button to search online for additional code snippets.

Using the Code Snippets Manager provides an easy way to see the code snippets that are available, and to reorganize them as desired.

Understanding Code Snippets

As with many things these days, a code snippet is just an XML file. Peeking inside a code snippet to see how they are made will help you when you create your own code snippets.

The Code Snippets Manager (see Figure 6.10) defines the location where each code snippet is stored on your system. To find the location of a specific code snippet, navigate to the code snippet in the Code Snippets Manager, and view the Location label near the top of the dialog.

Once you know the location of the code snippet on your system, you can use Explorer to navigate to the code snippet's directory and open the code snippet file. The Define a Property code snippet for Visual Basic is contained in the file DefineAProperty.snippet, and it looks like this:

```
<?xml version="1.0" encoding="UTF-8"?>
<CodeSnippets xmlns="http://schemas.microsoft.com/
➥VisualStudio/2005/CodeSnippet">
  <CodeSnippet Format="1.0.0">
    <Header>
      <Title>Define a Property</Title>
      <Author>Microsoft Corporation</Author>
      <Description>Defines a Property with a backing field.
      </Description>
      <Shortcut>Property</Shortcut>
    </Header>
```

```
<Snippet>
  <Declarations>
    <Literal>
      <ID>PropertyName</ID>
      <Type>String</Type>
      <ToolTip>Replace with property name.</ToolTip>
      <Default>NewProperty</Default>
    </Literal>
    <Literal>
      <ID>PropertyType</ID>
      <Type>
      </Type>
      <ToolTip>Replace with the property type.</ToolTip>
      <Default>Integer</Default>
    </Literal>
    <Object>
      <ID>PrivateVariable</ID>
      <Type>Object</Type>
      <ToolTip>Replace this with the private variable name.
➥</ToolTip>
      <Default>newPropertyValue</Default>
    </Object>
  </Declarations>
  <Code Language="VB" Kind="method decl"><![CDATA[Private
➥$PrivateVariable$ As $PropertyType$
Public Property $PropertyName$() As $PropertyType$
    Get
        Return $PrivateVariable$
    End Get
    Set(ByVal value As $PropertyType$)
        $PrivateVariable$ = value
    End Set
End Property]]></Code>
  </Snippet>
  </CodeSnippet>
</CodeSnippets>
```

The `Header` tag section defines the basic information about the code snippet that is displayed in the Code Snippet Manager. The `Snippet Declarations` section defines the replacements for the code snippet. The `Code` section defines the code snippet itself. The code snippet uses the `$` character to delimit the replacements in the snippet. Using the same replacement name throughout the snippet provides cascading replacements.

You can edit a code snippet file to modify the snippet. For example, if you would like to change the shortcut associated with a code snippet, you can modify the code snippet file `Shortcut` element.

Now that you know what a code snippet file looks like, you can build your own code snippets.

Building Your Own Code Snippets

To get the greatest benefit from code snippets, create your own or modify the existing ones to match how you code. You can approach this task in several ways.

You can build your own code snippets the hard way by manually creating the code snippet file contents yourself with your XML editor of choice. But this means that you need an intimate understanding of the snippet XML schema, and you have to do a lot of typing, typing, typing.

You could use the XML Code Editor provided in Visual Studio and then get some assistance with creating your code snippet. The XML Code Editor Code Snippet Picker provides a Snippet code snippet. This code snippet provides you with the correct XML layout for a code snippet XML file. Just insert the Snippet code snippet, tab through the code snippet to set the appropriate element values, and then add the code you want for the snippet itself.

Another choice is to locate an existing code snippet file that is similar to the snippet you want to create. Copy the file and then edit it as you desire. This is the best choice if you simply want an enhanced version of one of the existing snippets without modifying the original snippet.

By far the easiest way to create your own snippets or edit existing snippets is to use the open-source Snippet Editor created by Bill McCarthy, a developer from Australia and Microsoft MVP, in conjunction with Microsoft. You can download the Snippet Editor from http://msdn. microsoft.com/vbasic.

After downloading and installing the Snippet Editor, launch SnippetEditor.exe. By default, the Snippet Editor displays the Visual Basic code snippets in a folder hierarchy in the left pane. Navigate the folder hierarchy and double-click on a snippet to show the snippet details in the right pane, as shown in Figure 6.11.

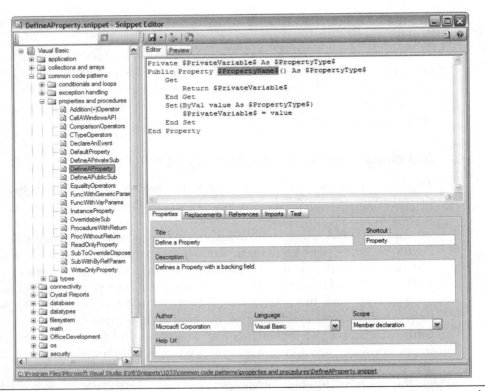

Figure 6.11 The open-source Snippet Editor provides a much easier way to create and edit snippets.

The Snippet Editor displays the same folder hierarchy shown in the Code Snippets Manager, except that the snippet name is displayed instead of the title. To see snippets for other languages, use the Option button (on the far right of the toolbar) to select the desired language(s).

The Snippet Editor allows you to edit existing code snippets or create new ones. It allows you to add code snippet folders and drag and drop code snippets between the folders. It also allows you to build a Visual Studio Content Installer, making it easier to share your code snippets with others. Most importantly, it allows you to search code snippets by keyword using the filter feature just above the folder hierarchy.

For example, if you want to find any code snippet having to do with properties, you can perform a search. Type **prop** in the Filter textbox and click the Apply button. The folder hierarchy in the left pane of the Snippet Editor is filtered to only those code snippets containing the text "prop."

You can view or edit any of the snippets. For example, you can update the VB Define a Property code snippet to prefix the private member variable with an underscore. You could even add all the code required to set the `DataStateChanged`. Navigate the filtered hierarchy to the DefineAProperty code snippet. Double-click on the code snippet to edit it. It appears in the right pane of the Snippet Editor, as shown in Figure 6.11.

The Editor tab in the top-right pane of the Snippet Editor allows you to edit the code snippet as desired. For this example, insert an underscore character before the `$PrivateVariable$` replacements in the Editor tab. The Preview tab provides a preview of what the code expansion looks like so that you can confirm your expected results.

The bottom-right pane of the Snippet Editor provides tabs to help you edit your code snippet. The Properties tab displays the code snippet's properties, such as the title, description, and shortcut.

The Replacements tab allows you to define the fields that are to be used as replacements when the code snippet is expanded. You can add new replacements, modify existing replacements, or delete a replacement.

The References tab defines which references need to be added when the code snippet is inserted into the Code Editor. Similarly, the Imports tab defines which imports need to be set.

Create your own code snippet by right-clicking the desired folder and selecting **Add New Snippet** from the context menu.

For example, suppose you want to create a snippet with a specialized `Property` statement that knows how to handle object instances. Right-click the properties and procedures node under common code patterns, and select **Add New Snippet**. Give the new code snippet an obvious name, such as InstanceProperty.

Double-click on the new InstanceProperty code snippet to edit it. On the Properties tab, give the code snippet a title, description, shortcut, and so on.

On the Replacements tab, add a replacement for the data type, private variable name, and property name. If you aren't sure what values to set, use an existing snippet as an example.

Then write the desired code in the Editor pane (or copy from one of the other snippets and edit it), using the replacements as needed. The result is similar to the following:

```
Private _$PrivateVariable$ As $PropertyType$
Public Property $PropertyName$() As $PropertyType$
    Get
```

```
        If _$PrivateVariable$ Is Nothing Then
            _$PrivateVariable$ = New $PropertyType$
        End If
        Return _$PrivateVariable$
    End Get
    Set(ByVal value As $PropertyType$)
        _$PrivateVariable$ = value
    End Set
End Property
```

Click the Preview tab to confirm the results. When you obtain the desired results, save the code snippet. The code snippet is automatically added to the Code Snippet Manager in the defined folder, so it is immediately ready for your use in the Code Editor.

Any time you find yourself typing the same set of code or looking up some syntax you do not use very often, consider building a snippet for that code. As you build your code snippet library, the code for many of your coding tasks will be at your fingertips.

Your code snippets are yours. Modify them, reorganize them, and create your own so that you can build a very efficient, personalized snippets library.

Building Along

For the Purchase Tracker sample application:

- If desired, build a code snippet that inserts the `Property` statement structure that includes all the code that calls the `DataStateChanged` method.

You can then use this snippet to create properties that include the majority of their required code.

Performing Unit Testing

No software is really done until it has been tested. When building your application, the first level of formal testing you perform is called unit testing. **Unit testing** is testing a particular "unit" of your application, normally methods of your classes. This testing is initially done by the developer as part of the process of confirming that each method is complete and correct.

To perform unit testing, you must first create a unit test. A **unit test** is a programmatic test used to exercise your code by directly calling methods, passing appropriate parameters, and evaluating the results produced against expected results.

Unit tests are also great for regression testing. **Regression testing** is retesting your code after it has been modified to ensure that other previously working methods won't fail as a result of your changes. This helps ensure that newly modified code does not adversely affect existing, unchanged code.

Immediately after completing development of a method, while the code in the method is still fresh in your mind, write the unit test for that method. Some software development methodologies, such as Test-Driven Development (TDD), suggest that you write the unit test *before* you create the method. That gives your method a target for success and helps you know when your method is done.

Either way, you begin creating your unit tests by creating a project in Visual Studio that is your unit test project. You then add a test class to the unit test project for each business object class. Each test class is marked with attributes to identify it as a test class. In each test class, you add code to test the business object methods in that class. Again, you use attributes to mark the methods as test methods. The exact attributes you use depends on your unit testing tool.

If you have an edition of Visual Studio Team System, such as Visual Studio Team Developer, features are built in to assist you with unit testing. Otherwise, you can use the open-source NUnit tool to build your unit tests.

This section describes the features of Visual Studio Team System for defining and executing unit tests. See the NUnit Web site (http://www.nunit.org/) or the Microsoft NUnit article at http://msdn.microsoft.com/library/default.asp?url=/library/en-us/dnaspp/html/aspnet-testwithnunit.asp for details on building unit tests with NUnit. See the "Additional Reading" section near the end of this chapter for information on using Visual Studio Team System to define other types of tests.

NOTE: The unit testing features built into Visual Studio are available *only* in the Visual Studio Team System editions. If you are using one of the other editions, you can use NUnit instead.

Building a Unit Test Project

The way you create your unit test depends on whether you are writing the test before or after building the code. If you build the code first, you can generate the test project from the code. If you build the test before the code, you need to build the test manually.

Building a Test Project from the Code Editor

One of the easiest ways to build your test project is to build it using the Code Editor after you have developed the code to test. You can use this technique to automatically build unit test methods for every method in every class in every project of your application.

To build a test project based on existing code using the Code Editor:

1. Right-click in the Code Editor and select **Create Unit Tests** from the context menu.
   The Create Unit Tests dialog is displayed, as shown in Figure 6.12.

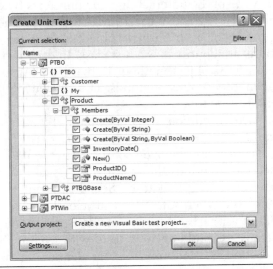

Figure 6.12   The Create Unit Tests dialog allows you to generate unit tests for the class members you specify.

2. Check the desired classes, properties, and methods to include in the test.
   The unit testing feature generates a unit test method for each property and method that you select.

The values that are checked by default depend on where you were in the Code Editor when you selected the Create Unit Tests option. If you were on the class definition, the class and all its members are selected. If you were on a specific member, only that member is selected.

3. Select the desired **Output project**. For a new test, select the default **Create a new Visual Basic test project...** option.

   If you already created a test project, you can add to it by selecting the project from this drop-down list.

4. Click **OK**.

   The New Test Project dialog is displayed (see Figure 6.13) for entry of the test project name.

Figure 6.13   The New Test Project dialog allows you to define the name of your unit test project.

5. Enter the name of the unit test project.

   Use standard naming conventions for your project name. If you have just one unit test project, you can name it using the project abbreviation with a suffix defining the type of project—for example, PTUnitTest.

   However, if you plan to have multiple unit test projects for your application, give the test a descriptive name based on what the unit test is testing.

6. Click **Create** to create the unit test project.

   Visual Studio creates the test project and adds it to Solution Explorer. Visual Studio then adds a class to the test project for each class selected for unit testing in the Create Unit Tests dialog (see Figure 6.12) and generates a test method within the class for each property and method selected for unit testing. It also adds an AuthoringTests.txt file to the project to provide you with guidance on authoring and running tests.

You can then add the required code to the unit tests to fully test the members of your classes.

If you later add classes or members that you want to test, you can repeat these steps and add tests to an existing test project. Select the existing test project in the Output project drop-down of the Create Unit Tests dialog (see Figure 6.12). You are not asked for a new project name.

Building a Test Project Using the Unit Test Wizard

You can build your test project from the menu using the Unit Test Wizard. This process builds the tests for existing code similar to the preceding process, but with the steps in a slightly different order.

To build a test project based on existing code using the Unit Test Wizard:

1. Select **Test | New Test** from the main menu bar.
   The Add New Test dialog is displayed, as shown in Figure 6.14.

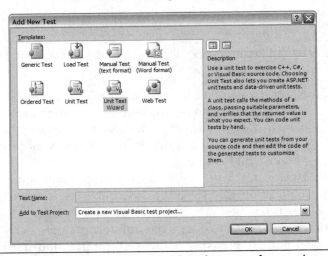

Figure 6.14   Use the Add New Test dialog to select the type of test to be created. This chapter describes only unit tests.

2. Select the **Unit Test Wizard** template and click **OK**.
   If you select the **Create a new Visual Basic test project...** option from the **Add to Test Project** drop-down list, the New Test Project dialog is displayed (see Figure 6.13).
   If you previously created a unit test project, you can add to it by selecting the project from the **Add to Test Project** drop-down list. You are not asked for the name of the test project. Instead, the

Create Unit Tests dialog is displayed (see Figure 6.12), so you can skip to step 5.

3. Enter the name of the unit test project.

Use standard naming conventions for your project name. If you have just one unit test project, you can name it using the project abbreviation with a suffix defining the type of project—for example, PTUnitTest.

However, if you plan to have multiple unit test projects for your application, give the test a descriptive name based on what the unit test is testing.

4. Click **Create** to create the unit test project.

Visual Studio creates the test project and adds it to Solution Explorer. It also adds an AuthoringTests.txt file to the project to provide you with guidance on authoring and running tests.

The Create Unit Tests dialog is then displayed (see Figure 6.12).

5. Check the desired classes, properties, and methods, and click **OK**.

Visual Studio adds a class to the test project for each class selected for unit testing in the Create Unit Tests dialog (see Figure 6.12). It also generates a test method within the class for each property and method selected for unit testing.

You can then add the required code to the unit tests to fully test the members of your classes.

Building a Test Project from Scratch

Sometimes you need to create a test project from scratch. For example, you may want to create the test before creating the code.

To build a test project from scratch:

1. Select **Test | New Test** from the main menu bar.
The Add New Test dialog is displayed (see Figure 6.14).

2. Select the **Unit Test template**.

If you select the **Create a new Visual Basic test project...** option from the **Add to Test Project** drop-down list, the New Test Project dialog is displayed (see Figure 6.13).

If you previously created a unit test project, you can add to it by selecting the project from the **Add to Test Project** drop-down list. Visual Studio then adds an empty unit test class to the selected unit test project. You can then skip these remaining steps.

3. Enter the name of the unit test project.

Use standard naming conventions for your project name. If you have just one unit test project, you can name it using the project abbreviation with a suffix defining the type of project—for example, PTUnitTest.

However, if you plan to have multiple unit test projects for your application, give the test a descriptive name based on what the unit test is testing.

4. Click **Create** to create the unit test project.

Visual Studio creates the test project, adds it to Solution Explorer, and creates an empty test class with an empty test method. It also adds an AuthoringTests.txt file to the project to provide you with guidance on authoring and running tests.

You can then add the required code to the unit tests. In this case, however, none of the code is added for you. You need to build it all from scratch.

Building a Test Project from Solution Explorer

Since a unit test project is just like any other type of project, you can also add a unit test project to a solution the same way you add other projects to a solution.

To build a test project from scratch using Solution Explorer:

1. Right-click the solution in Solution Explorer and select **Add** | **New Project** from the context menu, *or* select **File** | **Add** | **New Project** from the main menu bar.

The Add New Project dialog appears for selection of the project type and template.

2. Open the **Test Projects** node, and select **Test Documents** from the **Project types** tree view.

3. Select the **Test Project** template, and name the test.

Use standard naming conventions for your project name. If you have just one unit test project, you can name it using the project abbreviation with a suffix defining the type of project—for example, PTUnitTest.

However, if you plan to have multiple unit test projects for your application, give the test a descriptive name based on what the unit test is testing.

4. Click **OK**.

Visual Studio creates the test project, adds it to Solution Explorer, and creates an empty test class with an empty test method. It also adds an AuthoringTests.txt file to the project to provide you with guidance on authoring and running tests.

You can then add the required code to the unit tests. In this case, however, none of the code is added for you. You need to build it all from scratch.

Coding the Unit Test

The basic structure of the unit test code is generated automatically if you write the test from existing code. Otherwise, you have to create it all manually. Even if you select to write your tests from scratch, looking at the generated code can provide tips on building your tests.

The generated code defining the test class is as follows:

```
'''<summary>
'''This is a test class for PTBO.Product and is intended
'''to contain all PTBO.Product Unit Tests
'''</summary>
<TestClass()> _
Public Class ProductTest
```

There are two things to point out here. First, the generated code makes excellent use of XML comments to help you work with and maintain the unit tests. Second, the tests are identified with attributes. The testing runtime understands which classes are test classes by looking for the `TestClass` attribute.

The generated code for unit testing a property is as follows:

```
'''<summary>
'''A test for ProductName()
'''</summary>
<TestMethod()> _
Public Sub ProductNameTest()
    Dim target As Product = New Product

    Dim val As String = Nothing
    'TODO: Assign to an appropriate value for the property
```

```
    target.ProductName = val

    Assert.AreEqual(val, target.ProductName, _
        "PTBO.Product.ProductName was not set correctly.")
    Assert.Inconclusive("Verify the correctness of this test
➥method.")
End Sub
```

NOTE: As of this writing, the generated code for the `ProductIDTest` method is invalid if you specified the `ProductID` with a private setter, as described earlier in this chapter. You need to comment out or delete the `target.ProductID = val` statement in the test method to compile the test project.

The generated code for unit testing a method is as follows:

```
'''<summary>
'''A test for Create(ByVal Integer)
'''</summary>
<TestMethod()> _
Public Sub CreateTest()
Dim prodID As Integer 'TODO: Initialize to an appropriate value

    Dim expected As Product = Nothing
    Dim actual As Product

    actual = PTBO.Product.Create(prodID)

    Assert.AreEqual(expected, actual, _
        "PTBO.Product.Create did not return the expected value.")
    Assert.Inconclusive("Verify the correctness of this test
➥method.")
End Sub
```

NOTE: If your class has overloaded methods, the generated code names the methods XXXTest, XXXTest1, and XXXTest2, where XXX is the name of your method.

The generated unit test code in both examples makes use of XML comments to provide documentation on the test methods. The code uses the `TestMethod` attribute to define the method as a test method. For properties, the test methods get and set the values to test them. For methods, the code prepares the parameters and then calls the method.

Because the unit test code generator cannot anticipate what valid and invalid values are for your properties or for the parameters of your methods, it uses Task List comments (TODO) to draw your attention to the part of the test you need to customize. You need to modify the test code to define the appropriate values.

When adding code to the unit test, make use of the .NET Framework `Assert` class. The `Assert` class asserts that something is true. If it is not true, the code produces an error caught by the testing runtime. The testing runtime then displays the error as part of the unit test results, described later. The most commonly used `Assert` class methods are as follows:

- `AreEqual` tests whether the two specified values are equal and fails if they are not equal.
- `AreNotEqual` tests whether two specified values are not equal and fails if they are equal.
- `IsInstanceOfType` tests whether an object is of an expected type and fails if it is not.
- `Fail` specifies a failure. You use this method when you add custom code in a test method that checks a condition and that condition fails.
- `Inconclusive` denotes that a test result cannot be proven true or false. You will see many of these in the generated tests when the code generator does not have enough information to validate the results. This basically identifies tests that are not complete. You need to locate and change these statements with appropriate logic for your testing before you can run the test.

For example, the purpose of the `Product` class `Create` method is to create a populated instance of the `Product` class. The existing code has hard-coded values for an ID of 1, so that can be used for the testing.

Valid test cases for the `Create` method, as it is currently written, are as follows:

- Pass in an ID of 1 and assert that a valid `Product` object is returned.

- Pass in an ID of 1 and assert that the properties of the `Product` object are as expected.
- Pass in an ID of 0 and assert that an empty `Product` object is returned.
- Pass in an ID of 0 and assert that all the properties of the `Product` object are initialized.

You then write code in the method for each of these test cases. The resulting code for the `Create` method example is as follows:

```
''' <summary>
''' A test for Create(ByVal Integer)
''' </summary>
<TestMethod()> _
Public Sub CreateTest()
    Dim prodID As Integer
    Dim expected As Product = Nothing
    Dim actual As Product

    ' Test Case 1: Pass in an ID of 1,
    ' assert that a valid Product object is returned.
    prodID = 1
    actual = PTBO.Product.Create(prodID)
    Assert.IsInstanceOfType(actual, GetType(Product), _
    "PTBO.Product.Create did not return the expected data type.")

    ' Test Case 2: Pass in an ID of 1,
    ' assert that the properties of the Product object
    ' are as expected.
    Assert.AreEqual(actual.ProductID, 1, _
        "PTBO.Product.Create did not set " & _
        "the expected value for ProductID.")
    Assert.AreEqual(actual.ProductName, "Mithril Coat", _
        "PTBO.Product.Create did not set " & _
        "the expected value for ProductName.")
    Assert.AreEqual(actual.InventoryDate.Value, #4/1/2006#, _
        "PTBO.Product.Create did not set " & _
        "the expected value for InventoryDate.")

    ' Test Case 3: Pass in an ID of 0,
    ' assert that an empty Product object is returned.
```

```
prodID = 0
actual = PTBO.Product.Create(prodID)
Assert.IsInstanceOfType(actual, GetType(Product), _
"PTBO.Product.Create did not return the expected data type.")

' Test Case 4: Pass in an ID of 0,
' assert that the properties of the Product object
' are initialized.
Assert.AreEqual(actual.ProductID, 0, _
    "PTBO.Product.Create did not set " & _
    "the expected value for ProductID.")
Assert.AreEqual(actual.ProductName, Nothing, _
    "PTBO.Product.Create did not set  " & _
    "the expected value for ProductName.")
Assert.AreEqual(actual.InventoryDate.HasValue, False, _
    "PTBO.Product.Create did not set  " & _
    "the expected value for InventoryDate.")
End Sub
```

The code for the first test case sets the `prodID` parameter to 1 and calls the `Create` method. It then uses the `IsInstanceOfType` method of the `Assert` class to ensure that an instance of the `Product` class was returned. This could instead call `IsNotNull` to ensure that the instance was not `Nothing`.

The code for the second test case checks the value of each property against its expected value. It uses the `AreEqual` method of the `Assert` class to ensure that the values are equal.

The code for the third test case sets the `prodID` parameter to 0 and calls the `Create` method. It then again verifies that an instance of the `Product` class was returned.

The code for the fourth test case checks the value of each property to ensure that it was appropriately initialized.

The key to building good unit tests is to think through all the possible test cases for the class members. For properties, assign both valid and invalid data, and ensure that both are handled as appropriate for your application. For methods, pass in both valid and invalid parameters to ensure that your application handles both.

A good organizational technique for your unit tests is to number each test case and include it as documentation in the unit test method, as shown in the example in this section.

6. CLASS TOOLS AND TECHNIQUES

Running the Unit Test

Once you have created your unit tests, you can run them. Running tests automatically produces test results, saves the results, and displays a summary of the results.

To run a test project, set the test project as the startup project for the solution. Then start the project just like you would start any other project. The testing runtime executes the tests, showing you the progress in the Test Results window. When the test is complete, the Test Results window shows you a summary of the test results, as shown in Figure 6.15.

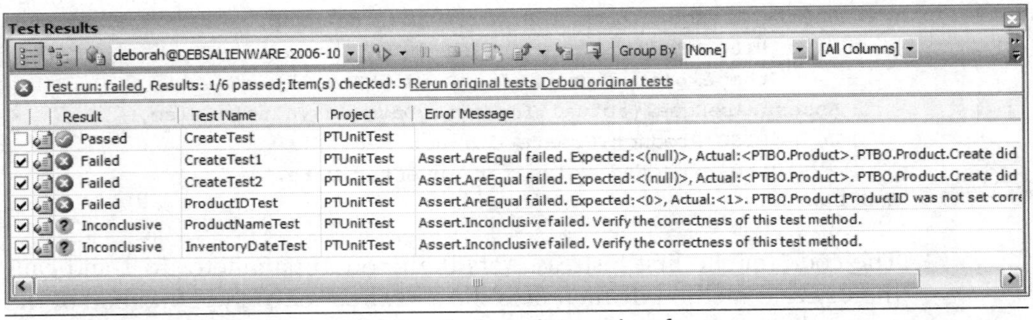

	Result	Test Name	Project	Error Message
☐	Passed	CreateTest	PTUnitTest	
☑	Failed	CreateTest1	PTUnitTest	Assert.AreEqual failed. Expected:<(null)>, Actual:<PTBO.Product>. PTBO.Product.Create did
☑	Failed	CreateTest2	PTUnitTest	Assert.AreEqual failed. Expected:<(null)>, Actual:<PTBO.Product>. PTBO.Product.Create did
☑	Failed	ProductIDTest	PTUnitTest	Assert.AreEqual failed. Expected:<0>, Actual:<1>. PTBO.Product.ProductID was not set corre
☑	Inconclusive	ProductNameTest	PTUnitTest	Assert.Inconclusive failed. Verify the correctness of this test method.
☑	Inconclusive	InventoryDateTest	PTUnitTest	Assert.Inconclusive failed. Verify the correctness of this test method.

Figure 6.15 The Test Results window displays the results of your tests.

The most important feature of this dialog is information on the results of your test. Notice that the CreateTest unit test passed. The other unit tests either failed or generated an inconclusive result. This is because the code generation does not provide you with a test that passes. You need to write custom code in each test. To pass all the unit tests, you need to update every unit test method, similar to how the `CreateTest` method was updated.

You can perform a number of other tasks from this dialog:

- The leftmost drop-down list in the Test Results toolbar allows you to select a test run to view. Every test run is automatically saved, and you can view any of the runs. The default is the latest test run.
- Buttons in the Test Results toolbar allow you to execute tests directly from this window.
- Buttons in the Test Results toolbar allow you to export or import test results.
- The rightmost controls in the Test Results toolbar allow you to organize the Test Results window contents by grouping, sorting, or filtering the results.

- The Show Code Coverage Results button in the Test Results toolbar (accessible from the Toolbar Options icon shown with double arrows at the far right) allows you to view your test's code coverage. This defines how much of your code was actually tested.

NOTE: You must run the unit test project without debugging (**Debug | Start Without Debugging**) in order to build the code coverage results.

See the "Additional Reading" section for more information on all of the many features available when executing tests and reviewing results.

Building Along

For the Purchase Tracker sample application:
- Optionally, build a unit test project, as defined in this section.

Execute your unit test project to confirm the operation of your business objects.

You can build a unit test project and create unit tests from existing code using the Visual Studio unit test generation features, or you can write the test completely by hand. Either way, you add your custom code to the unit tests for each possible test case. You can then execute the tests and view the results to confirm the operation of your application.

Implementing Master/Detail Classes

Master/detail is the name given to two entities that have a specific relationship whereby each master item has a set of detail items associated with it. The classic example of master/detail is an invoice. Each invoice header (master) has a set of invoice line items (detail) associated with it.

You can often recognize a master/detail relationship between business object entities because they are described using "has a." An invoice header *has a* set of invoice line items. A customer *has a* set of purchases.

In many cases, there may be several ways that a set of business objects could be related. The correct set of relationships that you define in your application depends on the purpose of your application.

For example, looking at `Customer`, `Product`, and `Purchase` business objects, their appropriate relationships depend on the purpose of the application:

- If the purpose is fulfillment, the focus is on retrieving products from inventory to fulfill orders. In this case, the `Purchase` class is implemented as an independent class with information from the `Product` and `Customer` classes as needed to fulfill the order. This does not implement a master/detail relationship.
- If the purpose is to understand how well a particular product sells, the `Purchase` class is implemented as a detail class for the `Product` master class (a product *has a* set of purchases). This allows you to easily see the set of purchases for a product.
- If the purpose is to track the purchases made by customers, the `Purchase` class is implemented as a detail class for the `Customer` master class (a customer *has a* set of purchases). This allows you to easily track which purchases each customer makes.

The purpose of the Purchase Tracker sample application is to track each customer's purchases. The `Purchase` class is then implemented as a detail class to the `Customer` master class.

The master business object, `Customer` in this case, is implemented as a normal class, as shown earlier in this chapter.

The detail business object, `Purchase` in this example, is often implemented as two classes: one to provide basic item information (`Purchase`), and the other to manage a set of items (`PurchaseList`). The `Purchase` class provides the basic information for a purchase. The `PurchaseList` class manages the list of purchases for a given customer.

This section details how to create the detail business object classes. As an example, it builds both the detail item class (`Purchase`) and the detail collection class (`PurchaseList`). It then defines the master/detail relationship between these classes and the master class (`Customer`).

Building the Detail Item Class

The class defined for a detail item is created the same way as any other class.

To build a detail item class:

1. Add the class to the business object Class Library project in Solution Explorer.

2. Inherit from the base business object class.
   This ensures that it behaves like a standard business object. The `Inherits` statement is as follows:

```
Public Class Purchase
    Inherits PTBOBase
```

3. Define appropriate properties and methods for the class.
   Be sure to call the `DataStateChanged` method from the base business object class in each property, as detailed in the preceding chapter.

For example, a `Purchase` class has properties for `PurchaseDate` and `Quantity` and a Create method. The `PurchaseDate` property is implemented as follows:

```
Private _PurchaseDate As Nullable(Of Date)
''' <summary>
''' Gets or sets the date of the purchase.
''' </summary>
Public Property PurchaseDate() As Nullable(Of Date)
    Get
        Return _PurchaseDate
    End Get
    Set(ByVal value As Nullable(Of Date))
        If (_PurchaseDate.HasValue<>value.HasValue) OrElse _
            (_PurchaseDate.HasValue AndAlso _
            value.HasValue AndAlso _
            _PurchaseDate.Value <> value.Value) Then
            Dim propertyName As String = "PurchaseDate"

            Me.DataStateChanged(EntityStateEnum.Modified)
            _PurchaseDate = value
        End If
    End Set
End Property
```

The `Quantity` property is implemented as follows:

```
Private _Quantity As Integer
''' <summary>
''' Gets or sets the quantity purchased
''' </summary>
Public Property Quantity() As Integer
    Get
```

```
            Return _Quantity
        End Get
        Private Set(ByVal value As Integer)
            If _Quantity <> value Then
                Dim propertyName As String = "Quantity"

                Me.DataStateChanged(EntityStateEnum.Modified)
                _Quantity = value
            End If
        End Set
    End Property
```

The `Create` method creates an instance of the Purchase as follows:

```
Public Shared Function Create(ByVal purchID As Integer) _
            As Purchase
    Dim purch As Purchase

    ' Create a new instance
    purch = New Purchase()

    ' Populate the object
    If purchID = 1 Then
        purch.PurchaseDate = #4/4/2006#
        purch.Quantity = 5
    End If

    If purchID = 2 Then
        purch.PurchaseDate = #4/6/2006#
        purch.Quantity = 12
    End If

    ' Reset the entity's state
    purch.DataStateChanged(EntityStateEnum.Unchanged)

    Return purch
End Function
```

NOTE: The code in the `Create` method that hard-codes the values is temporary until the data can be retrieved from a database, as described in Chapter 8, "Building the Data Access Layer."

Building Along

For the Purchase Tracker sample application:

- Add a **Purchase** class to the business object Class Library project (**PTBO**).
  You can create this class from Solution Explorer, as shown in the preceding chapter, *or* from Class Designer, as detailed earlier in this chapter.
- Set the **Purchase** class to inherit from the base business object class (**PTBOBase**).
  You can define the inheritance in the Code Editor, as shown in the preceding chapter, *or* from Class Designer, as detailed earlier in this chapter.
- Add class documentation using XML comments.
- Add properties to the **Purchase** class for **PurchaseDate** (Nullable(Of Date)), **Quantity** (integer), **ProductID** (integer), and **CustomerID** (integer).
  You can type the code for these properties in the Code Editor, as shown in the preceding chapter, *or* add the properties using Class Designer as shown in this chapter *or* use a property snippet, as shown in this chapter. In any case, be sure to include the code to call DataStateChanged in the PurchaseDate and Quantity properties.
- Add a **PurchaseID** property to the **Purchase** class.
  The PurchaseID property in the Purchase class is implemented like the ProductID in the Product class:

```
Private _PurchaseID As Integer
Public Property PurchaseID() As Integer
    Get
        Return _PurchaseID
    End Get
    Private Set(ByVal value As Integer)
        _PurchaseID = value
    End Set
End Property
```

- Add a **Create** method to the **Purchase** class to create an instance of the Purchase class. Be sure to add the Shared keyword to the declaration.

- In the **Create** method, set default values for at least *two* different purchases, as shown in this section.
  Be sure to also add default values for the **ProductID** and **CustomerID** properties.
- Modify the **Create** method to reset the object's entity state back to Unchanged after it sets the property values.
  This ensures that the entity state tracks the user's changes, not changes made to the properties when they are first populated.
- Add documentation for each property and method using XML comments.
  You can define the comments in the Code Editor, as shown in the preceding chapter, *or* in the Class Details window, as detailed earlier in this chapter.
- Add a **private constructor**, as shown in the preceding chapter, to ensure that all other code must use the Create method to create an instance of the class.

You now have the start of a Purchase class. If desired, build a unit test for this class to test it.

Building the Detail Collection Class

A **collection class** is a class that manages a set of objects. You can create your collection class in a number of ways, but using one of the built-in generic collection classes provides the greatest benefit.

A **generic** collection class is a collection that allows only items of a specific type to be added to the collection. There are a number of built-in generic collection classes. Using one of the built-in generic collection classes provides a generalized list that is type-safe and that supports adding only items of a particular type.

If you want your collection to be bound to user interface elements (which is demonstrated in the next chapter), use the System.ComponentModel.BindingList generic collection class. This makes the collection easy to work with in code and easy to bind to user interface elements such as grids.

NOTE: You can use other generic collections, such as List and Dictionary, without inheriting from a .NET Framework class. See the "Additional Reading" section for more information on using generics.

To create a detail collection class:

1. Add a class to the business object Class Library project in Solution Explorer.
2. Inherit from the `BindingList` generic collection class. The `Inherits` statement is as follows:

```
Public Class PurchaseList
    Inherits ComponentModel.BindingList(Of Purchase)
```

3. Define appropriate properties and methods for the class.

Because `BindingList` is a generic collection, it has the standard `(Of T)` syntax, where `T` is the specific data type that you want it to accept. In this example, the `BindingList` accepts only objects created from the `Purchase` class. This ensures that only `Purchase` objects are added to this collection.

If you want to follow the Factory method design pattern introduced in the preceding chapter, add a `Create` method to the detail collection class. In the `Create` method, create appropriate objects, and add them to the collection.

For the `PurchaseList` example, the `Create` method looks like this:

```
Public Shared Function Create(ByVal custID As Integer) As _
    PurchaseList
    Dim purchList As PurchaseList

    ' Create a new instance
    purchList = New PurchaseList

    ' Populate the object
    If custID = 1 Then
        purchList.Add(Purchase.Create(1))
        purchList.Add(Purchase.Create(2))
    End If

    Return purchList
End Function
```

NOTE: The code in the `Create` method that hard-codes the values is temporary until the data can be retrieved from a database, as described in Chapter 8.

Following the Factory method pattern, the `Create` method is shared. This method takes the customer ID as a parameter. This allows the collection class to collect the set of purchases just for this customer.

The code in the method creates an instance of the `PurchaseList` class. It then uses the `Add` method to add two purchases to the collection. The `Add` method calls the `Create` method of the detail item (`Purchase` in this case) to create each `Purchase` object before adding it to the collection. It returns the populated collection.

Building Along

For the Purchase Tracker sample application:

- Add a class project item to the business object Class Library project (**PTBO**).

  You can create this class from Solution Explorer, as shown in the preceding chapter, or from Class Designer, as detailed earlier in this chapter.

  Name the class **PurchaseList**.

- Set the **PurchaseList** class to inherit from the built-in **BindingList** generic collection.

- Add class documentation using XML comments.

- Add a **Create** method to the **PurchaseList** class to create an instance of the `PurchaseList` class. Be sure to add the `Shared` keyword to the declaration.

- In the **Create** method, add at least *two* purchases to the `PurchaseList` collection, as shown in this section.

- Add documentation for the **Create** method using XML comments.

  You can define the comments in the Code Editor, as shown in the preceding chapter, or in the Class Details window, as detailed earlier in this chapter.

- Add a **private constructor**, as shown in the preceding chapter, to ensure that all other code must use the `Create` method to create an instance of the class.

You now have the start of a `PurchaseList` class. If desired, build a unit test for this class to test it.

Establishing the Relationship

Now that the master and detail classes are created, it is time to establish the master/detail relationship. The relationship is established by defining a property in the master class that manages the detail collection class.

For example, the master class (`Customer`) contains a property to manage the detail collection class (`PurchaseList`) as follows:

```
Private _CustomerPurchases As PurchaseList
Public Property CustomerPurchases() As PurchaseList
    Get
        Return _CustomerPurchases
    End Get
    Private Set(ByVal value As PurchaseList)
        _CustomerPurchases = value
    End Set
End Property
```

When an object is created from the master class, code in the master class can assign this property to the appropriate detail collection class as follows:

```
cust.CustomerPurchases = PurchaseList.Create(custID)
```

In this example, each customer now *has a* list of purchases associated with it.

Building Along

For the Purchase Tracker sample application:
- Open the **Customer** class in the Code Editor.
- Add a **CustomerPurchases** property, as defined in this section.
- Modify the **Create** method to assign the **CustomerPurchases** property, as defined in this section.
- If you have not done so already, add the `Purchase` and `PurchaseList` classes to the class diagram (**MainEntitiesDiagram**).

The resulting class diagram is shown in Figure 6.16.

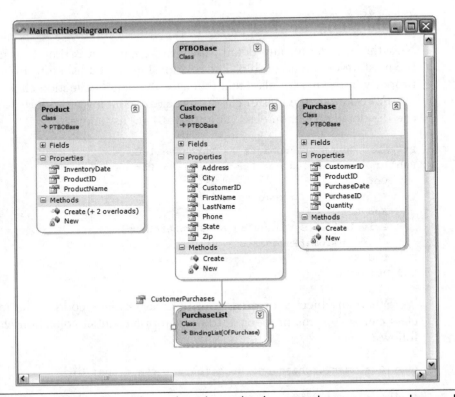

Figure 6.16 Class Designer shows the relationship between the `Customer` class and the `PurchaseList` class. It also depicts the relationship between the base business object class and the derived classes.

> **NOTE:** If you do not see the relationship between the `Customer` class and the `PurchaseList` class in your diagram, right-click the `CustomerPurchases` property in the `Customer` class, and select **Show as Association** from the context menu.

At this point, you have built your business object classes. Your user interface layer can now use them to get and retrieve data associated with the business objects. The details of this process are described in the next chapter.

Conclusion

What Did This Chapter Cover?

This chapter described some of the tools and advanced techniques that are available in Visual Studio and Visual Basic for working with classes. It provided information on working with Class Designer, inserting and creating code snippets, writing unit tests, defining master/detail object relationships, and using generic collections.

This chapter covered several real productivity enhancers:

- Using Class Designer can improve your productivity if you prefer a visual model for creating your classes, properties, and methods.
- Using snippets can provide a huge time savings, both in minimizing typing for common tasks and in negating the need to look up syntax for less frequently used tasks.
- Using the unit testing tools in Visual Studio Team System (or a tool such as NUnit with other editions of Visual Studio) helps ensure that you deliver high-quality code and don't need to spend as much time fixing bugs, because you will have found and fixed the majority of them during your unit testing.
- Implementing lists of objects using generics significantly minimizes the amount of code you need to manage the list.

The next chapter details how the user interface can use the business objects by implementing object binding.

Building Along

If you are "building along" with the Purchase Tracker sample application, this chapter added classes to your business object component. It optionally added a unit test project to your solution for unit testing of your business object class's properties and methods.

Since the user interface from the preceding chapter does not yet reference any information in the business object component, running the application provides the same results as at the end of the preceding chapter. However, if you created the unit test project, you can now test your business objects.

The next chapter binds the user interface of the Purchase Tracker sample application to the business object classes.

Additional Reading

Beck, Kent. *Test Driven Development: By Example*. Addison-Wesley, November 2002.

This book emphasizes patterns and refactorings and presents detailed information on using test-driven development techniques.

David, Jean-Luc, Tony Loton, Erik Gunvaldson, Christopher Bowen, and Noah Coad. *Professional Visual Studio 2005 Team System*. Wrox, May 2006.

This is a good starting point for learning Visual Studio Team System.

Kurata, Deborah. *Everyday Use of Generics*. CoDe magazine, March/April 2007.

This article provides details on what generics are and why they are an important tool to use every day. It includes information on using the generic List, SortedList, and Dictionary. It also details how to build generic classes and generic methods.

Kurata, Deborah. *Having Fun with Code Snippets*. CoDe magazine, January/February 2006.

Using code snippets can make it quick to add common code pieces to your application. Creating your own snippets allows you to create a library of custom code pieces and share them with other developers. This article provides details on using snippets and creating your own snippets in both VB and C#.

Try It!

Here are a few suggestions for trying some of the techniques presented in this chapter:

1. Add a property to the `SalesRep` class using Class Designer.
2. Try executing the `Create` methods in the `SalesRep` class using Object Test Bench.
3. Create a code snippet for defining a property, and include the extra code needed to call the `DataStateChanged` method.
   Use the XML Code Editor or the Snippet Editor. If desired, use the existing property code snippet as a starting point. Be sure to try out your snippet.
4. Add unit tests for each of the properties and methods in the `SalesRep` class.
   Use Visual Studio Team System if you have it; otherwise, try out NUnit. Run the unit tests to test all the code.
5. Build a `CustomerList` class, and define a master/detail relationship between your `SalesRep` class and the `CustomerList` class.
   The `CustomerList` class provides the set of customers for a `SalesRep`.

CHAPTER 7

BINDING THE USER INTERFACE TO THE BUSINESS OBJECTS

One Ring to rule them all,
One Ring to find them,
One Ring to bring them all and in the darkness bind *them.*
—J. R. R. Tolkien, "The Fellowship of the Ring"

Binding seems a little ominous. Haven't we been told since Visual Basic 2.0 that we should never use binding? It incorporated patterns that were not extensible, it did not use good programming practices, and it frequently didn't work as expected. But object binding—oh my precious yes—object binding is another thing entirely.

This chapter provides object binding fundamentals, including connect-the-dots binding and building user interfaces from business objects. It then provides details on enhancing your object binding to support validation. The Purchase Tracker sample application is used to demonstrate these techniques. Once you see all the things that object binding can do for you, you may be captivated by it as well.

What Does This Chapter Cover?

This chapter demonstrates the following techniques:

- Configuring a data source for object binding
- Using connect-the-dots binding
- Building a form from a business object
- Binding to a generic collection
- Binding to a DataTable
- Defining business/validation rules in properties
- Using the `ErrorProvider` control

- Building a `Validation` class
- Implementing `IDataErrorInfo`

Object binding is great fun. You can accomplish much with object binding by simply creating properties in your business object classes and then using Visual Studio to build forms from those business object classes. But to get the most from object binding, you also need to incorporate validation and display of data entry errors to the user. This chapter covers all these techniques.

NOTE: All the information on object binding in this chapter is for Windows forms only. Object binding for the Web is significantly different and is not covered in this book.

Understanding Object Binding

Before going through the details of how to use object binding, it is important to understand exactly what it is—and what it is not. Object binding is binding your business object properties to user interface elements. Object binding is not database binding in the strict sense of the term. It does not directly collect or bind any data from your database.

When you are using business object classes *without* object binding, the flow of data from the database to your user interface and back again requires these steps:

1. The business object calls the data access component to get the data from the database and sets the business object properties using that data.
   For example, the `Product` class calls the data access component, which uses a query or stored procedure to fill a DataTable from the Product table. The data access component returns the DataTable to the `Product` class, which assigns each field from the table to a property of the object. To illustrate, the line of code required to get the ProductName field from the DataTable and set the `ProductName` property is as follows:

   ```
   myProduct.ProductName = dt.Rows(0).Item("ProductName")
   ```

2. The user interface component accesses the business object properties to fill the values of the controls on the form.

   For example, each control on the ProductWin form is assigned to the value of the appropriate `Product` business object property. To illustrate, the line of code required to set the `Text` property of the Name `TextBox` control to the `ProductName` property of the `Product` business object is as follows:

   ```
   NameTextBox.Text = myProduct.ProductName
   ```

3. After the user makes any changes, the user interface component assigns the current values in the controls back to the business object properties.

   For example, the value in each control on the ProductWin form is assigned back to its associated `Product` business object property. To illustrate, the line of code required to set the `ProductName` property to the current value in the Name `TextBox` control is as follows:

   ```
   myProduct.ProductName = NameTextBox.Text
   ```

4. The business object component updates the DataTable using the property values and passes it back to the data access component, which updates the database with the changed data.

   For example, the value of each `Product` business object property is assigned to the associated field in the DataTable, and the result is passed to the data access component, which updates the Product table. To illustrate, the line of code required to set the ProductName field in the DataTable to the value of the `ProductName` business object property is as follows:

   ```
   dt.Rows(0).Item("ProductName") = myProduct.ProductName
   ```

Using object binding allows you to skip steps 2 and 3. Object binding automatically populates the controls on the user interface from the business object properties. As the users change the contents of the controls, object binding updates the associated business object properties, keeping them in synchronization.

That still leaves steps 1 and 4 for you. Chapter 8, "Building the Data Access Layer," provides information on building a data access component to handle steps 1 and 4. For now, this chapter hard-codes data in the business objects to use for trying out the binding.

In summary, object binding is the process of binding control properties directly to properties of your business objects. For example, you could bind the `Text` property of a `TextBox` control to the `ProductName` property of a `Product` business object. When the form is displayed, the runtime automatically displays the value of the `ProductName` property in the `TextBox`. And if the user changes the text in the `TextBox` control, the runtime modifies the `ProductName` property accordingly. This saves you from writing the code required to transfer data back and forth between the controls on the user interface and the business object properties.

Visual Studio provides design-time tools for working with your business objects as data sources for your user interface, making it easy to bind each control to its associated business object property. The only requirement for your business objects to work with these tools is that the business object class needs at least one public property. No specific constructors, interfaces, or attributes are needed.

Object Binding Versus Data Binding

Don't confuse the term *object binding* with the more generalized term *data binding*. Data binding is the broad term for binding control properties to data from any data source. Object binding is just one type of data binding. Some common types of data binding are as follows:

- Binding to tables in a database (Visual Studio generates code to define a typed DataSet and TableAdapters)
- Binding to stored procedures in a database (Visual Studio generates code to define a typed DataSet and TableAdapters)
- Binding to a business object (object binding does not generate code; it just sets control properties)
- Binding to an array or collection of data
- Binding to a Web service

When binding to a database, Visual Studio generates a significant amount of code and then binds the user interface to that generated code. Object binding binds to *your* code. That gives you much more control and greatly simplifies the maintenance of your application.

Using Object Binding

You use object binding by following these steps:

1. Build the business objects for your application.
2. Define a business object data source in the Windows Application project containing your user interface.
3. Bind properties of the controls on the form to business object properties.

Step 1 was covered in detail in the prior two chapters. This chapter demonstrates steps 2 and 3. Step 3 can be done by writing code or by using the visual tools provided in Visual Studio.

Although it is much easier to think about object binding as a direct binding of a control's property to a specific business object's property, object binding frequently uses a `BindingSource` component as an intermediary. A **BindingSource** is a component on a form that binds the controls on the form to the business object. Each control is bound to the `BindingSource` component, which in turn is bound to the business object. This makes it much easier to change the binding for all controls by changing the `BindingSource` without having to separately rebind each control.

You set the `BindingSource` to an individual business object instance in your code. The runtime then binds all the properties associated with that instance to the controls, thereby displaying the business object property values in the controls. And as the user changes the content of any controls, the business object property values are changed accordingly.

A form can contain multiple `BindingSource` components. For example, a ProductWin form can contain product data and display a drop-down list of product types. You can define a `BindingSource` component for the product data and a second `BindingSource` component for the product type data.

The next sections present a detailed example.

Configuring a Data Source

In Visual Studio, a **data source** defines the source of data, such as a business object or a database. To use a data source to bind your user interface, you need to configure the data source for the project containing your user interface, such as your Windows Application project.

For object binding, each data source represents a single business object class. This means that you configure a data source for each business object class that you want to bind. Luckily, this process is quick and easy.

When you use object binding, the data source is referred to as an **object data source**. This is technically accurate because at runtime, the binding binds to a specific business object. However, this can look a little confusing at design-time because each data source represents a single business object class. The Data Sources window displays each object data source with the class name and lists the public properties of the class. You then bind each property of the class to a control on the form.

This section describes how to create and configure a data source.

Creating a Data Source

Assuming that you have already created your business object classes, the first step in binding your user interface to your business objects is to define data sources for your business object classes.

To set up an object data source for your user interface:

1. Build your business object **Class Library** project.
   Only compiled business object classes are recognized by the Data Source Configuration Wizard and the Data Sources window.
2. Select the **Windows Application** project in Solution Explorer.

NOTE: Always ensure that the Windows Application project is selected in Solution Explorer before you work with the Data Sources window.

---

3. Select **Data | Show Data Sources** from the main menu bar.
   The Data Sources window is displayed.
4. Click the **Add New Data Source** link in the Data Sources window, *or* click the **Add New Data Source** button on the Data Sources window toolbar, *or* select **Data | Add New Data Source** from the main menu bar.

NOTE: The Add New Data Source link only appears when the Data Sources window is empty.

This launches the Data Source Configuration Wizard. The first page, shown in Figure 7.1, allows you to select the source of the data.

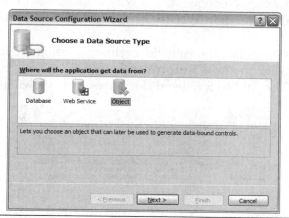

Figure 7.1   The Data Source Configuration Wizard helps you define data sources for your project.

5. Select **Object** for object binding, and click **Next**.
   The second page of the Data Source Configuration Wizard, shown in Figure 7.2, provides the list of classes for your selection.

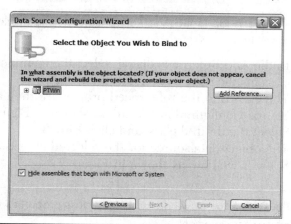

Figure 7.2   Only the classes that are in the current project or referenced by the current project are displayed.

6. Use the tree view to navigate to the class you wish to use for object binding.

   The tree view only lists the classes in the Windows Application project and classes in any component referenced by the Windows Application project.

   If you already have a reference to your business object Class Library component, the component appears in the Data Source Configuration Wizard, as shown later in Figure 7.4, and you can skip to step 9.

   Otherwise, you can add a reference using the following steps.

7. Click the **Add Reference** button.

   The Add Reference dialog appears, as shown in Figure 7.3.

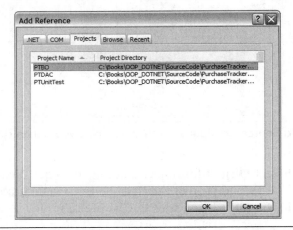

Figure 7.3   Select the Projects tab in the Add Reference dialog to display all the other projects in the current solution.

8. In the Add Reference dialog, select the component containing the class for the data source, and click **OK**.

   The classes in the referenced project are then added to the Data Source Configuration Wizard, as shown in Figure 7.4.

9. Select the desired class, and click **Finish**.

   The object data source for the selected class is added to the Data Sources window, as shown in Figure 7.5.

NOTE: The Data Sources window lists only class properties that are defined with a `Property` statement.

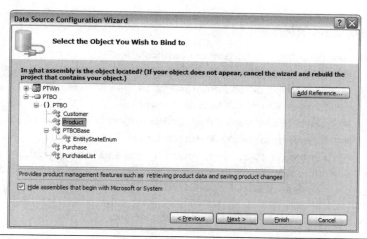

Figure 7.4 Select the desired business object class for the data source. Notice that the documentation that you defined for your class is provided below the tree view in this dialog.

Figure 7.5 The Data Sources window lists each data source available for binding. For object data sources, it lists the class name along with all its public properties.

Use the Data Source Configuration Wizard to define a data source for every business object class you plan to use for binding.

If you are curious about where the Data Sources window stores its information, it is in a set of XML files. Select the Windows Application project in Solution Explorer, and click the **Show All Files** button on the Solution Explorer toolbar. All the system files for the project are then accessible from Solution Explorer. Open the **My Project** node under the Windows Application project, and open the **DataSources** node under the **My Project** node to see the XML files for the data sources in the Data Sources window.

Creating data sources is quick and easy. Add a data source to the Windows Application project for any business object class that you want to use for binding to your user interface.

Building Along

For the Purchase Tracker sample application:

- Build the business object Class Library project (**PTBO**).
  Performing a build ensures that all the business object classes are available to the Data Sources window.
- Select the Windows Application project (**PTWin**) in Solution Explorer.
- Create an object data source for the **Product** class.
- Create an object data source for the **Customer** class.

Both data sources appear in the Data Sources window, along with all their public properties.

Adding Properties to a Data Source

The only absolute in software development is that things change. Over time, you may need to add or remove business object properties. The Data Sources window is smart about code changes. It automatically reflects any changes you make to your business object classes.

For example, the ProductWin form shown in Figure 7.6 has several elements that are not in the Data Sources window for the `Product` class. The `Product` class is missing product number, description, price, product type, and carried in stock/special order. The first three of these are basic properties that are added as described in this section. The last two are special cases that are discussed later in this chapter.

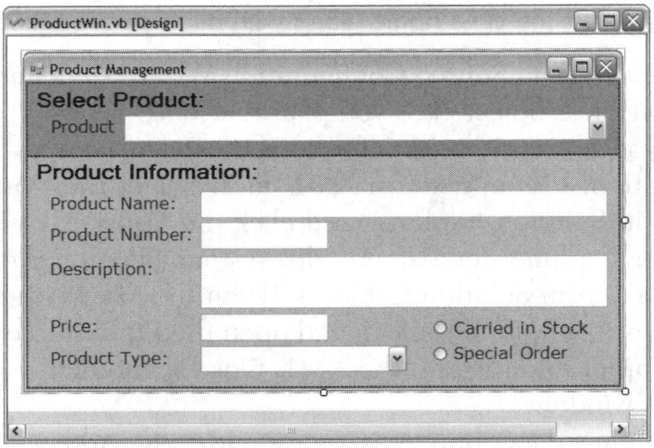

Figure 7.6   To bind a control on a form to a business object property, the business object class must have the associated property. Add properties to your business object class as needed.

To add a property to a data source:

1. Add the desired property to the business object class.
   You can create a property quickly using a code snippet, as shown in Chapter 6, "Class Tools and Techniques." Be sure to include all the code required to call `DataStateChanged`, as demonstrated in Chapter 5, "Building the Business Logic Layer."
   For example, the `Property` statement and associated backing variable for a `Description` property are as follows:

```
Private _Description As String
Public Property Description() As String
  Get
    Return _Description
  End Get
  Set(ByVal value As String)
    If _Description <> value Then
      Dim propertyName As String = "Description"
      Me.DataStateChanged(EntityStateEnum.Modified)
      _Description = value
    End If
  End Set
End Property
```

2. Build the business object Class Library project.

NOTE: Any time you add, remove, or change a property in the business object class, you *must* successfully rebuild the business object Class Library project before the change is reflected in the Data Sources window.

That's it. If the build completes successfully, all property changes are reflected in the Data Sources window.

NOTE: Ensure that the Windows Application project is selected in Solution Explorer before viewing or working with the Data Sources window.

Removing a property is even easier. Just delete the property from the class and rebuild the business object Class Library project. The Data Sources window then automatically removes the property from the data source.

Building Along

For the Purchase Tracker sample application:

- In the **Product** class, add **ProductNumber** (string), **Description** (string), and **Price** (decimal) properties.

  You can type the code for these properties in the Code Editor, *or* add the properties using Class Designer, *or* use the Define a Property code snippet. In any case, be sure to include the code to call `DataStateChanged`.

- Open the **Product** class in the Code Editor and add code to the **Create** method to define hard-coded values for these new properties. For example:

```
' Populate the object
If prodID = 1 Then
    prod.ProductID = 1
    prod.ProductName = "Mithril Coat"
    prod.InventoryDate = #4/1/2006#
    prod.ProductNumber = "LOTR-001"
    prod.Price = 3999999.99D
    prod.Description = "Beautiful silver coat made " _
        & "from Mithril. Great for today's corporate " _
        & "battles."
End If
```

- Build the business object Class Library project (**PTBO**).

The new properties appear in the Data Sources window.

Hiding Properties from a Data Source

There may be times that you want to hide business object properties so that they don't appear in the Data Sources window and are not available for binding. For example, you may have system management properties that your application needs but you don't want your user interface to display. Or maybe you added properties that are not yet completed and should be temporarily hidden from the Data Sources window.

You could just ignore these properties in the Data Sources window, but it is better to hide them. Hiding them ensures that you don't forget to ignore them. It also helps on projects with multiple developers, because the other developers can be confident that if the property is available in the Data Sources window, it can be bound to a user interface control.

If you use the techniques described later in this chapter to build an entire form from a business object class in the Data Sources window, Visual Studio creates a control for every business object property listed in the Data Sources window. Hiding extraneous properties prevents Visual Studio from creating unnecessary controls.

To hide business object properties from the Data Sources window:

1. Add the `BrowsableAttribute` to the property in the business object class, passing a parameter value of `false`.
   For example, the `InventoryDate` is not yet ready to appear in the user interface. You can prevent it from being displayed in the Data Sources window by setting the attribute as follows:

   ```
   <System.ComponentModel.BrowsableAttribute(False)> _
   Public Property InventoryDate() As Nullable(Of Date)
   ```

   See Chapter 5 for more information on attributes.
2. Build the business object Class Library project.

The `InventoryDate` property no longer appears in the Data Sources window.

Building Along

For the Purchase Tracker sample application:
- Open the **Product** class in the Code Editor.
- Modify the **InventoryDate** property so that it is hidden from the Data Sources window as detailed in this section.
- Build the business object Class Library project (**PTBO**).
The `InventoryDate` no longer appears in the Data Sources window.

The Data Sources window defines all the sources of data for the user interface. When using object binding, add a data source for every business object class that you plan to use for binding. And don't forget to rebuild your business object Class Library project after every property change to ensure that the changes are reflected in the Data Sources window.

Binding to Existing Controls

Once you have at least one data source set up in your Data Sources window, you can bind it to your user interface. The technique you use to set up the binding is slightly different, depending on whether you are working with existing controls or creating new controls. This section describes the former, and the next section details the latter.

The process of binding existing controls on a form to a data source is referred to as **connect-the-dots** binding. It is as easy as connecting point A to point B.

To bind an existing control to a business object property displayed in the Data Sources window:

1. Open the form you want to bind in the Forms Designer.
2. Open the Data Sources window.
   Position the Data Sources window so that you can easily see its contents and the Forms Designer at the same time.
3. Drag the desired property from the Data Sources window, and drop it *on* the appropriate control on the form to bind them.

Repeat this process for every control on the form that needs to be bound to the business object.

The first time you drop a property from an object data source to a form, Visual Studio adds a `BindingSource` component to the form's component tray and names it based on the name of your business object class. This component manages the binding between the form controls and the business object properties.

The default property of the control that you used as your drop target is bound to the `BindingSource` component for the property that was dragged from the Data Sources window. You can see this by using the Properties window to examine the control's `DataBindings` property.

For example, drag the `ProductName` property from the `Product` object data source in the Data Sources window and drop it on the Product Name `TextBox` control. This binds the `Text` property of the `TextBox` control to the `ProductName` property of the `Product` class by way of the `ProductBindingSource`. The result is shown in Figure 7.7.

7. BINDING THE USER INTERFACE TO THE BUSINESS OBJECTS

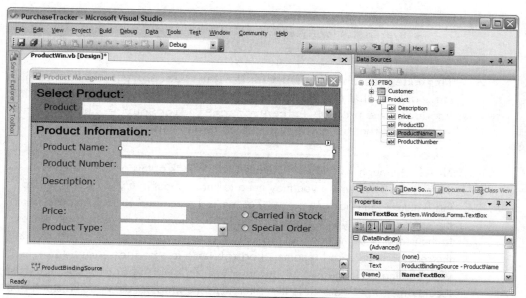

Figure 7.7 As shown in the Properties window, the `Text` property of the `NameTextBox` control is now bound to the `ProductName` property by way of the `ProductBindingSource`.

The binding information for the `BindingSource` component and for each bound control is retained in the form's partial class. When you perform the binding, Visual Studio sets the appropriate control properties.

NOTE: Viewing a form's partial class is detailed in Chapter 4, "Building the User Interface Layer."

The code Visual Studio adds to the partial class for the `BindingSource` component is as follows:

```
Me.ProductBindingSource.DataSource = GetType(PTBO.Product)
```

This defines that the `ProductBindingSource` is associated with the `Product` class in the PTBO project.

Visual Studio adds code to the partial class for each bound control as follows:

```
Me.NameTextBox.DataBindings.Add( _
    New System.Windows.Forms.Binding("Text", _
    Me.ProductBindingSource, "ProductName", True))
```

This code adds a binding entry for the `NameTextBox` control. The binding entry defines that the `Text` property of the `NameTextBox` is bound to the `ProductName` property in the `ProductBindingSource`. The last parameter defines that formatting is enabled to allow formatting of the value.

NOTE: Although you do not normally need to look at this generated code, there is one case where you may need to know about it. If you use the renaming feature (right-click any property or method name and select **Rename** from the context menu), you will see that the Rename renames only direct references to the property or method, not any occurrences in quoted strings. So if you use the rename feature and rename `ProductName` to `ProductShortName`, your binding no longer works, because it is still using `ProductName`. You must locate any partial class code that references the property as a quoted string and manually change its name.

Before you can successfully run the application, you need to write some code. So far, you have defined that the `BindingSource` component binds to a business object. And you have defined which properties of the business object are to appear in which control of the form. However, you did not define *which* business object it binds to.

To define which instance of the business object to bind to, assign the `DataSource` property of the `BindingSource` component to a business object instance as follows:

```
Dim myProduct = New Product
Me.ProductBindingSource.DataSource = myProduct
```

This example binds the controls in the user interface to a new instance of the `Product` class.

If you used the Factory method pattern to create your business objects as described in Chapter 5, you need to write only one line of code:

```
Me.ProductBindingSource.DataSource = Product.Create(1)
```

This code binds the controls in the user interface to the product with a product ID of 1.

In either case, you place this binding code in the form. The specific location in the form depends on when you want the binding to occur. If you want the binding to occur when the form is loaded, add this code to the form's `Load` event.

For example, assume that the preceding line of code is added to a form's `Load` event. When the form is loaded, the runtime calls the `Create` method of the `Product` class to create an instance of the class for a product with an ID of 1. By setting that instance as the `DataSource` for the `ProductBindingSource`, the runtime uses the properties associated with that instance to populate any controls on the form bound to the `ProductBindingSource`. So by writing only one line of code, when you run your application, your form appears populated with appropriate data.

If the user changes a value in a control on the form, the runtime assigns the revised value to the associated property.

NOTE: The business object property is assigned to the value from the control when the user leaves the control. By default, if the user modifies a value and then closes the form before leaving the control, the bound property is not changed. However, if you add code to call `Me.Validate`, as described in Chapter 8, the current control's value is assigned to its associated property even if the user does not leave the control.

Building Along

For the Purchase Tracker sample application:
- Open the **ProductWin** form in the Forms Designer.
- Open the **Data Sources** window.
- Bind the **Product Name**, **Product Number**, **Description**, and **Price** `TextBox` controls to their associated **Product** class properties by dragging the appropriate property from the Data Sources window and dropping it on the control.
- Remove any current code in the form's **Load** event.
  Any code inserted into this event in prior "Building Along" activities is no longer needed with object binding.
- Add the one line of code to the form's **Load** event that assigns the **DataSource** property of the **BindingSource** to the instance of the business object returned from the `Create` method as shown in this section.

Run the application. It displays your splash screen and then shows the MDI parent form. Select **Products | Manage Products** to display the ProductWin form. If you bound each of the controls as defined and you had set initial values for each property in the `Create` method for the `Product` class, the form is populated and looks similar to Figure 7.8.

You can change the value in any of the controls. However, this chapter does not provide the code to actually save the property values, so each time you run the application, the properties are returned to the hard-coded values you set in the `Create` method. (Data is retrieved from a database and saved back to the database in Chapter 8.)

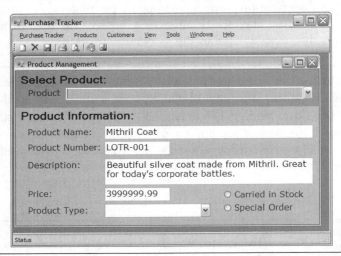

Figure 7.8   When you add one line of code, your form now displays the values of the bound properties.

Using object binding to bind data to a form is easy (and actually fun) to do. Just set up your data source, drag and drop from the data source to the controls, and add one line of code.

Binding to New Controls

Now for the really fun part. In addition to binding to existing controls, as described in the preceding section, you can use the features of the Data Sources window to add new controls to a form. Or you can use it to automatically create controls for all of the business object properties.

Adding New Controls Using the Data Sources Window

If you want to add a new control to a form, you can add the control from the Forms Designer toolbox, add the associated `Label` control, and then bind the new control using the techniques from the preceding section. But the Data Sources window provides a shortcut for this process. If you drag a property from the Data Sources window and drop it on the Forms Designer, Visual Studio creates the control, binds it, and creates the associated `Label` control. All you need to do is drag and drop!

To add a new control to a form:

1. Open the form in the Forms Designer.
2. Open the Data Sources window.
   Position the Data Sources window so that you can easily see its contents and the Forms Designer at the same time.
   If a Forms Designer window is active, the Data Sources window changes so that each object data source and each property under the object data source displays an icon to the left of the name, as shown in Figure 7.7. This icon indicates the type of control that Visual Studio creates if you drag the item to the Forms Designer.
3. Drag a property from the Data Sources window, and drop it on the Forms Designer.

Visual Studio automatically creates the control associated with the dropped property and binds it. It even gives the control a valid name using the property name and the control type, such as `ProductIDTextBox`—no lame `TextBox1` name. In addition, Visual Studio creates an appropriate `Label` control. Visual Studio is smart about generating the text for the `Label` control. It breaks the property name into separate words based on either alphabetic casing or underscores.

For example, if you drag the `ProductID` property from the Data Sources window and drop it in the ProductWin form, Visual Studio creates a `TextBox` control for the `ProductID` and an appropriate `Label` control.

But what if you don't want the property to render as a `TextBox` control? You can change the type of control that is rendered using the Data Sources window.

To change the default control type associated with a property:

1. Ensure that a Forms Designer is active.
2. Open the Data Sources window.

3. Click a property in the Data Sources window.
   The property item changes to a drop-down control list.
4. Drop down the control list and select the desired control type.
   Select Customize from the list to select a control type that is not on the list.

You can select just about any type of control, including third-party and custom controls.

NOTE: Before a third-party control can be added as a control type in the Data Sources window, it must first be added to the Forms Designer toolbox.

When you drag the control from the Data Sources window to the Forms Designer, Visual Studio renders the type of control you selected as the default control type for the property. The property retains its default control type in the Data Sources window.

Creating a Form from the Data Sources Window

But wait—there's more! You can use the Data Sources window to create all the controls for a business object and bind them.

To create a new bound form:

1. Add a project item to the Windows Application project using the **Inherited Form** template, and inherit from your base form class.
   This process was detailed in Chapter 4. (If you don't have a base form class, use the normal **Windows Form** template.)
   An empty form appears in the Forms Designer.
2. Open the Data Sources window.
   Position the Data Sources window so that you can easily see its contents and the Forms Designer window at the same time.
3. In the Data Sources window, click the object data source you want to bind to this form.
   The item changes to a drop-down control list.
4. Use the drop-down control list to define how Visual Studio renders controls on the form for this object data source.

The object data source can be rendered as Details, DataGridView, or None, or you can select Customize from the control list to select a control type that is not on the list.

For a data entry form, set the control type for the object data source to **Details**. Visual Studio renders individual controls for each property in the object data source, along with associated `Label` controls.

Select **DataGridView** to render the properties in the object data source as columns in a grid.

5. Drag the object data source node from the Data Sources window and drop it on the form.

NOTE: If you plan to use `Panel` or other container controls on the form, as in Figure 7.8, place the `Panel` controls or other containers on the form first, and then drag the object data source node and drop it on the desired container.

Bang! Visual Studio automatically creates the controls as you specified and binds them. If you selected Details rendering, Visual Studio creates a control based on the default control type for each object data source property in the Data Sources window. It sets each control's `Name` property based on the name of the associated business object property and control type. Visual Studio also defines an appropriate `Label` control for each control it creates. If you selected DataGridView rendering, Visual Studio defines a grid with appropriate columns and column header text.

For example, if you set up the `Customer` object data source to render as Details and then drag the `Customer` node from the Data Sources window and drop it on a form, Visual Studio creates a `TextBox` control for every property, binds it, names it, and creates a `Label` control, as shown in Figure 7.9.

Notice that this process created two components in the form's component tray. The `BindingSource` is the component that manages the binding. The `BindingNavigator` added VCR-style controls to the top of the form. This type of user interface is not recommended for most business applications. (How often does a user want to sequentially navigate through every customer, for example?) You can delete the `BindingNavigator` component, and Visual Studio automatically deletes the VCR-style controls.

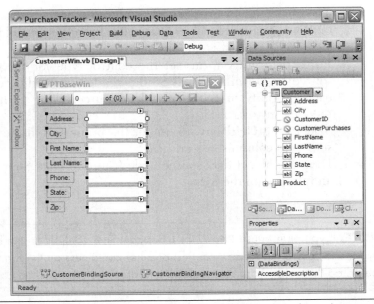

Figure 7.9   You can drag and drop an object data source node from the Data Sources window to generate all the controls on a form.

The labels created for the controls are generated based on the property names. Visual Studio is smart enough to add spaces between words based on underscores or alphabetic casing. This provides a great starting point for your user interface.

The controls are added in alphabetical order, which may not be the most logical order or placement for your users. You can move and size the controls as desired. After you have the controls in their desired order, use the Tab Order view, as described in Chapter 4, to reset the tab order.

All you need then is that one line of code in the form's `Load` event to define the instance of the business object that is bound to the controls:

```
Me.CustomerBindingSource.DataSource = Customer.Create(1)
```

When you run the application, the runtime automatically populates the controls on the form as shown in Figure 7.10. Notice that the form also supports the `Enter` and `Leave` event feature because it inherited from the base form class.

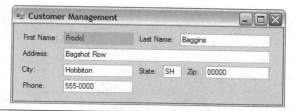

Figure 7.10 With a little rearranging, the form is complete and automatically displays the data associated with the defined business object.

The Data Sources window allows you to create all the controls on a form and bind them to a business object with one drag-and-drop operation and one line of code. It has the flexibility to allow you to define the type of control to render for each property in the object data source.

Using these techniques can make quick work of building and maintaining your user interface.

Building Along

For the Purchase Tracker sample application:

- Add a form project item to the Windows Application project (**PTWin**) using the **Inherited Form** template, and inherit from your base form class (**PTBaseWin**).
  Name the form **CustomerWin**.
- In the Data Sources window, select the **Customer** node and use the drop-down control list to select **Details** as the type of control to render.

NOTE: If your Data Sources window appears empty, ensure that the Windows Application project (PTWin) is the active project in Solution Explorer.

- In the Data Sources window, select the **CustomerPurchases** property and use the drop-down control list to select **None** as the type of control to render.
  The `CustomerPurchases` property is not rendered on the CustomerWin form.

7. BINDING THE USER INTERFACE TO THE BUSINESS OBJECTS

- In the Data Sources window, select the **CustomerID** property and use the drop-down control list to select **None** as the type of control to render.
  Normally, you don't show IDs to the user.
  Alternatively, you could set the `BrowsableAttribute` for the `CustomerID` property in the `Customer` class and rebuild the business object Class Library project to hide the `CustomerID` property from the Data Sources window.
- If you want to use the same conceptual user interface style for your CustomerWin form as with the ProductWin form, add two `Panel` controls to the **CustomerWin** form and set their `Dock` properties as you did with the ProductWin form in Chapter 4.
- Drag the **Customer** node from the Data Sources window to the **CustomerWin** form to create the controls on the form.
  The CustomerWin form appears similar to Figure 7.9.
  If you added `Panel` controls, drop the `Customer` node in the bottom panel to add the controls to that panel.
- Remove the **BindingNavigator** component from the form.
- Update the arrangement, caption, and tab order of the controls so that the form appears similar to Figure 7.10.
  If you added `Panel` controls, the bottom panel appears similar to Figure 7.10, and the top panel is empty at this point.
- Add the one line of code to the form's **Load** event that assigns the **DataSource** property of the **BindingSource** to the instance of the business object returned from the `Create` method.
- Open the MDI parent form (**PTMDIParentWin**) in the Code Editor.
- In the MDI parent form (**PTMDIParentWin**), create the **Click** event handler for the **Manage Customers** option on the **Customers** menu, and add code to display the **CustomerWin** form, as described in Chapter 4.

Run the application. It displays your splash screen and then shows the MDI parent form. Select **Customers | Manage Customers** to display the CustomerWin form. If you built the form using binding as defined, and you had set initial values for each property in the `Create` method for the `Customer` class, the form is populated similar to Figure 7.10.

Notice that as you tab through the form, the background color of each control changes. This demonstrates the benefit of inheritance. By simply inheriting from the base form class, you have the code to handle the `Enter` and `Leave` events on this form.

Binding to Radio Buttons

Some controls require special handling for them to bind correctly. Radio buttons are an example, because they basically require that one property map to multiple controls, which is not possible. So to bind to radio buttons, you need a property for the set of radio buttons *and* a property for each radio button.

Normally, there is only one stored value for a set of radio buttons. This value is managed using the business object property defined for the set of radio buttons. For example, the set of stock type radio buttons, shown in Figure 7.8, is stored as a stock type value of S for Carried in Stock and O for Special Order. This value is managed with a StockType property.

However, the radio buttons don't understand the StockType values. Radio buttons can only be on (true) or off (false). So the business object must also have Boolean properties for each radio button. This example has two radio buttons so needs two Boolean properties: CarryInStock and OrderOnly.

Code in the StockType property maps the stock type values to the appropriate Boolean property values using code similar to the following:

```
Public Property StockType() As String
    Get
        Dim returnValue As String = String.Empty
        If CarryInStock = True Then
            returnValue = "S"
        ElseIf OrderOnly = True Then
            returnValue = "O"
        End If
        Return returnValue
    End Get
    Set(ByVal value As String)
        ' Also assign the appropriate Boolean
        Select Case value
            Case "S"
                CarryInStock = True
            Case "O"
                OrderOnly = True
        End Select
    End Set
End Property
```

When code in the application gets the `StockType` property, the code checks the Boolean properties. It returns an `S` if the `CarryInStock` property is `True` or `O` if the `OrderOnly` property is `True`. When code sets this property, the property sets the appropriate Boolean property to `True`.

To bind to a radio button:

1. Add a property to the business object class for each radio button. You can create these properties quickly using a code snippet, as shown in Chapter 6. Be sure to include all the code required to call `DataStateChanged`, as demonstrated in Chapter 5.

   For example, for a set of stock type radio buttons, add properties to the `Product` class for `CarryInStock`, `OrderOnly`, and any other desired stock type.

2. Add code to the `Property` statement for each property to reset the related properties when this property is set.

   Radio buttons work in a set so that when one radio button is turned on, the others are turned off. The same is true of the associated properties. When one is set on, the others need to be set off. For example:

   ```
   If CarryInStock = True Then
       OrderOnly = False
       ' Set every other stock type to False here
   End If
   ```

3. Add a property in the business object class for the set of radio buttons, and add code similar to that shown in this section.

   You can create a property quickly using a code snippet, as shown in Chapter 6. This property does *not* need to call the `DataStateChanged` method.

   For example, a `StockType` property in the `Product` class handles the set of stock type radio buttons.

4. Build the business object Class Library project.

   This ensures that all changes made to the business object class appear in the Data Sources window.

5. If the radio buttons are already on the form, bind each radio button to its associated property by dragging the property from the Data Sources window and dropping it on the `RadioButton` control.

6. If the radio buttons are not already on the form, select each associated property in the Data Sources window and use the drop-down control list to select RadioButton as the type of control to render.

Then drag each property from the Data Sources window and drop it on the form.

By default, a Boolean property renders as a `CheckBox` control. To instead render as a `RadioButton` control, drop down the control list for each Boolean property, and select RadioButton from the list.

This example demonstrates the use of two radio buttons in a set. Use the same steps to define any number of radio buttons in a set. Define a property for each of the radio buttons. Add code to the property for each radio button to turn off all the other radio buttons. Add code to the property for the set of radio buttons to turn on the appropriate radio button based on the property value.

Binding to radio buttons is a bit more work, but it's possible using the techniques described in this section.

Building Along

For the Purchase Tracker sample application:

- Open the **Product** class in the Code Editor.
- Add **CarryInStock**, **OrderOnly**, and **StockType** properties.
- Add code in the `Property` statement for the **CarryInStock** and **OrderOnly** properties to turn off the other property when the property is set.

For example, the code for `CarryInStock` is as follows:

```
Public Property CarryInStock() As Boolean
    Get
        Return _CarryInStock
    End Get
    Set(ByVal value As Boolean)
        If _CarryInStock <> value Then
            Dim propertyName As String = "CarryInStock"
            Me.DataStateChanged(EntityStateEnum.Modified)
            _CarryInStock = value

            ' If this is true,
            ' set the other choice(s) to false
            If CarryInStock = True Then
                OrderOnly = False
            End If
```

```
     End If
   End Set
End Property
```

The code for `OrderOnly` is similar.

- Add code in the `Property` statement for the **StockType** property to set the other two properties based on the property value using the code shown in this section.
- Add code to the **Create** method in the **Product** class to define a hard-coded value for the **StockType** property. There are only two valid values, O or S. Set it to O.
- Build the business object Class Library project (**PTBO**).
- Bind the **CarryInStock** and **OrderOnly** properties to the appropriate **RadioButton** controls already on the **ProductWin** form.

Run the application. It displays your splash screen and then shows the MDI parent form. Select **Products | Manage Products** to display the ProductWin form. The Special Order radio button value is set. If you click the Carried in Stock radio button, the Special Order radio button is turned off.

Binding to Grids

Sometimes the user wants to work with a list of objects. You can display this list using a grid. Grids are most helpful to the user when working with a relatively small list. It is much more useful and manageable to view a grid containing a dozen or so entries instead of a grid with hundreds of thousands of entries.

To minimize the number of entries in a grid, a common technique is to perform data filtering. The grid then displays the filtered list of information. This allows the user to focus on the specific items that are most beneficial to achieve a particular objective.

For example, your application might track hundreds of thousands of purchases (or more). One customer, however, has a more reasonable number of purchases. Because the application's goal is to track purchases for a particular customer, this filtering makes sense to assist the users in achieving their goals.

Binding to a Grid

The steps required to bind a grid to a business object are basically the same as with any other control. However, the business object class itself is a little more complex, because the grid binds to a list of objects, not a single object.

A grid contains multiple objects, so the object data source that you bind to the grid needs to provide multiple objects. This is most commonly done with a collection class, as described in Chapter 6. Chapter 6 defined a detail item class (`Purchase`) that manages a single item and a detail collection class (`PurchaseList`) that manages the list of items.

To bind a collection class to a grid:

1. Create an object data source for the collection class.
   The collection class appears in the Data Sources window, as shown in Figure 7.11. Notice that the properties of the collection class that are listed in the Data Sources window are actually the properties of the objects contained within the collection. For example, the `Purchase` class properties are listed for the `PurchaseList` object data source.

Figure 7.11 An object data source for a collection class provides the properties of the items within the collection.

2. Create a new form for the grid by adding a project item to the Windows Application project using the **Windows Form** template. This process was detailed in Chapter 4.
   Alternatively, you can add the grid to an existing form.
3. In the Data Sources window, click the object data source node for the collection class and use the drop-down control list to select DataGridView as the type of control to render.

4. Drag the object data source node for the collection class from the Data Sources window, and drop it on the form.

NOTE: If you plan to use `Panel` or other container controls on the form, as in Figure 7.8, place the `Panel` controls or other containers on the form first, and then drag the object data source node and drop it on the desired container.

Visual Studio adds a grid to the form, with a column for every property listed under the object data source node in the Data Sources window.

5. Add the line of code that defines the collection class instance that is bound to the `BindingSource`.

To perform the binding when the form opened, add code like this to the form's `Load` event:

```
Me.PurchaseListBindingSource.DataSource = _
                        PurchaseList.Create(1)
```

This line of code calls the `Create` method of the `PurchaseList` class to create an instance of the `PurchaseList`. If you look at this `Create` method code shown in Chapter 6, you will see that it in turn creates an instance of the `Purchase` class for every purchase and adds it to the collection. Because the list is filtered to the purchases for the customer with a `CustomerID` of 1, a reasonable number of `Purchase` instances are created. The resulting instances are displayed in the grid.

You can edit the resulting form as desired. For example, you can remove the `BindingNavigator` component and move and size the grid. If you want the grid to fill the entire contents of the form and resize as the form is resized, click the grid and select the smart tag. Then select **Dock in Parent container**.

NOTE: If you later add properties to the class, they appear in the Data Sources window, but they are not automatically added to your grid. You must add them manually, as defined later in this section.

When you run the application, the runtime populates the grid with the values from the collection class, similar to Figure 7.12.

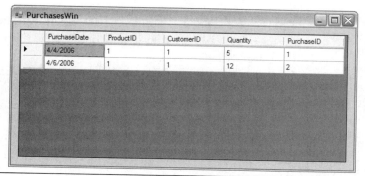

Figure 7.12 Visual Studio automatically generates the grid with appropriate columns from the object data source.

Notice that the form does not yet provide a facility for the user to define a customer filter. Currently, it hard-codes the filter to obtain only purchases for a `CustomerID` of 1. The filter feature is added later in this chapter.

Use the techniques described in this section any time you want to display a list of business object data in a grid.

Building Along

For the Purchase Tracker sample application:

- Add a form project item to the Windows Application project (**PTWin**) using the **Windows Form** template.
  Name the form **PurchasesWin**.
  This form is not a data entry form and therefore does *not* need to inherit from your base form class.

- If you want to use the same conceptual user interface style for your PurchasesWin form as with the ProductWin form, add two `Panel` controls to the **PurchasesWin** form, and set their `Dock` properties as you did with the ProductWin form in Chapter 4.

- Since the **Customer** object data source already has a **CustomerPurchases** property in the Data Sources window to manage the list of purchases for a customer (as detailed at the end of Chapter 6), you don't need to create an object data source for the `PurchaseList` class.
  You can use the existing `CustomerPurchases` property for the data source, or you can create a `PurchaseList` object data source, as described in this section.

- In the Data Sources window, click the **CustomerPurchases** property (or `PurchaseList` object data source) and use the drop-down control list to select **DataGridView**.
- Drag the **CustomerPurchases** property from the Data Sources window to the **PurchasesWin** form to create the bound grid.

  If you added `Panel` controls, drop the `CustomerPurchases` property in the bottom panel to add the grid to that panel.

  If you created a `PurchaseList` object data source, you can use it instead. Drag it to the form instead of the `CustomerPurchases` property.
- Remove the **BindingNavigator** component from the form.
- If you added `Panel` controls to the form, use the smart tag to set the **Dock in Parent container** property; otherwise, don't set this property.
- Add the one line of code to the form's **Load** event that assigns the **DataSource** property of the **BindingSource**. The exact code depends on the data source you used.

  If you used the `CustomerPurchases` property, the line of code is as follows:

  ```
  Me.CustomerPurchasesBindingSource.DataSource = _
                    Customer.Create(1).CustomerPurchases
  ```

  This code fills the grid with the purchases defined for the customer with a `CustomerID` of 1.

  If you used the `PurchaseList` object data source, the line of code is as follows:

  ```
  Me.PurchaseListBindingSource.DataSource = _
                    PurchaseList.Create(1)
  ```

  This code fills the grid with the purchases defined for the customer with a `CustomerID` of 1.
- In the MDI parent form (**PTMDIParentWin**), create the **Click** event handler for the **View Purchases** option on the **Purchase Tracker** menu, and add code to display the **PurchasesWin** form, as described in Chapter 4.

Run the application. It displays your splash screen and then shows the MDI parent form. Select **Purchase Tracker | View Purchases** to display the PurchasesWin form. Your hard-coded data appears as shown in Figure 7.12.

Specifying a Read-Only Grid

If you look closely at Figure 7.12, you may notice that that space is added to the bottom of the grid for entry of a new purchase. By default, grids created using the Data Sources window are editable. In some cases this is desired, but in other cases you may want a read-only grid.

To specify a read-only grid:

1. Select the grid in the Forms Designer.
2. Click the grid's smart tag.
3. Uncheck **Enable Adding**, **Enable Editing**, and **Enable Deleting** on the smart tag menu.

The grid is then read-only.

You can use this technique to allow the user to make some changes, but not all types of changes. For example, you could uncheck **Enable Deleting** but check **Enable Adding** and **Enable Editing** or any other combination.

Building Along

For the Purchase Tracker sample application:

- Open the **PurchasesWin** form in the Forms Designer.
- Modify the grid properties so it is read-only.

Run the application. It displays your splash screen and then shows the MDI parent form. Select **Purchase Tracker | View Purchases** to display the PurchasesWin form. The grid no longer provides space for adding new entries nor does it allow editing or deleting.

Modifying Grid Columns

The grid shown in Figure 7.12 includes ProductID and CustomerID columns. The CustomerID is not needed because the list is already filtered for a particular customer. The ProductID would be more useful as a product name (see the next section). It is important to tailor the grid to the data that the user needs to work with.

To add, remove, or edit columns in the grid:

1. Select the grid in the Forms Designer.
2. Click the grid's smart tag.
3. Select **Edit Columns** from the smart tag menu to add, remove, or reorder columns, or set other column properties, such as the column's width.

The grid's smart tags make it easy to add, remove, or edit columns in the grid. Alternatively, you can modify grid attributes and styles in code. Create a method in the form's class for setting the grid attributes, and call that method from the form's `Load` event.

Building Along

For the Purchase Tracker sample application:
- Open the **PurchasesWin** form in the Forms Designer.
- Remove the **CustomerID** and **ProductID** columns from the grid.
- Edit the titles of the other columns to display separate words instead of the concatenated titles. Set the column widths as needed.

Run the application. It displays your splash screen and then shows the MDI parent form. Select **Purchase Tracker** | **View Purchases** to display the PurchasesWin form. Review your changes to the grid.

Displaying Related Object Properties

In most applications, the users don't care about IDs; they are interested in logical key information. For example, the `Purchase` class includes a `ProductID` property that identifies the product associated with this purchase. Instead of displaying the ProductID to the user, it is often more useful to display the product name.

Because these related object properties are not properties of the class, they don't appear in the Data Sources window. So a little more work is involved to include them in the grid.

To display related object properties in a grid:

1. Open the class associated with the object data source for the grid in the Code Editor.

2. Add a property to the class to retain an instance of the related class.

For the purchases example, the `Purchase` class needs a `ProductInstance` property, as follows:

```
Private _ProductInstance As Product
Public Property ProductInstance() As Product
    Get
        Return _ProductInstance
    End Get
    Private Set(ByVal value As Product)
        _ProductInstance = value
    End Set
End Property
```

3. When setting the associated ID property, set the instance property for the specified ID.

For the purchases example, modify the setter in the `ProductID` `Property` statement as follows:

```
Private Set(ByVal value As Integer)
    _ProductID = value
    ProductInstance = Product.Create(ProductID)
End Set
```

When the `ProductID` property in the `Purchase` class is set, this code creates an instance of the related `Product` class. The `Product` class instance then provides access to all the `Product` class properties.

If you build the business object Class Library component at this point, you see the related class properties under the object data source in the Data Sources window. For example, the `Product` class properties are listed under the `PurchaseList` object data source, as shown in Figure 7.13.

NOTE: You can drag and drop these related properties to bind them to controls on the form. However, they cannot be used to bind columns in a grid. The grid requires that all properties be direct properties of the object bound to the grid, not related properties.

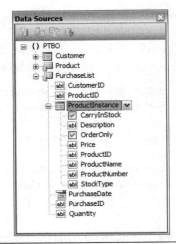

Figure 7.13   When you add a reference to an instance of a related class, that class's properties are also displayed in the Data Sources window.

4. Add a read-only property to the class for each desired property in the related class.

   Only properties directly in the object data source that is bound to the grid can bind to columns in the grid. To bind columns to related properties, you must add a property to the class for each property in the related class that you want to include in the grid. Use the instance of the related class to retrieve the property's value.

   To include a product name column in the grid, for example, define a read-only `ProductName` property in the class as follows:

```
Public ReadOnly Property ProductName() As String
    Get
        Return ProductInstance.ProductName
    End Get
End Property
```

NOTE: This is needed *only* for adding grid columns. If you want to add the associated control to the form and bind it, you do *not* need to perform this step.

5. Build the business object Class Library project.
6. Add a new column to the grid for each desired property using the grid's smart tag.

When you run the application, the related property values appear in the grid.

Using this technique, you can expose properties of related classes to display a more complete set of information in the grid.

Building Along

For the Purchase Tracker sample application:

- Open the **Purchase** class in the Code Editor.
- Add a **ProductInstance** property, as described in this section.
- Modify the **ProductID** property to create the appropriate instance of the **Product** class using code shown in this section.
- Add **ProductName** (string) and **ProductNumber** (string) read-only properties that return the values from the associated instance of the Product class, as shown in this section.
- Build the business object Class Library project (**PTBO**).
- Open the **PurchasesWin** form in the Forms Designer.
- Add columns to the grid for the **ProductName** and **ProductNumber** properties.

NOTE: Don't use **ProductName** as the name of your column. **ProductName** is a built-in property of the Control class that returns the name of the assembly containing the control. (For more information, in the Code Editor for one of your forms, type Me.ProductName and look at the Intellisense.)

To prevent naming conflicts, after adding the column to the grid, rename the column (*not* the property). Click the smart tag for the grid, select **Edit Columns**, and change the **"(Name)"** for the **ProductName** column to **ProductNameColumn**.

Run the application. It displays your splash screen and then shows the MDI parent form. Select **Purchase Tracker | View Purchases** to display the PurchasesWin form. Your new columns appear and are populated. The data in the columns is set based on the hard-coded data in the Create method of your Product class.

Binding to Combo Boxes

Often you need to display lists of choices in your user interface. For example, you may want to display a list of all the products for the user to select the product to edit. Or, you may want to provide a list of product types, states, or payment plans to assist the user with data entry. These lists are often implemented using combo boxes.

For example, the ProductWin form, shown in Figure 7.14, contains two combo boxes. The Product combo box allows the user to select the product to edit. The code uses this selection to programmatically retrieve the desired product. The Product Type combo box assists the user with data entry. Instead of requiring the user to type in an appropriate product type, the types are listed for user selection. The selected value is then stored with the product data.

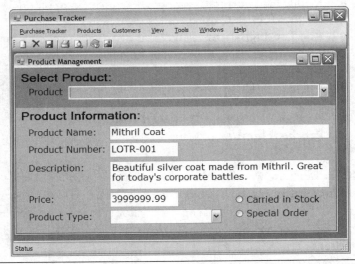

Figure 7.14   Combo boxes are often used on a form to provide the user with a defined set of choices.

The two most common ways to use a combo box in your user interface are:

- **Programmatic.** You define a list of choices and display them in a combo box. When the user makes a selection, you use the selected value in your code to proceed based on the user's choice.

Filtering and item selection are prime examples of programmatic use of a combo box. You present a list of choices and the user selects how to filter the data or which item to display. The application uses that choice to filter or select the data. The Product combo box in the ProductWin form (see Figure 7.14) illustrates programmatic use of a combo box.

■ **Data entry.** You define a list of valid values for data entry and display them in a combo box. When the user makes a selection, the value is retained. When the user selects to save, you store the selection with the form's data.

The Product Type combo box, shown in Figure 7.14, provides the user with data entry assistance by offering a list of valid product types. The user selects the desired type, and that type is retained with the other product data.

Why worry about this difference in combo box usage? Because the details of binding are slightly different, depending on whether you need the combo box for programmatic use or for end-user data entry.

Binding a Combo Box for Data Entry

Combo boxes help users enter valid data into your application by providing a limited list of valid values. Examples include a product type, a state or province code, or a payment type (cash, credit card, and so on). Instead of typing in a value, the users select a value from the list. Then the users don't need to memorize the list of valid values, and you don't need to write code to ensure that their entered value is valid.

When you provide a combo box for data entry, you ultimately assign the user's selection to one of the business object class properties. For example, the user's selection in a Product Type combo box is assigned to a `ProductType` property in the `Product` class.

To bind to a combo box for data entry:

1. Define the data structure for the list of valid values in your code. Because the binding in Visual Studio allows you to bind to many different types of structures, you have many choices. You can use anything from an array to a DataSet to a generic collection, such as a `List`.

2. Define a property for the data entry value in the business object class.

For the Product Type combo box example, the property is `ProductType` in the `Product` class.

If this property did not previously exist, be sure to build the business object Class Library component after you add this property to ensure that the Data Sources window has access to the new property.

3. Set up the binding.

This step involves setting up the combo box for binding and adding the one line of code that associates the data structure defined in step 1 with the `DataSource` property of the `BindingSource`.

When binding to a combo box for data entry, *three* `ComboBox` control properties need to be set:

`DisplayMember` defines the property containing the data you want displayed in the combo box. This is often a name or description. For the Product Type combo box example, this is the logical name of the product type ("Clothing," "Leather goods," and so on).

`ValueMember` defines the property containing the data you want saved when the user makes a selection. This is the value that the business object saves with the other business object data. If you want to save the actual string product type, you set this to the same property as the `DisplayMember`. For more flexibility and changeability, you may want to store a numeric value that is associated with each product type (1, 2, and so on) instead.

`SelectedValue` defines the business object property to which the selected `ValueMember` is assigned. This is the property defined in step 2. For the Product Type combo box example, this is the `ProductType` property.

That's it. The binding takes care of the rest. When the user drops down the combo box, all the data defined by the `DisplayMember` is displayed. When the user selects a value from the combo box, the runtime automatically retrieves the information defined in the `ValueMember` and assigns it to the property defined in the `SelectedValue`.

These steps are discussed in detail in the next sections.

Selecting the Data Structure

The first step to binding a combo box is to select the data structure for storing the list of values for display in the combo box. With the binding features in Visual Studio, you have many different data structures to choose from.

One data structure option is a collection class. Create a class for the item, such as `ProductType`. Create a class to manage the list of items, such as `ProductTypeList`, as described in Chapter 6. Then bind the `BindingSource` for the combo box to an instance of the collection class. The runtime creates an instance of the `ProductType` class for each product type, adds the instance to the collection, and displays the results in the combo box. This is similar to the techniques for binding to a grid described in the previous section.

Another data structure option is a DataTable. A **DataTable** is an ADO.NET structure that contains all the rows for a particular table. It manages the list of all the objects as a set of rows. Populate the DataTable (from a database or in the code), and then bind the `BindingSource` for the combo box to the resulting DataTable.

Either option seems like too much work to do for every kind of list that you want to display on your user interface. Your application may require product types, customer types, purchase types, payment types, states or provinces, credit card types, and so on. If you think about it, most types are basically the same.

Normally, a type consists of two parts: a string to display to the user and a value that is stored with the other business object data. Because most types are very similar, it makes sense to build a general class to support types.

Once you build a class to support types, you can then bind to this class any time types are needed in your application. This section presents two approaches for building a generalized mechanism for supporting types. The first approach uses a collection class. The second approach uses a DataTable.

Building a Collection Class to Support Types

Using a collection class to support types provides an object-centric approach to managing all the types in your application. Each valid item is defined as an individual instance of a class and is added to the collection.

To build a general class to support types using a collection class approach:

1. Add a class to the business object Class Library project.
   This is the generalized class that supports any type.
   Give it a clear name, such as `TypeEntry`.
2. Add two read-only properties: one for the name to display in the combo box and one for the associated value.

Give the properties clear names such as `TypeName` and `TypeValue`. The `TypeName` defines the information displayed in the combo box, and the `TypeValue` defines the value assigned when the user selects the item.

3. Add an `Enum` or some other mechanism for defining the valid kinds of types that the general type class supports (or add code to retrieve them from a table).

```
Public Enum TypeEnum
    ProductType = 1
    CustomerType = 2
    States = 3
End Enum
```

4. Add a `Create` method that creates an instance of the `TypeEntry` class.
   See Chapter 6 for an example of defining a `Create` method for a detail item class.

5. Add another class to the business object Class Library project, and make it a collection class by inheriting from `BindingList(Of TypeEntry)`.
   This is the generalized class that supports any list of types.
   Give it a clear name, such as `TypeList`.
   See Chapter 6 for more information on inheriting from `BindingList`.

6. Add a `Create` method that creates an instance of the `TypeList` class for a specific kind of type:

```
Public Shared Function Create(ByVal TypeID As TypeEnum) _
                                        As TypeList
```

   See Chapter 6 for a detailed example of defining a `Create` method for a detail collection class.

7. Build the business object Class Library project.

The resulting collection class is then ready to be used for binding.

Building a Class That Uses a DataTable to Support Types

Using a DataTable to support types provides a data-centric approach to managing all the types in your application. Each valid type is defined as a row in the DataTable. Using a DataTable can provide better performance when there are large numbers of valid types, because it does not require creating individual objects for each type.

To build a general class to support types using a DataTable approach:

1. Add a class to the business object Class Library project.
   This is the generalized class that supports any list of types.
   Give it a clear name, such as `TypeList`.

NOTE: This approach needs only one class—the class that provides the list. It does not need a detail item and a detail collection class, as in the prior approach.

NOTE: This class is given the same name as the detail collection class in the prior example because it performs the same function even though it performs the function very differently. If you want to write code for both the collection class approach and this data-centric approach, use a different class name here.

---

2. Add two read-only properties: one for the name to display in the combo box and one for the associated value.
   Give the properties clear names, such as `TypeName` and `TypeValue`. The `TypeName` defines the information displayed in the combo box, and the `TypeValue` defines the value assigned when the user selects the item.

NOTE: These property names must exactly match the names of the fields in the DataTable. If the name in the underlying database does not match, use aliases when building the DataTable to change the name to the property name.

Because the data comes from the DataTable, the properties don't need to return any values. The properties are defined only for use in the Data Sources window.

```
Public ReadOnly Property TypeName() As String
    Get
        Return String.Empty
    End Get
End Property
```

```
Public ReadOnly Property TypeValue() As Object
    Get
        Return Nothing
    End Get
End Property
```

3. Add an `Enum` or some other mechanism for defining the valid kinds of types that the general type class supports (or add code to retrieve them from a table):

```
Public Enum TypeEnum
    ProductType = 1
    CustomerType = 2
    States = 3
End Enum
```

4. Add a `Create` method that returns a `DataTable` object for a specific kind of type:

```
Public Shared Function Create(ByVal TypeID As TypeEnum) _
                                        As DataTable
```

NOTE: You need to import the `System.Data` namespace to access the `DataTable` class without using the namespace qualifier (`System.Data.DataTable`). See Chapter 3, "Building Projects," for more information on importing namespaces.

---

5. Build the business object Class Library project.

The resulting class is then ready to be used for binding.

Building Along

For the Purchase Tracker sample application, the DataTable approach is used as follows.

NOTE: You can use the collection class approach instead if desired. You then need to follow the steps in the preceding section, not the following steps.

- Add a class project item to the business object Class Library project (**PTBO**).
  Name the class **TypeList**.
- Add **TypeName** and **TypeValue** read-only properties to the class, as defined in this section.
- Define an `Enum` in the class to hold the kinds of types managed by this class.
- Define a **Create** method in the class that returns a `DataTable` object.

Because the sample application does not yet have a data access component to fill the DataTable, temporarily create the `DataTable` object in the `Create` method, as follows:

```
Public Shared Function Create( _
    ByVal TypeID As TypeEnum) As DataTable
    Dim dt As New DataTable

    ' Add the columns
    dt.Columns.Add(New DataColumn("TypeName"))
    dt.Columns.Add(New DataColumn("TypeValue"))

    ' Add the rows
    Select Case TypeID
        Case TypeEnum.CustomerType
            dt.Rows.Add("Corporate", 1)
            dt.Rows.Add("Education", 2)

        Case TypeEnum.ProductType
            dt.Rows.Add("Clothing", 1)
            dt.Rows.Add("Weapons", 2)
            dt.Rows.Add("Leather goods", 3)
    End Select

    Return dt
End Function
```

NOTE: Added `DataColumn` objects are strings unless you specify otherwise.

> ■   Build the business object Class Library project (**PTBO**).
> At this point, you have not yet defined the binding to the ComboBox control, so there are no new features to try out.

Defining a Property in the Business Object Class

When you work with combo boxes defined for data entry, the purpose of the list of types is to provide a set of choices for a specific business object property. Before you can complete the binding, you need to define that business object property.

For example, for a Product Type combo box, the selected product type must be retained with all the other `Product` object properties. This requires that you create a `ProductType` property in the `Product` class and that you bind that property to the user-selected value from the combo box.

To define a property in the business object class for the combo box selection:

1. Add a property in the business object class.
   Use the same style of `Property` statement used for the other properties in the business object classes.
   For example, a `ProductType` property is defined as follows:

```
Private _ProductType As Integer
Public Property ProductType() As Integer
  Get
    Return _ProductType
  End Get
  Set(ByVal value As Integer)
    If _ProductType <> value Then
      Dim propertyName As String = "ProductType"
      Me.DataStateChanged(EntityStateEnum.Modified)
      _ProductType = value
    End If
  End Set
End Property
```

2. Build the business object Class Library project.
   This ensures that the new property appears in the Data Sources window.

Building Along

For the Purchase Tracker sample application:

- Open the **Product** class in the Code Editor.
- Add the **ProductType** property, as described in this section.
- Modify the **Create** method of the **Product** class to set an initial value for the property using a valid value, as defined in the `TypeList` class.
- Build the business object Class Library project (**PTBO**).

At this point, you have not yet defined the binding to the ComboBox control, so there are no new features to try out.

Setting Up the Binding

You now have the list of valid values to display in the combo box, using either a collection class or a DataTable. You also have a business object property to assign the value that the user selected from the list. The last step is to set up the binding.

To set up the binding for a data entry combo box:

1. Create an object data source for the class that manages the list of valid types.

    If you are using a collection class, this is the collection class. If you are using a DataTable, this is the class defined to manage the DataTable. In either case, the name of the class was defined as `TypeList`.

    The result is shown in Figure 7.15.

Figure 7.15   The generalized type class appears in the Data Sources window.

2. Drag the **TypeList** node from the Data Sources window and drop it on the `ComboBox` control.

   If you're creating a new combo box, use the drop-down control list for the `TypeList` node in the Data Sources window, and select ComboBox as the control to render. (If ComboBox is not available as a selection, use the Customize option to add it.) Then drag the node and drop it on the form.

NOTE: If you define a specific control type for an object data source and then drag that object data source onto a form, Visual Studio does not create a label. It only creates labels when you drag properties or use the Details option.

Visual Studio adds another `BindingSource` component to the form. This `BindingSource` is the source of the data for the combo box. Because it is generalized for any type, you can use it as the source of data for any data entry combo box.

3. Use the smart tag on the `ComboBox` control to change the `ValueMember` property to `TypeValue`.

   Visual Studio automatically sets the `DisplayMember` and `ValueMember` properties of the `ComboBox` control to the `TypeName` property.

4. Drag the associated business object property from the Data Sources window and drop it on the `ComboBox` control. This is the business object property that will store the user's selection.

   Visual Studio automatically sets the `SelectedValue` property of the `ComboBox` control to the business object property.

   This process is referred to as **double binding** because you first bind the object data source providing the list of choices and then bind the property of the business object that stores the user-selected value.

5. Use the smart tag on the `ComboBox` control to confirm that the binding properties are as follows:

   DisplayMember is assigned to the property of the `TypeList` class that defines the information to display to the user. For the Product Type combo box example, this is the `TypeName` property.

ValueMember is assigned to the property of the `TypeList` class that defines the value to save. For the Product Type combo box example, this is the `TypeValue` property.

SelectedValue is assigned to the business object property used to retain the user-selected value. For the Product Type combo box example, this is the `ProductType` property from the `ProductBindingSource`.

6. Add the line of code that sets the `BindingSource`.

If the combo box is bound when the form is opened, add code like this to the form's `Load` event:

```
Me.TypeListBindingSource.DataSource = _
     TypeList.Create(TypeList.TypeEnum.ProductType)
```

This line of code calls the `Create` method of the `TypeList` class to create the `DataTable` object and assigns the resulting `DataTable` object as the data source. If you used a collection class, call the `Create` method of the collection class instead.

When you run the application, the runtime automatically populates the combo box with the list of valid values.

If you open the designer-generated partial class for the form and look at the code for the combo box, you will see that it sets the basic binding properties as follows:

```
Me.ProductTypeComboBox.DataSource = Me.TypeListBindingSource
Me.ProductTypeComboBox.DisplayMember = "TypeName"
Me.ProductTypeComboBox.ValueMember = "TypeValue"
```

It defines the second binding by adding it directly to the `DataBindings` collection as follows:

```
Me.ProductTypeComboBox.DataBindings.Add(New _
     System.Windows.Forms.Binding("SelectedValue", _
     Me.ProductBindingSource, "ProductType", True))
```

This code binds the `SelectedValue` property of the `ComboBox` control to the `ProductType` business object property using the `ProductBindingSource`. Notice how this uses the string name of business object property. If you ever change the property's name, this code does not generate an error at compile time, but generates a runtime error.

Building Along

For the Purchase Tracker sample application:

- Select the Windows Application project (**PTWin**) in Solution Explorer.
- Create an object data source for the **TypeList** class.
- Open the **ProductWin** form in the Forms Designer.
- Drag the **TypeList** node from the Data Sources window and drop it on the **Product Type** ComboBox control.
  This provides the list of values to appear in the Product Type combo box.
- Drag the **ProductType** property under the **Product** node in the Data Sources window and drop it on the **Product Type** ComboBox control.
  This performs the double binding.
- Add the one line of code to the form's **Load** event that assigns the **DataSource** property of the **TypeBindingSource** to an instance of the **TypeList** class.

Run the application. It displays your splash screen and then shows the MDI parent form. Select **Products | Manage Products** to display the ProductWin form. The value in the Product Type combo box defaults to the value of the ProductType property you set in the Create method. When you drop down the list, you see the set of valid Product Type values.

If you run the application again, you will see that it does not retain your selected value. It displays the default value you set in the Create method. This is because the Create method hard-codes the default values. This is enhanced in Chapter 8.

By building a generalized type class, you have reusable code for all the types in your application. You can include this class in your framework to reuse it in other applications.

To use the TypeList class, define an object data source for the class. Then drag the TypeList node from the Data Sources window, and drop it on every ComboBox control used for data entry. Finally, create the one line of code, passing the appropriate parameter to select the kind of type that you need. This technique is useful any time you need to display a list of values to the user.

NOTE: Although this section focused on ComboBox controls, these techniques work for any list-based control, such as the ListBox control.

Binding a Combo Box for Programmatic Use

Not all combo boxes are used for data entry. Often you need to give the users a set of choices that are handled programmatically. For example, suppose you want to allow the users to choose how to filter a grid or which item to view or edit. You may want to provide a list of reports they could select, or operations they could perform.

When you provide a combo box for programmatic use, you do not assign the user's selection to a business object property. Instead, you write code to react based on the user's selection.

To bind to a combo box for programmatic use:

1. Define the data structure for the list of valid values in your code. Because the binding in Visual Studio allows you to bind to many different types of structures, you have many choices. You can use anything from an array to a DataSet to a generic collection, such as a `List`.

2. Set up the binding.
   This step involves setting up the combo box for binding and adding the one line of code that associates the data structure defined in step 1 with the `DataSource` property of the `BindingSource`.
   When binding to a combo box for programmatic use, *two* `ComboBox` control properties need to be set:
   `DisplayMember` defines the property containing the data you want displayed in the combo box. This is often a name or description. For the Product combo box example, this is the `ProductName` property to display the product names in the list.
   `ValueMember` defines the property containing the data you need as the value of the combo box selection in your code. For the Product combo box example, you set this to the `ProductID` property so that your code has access to the product's ID.

NOTE: Do *not* set the `SelectedValue` property. If you do, the combo box behaves oddly because it is attempting to retain your selection.

---

3. Add code to the appropriate event to programmatically respond to the user's selection.

You normally use the `SelectedValueChanged` event of the `ComboBox` control for this. When the user selects a new value, your code responds accordingly. In the Product combo box example, the code retrieves a different product for reviewing or editing.

These steps are discussed in detail in the next sections.

Selecting the Data Structure

The first step to binding a combo box is to select the data structure for storing the list of choices for display in the combo box. The data structure you choose depends on where the information for the list resides, the number of list entries, and your personal preferences.

The built-in generic `List` class is a good choice if you are displaying a list of choices that are hard-coded in your application, like a sort order (Ascending, Descending, None) or display options (single document, multiple document, default). Create a generic `List` in your code, add the choices to the `List`, and bind the `ComboBox` control as follows:

```
Dim sortTypeList As New List(Of String)
sortTypeList.Add("Ascending")
sortTypeList.Add("Descending")
sortTypeList.Add("None")

SortTypeComboBox.DataSource = sortTypeList
```

This code binds the combo box directly to the `List` without using the Data Sources window or a `BindingSource`. This straight-forward binding is great when binding to simple lists of choices.

Another data structure option is to use a collection class. Build a business object class that defines a choice, and then build a collection class to manage the set of choices, as described in Chapter 6. The runtime creates an instance of the business object class for every choice in the list. A collection class is a good data structure to use if you have a reasonably sized list of items that are stored in a database or some other source.

A DataTable, like the one used when binding to a data entry combo box, is also a good data structure option. Build a class that contains the property names to be associated with the `ComboBox` control's `DisplayMember` and `ValueMember`. Add the code to populate the DataTable with the list of choices. The runtime then populates the DataTable and displays the set of choices in the list. If you have a large set of choices stored in a database, this option can provide much better performance than a collection class. It is perfect for presenting read-only lists for selection, such as a list of customer or product names, when it is not efficient or necessary to create an instance for each item. And from a work-flow perspective, it is highly likely that the user would edit only a few items at a time, making it wasteful to create potentially hundreds of thousands of individual item instances.

The steps required to build a collection class or to build a class that uses a DataTable are similar to those described in the preceding section. To see the minor differences between building these classes for a generalized data entry type and for programming use, the DataTable method is detailed here. This specific example implements a combo box for display of a list of items. The user selects from the list to define which item to review or edit. The code uses the user's selection to retrieve and display the desired item.

To build a class to manage a list of choices using a DataTable approach:

1. Add a class to the business object Class Library project.
   This is the class that manages the list of choices.
2. Add two read-only properties: one for the name to display in the combo box and one for the associated value.
   Give the properties the same names as the associated field names in the DataTable.

NOTE: These property names must exactly match the names of the fields in the `DataTable`. If the name in the underlying database does not match, use aliases when building the `DataTable` to change the name to the property name.

Because the data comes from the `DataTable`, the properties don't need to return any values. The properties are defined only for use in the Data Sources window.

```
#Region " Public Properties"
    Public ReadOnly Property ProductName() As String
        Get
            Return String.Empty
        End Get
    End Property
```

```
        Public ReadOnly Property ProductID() As Integer
            Get
                Return Nothing
            End Get
        End Property
    #End Region
```

3. Add a `Create` method that returns a `DataTable` object.

NOTE: You need to import the `System.Data` namespace to access the `DataTable` class without using the namespace qualifier (`System.Data.DataTable`). See Chapter 3 for more information on importing namespaces.

---

4. Build the business object Class Library project.

The resulting class is then ready to be used for binding.

Building Along

For the Purchase Tracker sample application, the DataTable approach is used as follows.

NOTE: You can use the collection class approach instead if desired. You then need to follow the steps detailed earlier for building a collection class and not the following steps.

- Add a class project item to the business object Class Library project (**PTBO**).
  Name the class **ProductList**.
- Add **ProductName** and **ProductID** read-only properties to the class, as defined in this section.
- Define a **Create** method in the class that returns a `DataTable` object.
  Because the sample application does not yet have a data access component to fill the `DataTable`, temporarily create the `DataTable` object in the `Create` method as follows:

```
Public Shared Function Create() As DataTable
    Dim dt As New DataTable

    ' Add the columns
    dt.Columns.Add(New DataColumn("ProductName"))
    dt.Columns.Add(New DataColumn("ProductID"))

    ' Add the rows
    dt.Rows.Add("Mithril Coat", 1)
    dt.Rows.Add("Anduril", 2)

    Return dt
End Function
```

In Chapter 8, you replace this code with code that accesses the database.

■ Modify the **Create** method in the **Product** class to add at least one additional set of sample data.

For the hard-coded values to work properly, the ProductID values defined in the Create method of the ProductList class need to have a match in the Create method of the Product class. So, you may want to add more test data in the Product class so that you can test more than one product.

```
If prodID = 2 Then
    prod.ProductID = 2
    prod.ProductName = "Anduril"
    prod.InventoryDate = #4/8/2006#
    prod.ProductNumber = "LOTR-002"
    prod.Price = 499.99D
    prod.Description = "Flame of the West, " _
                     & "sword of the king."
    prod.StockType = "S"
    prod.ProductType = 2
End If
```

■ Build the business object Class Library project (**PTBO**).

At this point, you have not yet defined the binding to the ComboBox control, so there are no new features to try out.

Setting Up the Binding

You now have the list of choices to display in the combo box, using either a collection class or DataTable. The next step is to set up the binding.

To set up the binding for a list of choices displayed in a combo box:

1. Create an object data source for the class that manages the list of choices.

   If you are using a collection class, this is the collection class. If you are using a DataTable, this is the class defined to manage the DataTable.

2. Drag the object data source node from the Data Sources window and drop it on the `ComboBox` control.

   If you're creating a new combo box, use the drop-down control list for the object data source node in the Data Sources window, and select ComboBox as the control to render. (If ComboBox is not available as a selection, use the Customize button to add it.) Then drag the node and drop it on the form.

NOTE: If you define a specific control type for an object data source and then drag that object data source onto a form, Visual Studio does not create a label. It only creates labels when you drag properties or use the Details option.

Visual Studio adds another `BindingSource` component to the form. This `BindingSource` is the source of the data for the combo box.

Visual Studio then automatically sets the `DisplayMember` and `ValueMember` properties of the `ComboBox` control based on the object data source properties.

3. Use the smart tag on the `ComboBox` control to confirm that the binding properties are as follows:

   `DisplayMember` is assigned to the property that defines the information to display to the user. For the Product combo box example, this is the `ProductName` property.

   `ValueMember` is assigned to the property that is used in the code. For the Product combo box example, this is the `ProductID` property.

   `SelectedValue` is set to none.

4. Add the line of code that sets the `BindingSource`.
   If the combo box is bound when the form is opened, add code like this to the form's `Load` event:

```
Me.ProductListBindingSource.DataSource = _
                        ProductList.Create
```

This line of code calls the `Create` method of the `ProductList` class to create the `DataTable` object and assigns the resulting `DataTable` object as the data source. If you used a collection class, call the `Create` method of the collection class instead.

When you run the application, the runtime automatically populates the combo box with the list of valid values. By default, the combo box selects the first entry. If you want the combo box selection to be blank when the form is first loaded, set the `SelectedValue` property of the combo box to a value that is not valid. For example, since 0 is not a valid Product ID, you could set the `SelectedValue` to 0 by adding this line after the binding code line:

```
ProductComboBox.SelectedValue = 0
```

Then, when you run the application, the combo box appears empty. You can then drop down the list to see the choices. However, selecting a choice does not yet do anything. You need code to respond to the selection, as covered in the next section.

Building Along

For the Purchase Tracker sample application:
- Select the Windows Application project (**PTWin**) in Solution Explorer.
- Create an object data source for the **ProductList** class.
- Open the **ProductWin** form in the Forms Designer.
- Drag the **ProductList** node from the Data Sources window and drop it on the **Product** ComboBox control.
- Add the one line of code to the form's **Load** event that assigns the **DataSource** property of the **ProductListBindingSource** to an instance of the **ProductList** class.
- Add the line of code to the form's **Load** event that sets the selected value of the combo box to an invalid value so it appears empty.

Run the application. It displays your splash screen and then shows the MDI parent form. Select **Products** | **Manage Products** to display the ProductWin form. The value in the Product combo box is initially empty. When you drop down the list, you see the set of valid product choices, as defined in the `Create` method of the `ProductList` class.

Responding Programmatically

The last step in binding a combo box for programmatic processing is to write the code to respond to the user's selection. How you respond depends entirely on what you need the selection to do. For example, if the list displays a set of sort options, you respond by performing the selected sort. If the list displays filter criteria to filter a set of data, you respond by filtering the data.

Regardless of what code you write, where you write the code normally is the same: the `SelectedValueChanged` event for the `ComboBox` control. For example:

```
Private Sub ProductComboBox_SelectedValueChanged( _
    ByVal sender As Object, _
    ByVal e As System.EventArgs) _
    Handles ProductComboBox.SelectedValueChanged
     If ProductComboBox.SelectedValue IsNot Nothing Then
         ' Your code here
     End If
End Sub
```

This code checks the `SelectedValue` property of the `ComboBox` control. If that property has a value, the code uses that value to proceed appropriately.

Using the Product combo box from earlier in this section as an example, when the user selects a product from the Product combo box, the code rebinds all the data entry controls on the form to the selected `Product` class instance. Because all the data entry controls are bound to the `BindingSource` on the form, you only need to change the `DataSource` of the `BindingSource`. The runtime then repopulates all the controls with values from the selected product, allowing the user to review or edit that product.

The code in the `SelectedValueChange` event for the Product combo box is as follows:

```
Private Sub ProductComboBox_SelectedValueChanged( _
    ByVal sender As Object, _
    ByVal e As System.EventArgs) _
    Handles ProductComboBox.SelectedValueChanged
      Dim selectedID As Integer
      If ProductComboBox.SelectedValue IsNot Nothing Then
          selectedID = DirectCast(ProductComboBox.SelectedValue, _
                                                            Integer)

          Me.ProductBindingSource.DataSource = _
                              Product.Create(selectedID)
      End If
End Sub
```

If the user selects an entry in the combo box, the runtime sets the
`SelectedValue` to the ProductID for the selected entry and generates
the SelectedValueChanged event. The code in this event converts the
SelectedValue, which is of type `Object`, to an integer. The integer ID
is then passed to the `Create` method in the `Product` class. This creates
an instance of the `Product` class for the product defined with the specified ID. The `DataSource` property of the `ProductBindingSource` is
assigned to this product instance, causing the runtime to display the data
for the product in the bound controls on the form.

Building Along

For the Purchase Tracker sample application:

- Open the **ProductWin** class in the Code Editor.
- Add the code to the **SelectedValueChanged** event, as described in
  this section.
- Delete the code from the form's **Load** event that sets the
  ProductBindingSource, because it is now set in the
  SelectedValueChanged event instead.

Run the application. It displays your splash screen and then shows the
MDI parent form. Select **Products | Manage Products** to display the
ProductWin form. The value in the Product combo box is initially empty.
When you drop down the list, you see the set of valid product choices, as
defined in the `Create` method of the `ProductList` class. If you select a
product, the property values for the selected product fill the form.

This section detailed how to bind to a combo box and then programmatically respond to the users' selection. You can use the techniques presented in this section any time you want to provide a list of choices to the users and then proceed in the code based on their selection. Once you know the basic techniques, you can implement any combo box.

Building Along

For the Purchase Tracker sample application:

- Add a class project item to the business object Class Library project (**PTBO**).
  Name the class **CustomerList**.
  This class provides the list of customers for both the CustomerWin form and the PurchasesWin form.
- Add **CustomerName** and **CustomerID** read-only properties to the class.
- Define a **Create** method in the class that returns a `DataTable` object.
  Because the sample application does not yet have a data access component to fill the `DataTable`, temporarily create the `DataTable` object in the `Create` method as follows:

```
Public Shared Function Create() As DataTable
    Dim dt As New DataTable

    ' Add the columns
    dt.Columns.Add(New DataColumn("CustomerName"))
    dt.Columns.Add(New DataColumn("CustomerID"))

    ' Add the rows
    dt.Rows.Add("Baggins, Frodo", 1)
    dt.Rows.Add("Baggins, Bilbo", 2)

    Return dt
End Function
```

In Chapter 8, you replace this code with code that accesses the database.

- Modify the **Create** method in the **Customer** class to add at least one additional set of sample data.

For the hard-coded values to work properly, the `CustomerID` values defined in the `Create` method of the `CustomerList` class need to have a match in the `Create` method of the `Customer` class. So you may want to add more test data in the `Customer` class so that you can test more than one customer.

```
If custID = 2 Then
    cust.CustomerID = 2
    cust.LastName = "Baggins"
    cust.FirstName = "Bilbo"
    cust.Address = "Bagshot Row"
    cust.City = "Hobbiton"
    cust.State = "SH"    ' The Shire
    cust.Zip = "00000"
    cust.Phone = "555-0001"

    cust.CustomerPurchases = _
        PurchaseList.Create(custID)
End If
```

- Build the business object Class Library project (**PTBO**).
- Select the Windows Application project (**PTWin**) in Solution Explorer.
- Create an object data source for the **CustomerList** class.
- In the Data Sources window, select the **CustomerList** node and use the drop-down control list to select **ComboBox** as the type of control to render.
- Open the **CustomerWin** form in the Forms Designer.
- Drag the **CustomerList** node from the Data Sources window and drop it on the **CustomerWin** form to create the **CustomerList** combo box, and add an appropriate `Label` control.
  If you created panels on the CustomerWin form, drag the `CustomerList` node to the top panel.
  This combo box allows the user to select which customer to view and edit.
- Add code to the form's **Load** event that assigns the **DataSource** property of the **CustomerListBindingSource** to an instance of the **CustomerList** class as follows:

```
Private Sub CustomerWin_Load( _
    ByVal sender As Object, _
    ByVal e As System.EventArgs) Handles MyBase.Load
```

```
        Me.CustomerListBindingSource.DataSource = _
                                    CustomerList.Create
        CustomerListComboBox.SelectedValue = 0
End Sub
```

- Add code to the **SelectedValueChanged** event for the **CustomerList** combo box to respond to the user's selection:

```
Private Sub _
  CustomerListComboBox_SelectedValueChanged( _
  ByVal sender As Object, _
  ByVal e As System.EventArgs) _
  Handles CustomerListComboBox.SelectedValueChanged
    Dim selectedID As Integer
    If CustomerListComboBox.SelectedValue _
                            IsNot Nothing Then
      selectedID = DirectCast( _
          CustomerListComboBox.SelectedValue, Integer)
      Me.CustomerBindingSource.DataSource = _
          Customer.Create(selectedID)
    End If
End Sub
```

- Delete the code from the form's **Load** event that sets the **CustomerBindingSource**, because now it is set in the `SelectedValueChanged` event instead.
- Open the **PurchasesWin** form in the Forms Designer.
- Drag the **CustomerList** node from the Data Sources window and drop it on the **PurchasesWin** form to create the **CustomerList** combo box, and add an appropriate `Label` control.
  If you created panels on the PurchasesWin form, drag the `CustomerList` node to the top panel.
  This combo box allows the user to filter the list of purchases to those for one particular customer.
- Add code to the form's **Load** event that assigns the **DataSource** property of the **CustomerListBindingSource** to an instance of the **CustomerList** class as follows:

```
Private Sub PurchaseWin_Load( _
   ByVal sender As Object, _
   ByVal e As System.EventArgs) Handles MyBase.Load
```

```
        Me.CustomerListBindingSource.DataSource = _
                                CustomerList.Create
        CustomerListComboBox.SelectedValue = 0
End Sub
```

- Add code to the **SelectedValueChanged** event for the **CustomerList** combo box to respond to the user's selection. The exact code depends on the object data source you used.

If you used the `CustomerPurchases` property, the code is as follows:

```
Private _
  Sub CustomerListComboBox_SelectedValueChanged(_
  ByVal sender As Object, _
  ByVal e As System.EventArgs) _
  Handles CustomerListComboBox.SelectedValueChanged
   Dim selectedID As Integer
   If CustomerListComboBox.SelectedValue _
                            IsNot Nothing Then
     selectedID = DirectCast( _
       CustomerListComboBox.SelectedValue, Integer)
     Me.CustomerPurchasesBindingSource.DataSource = _
       Customer.Create(selectedID).CustomerPurchases
   End If
End Sub
```

This code retrieves the selected ID from the combo box and uses it to create the appropriate `Customer` object. It then assigns the `DataSource` property to the `CustomerPurchases` property of that `Customer` object.

If you used the `PurchaseList` object data source, the code is as follows:

```
Private _
  Sub CustomerListComboBox_SelectedValueChanged( _
  ByVal sender As Object, _
  ByVal e As System.EventArgs) _
  Handles CustomerListComboBox.SelectedValueChanged
   Dim selectedID As Integer
   If CustomerListComboBox.SelectedValue _
                     IsNot Nothing Then
```

```
            selectedID = DirectCast( _
                CustomerListComboBox.SelectedValue, Integer)
            Me.PurchaseListBindingSource.DataSource = _
                PurchaseList.Create(selectedID)
        End If
    End Sub
```

This code retrieves the selected ID from the combo box and uses it to create the appropriate `PurchaseList` object. It then assigns the `DataSource` property to this `PurchaseList` object instance.

■ Delete the code from the form's **Load** event that sets the **BindingSource**, because now it is set in the `SelectedValueChanged` event instead.

At this point, you have all the user interface and code in place for the CustomerWin, ProductWin, and PurchasesWin forms. You also have the business object classes for `Customer`, `CustomerList`, `Product`, `ProductList`, `Purchases`, `PurchaseList`, and `TypeList`.

Run the application. It displays your splash screen and then shows the MDI parent form. You can select to view customers, products, and customer purchases. Wow!

Handling User Entry Errors

If the user always did everything right and never did anything wrong, your user interface code would be complete. But presuming perfection from the user is not a viable expectation for your application. Instead, you need to follow defensive coding techniques and assume that the user won't put in valid data.

The best way to implement user-entry validation is to use the built-in object binding features. Just add code to the properties in the business object classes to validate the property values. Then use the `ErrorProvider` control error icon to display any errors to the user. Using object binding, the .NET runtime automatically sets the `ErrorProvider` error icon text based on your validation code.

Displaying an Error

The **ErrorProvider** is a build-in component that you add to your forms to display validation errors to the user. If the user enters invalid data into a control on the form, the `ErrorProvider` component places an error icon next to the control. When the user positions the cursor over the error icon, a ToolTip appears, displaying the error message for the control, as shown in Figure 7.16.

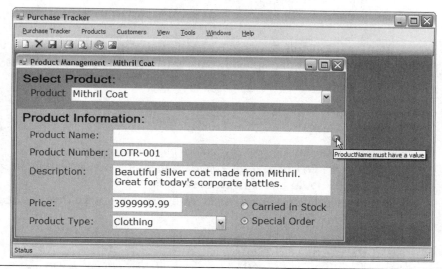

Figure 7.16 When a property is invalid, the `ErrorProvider` displays an error icon with ToolTip text describing the error.

Using the `ErrorProvider` is better than displaying an error in a message box, because once the message box is dismissed, the error message is no longer visible. Plus, a message box interferes with the user's data entry flow. Using the `ErrorProvider`, the user can enter all the data for the form and then look at which controls have an error icon without having the interruption of a message box.

You can implement the `ErrorProvider` functionality manually using methods of the `ErrorProvider` component to position the error icon and identify the error text. But if you are using object binding, the `ErrorProvider` can be set up to work automatically.

To display an error message when using object binding:

1. Open the form in the Forms Designer.
2. Add the **ErrorProvider** control to the form.
   The control appears in the component tray.
3. In the Properties window for the `ErrorProvider`, set the `DataSource` property to the `BindingSource` for the business object associated with the form.
   You may also want to turn off the icon blinking, because many users find it irritating. In the Properties window, set the `BlinkStyle` property of the `ErrorProvider` to `NeverBlink`.

Implementing an `ErrorProvider` control provides a very clean and user-friendly means of displaying data entry errors to the user. And it works well with object binding.

Building Along

For the Purchase Tracker sample application:

- Add the **ErrorProvider** control to each of the data entry forms: **ProductWin** and **CustomerWin**.
- Bind each **ErrorProvider** to the business object **BindingSource** for the form.
  For the **ProductWin** form, bind the **ErrorProvider** to the **ProductBindingSource**.
  For the **CustomerWin** form, bind the **ErrorProvider** to the **CustomerBindingSource**.

The application does not yet provide any validation code, so you won't see an error icon appear yet when you run the application.

Adding Validation to the Properties

It is often tempting to add data entry validation code directly in the forms. But good programming practices dictate that all the business rules for an application are in the business objects, including validation. And with object binding in place, this is easy to do.

As the user leaves a control on the form, the runtime automatically assigns the control's value to the associated property in the business object. Code in the setter for the property is then executed, providing an excellent opportunity to perform real-time validation as the user moves through the form.

Even if the user did not change the value, the setter is executed. This is why you added code to the properties to check if the value was actually changed before assigning the new value.

To validate a property:

1. Define the appropriate validation rules for the property.
2. Add code to the property setter to validate the user-entered value against the defined rules.

Repeat these steps for every property that requires validation.

For example, the following are sample validation rules for the properties in the `Product` class:

- The product name is required.
- The product name has at least 5 characters.
- The product name has at most 24 characters.
- The product number is required.
- The product number has at most 10 characters.
- The description has at most 1,200 characters.
- The price must be numeric.
- The product type must be one of the defined types. (This is already handled by the use of a combo box, which limits the selection to valid values.)

You can implement the first rule by checking for a null or empty value in the `ProductName` property:

```
Set(ByVal value As String)
    If _ProductName <> value Then
        Dim propertyName As String = "ProductName"
        If String.IsNullOrEmpty(value) Then
            Throw New InvalidOperationException("Product Name " _
                                        & "must have a value")
        End If

        Me.DataStateChanged(EntityStateEnum.Modified)
        _ProductName = value
    End If
End Set
```

The Product Name `TextBox` control is bound to the `ProductName` property. So when the user leaves the Product Name `TextBox`, the runtime executes the `ProductName` property setter and if the control is empty this code generates an exception. The runtime catches the exception and automatically displays an error icon, as shown in Figure 7.16.

NOTE: Any unexpected exception generated by any code in any `Property` statement, or code called by any `Property` statement, is also caught by the object binding and displayed in the `ErrorProvider` error icon. For example, if you have a casting error at runtime, it is caught by the object binding code and displayed in the error icon ToolTip. This can mask critical runtime errors.

Because the property setter generates an exception, the user is trapped in the control until the problem is remedied. You can have more control over the validation by implementing the `IDataErrorInfo` interface, as described in the next section.

Implementing Validation

You could implement validation for your application by writing code in every `Property` statement to check each business rule and throw an exception, as demonstrated in the preceding section. However, a more complete, flexible, and reusable solution is to develop a library of validation code that can be used by your properties. And by implementing the `IDataErrorInfo` interface, you can also reuse the code that displays validation errors without having to throw exceptions.

Defining a Validation Class

A `Validation` class is a generalized class that includes any methods needed to validate data for your application. It can perform required value checking, string length checking, numeric checking, date range checking, and so on. It can also maintain a collection of the validation errors instead of throwing exceptions. This allows the user to move through the user interface even if validation errors occur.

If you build multiple applications, consider creating another Class Library project for this common code that can be reused by each of the applications. You can add this new project to your framework. If you are responsible for only one application, you can put the `Validation` class in the business object Class Library project.

The first step of building a `Validation` class is to add a class to the project and give it a clear name, such as `Validation`.

In the `Validation` class, define a collection that stores the list of validation errors. The collection allows only string values, and it must provide a key so that you can easily access all the validation errors for a particular property. The best collection for this purpose is the built-in generic `Dictionary` class.

Define the `Dictionary` using a private property in the `Validation` class as follows:

```
Private _ValidationList As Dictionary(Of String, String)
Private Property ValidationList() As Dictionary(Of String, String)
    Get
        Return _ValidationList
    End Get
    Set(ByVal value As Dictionary(Of String, String))
        _ValidationList = value
    End Set
End Property
```

Notice the generic `Dictionary(Of  String, String)` syntax. This defines that the `Dictionary` key is of type `String` and the value put into the `Dictionary` is of type `String`. This `Dictionary` contains the list of all validation error messages, keyed on the name of the property causing the validation error.

Initialize this collection when an instance of the `Validation` class is created by adding code to the constructor for the `Validation` class as follows:

```
Public Sub New()
    ' Create the list to contain the validation errors
    ValidationList = New Dictionary(Of String, String)
End Sub
```

If the user makes the same error repeatedly, you don't want to keep adding the message to the list of validation errors. You do, however, want to add multiple error messages for the same property if those messages are different. For example, the `ProductName` property could have two validation errors that would appear as "Property Name must have a value; Property Name must be at least 5 characters".

To ensure that validation errors are handled correctly, validation error messages are added to this collection only from within the `Validation` class. So the code to add an error to the collection is defined in a private method as follows:

```
''' <summary>
''' Adds a validation error to the collection
''' </summary>
''' <param name="propertyName">Property with the error</param>
''' <param name="message">Message to be displayed
''' to the user</param>
''' <remarks></remarks>
Private Sub AddValidationError(ByVal propertyName As String, _
    ByVal message As String)
    ' If the property already has a message, add this message
    If ValidationList.ContainsKey(propertyName) Then
        Dim existingMessage As String = _
                            ValidationList(propertyName)
        If existingMessage.Contains(message) Then
            ' Do nothing - this message is already displayed
        Else
            ' Append the new message to the existing message
            ValidationList(propertyName) &= "; " & message
        End If
    Else
        ' Add the message to the validation list
        ValidationList.Add(propertyName, message)
    End If
End Sub
```

This method takes the property name and validation error message as parameters. The method first determines if the defined property has validation messages using the `Dictionary`'s `ContainsKey` method. If not, it adds the message to the collection, using the property name as the key.

If this property has existing validation messages, this code determines whether the new validation message is already in the list. If so, it does nothing. If not, it concatenates the new message onto any existing message(s). This results in a single message for each control that contains a concatenated list of all the control's validation error messages. This single message is then easy to display as a single string in the `ErrorProvider` error icon ToolTip.

Because the `ValidationList` collection is private, you need to provide some public properties and methods in the `Validation` class that the business object class can call to obtain information about the validation errors. One such public property is `Count`:

```
Public ReadOnly Property Count() As Integer
    Get
        Return ValidationList.Count
    End Get
End Property
```

The `Count` property provides the number of entries in the `ValidationList` collection for a particular business object. Given that there can be at most one entry for each property, `Count` basically defines the number of properties of the business object that have validation errors. The `Dictionary` `Count` property provides the value for the `Validation` class `Count` property.

A public read-only `Item` property provides the validation error message for a specific property given the key, which is the property name. The `Item` property code is as follows:

```
''' <summary>
''' Gets the validation errors for the defined property
''' </summary>
''' <param name="propertyName">Name of the property</param>
Public ReadOnly Property Item(ByVal propertyName As String) _
                                                    As String
    Get
        If ValidationList.ContainsKey(propertyName) Then
            Return ValidationList.Item(propertyName)
        Else
            Return Nothing
        End If
    End Get
End Property
```

This code determines whether any validation errors exist for the defined property. If so, it uses the `Item` method of the `Dictionary` to return the validation error string.

Adding a `ToString` method allows the `Validation` class to provide all the validation errors in one string. This could be used to summarize the entire set of validation errors for a business object. The code for the `ToString` method is as follows:

```
''' <summary>
''' Converts the collection of validation errors
''' into a single string
''' </summary>
''' <returns></returns>
''' <remarks></remarks>
Public Overrides Function ToString() As String
    Dim sb As New System.Text.StringBuilder
    For Each s As String In ValidationList.Values
        sb.AppendLine(s)
    Next
    Return sb.ToString
End Function
```

The `Overrides` keyword is required because the `ToString` method is already provided by the `Object` type, which is the base class for all reference types (including your classes). This method uses the `StringBuilder` class, which provides higher-performance string manipulation when appending a large number of strings. Depending on the number of validation rules you have in your business object classes, using the `StringBuilder` class may not be necessary in this method. You could just append all the validation messages into one string using the string append character (`&`).

Now that the collection is in place and ready for validation error messages, you can write a public method in the `Validation` class for each type of validation you need to perform.

For example, the code required to validate a required value is as follows:

```
''' <summary>
''' Checks for a required value in a property
''' </summary>
''' <param name="propertyName">Name of the property</param>
''' <param name="value">Value of the property</param>
''' <returns>True if the property has a value;
```

```
''' false if the property has no value</returns>
''' <remarks></remarks>
Public Function ValidateRequired(ByVal propertyName As String, _
        ByVal value As String) As Boolean
    Dim newMessage As String = String.Empty

    If String.IsNullOrEmpty(value) Then
        newMessage = String.Format("{0} is required, " _
                    "please enter a valid value", propertyName)
        ' Add the message to the validation list
        AddValidationError(propertyName, newMessage)
        Return False
    Else
        Return True
    End If
End Function
```

This function checks the property's value. If it is null or empty, the code adds a validation error and returns `False`. If it has a value, it returns `True`.

NOTE: Consider using a Resource file for each of your message strings, as described in Chapter 4.

Another useful method is one that clears all the errors for a property. When the user fixes the validation issue, you want to ensure that the message no longer appears. The method to clear the errors for a property is as follows:

```
''' <summary>
''' Clears the validation for a property
''' </summary>
''' <param name="propertyName">Name of the property</param>
''' <remarks>Should be called before any other validation
''' is called</remarks>
Public Sub ValidateClear(ByVal propertyName As String)
    ' If the property doesn't have any messages, this is done
    If ValidationList.ContainsKey(propertyName) Then
        ' Otherwise, remove the entry
        ValidationList.Remove(propertyName)
    End If
End Sub
```

This code first checks whether there are any validation errors in the collection for the property. If so, it removes them. If not, it does nothing.

Add other validation methods to the `Validation` class as desired. For example, a method to validate a property's maximum length is as follows:

```
''' <summary>
''' Validates the maximum length of a field
''' </summary>
''' <param name="propertyName">Name of the Property to
''' validate</param>
''' <param name="value">Value of the Property to validate</param>
''' <param name="maxLength">Maximum length</param>
''' <returns></returns>
''' <remarks></remarks>
Public Function ValidateLength(ByVal propertyName As String, _
    ByVal value As String, ByVal maxLength As Integer) As Boolean
    Dim newMessage As String = String.Empty
    If Not String.IsNullOrEmpty(value) AndAlso _
                        value.Length > maxLength Then

        newMessage = String.Format( _
                        "{0} has a maximum size of {1}", _
                        propertyName, maxLength)
        ' Add the message to the validation list
        AddValidationError(propertyName, newMessage)
        Return False
    Else
        Return True
    End If
End Function
```

When you have finished adding any other validation methods to the `Validation` class, it is ready to be used by the business object classes.

By building a generalized `Validation` class, you can encapsulate all the validation processing in one class. You can use this class to perform validation in any business object in your application.

Building Along

For the Purchase Tracker sample application:
- Add a class project item to the business object Class Library project **(PTBO)**.

> Name the class **Validation**.
> - Create the code in the **Validation** class, as defined in this section.
> - Optionally, replace the hard-coded validation error strings in the Validation class methods with resource strings such as the ValidationRequired resource string you created in Chapter 4.
>
> If you run the application at this point, the Validation class does not do anything, because the business objects do not use it yet.

Using the Validation Class

The Validation class can be used by every business object in your application that requires property validation. So you could create an instance of the Validation class in every business object. Alternatively, it would be easier to create the Validation instance in the base business object class. Every business object that inherits from the base business object class then has its own instance of the Validation class.

In the base business object class, define a property for the Validation instance as follows:

```
Private _ValidationInstance As Validation
''' <summary>
''' Gets or sets the validation instance for the business objects
''' </summary>
''' <value>Instance of the Validation class</value>
''' <returns>Instance of the Validation class</returns>
''' <remarks>By using one instance of the Validation class for
''' a business object, all validation errors/rules will be
''' managed as one unit</remarks>
Protected Property ValidationInstance() As Validation
   Get
      Return _ValidationInstance
   End Get
   Private Set(ByVal value As Validation)
      _ValidationInstance = value
   End Set
End Property
```

The instance of the Validation class is protected to ensure that it is used only by the business objects that inherit from this base business object class. The setter is private to ensure that no code outside the base business object class can create the instance. This gives the base business object class better control over the validation.

In the constructor of the base business object class, create the instance of the `Validation` class:

```
Public Sub New()
  ' Create the instance of the validation class
  ValidationInstance = New Validation
End Sub
```

Although it is not absolutely necessary, you can expose a property in the base business object class that defines whether the business object is valid:

```
'''  <summary>
'''  Gets a flag defining whether the business object is valid
'''  </summary>
'''  <value>Flag</value>
'''  <returns>True if it is valid;False if not valid</returns>
'''  <remarks></remarks>
Public ReadOnly Property IsValid() As Boolean
  Get
      Return (ValidationInstance.Count = 0)
  End Get
End Property
```

The application can call this method to easily determine if the business object properties are valid.

You need to make one more change to the base business object class. To display the errors from the `Validation` class in the `ErrorProvider` error icon, you need to implement the `IDataErrorInfo` interface in the class:

```
Public Class PTBOBase
    Implements System.ComponentModel.IDataErrorInfo
```

This interface implements two properties: `Error` and `Item`. Add code to the `Error` property to return a string containing all the errors for a business object:

```
''' <summary>
''' Gets the validation errors in a formatted string
''' </summary>
''' <value></value>
''' <returns></returns>
''' <remarks>This property should not be browsable in the
''' Properties window or Data Sources window</remarks>
<System.ComponentModel.BrowsableAttribute(False)> _
Public ReadOnly Property [Error]() As String _
    Implements System.ComponentModel.IDataErrorInfo.Error
    Get
      Return ValidationInstance.ToString
    End Get
End Property
```

> **NOTE:** The name of this method has square brackets around it because `Error` is a keyword.

This code sets the `BrowsableAttribute` to `False` to ensure that the `Error` property does not appear in the Data Sources window. It is a read-only property, so only has a getter. The code in the getter uses the `ToString` method of the `Validation` class to return the list of all validation errors for the business object.

Add code to the `Item` property to return the validation errors for one specific property as follows:

```
''' <summary>
''' Gets the validation errors for a particular property
''' </summary>
''' <param name="propertyName">Name of the property</param>
''' <value></value>
''' <returns></returns>
''' <remarks>This property should not be browsable in the
''' Properties window or Data Sources window</remarks>
<System.ComponentModel.BrowsableAttribute(False)> _
Default Public ReadOnly Property Item( _
    ByVal propertyName As String) As String _
    Implements System.ComponentModel.IDataErrorInfo.Item
    Get
```

```
        Return ValidationInstance.Item(propertyName)
    End Get
End Property
```

This code sets the `BrowsableAttribute` to `False` to ensure that the `Item` property does not appear in the Data Sources window. It is a read-only property, so only has a getter. The code in the getter uses the `Item` method of the `Validation` class to return the validation errors for the specified business object property.

Each business object `Property` statement can then call any of the `Validation` methods. To ensure that the validation for all the properties is handled by the same instance of the `Validation` class, always access the `Validation` methods using the `ValidationInstance` property.

For example, for the `ProductName` property, the `Product` business object validation rules require that the property contains a value and that the maximum length is 24 characters. You add the calls to the `Validation` class directly in the setter for the property:

```
Set(ByVal value As String)
    If _ProductName <> value Then
        Dim propertyName As String = "ProductName"
        ValidationInstance.ValidateClear(propertyName)
        ValidationInstance.ValidateRequired(propertyName, value)
        ValidationInstance.ValidateLength(propertyName, value, 24)
        Me.DataStateChanged(EntityStateEnum.Modified)
        _ProductName = value
    End If
End Set
```

The setter first calls the `ValidateClear` method to ensure that any prior messages for the property are cleared. It then calls the `ValidateRequired` and `ValidateLength` methods to perform the required validation. If the user enters an invalid value, the `Validation` class adds the appropriate error string to the `ValidationList` dictionary, and the `IDataErrorInfo` takes care of displaying the `ErrorProvider` error icon, as shown in Figure 7.16.

The most interesting part about this code is that it provides immediate validation as the user moves through the form, and it displays the results of the validation in the user interface, yet it required no changes whatsoever to the user interface code.

Building Along

For the Purchase Tracker sample application:
- You already created a base business object class (**PTBOBase**) in Chapter 5, so open the **PTBOBase** class in the Code Editor.
- Add the **ValidationInstance** property and create the instance in the constructor as shown in this section.
- Implement the **IDataErrorInfo** interface as shown in this section.
- Modify the setter for each updateable business object property in the **Product** and **Customer** classes to call the appropriate validation methods based on the property's validation rules.
  Be sure to always call `ValidateClear` first to clear any prior messages for the property.

Run the application. It displays your splash screen and then shows the MDI parent form. Display one of the data entry forms, and enter invalid data as defined by your business rules. An error icon appears for each invalid entry. Notice also that you can move around the controls on the form, even if some of the controls have errors. When you correct the invalid entry, the error icon disappears.

By building a `Validation` class and managing the instance of that class in your base form class, you can easily add validation to any business object class in your application. Simply add calls to the `Validation` class methods in the desired business object `Property` statements. Any user interface elements bound to those business object properties are then validated and an error icon is automatically displayed for any validation errors.

Conclusion

What Did This Chapter Cover?

This chapter detailed the process of implementing object binding in your application. It included the drag-and-drop process of building a user interface from a business object. It also described the more complex code you need to implement validation and display data entry errors to the end user.

This chapter covered several real productivity enhancers:

- Binding a form's controls to business object properties prevents the need to write any code that copies the values between the controls and the business object properties.
- By building the business object with its properties first, you can use the Data Sources window to quickly build a form to display and edit those properties.
- Binding a control such as a grid to a collection class allows you to easily provide the users with a set of data to view or edit.
- Binding to a class that exposes a DataTable gives you the performance of binding to the data.
- Implementing a standard `TypeList` class provides a quick and easy way to handle lists of valid values for your objects' properties, such as customer types, product types, payment types, and so on.
- Although the `Validation` class may take a while to create, once you have it in place, you can use it to validate any property in your application.
- Implementing the `IDataErrorInfo` interface may look complex, but with a little code in the base business object class, all your object properties can display their validation errors in the user interface, with no validation code required in the user interface.

The next chapter demonstrates how to create the database, define queries, build a data access component, and reference the data access component from your business objects.

Building Along

If you are "building along" with the Purchase Tracker sample application, this chapter bound all the forms you created in Chapter 4 and in this chapter to the business object classes you created in Chapters 5 and 6, pulling together the pieces of your application. It also implemented the selection criteria for each form, providing a Product and Customer drop-down list.

You can run the Purchase Tracker sample application and view the Product, Customer, and Purchases forms. You cannot save any changes, because the database code is not yet in place.

When building production-level applications, you may want to consider enhancing the binding features as follows:

- **Sorting**

  By default, a `DataGridView` control that is bound to a business object that inherits from `BindingList` does not know how to sort itself. So if you need to allow the user to sort columns by clicking a column header, you need to perform that sorting.

  The code needed to perform sorting is long and complex. You start by overriding the `ApplySortCore` method of the `BindingList`. You then have to create a class that implements `IComparer`. This code is beyond the scope of this book, but you can find more information about this technique by searching on `ApplySortCore` in the help system.

  Add the sorting code to a base business object list class, and inherit from that class for all classes that manage a list and require sorting.

- **Deleting**

  If your user interface displays one item, such as a product, and allows the user to delete the item, you can immediately perform the delete, and everything works fine.

  If your user interface displays a grid bound to a business object that inherits from `BindingList`, and the grid allows the user to delete any number of items before saving changes, you need to write more code. When the user deletes an item from the grid, the item is also deleted from the `BindingList`. If you immediately delete the item from the database at that time, there is no problem. But if you allow the user to make multiple changes to the grid before saving, you have a problem.

  When working with a grid that the user can modify extensively before performing a save operation, the save code needs to iterate through the resulting `BindingList` and save any changes to the database. But deleted items are deleted from the `BindingList`, so you don't have them anymore to know to delete them from the database. To handle this, you either need to create a copy of the `BindingList` and use that to determine which items need to be deleted, or you can create a separate list of deleted items that you can process when the user saves.

The next chapter replaces the hard-coded data values in your business objects with actual values from a database. The application will then be able to retrieve and save data.

Additional Reading

Kurata, Deborah. *Object Binding Tips and Tricks*. *CoDe* magazine, March/April 2006.

This article provides tips and tricks for using object binding.

Noyes, Brian. *Data Binding with Windows Forms 2.0*. Addison-Wesley, 2006.

This book provides further information on data binding, but all of it is in C#.

Try It!

Here are a few suggestions for trying some of the techniques presented in this chapter:

1. Add other methods to the `Validation` class, such as `ValidateNumeric` to ensure an entered value is a number and `ValidateDateRange` to check that a date is between two other dates.

   Add calls to these methods in appropriate properties in your business objects.

2. Add an object data source for the `SalesRep` business object class.

3. Bind the properties in the SalesRep object data source to the controls on the Sales Rep form.

   Run the application. The Sales Rep form displays the data as defined in the `Create` method of the `SalesRep` class.

4. Add the `ErrorProvider` component to the Sales Rep form, and bind it to the SalesRep `BindingSource`.

5. Add calls to the `Validation` class in the property setters for the `SalesRep` class.

   Run the application. Because the `SalesRep` class already inherits from the base business object class, the validation works with no other changes.

CHAPTER 8

BUILDING THE DATA ACCESS LAYER

Try not! Do, or do not; there is no try.
—**Yoda the Jedi Master,** *The Empire Strikes Back*

Most applications need to "do" data. They need somewhere to store all the information for products, customers, purchases, samples, contacts, members, and so on. They also need to retrieve that information for use in the application, and apply changes to that information.

All of this is handled in the application's data access layer. The data access layer can access data from any source, such as a configuration file, other external file, or database. Because the majority of applications use some type of database, this chapter focuses on building a data access layer to access a relational database.

When you build a data access layer to access a database, the data access layer includes the database to store the data. It includes the queries to retrieve the data from the database and save changes back to the database. And, it includes the data access component that calls the queries and provides the interaction between the database and your business objects.

This chapter describes how to build a database, write queries, and create a database project using the tools within Visual Studio. It covers how to use Visual Studio to manage connection strings. Finally, it details how to build a data access component for accessing the database from your application.

What Does This Chapter Cover?

This chapter demonstrates the following techniques:

- Building a database using Server Explorer
- Creating sample data using the Results Pane

- Building stored procedures using Query Builder
- Managing stored procedures with a Database project
- Handling connection strings using `My.Settings`
- Calling stored procedures and queries using ADO.NET
- Accessing the data access component from the business objects

Most of the popular database products work well with ADO.NET, the .NET Framework's data access library, including Microsoft SQL Server, Microsoft Access, Oracle, and MySQL. With ADO.NET, you can handle connection strings, call queries, and build a data access component to access your data using any of these database products.

However, not all the database products support all the Visual Studio database features. For example, using Microsoft Access and the OleDb data provider, you can only view your tables and views from Visual Studio. You cannot update your table structure or queries. Notes throughout this chapter identify which features may or may not be available for your database product.

The examples in this chapter use SQL Server 2005 Express Edition (SQL Server Express). SQL Server Express is a free download from Microsoft.

NOTE: Although the examples use SQL Server Express, you can use the features in this chapter with any other database product, except as noted.

SQL Server Express

SQL Server Express is a full database management system that you can distribute royalty-free with your application. It can function as a client database server for single-user applications, as a basic shared database server for multiple users, or as a file-based database server. The file-based feature is similar to Microsoft Access. It allows you to deliver the database by simply copying the database file, making the deployment process a breeze.

NOTE: Using the file-based feature, you must deploy the file on the user's computer. You cannot put the file on a shared drive, as you could with Microsoft Access. That makes this feature useful for only single-user applications.

The notable differences between SQL Server Express and other editions of SQL Server include the maximum database size (4 GB), the amount of RAM it uses (1 GB), its limit to single-processor systems, and its lack of built-in management tools.

SQL Server Express is fully compatible with other editions of SQL Server. You can create a database with SQL Server Express and use it in any other SQL Server edition. This allows you to use SQL Server Express for your development and testing and then deploy with a higher-end edition of SQL Server. (But since the Developer Edition of SQL Server is so inexpensive, most developers choose it over the Express Edition to get the additional management tools.)

You can have multiple versions of SQL Server installed on one computer. For example, you could have SQL Server 2000, SQL Server 2005, and SQL Server Express all installed on your computer. When each version of SQL Server is installed, it is given a unique name based on the name of the computer on which it was installed. For SQL Server Express, the default name is the computer name with "\SQLExpress" appended to it.

Building a Database

Visual Studio provides many ways to store your data. You can write it to a text file, you can serialize it to XML, you can save it as a byte stream, and so on. But by far the most common technique for data storage is to use a database.

This section describes the tools within Visual Studio for building your database.

Defining the Database

The first step in building the database for your application is to create the database itself. If you are using SQL Server, you can create your database using SQL Server management tools or directly from within Visual Studio using Server Explorer.

NOTE: If you are using a database product other than SQL Server, you can use the database product's management tools to create the database. For example, if you are using Microsoft Access, it provides its own set of tools to create the database.

To create a SQL Server database using Server Explorer:

1. Open Server Explorer (**View** | **Server Explorer**).
2. Right-click the **Data Connections** node and select **Create New SQL Server Database** from the context menu.
   This displays the Create New SQL Server Database dialog.
3. Select the name of the SQL Server you want to use.
   If you have more than one edition of SQL Server installed, the set of SQL Server names are listed for your selection. If you are on a network, any other computers that have a publicly accessible SQL Server installed are also included on the list.

NOTE: You may not see your SQL Server Express Edition appear in this list. If not, you can type it in as *your machine name***\SQLExpress** or as **(local)\ SQLExpress** or just **.\SQLExpress**.

---

4. Define the appropriate information to log into the selected SQL Server.

NOTE: By default, SQL Server Express is installed with **Windows Authentication** in place.

---

5. Define the name of the database.
   Use standard naming conventions for your database name. One recommended standard is to use the same name as the application name if the purpose of the database is to support only the one application.
   The resulting dialog looks similar to Figure 8.1.
6. Click **OK**.
   The database is created in the defined SQL Server instance, and a connection to the database is added to Server Explorer, as shown in Figure 8.2.

Use these steps any time you need to create a new SQL Server database.

Figure 8.1 The Create New SQL Server Database dialog allows you to define a new database.

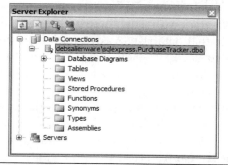

Figure 8.2 Server Explorer lists your data connections. For each data connection, it lists all the tables, views, stored procedures, and other information associated with the database.

Building Along

For the Purchase Tracker sample application:

- Download and install SQL Server Express, or select one of your existing installed SQL Server editions to use for the "Building Along" activities.

> **NOTE:** Even if you have always used Microsoft Access or MySQL in the past, you may want to give SQL Server Express a try for this sample application. It's free and easy to download and install.
>
> However, you can continue with the "Building Along" using a product other than SQL Server. You then need to use the database product's management tools to create the database, and use the information in the next section to connect to the database from Visual Studio.

> ■   Create the database using the steps described in this section.
>   Name the database **PurchaseTracker**.
> The database appears in Server Explorer similar to Figure 8.2.

Connecting to the Database

Before you can work with a database within Visual Studio, you must define a connection to that database. A **connection** defines the details that Visual Studio needs to access the database, such as the name of the database product, the name of the database, and security information such as a username and password.

When creating a new database, as described in the preceding section, the connection is created for you. You can view or change the connection information by right-clicking the data connection in Server Explorer and selecting **Modify Connection** from the context menu.

If you already have an existing database that you want to access from Visual Studio or if you created your database using a database product other than SQL Server, you can connect to it using Server Explorer.

> **NOTE:** You can connect to any type of database that has a .NET data provider, including Microsoft Access, Oracle, and MySQL.

To connect to an existing database:

1. Click the **Connect to Database** button on the Server Explorer toolbar, *or* right-click **Data Connections** in Server Explorer and select **Add Connection** from the context menu.

This displays the Choose Data Source dialog, as shown in Figure 8.3.

NOTE: If you have ever previously created a data connection in Visual Studio, you may see the Add Connection dialog first, as shown later in Figure 8.4. Click the Change button on the Add Connection dialog to display this dialog.

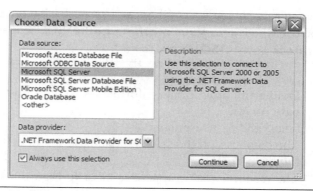

Figure 8.3   Select the desired type of data source that you want to connect to, along with the appropriate data provider, in the Choose Data Source dialog.

2. Select the type of data source for the connection, select the data provider, and click **Continue**.

Select **Microsoft SQL Server** to connect to a SQL Server 2000 or SQL Server 2005 database, either as a client database or as a server database.

Select **Microsoft SQL Server Database File** to use a file-based database. This allows you to deploy a single file instead of installing a database.

Select **Microsoft Access Database File** for a Microsoft Access database. The data provider then defaults to the OleDb data provider.

Select **Microsoft ODBC Data Source** for any other database product that supports an ODBC connection, such as MySQL.

The Add Connection dialog is then displayed.

NOTE: Depending on the data provider you selected, the Add Connection dialog may request different information than described here.

3. Select the name of the database server you want to connect to. If you selected a SQL Server data source, and you have more than one edition of SQL Server installed, the set of SQL Server names are listed for your selection. If you are on a network, any other computers that have a publicly accessible version of SQL Server installed are also included in the list.

NOTE: You may not see your SQL Server Express Edition appear in this list. If not, you can type it in as *your machine name***SQLExpress** or as **(local)\ SQLExpress** or just **.\SQLExpress**.

---

4. Define the appropriate information to log into the selected database server.
5. Select the database name. The databases in the selected database server instance are listed in the drop-down. The resulting dialog appears similar to Figure 8.4.

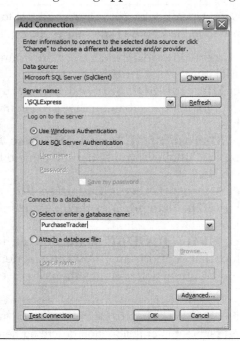

Figure 8.4   The Add Connection dialog allows you to define a connection to a database and then test that connection.

6. Click **Test Connection** to test the connection to your database.
7. Click **OK**.

The connection is then added to Server Explorer, shown in Figure 8.2. If you connect to an existing database, you see all the tables, views, stored procedures, and other database objects for the database in Server Explorer.

NOTE: By default, you cannot remotely connect to a SQL Server Express database. That means that unless you change the settings, you cannot access a SQL Server Express database that resides on another computer.

To allow for remote connections to a SQL Server Express database, you need to enable TCP/IP for that SQL Server by using the SQL Server Configuration Manager application (**Start | All Programs | Microsoft SQL Server 2005 | Configuration Tools | SQL Server Configuration Manager**). Expand the SQL Server 2005 **Network Configuration** node, and click the **Protocols** node. The protocols then appear in the right pane. Right-click **TCP/IP** and select **Enable** to enable it.

Any time you want to work with a database using the Visual Studio tools, you must first have a connection to that database defined in Server Explorer.

Creating a Table

After you create a database, the next step is to create the tables within the database. Or, if you are working with an existing database, you can add tables as needed. A table represents a particular business entity or defines a relationship between business entities.

A **table** is a set of rows and columns that store the data associated with a particular entity, such as products. A **column** defines each data element associated with the entity, such as ProductName and Price. A **row** contains the actual data in each data element for a particular item, so the "Mithril Coat" row has values for ProductName, Price, and so on.

The tables defined in a database appear under the data connection for the database in Server Explorer. The columns in each table appear under the table name. This allows you to view the table and column information directly from Visual Studio.

The process of defining the appropriate set of tables and columns for your application is accomplished during the design phase, as described in Chapter 2, "Designing Software." Once you know what tables and columns you need, you can create each table and its associated columns. If you are using SQL Server, you can add tables and columns directly from Server Explorer.

NOTE: If you are using a database product other than SQL Server, you can view the tables and columns from Server Explorer, but you cannot create or modify tables. Use the database product's management tools to create and modify the tables. For example, if you are using Microsoft Access, it provides its own set of tools.

To create a new SQL Server table:

1. Right-click the **Tables** folder under the data connection in Server Explorer and select **Add New Table** from the context menu, *or* select the data connection and select **Data** | **Add New** | **Table** from the main menu bar.
   This displays the Table Designer.
2. Enter the column name, data type, and any other column properties for each column in the table.
   Don't worry about the table keys at this point. They are discussed later in this chapter.
   The result appears similar to Figure 8.5.
3. Select **File** | **Save** from the main menu bar to save the table.
   This displays the Choose Name dialog for entry of the table name.
4. Enter the table name, and click **OK**.
   Use standard naming conventions for your table name. One recommended standard is to use the entity's singular name, such as Product or Customer.
   The table is then added to the database and appears in Server Explorer, as shown in Figure 8.6.

Use the steps in this section any time you need to add a new table or modify columns in a SQL Server database.

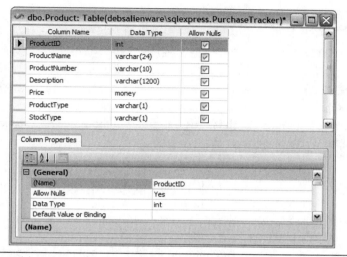

Figure 8.5   The Table Designer allows you to define all the columns in the table.

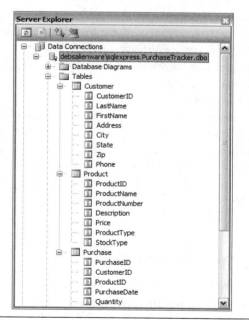

Figure 8.6   The Server Explorer lists each table and each column in the table, making it easy to see the list of columns while working in Visual Studio.

Building Along

For the Purchase Tracker sample application:

NOTE: If you are using a product other than SQL Server, you need to use the database product's management tools to create the tables. If you created a connection to the database, as described in the preceding section, the new tables appear in Server Explorer.

- Add a **Product** table to the **PurchaseTracker** database, and enter all the columns, as shown in Figure 8.5.
  The Product table stores basic information on the products available for purchase.
- Add a **Customer** table to the **PurchaseTracker** database, and enter all the columns, as shown later in Figure 8.7.
  The Customer table stores basic information on the customers that purchase products.
- Add a **Purchase** table to the **PurchaseTracker** database and enter all the columns, as shown in Figure 8.6.
  The data type for the PurchaseDate column is datetime. All the other columns have a data type of int.
  The Purchase table stores information about each customer's purchases. The Purchase table includes a column for the CustomerID from the Customer table to define the customer who purchased the product. The Purchase table also includes a column for the ProductID from the Product table to define the product that was purchased.

You can view the new tables with all their columns in Server Explorer, as shown in Figure 8.6.

Defining the Primary Key

A **primary key** is a unique identifier assigned to each row in a table. It is used to uniquely identify the row and to join related data in different tables to the row. For example, each row in the Product table has an assigned ProductID as the primary key. Each purchase in the Purchase table has a product associated with it, so the ProductID is stored in each Purchase row. This ProductID can be used to find all purchases for a particular product.

It is best to define primary keys that are meaningless—that is, keys that have no intrinsic meaning. For example, the product number (which is a string) should not be the key. If the product number were used as a key, it would take up more space than a numeric key, and it would run the risk of needing correction. If there were 30 different purchases for product LOTR-001, and then management decided to change the abbreviation in the product numbers to be more specific (FOTR, TTT, ROTK), every one of the 30 rows would need to be updated to FOTR-001. And since the primary key cannot be updated, this means creating new rows and copying all of the data. You can avoid these problems by using meaningless keys. (See Chapter 2 for more information on defining keys, including a real-life example of the importance of meaningless keys.)

NOTE: For non-*Lord of the Rings* fans, these product number abbreviations are the abbreviations for each of the three *Lord of the Rings* books/movies.

To prevent these types of problems, define a unique meaningless number for each row to use as the primary key, such as a counter or globally unique identifier (GUID). If you are using SQL Server, you can define the primary key as an Identity column. A column defined as an **Identity column** is automatically assigned a system-generated sequential value that uniquely identifies the row in the table. In Microsoft Access, this is called an AutoNumber column.

You can set the primary key for a SQL Server table using Server Explorer.

NOTE: If you are using a database product other than SQL Server, use the database product's management tools to define the primary key.

To define a primary key for a SQL Server table:

1. Double-click on a table in Server Explorer to open the Table Designer for the table.
2. Insert a column in the table to be used as the primary key.
   Or select an existing column if you already created an ID column for the table.

8. BUILDING THE DATA ACCESS LAYER

Use standard naming conventions for your primary key. One recommended standard is to use the table name with a suffix of "ID." For example, ProductID is the primary key in the Product table.

3. Ensure that the **Allow Nulls** checkbox is not checked for the column in the Table Designer.

   A primary key field cannot be null.

4. Select the column in the Table Designer, and open the **Identity Specification** node on the **Column Properties** tab (see Figure 8.7).

5. Set the **Is Identity** value to **Yes**.

   When **Is Identity** is set, SQL Server automatically sets the value for the primary key to a unique value as each row is created in the table.

6. Right-click the column in the Table Designer, and select **Set Primary Key** from the context menu, *or* click the column and select **Table Designer | Set Primary Key** from the main menu bar.

   A key icon is then displayed next to the key column, as shown in Figure 8.7.

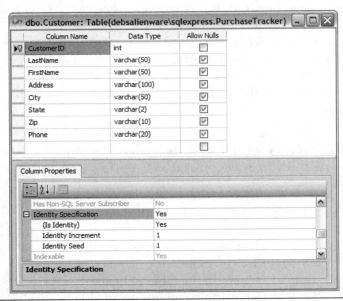

Figure 8.7 Primary keys should be meaningless, non-null values. Use the Identity Specification to allow SQL Server to manage the assignment of unique primary key values to each row in the table.

Use the techniques described in this section to create a primary key for each SQL Server table in your database.

Building Along

For the Purchase Tracker sample application:

NOTE: If you are using a product other than SQL Server, you need to use the database product's management tools to define the primary keys.

- Double-click on the **Product** table in Server Explorer to open the Table Designer.
- Select the **ProductID** column.
- Set the information in the **Identity Specification** node, as described in this section.
- Set the column as the primary key.
- Repeat for the **CustomerID** in the **Customer** table and the **PurchaseID** in the **Purchase** table.

Each key is then shown with a key icon (see Figure 8.7).

Defining System Columns

Each table in your database contains all of the data for an entity, along with a unique primary key. But you may want to add other columns to each table for system management or audit tracking.

The most common system columns are as follows:

LastUpdateDate defines the date and time that a row was last updated.

LastUpdateUser defines the username (or user ID) of the user who performed the last update.

NOTE: Some applications also use a RowTimeStamp column. A **TimeStamp** is a SQL Server data type that SQL Server sets automatically each time a row is updated in the database. The TimeStamp is used during the save operation to ensure that the row was not changed by someone else between the time the row was retrieved and the time it was saved. This provides for concurrency checking. Other database products provide similar data types. See the "Additional Reading" section for references to database books for more information on this topic.

Some applications also define CreateDate and CreateUser columns to provide additional audit information on the date and the user who created the row.

Think about the data that you may need to resolve issues with the database or provide management audit information. Add this information to each table as standard system columns.

Building Along

For the Purchase Tracker sample application:

NOTE: If you are using a product other than SQL Server, you need to use the database product's management tools to add the system columns to the tables.

- Double-click on the **Product** table in Server Explorer to open the Table Designer.
- Add the **LastUpdateDate** and **LastUpdateUser** columns, as described in this section.
- Repeat for the **Customer** and **Purchase** tables.
  To save time, you can copy the two new columns from the Product table and paste them into the Customer and Purchase tables.

The new columns appear in Server Explorer.

Building a Database Diagram

It is sometimes useful to see a pictorial view of your database, or a portion of it. That is the purpose of SQL Server's database diagram feature.

NOTE: If you are using a database product other than SQL Server, some of the database product's management tools provide database diagramming features.

NOTE: If you are using SQL Server 2000 instead of SQL Server 2005, you cannot add database diagrams from within Visual Studio. You must instead use Enterprise Manager to create your diagrams.

To build a database diagram for a set of SQL Server 2005 tables:

1. Right-click the **Database Diagrams** folder under the data connection in Server Explorer and select **Add New Diagram** from the context menu, *or* select the data connection and click **Data | Add New | Diagram** from the main menu bar.
   This displays the Add Table dialog.
2. Select one or more tables to include in the diagram, and click **Add**. Then click **Close**.
   The tables are added to the Database Designer. Drag the tables in the Database Designer to lay out the diagram as desired.
   The result appears similar to Figure 8.8.

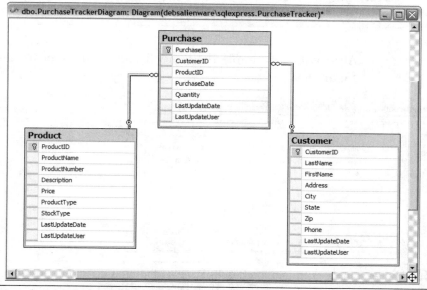

Figure 8.8 The database diagram for the Purchase Tracker sample application includes tables for customer, product, and purchase information.

Inserting Sample Data

To test your code, you need some sample data in your tables. Use the Results Pane of the Query Builder to enter sample data.

NOTE: This feature works with most database products, including SQL Server and Microsoft Access.

To enter sample data into a table:

1. Right-click the table in Server Explorer and select **Show Table Data** from the context menu, *or* click the table and select **Data |** **Show Table Data** from the main menu bar.
   This displays the Results Pane of the Table Designer.
2. Type sample data into each column.

NOTE: If you identified the ID column as an Identity or AutoNumber column, do not enter a value for the ID column. The ID is assigned automatically.

After entry of sample data, the Results Pane appears similar to Figure 8.9.

	ProductID	ProductName	ProductNumber	Description	Price	ProductType	StockType
▶	1	Mithril Coat	LOTR-001	Beautiful silver coat made fr...	3999999.9800	1	O
	2	Anduril	LOTR-002	Flame of the West, sword of...	499.9900	2	S
	3	One Ring	LOTR-010	The One Ring to rule them all	699.9500	4	S
*	NULL	NULL	NULL	NULL	NULL	NULL	NULL

Figure 8.9   Enter sample data into the Results Pane so that you have data to use for testing.

Use the techniques described in this section to enter sample data into your application. You can also use these techniques to view or edit existing data in the table.

Building Along

For the Purchase Tracker sample application:
- Add sample data to the **Product** table using the technique described in this section.
  The result for the Product table could look something like Figure 8.9.
- Repeat for the **Customer** table.
- Repeat for the **Purchase** table.
  Be sure that the ProductID and CustomerID columns in the Purchase table are valid IDs from the Product and Customer tables.

At this point, you have not yet added code to retrieve values from the tables, so you won't be able to see your sample data in your application yet.

With the tables created, the columns defined, and the primary keys set, the database is ready for use. By entering sample data, you can more easily test the code that accesses the database.

Building Stored Procedures

A **stored procedure** is a software routine that is stored in the database and run within the context of the database.

NOTE: Stored procedures are supported by many database management products, such as SQL Server and Oracle. Microsoft Access has QueryDefs, which are similar in concept to a stored procedure but with a slightly different syntax.

Stored procedures frequently perform CRUD (create, read, update, and delete) operations on data in the database. They can also perform other, more complex data operations, such as increasing the price of every product by 10%. Stored procedures can take input parameters, return tabular or scalar results, and return output parameters.

For example, to retrieve product data for a particular product, you can build a stored procedure that defines the ProductID as an input parameter, retrieves all the columns in the Product table for the defined ProductID, and returns them as a tabular result. To save product data, you can build a stored procedure that takes all the product columns as input parameters and updates them in the database.

You can call stored procedures (or QueryDefs) from your application so that your code does not need to interact directly with the database. This approach is recommended over adding SQL statements directly to your application for the following reasons:

- Code in the stored procedure runs within the context of the database, making the stored procedure more efficient than a SQL statement.
- Structural changes to the database can often be handled by modifying stored procedures, so you don't have to change your application code.
- Stored procedures can enhance your database's security, preventing SQL injection attacks.
- Stored procedures can reduce network traffic, especially when the stored procedure needs to work with many rows but return only one value, such as when calculating a total.
- You can reuse stored procedures anywhere in your application or in any application that accesses the database.

Most applications need four basic types of stored procedures:

- Retrieve stored procedures with an ID parameter that retrieves all columns for one row.
- Retrieve stored procedures that retrieve name and ID values of all rows for use in lists, such as a combo box for selecting a customer or product.
- Retrieve stored procedures that retrieve all columns for a set of rows filtered by a parameter for use in grids.
- Save stored procedures for saving any changes made to a row.

This section describes how to create stored procedures.

Creating a Stored Procedure

SQL Server stored procedures are basically a set of Transact-SQL (T-SQL) statements. Writing T-SQL statements may be a little daunting if you have not done it before. This section describes the basics of creating a SQL Server stored procedure. The next section describes how to generate your T-SQL statements using Query Builder.

> **NOTE:** The rest of this section details how to create SQL Server stored procedures. If you are using a different database management product, you can use that product's tools to create your stored procedures or QueryDefs.

> **NOTE:** With SQL Server 2005, you can also write procedures by creating Common Language Runtime (CLR) methods in languages such as Visual Basic or C#. This type of procedure is designed for very specific cases in which T-SQL procedures can't be used. Generally, they're designed to replace Extended Stored Procedures written in C++. They are not commonly used for simple data access.
>
> The CLR can also be used to create User-Defined Types, Functions, and Aggregates. But again, these are for very special cases and should not be implemented without a thorough understanding of their impact on security, performance, and your development patterns. For more information on writing CLR stored procedures, see the "Additional Reading" section for references to database books that cover this topic.

To create a SQL Server stored procedure:

1. Right-click the **Stored Procedures** folder under the data connection in Server Explorer and select **Add New Stored Procedure** from the context menu, *or* select the data connection and select **Data** | **Add New** | **Stored Procedure** from the main menu bar. This generates a skeleton of a stored procedure and displays it in the Code Editor:

```
CREATE PROCEDURE dbo.StoredProcedure1
      /*
      (
      @parameter1 int = 5,
      @parameter2 datatype OUTPUT
      )
      */
AS
      /* SET NOCOUNT ON */
      RETURN
```

The /* and */ are T-SQL comment markers. Everything between the markers is a comment.

2. Change the name of the stored procedure.
   The skeleton code identifies the stored procedure using a standard prefix and a default name:

   `dbo.StoredProcedure1`

   The `dbo` prefix is an abbreviation for database owner that qualifies the stored procedure name. The `dbo` is a predefined user who has implied permissions to perform all activities in the database. Normally you want to retain this prefix.
   Change the default stored procedure name using good naming conventions. Some naming conventions define the stored procedure name using the entity name, the operation name, and `_sp` to define it as a stored procedure. An example is `ProductRetrieveByID_sp`. Stored procedures must have unique names.

NOTE: You cannot change the name of the stored procedure after you save it. If you do change the name and save the stored procedure, Visual Studio instead creates a new stored procedure with the new name.

---

3. Modify the parameter list as needed to pass parameters into or out of the stored procedure.
   The at sign (`@`) denotes a parameter for the stored procedure. Define each parameter, along with its data type, any default value, and whether it is passed in to the procedure or output from the procedure.
   It is highly recommended that the parameter names match the associated column names. This makes it easier to write more generalized code. For example, your application can use the field names in a DataSet to automatically build the parameter names for the stored procedure.
   If the stored procedure has no parameters, remove this section from the stored procedure.
   Also, be sure to remove the comment markers from the parameter list.
4. Write the T-SQL statement(s) for your stored procedure after the `AS` clause.
   See the next section for assistance in building your T-SQL statements.

5. Save the stored procedure just like you save any other code file. The stored procedure is saved directly into the database.

NOTE: The stored procedure *must* be correct before it can be saved, because it is saved directly into the database. If you have an error, you get a dialog that says something like "The operation could not be completed." Check your column names, table names, and T-SQL syntax to correct the problem.

It is always a good idea to test the stored procedure after you write it. Retrieve, update, and delete stored procedures provide valid results only if you have some data in the database, so be sure to create sample data before you write your stored procedures.

Test the stored procedure by right-clicking anywhere on the stored procedure in the Code Editor and selecting **Execute** from the context menu. If the stored procedure has parameters, the Run Stored Procedure dialog appears. It allows you to enter test values for your parameter(s), as shown in Figure 8.10.

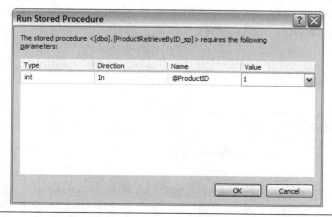

Figure 8.10 The Run Stored Procedure dialog is displayed only if your stored procedure requires parameters.

The result of the execution of the stored procedure is displayed in the Output window, as shown in Figure 8.11.

8. BUILDING THE DATA ACCESS LAYER

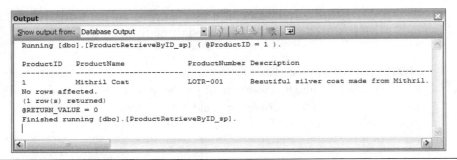

Figure 8.11 If the stored procedure executes successfully, the results are displayed in the Output window. Notice that the columns in the Output window are sized to their maximum size as defined in the table, so you need to scroll to see all of the data.

Follow these steps to create all the stored procedures for your application. If step 4 appears a little daunting, don't worry. A Query Builder feature is available to help you build your queries, as described in the next section.

Or, if you really want to make quick work of building your stored procedures, you can create a stored procedure generator. Since stored procedures are simple text files, it is easy to read the database and concatenate the appropriate strings to automatically build all your CRUD stored procedures. See the "Additional Reading" section for the reference to a *CoDe* magazine article that details the steps of building a stored procedure generator.

Building Along

For the Purchase Tracker sample application:

NOTE: If you are using Microsoft Access, you can create these as QueryDefs instead of stored procedures.

■ Create a new stored procedure as described in this section.
   This stored procedure retrieves all the product data for a particular product using the **ProductID** as a parameter.
■ Change the name of the stored procedure to **dbo. ProductRetrieveByID_sp**.

The resulting procedure line is as follows:
```
CREATE PROCEDURE dbo.ProductRetrieveByID_sp
```

- Pass the **ProductID** column as a parameter.
  The resulting parameter list is as follows:
```
(
        @ProductID int
)
```
  Be sure to remove the comment markers from around the parameter. Don't worry about the contents of the stored procedure for now; it is created in the next section.
- Save the stored procedure.
- Follow similar steps to create a new stored procedure to retrieve all of the customer data for a particular customer using the **CustomerID** as a parameter.
  Name this stored procedure **CustomerRetrieveByID_sp**.
- Follow similar steps to create a new stored procedure to retrieve all the purchases for a particular customer using the **CustomerID** as a parameter.
  Name this stored procedure **PurchaseRetrieveByCustomerID_sp**.
- Create a new stored procedure to retrieve all products using no parameter.
  Name this stored procedure **ProductRetrieveList_sp**.
- Create a new stored procedure to retrieve all customers using no parameter.
  Name this stored procedure **CustomerRetrieveList_sp**.

Be sure to save each of these stored procedures. However, you cannot test them yet because they don't contain any T-SQL statements.

Each of these five stored procedures and their parameters appear in Server Explorer.

Generating a T-SQL Statement

If you don't know how to use T-SQL, building T-SQL statements can be challenging. And if you do know how to use T-SQL, building T-SQL statements can be tedious, boring, and error-prone. The Query Builder can help you build your T-SQL statements.

NOTE: The rest of this section details how to generate SQL Server stored procedures. If you are using a different database management product, you can use that product's tools to create your stored procedures or QueryDefs.

Query Builder is accessible from within the Code Editor when you're working with SQL Server stored procedures. Query Builder refers to each T-SQL statement in your stored procedure as a query.

The Query Builder allows you to work with your query in three ways:

- Visually using the **Diagram Pane** at the top of the window
- Tabularly by entering values in a grid using the **Criteria Pane**
- Syntactically by building the SQL statements in the **SQL Pane**

Any change you make to one pane is made to all the panes. For example, if you modify the Diagram Pane, the modification appears in the Criteria and SQL Panes. This allows you to see the T-SQL statement as it is being built. An example query is shown in Figure 8.12.

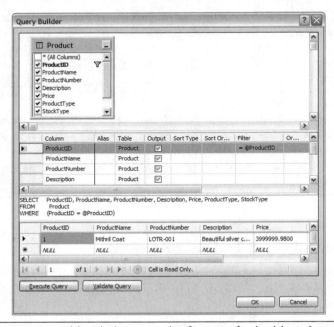

Figure 8.12   The Query Builder dialog provides features for building the T-SQL statements for your stored procedures. Starting at the top, the window is divided into Diagram, Criteria, SQL, and Results panes.

You can turn any of the panes on or off by right-clicking in the Query Builder, selecting **Pane**, and then checking/unchecking the pane in the context menu.

To create a T-SQL statement using the Query Builder:

1. Double-click on the stored procedure in Server Explorer to open it in the Code Editor.
2. Right-click in the Code Editor after the AS clause in the stored procedure, and select **Insert SQL** from the context menu.

   The Query Builder first displays the Add Table dialog, shown in Figure 8.13. This dialog allows you to select the database objects to use in your query.

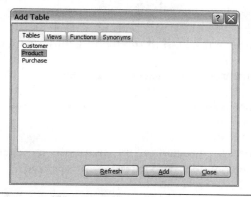

Figure 8.13   Use the Add Table dialog to select the tables for your query.

3. Select one or more tables and click **Add**. When you are finished, click **Close**.

   The Query Builder dialog is displayed (see Figure 8.12).
4. Select the columns to output from your stored procedure by checking the column names in the **Diagram Pane**, *or* by checking the **Output** checkbox for the column in the **Criteria Pane**, *or* by typing the list of column names in the SELECT statement in the **SQL Pane**.
5. Define the parameters to pass into the stored procedure by entering the parameter names in the **Filter** for the column in the **Criteria Pane**, *or* by typing the parameters in the WHERE clause in the **SQL Pane**.

   In T-SQL, parameter names are prefixed with the @ character.

NOTE: When you reference a stored procedure's parameter, be sure to prefix it with the @ character, as shown in the Filter clause in Figure 8.12.

---

6. When you finish building your query, click **Execute Query** in the Query Builder to test it.

   If your query has parameters, the Query Parameters dialog is displayed for entry of test parameters.

   The result of the query execution appears in the **Results Pane** at the bottom of the Query Builder, as shown in Figure 8.12.

7. When the query is complete and tested, click **OK**.

   The Query Builder writes the resulting query into your stored procedure.

The query is inserted in the Code Editor as follows:

```
CREATE PROCEDURE dbo.ProductRetrieveByID_sp
      (
      @ProductID int
      )
AS
      SELECT        ProductID, ProductName, ProductNumber,
➥Description, Price, ProductType, StockType
      FROM          Product
      WHERE    (ProductID = @ProjectID)
RETURN
```

To make it easier to work with the columns in your table and for later maintenance, put each column on its own line in the stored procedure, as follows:

```
ALTER PROCEDURE dbo.ProductRetrieveByID_sp
      (
      @ProductID int
      )
AS
      SELECT    ProductID,
                ProductName,
                ProductNumber,
                Description,
                Price,
```

```
          ProductType,
          StockType
FROM      Product
WHERE     (ProductID = @ProductID)
RETURN
```

Notice that after you save the stored procedure the first time, the CREATE keyword at the beginning of the procedure changes to ALTER. From this point forward, you are altering an existing stored procedure.

Use the Query Builder any time you need to insert a T-SQL statement into a stored procedure.

Building Along

For the Purchase Tracker sample application:

NOTE: If you are using Microsoft Access, you can use the Microsoft Access management tool to detail each QueryDef.

- Open the **ProductRetrieveByID_sp** stored procedure in the Code Editor.
- Launch the Query Builder and add the **Product** table to the query.
  The Product table is added to the FROM clause in the SQL statement.
- Select **Product** table columns in the **Diagram Pane**, as shown in Figure 8.12.
  The columns are added to the SELECT clause in the SQL statement.
- Add the **@ProductID** parameter as a filter using the **Criteria Pane**, as shown in Figure 8.12.
  The parameter is added to the WHERE clause in the SQL statement.
- Click **Execute Query** to try out the resulting query.
  The result of the query is shown in the Results Pane, as shown in Figure 8.12. Your result may vary if you entered different sample data.
- When the query returns the desired result, click OK to write the query to the stored procedure and save the completed stored procedure.
- Follow similar steps to add a T-SQL statement to the **CustomerRetrieveByID_sp** stored procedure.

Return all **Customer** table columns using the **@CustomerID** parameter as the filter. This returns all data for a particular customer.

- Follow similar steps to add a T-SQL statement to the **PurchaseRetrieveByCustomerID_sp** stored procedure.
Return all **Purchase** table columns using the **@CustomerID** parameter as the filter. This returns all the purchases for a particular customer.

- Follow similar steps to add a T-SQL statement to the **ProductRetrieveList_sp** stored procedure.
Return only the **ProductID** and **ProductName** columns from the **Product** table using no filter. This returns identification information for all the products. The application uses this stored procedure to display the list of products for user selection.

- Follow similar steps to add a T-SQL statement to the **CustomerRetrieveList_sp** stored procedure.
Return only the **CustomerID** and **CustomerName** columns from the **Customer** table using no filter. This returns identification information for all the customers. The application uses this stored procddure to display the list of customers for user selection.
Since there is no CustomerName column in the Customer table, return it using the following syntax:

```
CREATE PROCEDURE dbo.CustomerRetrieveList
AS
    SELECT CustomerID,
           LastName + ', ' + FirstName AS CustomerName
    FROM   Customer
           RETURN
```

This defines an additional column in the query results. The As clause defines an alias, giving the additional column a name.

Be sure to test and then save each of the updated stored procedures.

Creating a Save Stored Procedure

So far all of the stored procedures created in this chapter have retrieved data from the database. You also need to define stored procedures to save data. The T-SQL statements you need to save data are different for inserts, updates, and deletes, so you need multiple T-SQL statements to perform your save logic.

NOTE: The rest of this section details how to create SQL Server stored procedures for saving data. If you are using a different database management product, you can use that product's tools to create your stored procedures or QueryDefs.

There are two primary techniques for creating a save stored procedure:

- Create three separate stored procedures: one to perform updates, one for deletes, and one for inserts.

NOTE: For auditing purposes, some applications do not allow the users to delete data. Instead, you can add a Status system column to each table, defining whether a row is active or deleted. In that case, you don't need delete functionality in your stored procedures, because a delete is simply an update of the Status column.

- Create one stored procedure that has separate logic for updates, deletes, and inserts.

The first option has the benefit of writing single-purpose stored procedures. However, if you have many tables, this can lead to a very large number of stored procedures that you have to manage and maintain. The second option keeps all the save logic in one location.

NOTE: If you are using Microsoft Access, you must create a separate QueryDef for updates, deletes, and inserts, because QueryDefs don't support branching logic.

To create a single SQL Server save stored procedure:

1. Follow the instructions provided earlier in this chapter for creating a stored procedure.
   Use good naming conventions for your save stored procedure name. Some naming conventions define the stored procedure

8. BUILDING THE DATA ACCESS LAYER

name using the entity name, the operation name, and _sp to define it as a stored procedure. An example is `ProductSave_sp`. Stored procedures must have unique names.

2. Add a parameter for each column in the table that can be saved, plus a parameter for **RowState**.

   These parameters are used to pass the changed data to the stored procedure.

   If you defined system columns, don't add a parameter for the LastUpdateDate column, because the stored procedure sets it. This ensures that one standard time zone is used for all database operations.

   The `RowState` parameter defines whether the data needs to be inserted, updated, or deleted.

   For example, the parameter list to save the data in a Product table is as follows:

```
CREATE PROCEDURE dbo.ProductSave_sp
        @ProductID          int,
        @ProductName        varchar(24),
        @ProductNumber      varchar(10),
        @Description        varchar(1200),
        @Price              money,
        @ProductType        varchar(1),
        @StockType          varchar(1),
        @LastUpdateUser     varchar(50),
        @RowState           varchar(50)
AS
```

3. Use `IF` T-SQL statements to perform the appropriate logic based on the `RowState`.

   The `RowState` is the object's `EntityState`, as described in Chapter 5, "Building the Business Logic Layer." Be sure to use the same values in the `IF` statements as defined in your `EntityStateEnum`.

4. Use the Query Builder to create the T-SQL statement for each `IF` statement.

   By default, the Query Builder constructs select queries for data retrieval. You can change the type of query by right-clicking in the Query Builder and selecting **Change Type**. Change the type to **Insert Values** for insert, **Delete** for delete, and **Update** for update.

A sample T-SQL statement for the insert operation is as follows:

```
IF  @RowState = 'Added'
    BEGIN
        INSERT INTO Product
                        (ProductName,
                        ProductNumber,
                        Description,
                        Price,
                        ProductType,
                        StockType,
                        LastUpdateDate,
                        LastUpdateUser)
            VALUES      (@ProductName,
                        @ProductNumber,
                        @Description,
                        @Price,
                        @ProductType,
                        @StockType,
                        GETDATE(),
                        @LastUpdateUser)
        /* Return the inserted row */
        SELECT  ProductID = @@Identity)
    END
```

Notice that the ProductID is not inserted into the new row. The ProductID column is an Identity column, so SQL Server automatically assigns a unique value. The LastUpdateDate column is inserted into the new row, even though it was not passed in as a parameter. The GETDATE T-SQL function retrieves the system date, and the result is assigned to the LastUpdateDate column.

The last statement is a SELECT statement that returns the new ProductID. SQL Server automatically assigns the ID when the row is inserted. The result of that assignment is available using the @@Identity value.

A sample T-SQL statement for the update operation is as follows:

```
IF  @RowState = 'Modified'
    BEGIN
        UPDATE Product
        SET     ProductName =     @ProductName,
                ProductNumber =   @ProductNumber,
```

```
          Description =      @Description,
          Price =           @Price,
          ProductType =     @ProductType,
          StockType =       @StockType,
          LastUpdateDate = GETDATE(),
          LastUpdateUser = @LastUpdateUser
   WHERE
          ProductID =       @ProductID
END
```

The product values are changed for the row where the ID matches the passed-in ID. Notice that ProductID is not updated because the primary key is not an updatable value.

A sample T-SQL statement for the delete is as follows:

```
IF @RowState = 'Deleted'
   BEGIN
      DELETE FROM Product
      WHERE         ProductID = @ProductID
   END
```

Stored procedures are the recommended mechanism to retrieve data from the database and store data back to the database. You can see by the amount of work that is required to build these that a stored procedure generator can be very useful. See the "Additional Reading" section for more information on a stored procedure generator.

Building Along

For the Purchase Tracker sample application:

NOTE: If you are using Microsoft Access, you can use the Microsoft Access management tool to create each QueryDef.

■ Create a new stored procedure to save **Product** table data using the techniques and code detailed in this section.
Name the stored procedure **ProductSave_sp**.

- Create a new stored procedure to save **Customer** table data using the techniques detailed in this section.
Name the stored procedure **CustomerSave_sp**.
Be sure to test and then save each of these stored procedures. The new stored procedures appear in Server Explorer.

Using a Database Project

There are several issues with creating stored procedures directly into the database. For one, you are creating the stored procedure directly into the database. There is no versioning. There is no way to go back if you make an inadvertent change. There is no way to check them out, making it possible for two developers to work with the same stored procedure at the same time. And if you have a syntax error, you cannot save until you fix it. The purpose of a database project is to allow you to manage a set of database scripts, such as stored procedure scripts, separately from the database itself. This makes it possible to manage stored procedures just like you manage your other source code files.

A database project is a type of project that you add to your solution. Its only purpose is to manage database scripts. A **database script** is a set of commands that can be executed against a database. These scripts can include commands for building a table, modifying table columns, creating new stored procedures, updating existing stored procedures, and so on.

NOTE: The rest of this section details how to create a database project for SQL Server. You cannot use this feature with Microsoft Access databases.

When you want to edit a stored procedure, you instead edit the script for the stored procedure. You can then save the script at any time, even if it has syntax errors. When the stored procedure script is correct, you can run the script to apply the stored procedure change to the database.

To add a database project to your solution:

1. Right-click the solution in Server Explorer and select **Add | New Project** from the context menu, *or* select **File | Add | New Project** from the main menu bar.
This displays the New Project dialog.

8. BUILDING THE DATA ACCESS LAYER

2. Navigate to the **Other Project Types** and select **Database**.
   The set of database project templates are listed in the right pane.
3. Select the **Database Project** template.
4. Enter the name for the project.
   Use standard naming conventions for your project name.
5. Select the desired location for the project.
   The location defaults to the appropriate directory based on the solution location.
6. Click **OK**.
   The Add Database Reference dialog appears, as shown in Figure 8.14. This allows you to associate a specific connection with the database project.

Figure 8.14 The Add Database Reference dialog allows you to associate a data connection with a particular Database project.

7. Select the desired reference or add a new reference and click **OK**.
   Visual Studio adds the database project to your solution, as shown in Figure 8.15.

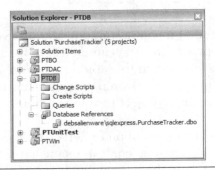

Figure 8.15 The Database project appears in Solution Explorer.

Once you have the database project in place, you can generate scripts for all of your existing stored procedures. This creates a code file for each stored procedure.

To generate a script for an existing stored procedure:

1. Right-click the stored procedure in Server Explorer and select **Generate Create Script to Project** from the context menu. Visual Studio generates the stored procedure script and adds it under the Create Scripts folder in Solution Explorer.

Repeat this step for each stored procedure in your database.

NOTE: If you have many stored procedures, this may be very tedious. It may be better to use your SQL Server management tools, which provide a feature to create scripts for all of your stored procedures in one step.

If you need to make a change to the stored procedure, edit the script. When the script is correct, apply the change to the database by right-clicking the script and selecting **Run** from the context menu. The script runs against the database defined as the default database reference in the Database project. The Output window displays any errors that occur when running the script. If the script runs successfully, the stored procedure is updated in the database.

You can create new stored procedures using scripts instead of creating them directly in the database. To create a script, right-click the **Create Scripts** folder in Solution Explorer, and select **Add SQL Script** from the context menu.

Using a database project gives you much better control over the stored procedures in your application.

Building Along

For the Purchase Tracker sample application:

NOTE: If you are using Microsoft Access, you cannot build a database project for your database. Skip this "Building Along." It does not impact the sample application.

8. BUILDING THE DATA ACCESS LAYER

- Create a new database project using the **Database Project** template, as described in this section.
  Name the project **PTDB**.
- Associate the connection to the **PurchaseTracker** database with this database project.
- Generate a script for each stored procedure in the database, as detailed in this section.

The new project appears in Solution Explorer with the scripts defined under the Create Scripts folder.

Building a Data Access Component

The data access layer defines how your application works with data. This layer includes the database. It includes queries defined as structured query language (SQL) statements, views, or stored procedures. And it includes a data access component that calls these queries to retrieve data or save changes to the data.

The data access component (DAC) contains the code required to access the database. It includes the code that connects to the database, prepares query parameters, calls queries, and returns the results. This code is somewhat complex, but it can be written in a generalized fashion so that one set of code can be used to query any table in the database.

This means that all of your business object classes can call one common DAC to retrieve data from the database and then store any data changes back to the database. This keeps all of the data access code encapsulated in one component.

You can build your DAC to use a vendor-specific data provider, such as Microsoft SQL Server or Oracle. Or you can use a more general data provider, such as ODBC or the newer OleDb, to access databases such as Microsoft Access and MySQL. Or you can use the new DbProviderFactory to build a data access component that can access any of these.

This section provides the steps for building a DAC component that you can use in any application that needs to access a database. It also describes how to call the DAC from the business objects.

Creating the DAC

The key piece of code in the data access layer is the DAC. The DAC is defined as a separate project in the solution because it is independent of any business logic. The DAC is composed of one or more classes that provide access to the database by calling SQL statements, stored procedures, or other queries (such as QueryDefs).

To create the DAC:

1. Create a project for the data access layer, as described in Chapter 3, "Building Projects."
2. Open the **Project Designer** for the DAC Class Library project. Right-click the project in Solution Explorer and select **Properties** from the context menu, *or* select **Project | Properties** from the main menu bar, *or* double-click on the **My Project** folder under the project in Solution Explorer to open the Project Designer.
3. Select the **References** tab.
4. Ensure that there is a reference to `System.Data`, as shown in Figure 8.16. If not, use the Add button to add the reference.
   To make the classes in this library easier to use in the code, check `System.Data` in the Imported Namespaces list, as shown in Figure 8.16.

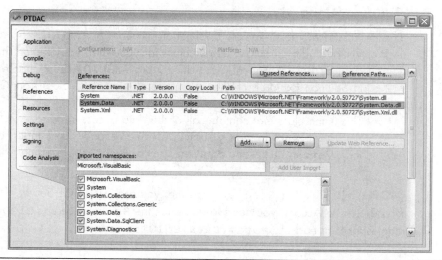

Figure 8.16 The References tab in the Project Designer for the DAC defines the references to the .NET Framework database libraries.

At this point, decide which data provider you will use in your DAC and import its associated library using the Imported Namespaces list shown in Figure 8.16. The common data providers and their associated libraries are:

- For SQL Server, import the `System.Data.SqlClient` namespace.
- For Access using OleDb, import the `System.Data.OleDb` namespace.
- For any ODBC data source, import the `System.Data.Odbc` namespace.
- To support *any* data source from *any* data provider, import the `System.Data.Common` namespace.

If you select one of the first three options, the code in the DAC is basically the same; only the library names are different. If you select the last option, you need to implement the DbProviderFactory, which is a little more complex and beyond the scope of this book. See the "Additional Reading" section for more information.

Your DAC project is then ready. You can then add all of the code required to access data as described in the next sections.

Building Along

For the Purchase Tracker sample application:

- Visual Studio created a default class for you when you created the data access component Class Library project (**PTDAC**) in Chapter 3. In *Solution Explorer*, change the name of this default class from Class1 to **DAC**.
  This is the class that contains all of the data access code.
- Add a reference to the `System.Data` namespace, and import both the `System.Data` and `System.Data.SqlClient` namespaces.

NOTE: This "Building Along" assumes that you are using SQL Server. If you are using Access, you need to reference the `System.Data.OleDb` namespace instead of `System.Data.SqlClient`.

At this point, there is no code in your data access component yet, so there are no new features to try out.

Defining the Connection String

Before the code in your application can access a database, it needs to connect to the database. That is normally done using a connection string. A **connection string** is a concatenated set of connection parameters that is used by .NET Framework database library methods to connect to the database.

Connection strings are not easy to define. The information in a connection string depends on the type of connection in a rather complex way. The best way to get the correct set of information for your connection string is to use Server Explorer.

To view the correct connection string for your database:

1. Open Server Explorer (**View | Server Explorer**).
2. Right-click the data connection and select **Modify Connection** from the context menu.
   This displays the Modify Connection dialog.
3. Click the **Advanced** button at the bottom of the dialog.
   The Advanced Properties dialog displays the valid connection string at the bottom of the dialog, as shown in Figure 8.17.

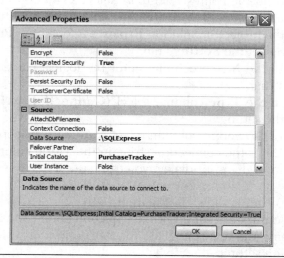

Figure 8.17   The Advanced Properties dialog for the connection displays the connection string used to connect to the database. You can select and copy it to the Clipboard to ensure that you have a valid connection string.

NOTE: The connection string for an Access database looks very different. For example:

```
Provider=Microsoft.Jet.OLEDB.4.0; Data Source="C:\Data\PT.MDB"
```

Once you have a valid connection string, you need to put it somewhere in the application. The easiest place to define the connection string is in the application settings.

Recall from Chapter 4, "Building the User Interface Layer," that there are two types of application settings: user-scoped and application-scoped. Chapter 4 detailed user-scoped settings to store each form's last user-defined location and size at runtime. Connection strings use application-scoped settings. Application-scoped settings are associated with the application, so users cannot change them at runtime.

To set the connection string in the application settings:

1. Open the **Project Designer** for the DAC Class Library project. Right-click the project in Solution Explorer and select **Properties** from the context menu, *or* select **Project | Properties** from the main menu bar, *or* double-click on the **My Project** folder under the project in Solution Explorer to open the Project Designer.
2. Select the **Settings** tab.
3. In the **Name** column, enter the logical name for the connection string.
4. In the **Type** column, select (**Connection string**) as the type for the setting.
5. In the **Scope** column, select **Application** scope.
6. Enter the connection string in the **Value** column. If you copied it from the prior dialog, you can paste it here.

The result is shown in Figure 8.18.

All settings are stored in the app.config file. You can view the settings by opening the app.config file for the project in which you defined the application setting.

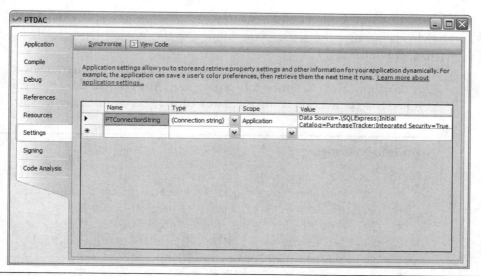

Figure 8.18   Use application settings to define your connection string.

NOTE: Because the app.config file is deployed and viewable, take precautions to avoid revealing sensitive information in the connection string, such as passwords or server paths. Consider using encryption to encrypt the connection string in the app.config file.

Even though Visual Studio allows you to create an app.config file for a Class Library project, the .NET Framework does not provide a configuration file model for class libraries. This means that when you run the application, the app.config file for any class library is ignored. You have to manually copy any settings (including the connection string) from the app.config file defined for any Class Library project into the app.config file for the application, which is defined in the startup Windows Application project.

NOTE: When you build the application, the app.config file for the startup Windows Application project is renamed with the name of the Windows Application project with a .config extension. This is the only configuration file the application accesses.

The app.config file for your Class Library project may *appear* to work. This is because the setting you defined in the Project Designer is used as the default.

Using application settings to store the connection string makes it easy for the application to connect to a database. Any code in the DAC can reference the connection using `My.Settings.PTConnectionString`.

Building Along

For the Purchase Tracker sample application:
- Copy the connection string for the PurchaseTracker database from Server Explorer to the Clipboard, as detailed in this section.
- Create a setting for the connection string in the data access component Class Library project (**PTDAC**), as detailed in this section. Name the setting **PTConnectionString**.
- Paste the connection string from the Clipboard to the **Value** column of the new setting.
- Open the app.config file for the data access component Class Library project (**PTDAC**). Copy the entire `connectionStrings` tag, and paste it into the app.config file for the Windows Application project (**PTWin**).

At this point, there is no code in your data access component yet, so there are no new features to try out.

Calling a Stored Procedure

If you defined stored procedures for your application, the DAC needs a method that calls a stored procedure and returns the results of the procedure.

NOTE: Although this section refers to "stored procedures," the code in this section works equally well with QueryDefs.

Looking back at the stored procedures created earlier in this chapter, you see that some stored procedures require parameters, like retrieve stored procedures that retrieve an item by ID, and save stored procedures. Other stored procedures do not require parameters, such as retrieve stored procedures that retrieve all rows from a table. To support this requirement, the DAC method that executes a stored procedure needs two overloads—one with parameters and one without.

But what about the value returned from the DAC method? At this point, you need to decide on the type of object to return from the method. The .NET Framework database library, ADO.NET, provides many choices. Here are the three most common:

DataReader is a read-only, forward-only stream of data from a database. You access each row of data using the `Read` method of the DataReader.

DataTable is an in-memory cache of data that contains all the selected rows and columns. When calling a stored procedure, the DataTable contains all the information defined by a single `SELECT` statement.

DataSet is an in-memory cache of data that contains all the rows and columns in multiple selections of data. When calling a stored procedure, the DataSet contains all of the information defined by any number of `SELECT` statements. The result of each `SELECT` statement is defined as separate DataTable objects within the DataSet.

NOTE: Microsoft Access does not support multiple `SELECT` statements in one QueryDef. You can still use a DataSet, but it always contains only one DataTable.

Your DAC could have a set of methods that provide each of these objects. That gives the business object the option to use whichever object makes the most sense based on the requirements. As an example, this section develops the methods that return a DataTable.

The DAC method to call a stored procedure with parameters is as follows:

```
''' <summary>
''' Calls a stored procedure and returns the result
''' </summary>
''' <param name="storedProcedureName">Name of the stored
```

```vb
''' procedure to execute</param>
''' <param name="arrParam">Parameters required by the stored
''' procedure</param>
''' <returns>DataTable containing the result</returns>
''' <remarks></remarks>
Public Shared Function ExecuteDataTable( _
    ByVal storedProcedureName As String, _
    ByVal ParamArray arrParam() As SqlParameter) As DataTable
    Dim dt As DataTable

    ' Open the connection
    Using cnn As New SqlConnection(My.Settings.PTConnectionString)
        cnn.Open()

        ' Define the command
        Dim cmd As New SqlCommand
        cmd.Connection = cnn
        cmd.CommandType = CommandType.StoredProcedure
        cmd.CommandText = storedProcedureName

        ' Handle the parameters
        If arrParam IsNot Nothing Then
            For Each param As SqlParameter In arrParam
                cmd.Parameters.Add(param)
            Next
        End If

        ' Define the data adapter and fill the dataset
        Dim da As New SqlDataAdapter(cmd)
        dt = New DataTable
        da.Fill(dt)

    End Using

    Return dt
End Function
```

This method is named `ExecuteDataTable` because it executes a stored procedure and returns a DataTable. Notice that this method is public and shared. This means that any code that references this component can use these methods without creating an instance of the DAC class.

NOTE: To modify this method to take a SQL string instead of a stored procedure name, modify the `storedProcedureName` parameter to be `SQLString`. Then change the `CommandType` property of the `SqlCommand` object in the code to be `CommandType.Text`, and assign the `CommandText` property to the `SQLString` parameter.

The `ExecuteDataTable` method has two parameters. The first is the name of the stored procedure.

The second parameter is a set of `SqlParameter` objects that specify the parameters to pass to the stored procedure. Notice the `ParamArray` keyword. This keyword allows the calling code to pass in any number of parameters of the defined type. In this example, the calling code can pass in any number of `SqlParameter` objects. The .NET runtime inserts each `SqlParameter` passed in to this method into the `arrParam` array. (Examples of passing parameters to this method are provided later in this chapter.)

The code begins by defining a new `Connection` object using the connection string identified in the `PTConnectionString` setting (described earlier in this chapter). It then uses the `Connection` object to open the connection to the database. Notice that this code uses the `Using` statement. When you define the connection in a `Using` block, the connection is automatically closed and disposed at the end of the block, even if an error occurs.

The code then sets up the `SqlCommand` object. The `SqlCommand` object defines the stored procedure or SQL text to execute. The `Connection` property associates the command with an open connection. The `CommandType` property defines whether the command is a stored procedure or SQL statement, and the `CommandText` property defines the stored procedure name or SQL statement text.

If there are any parameters, the code loops through each parameter and adds it to the `SqlCommand` object's `Parameters` collection.

The code then creates a new `SqlDataAdapter` object for the command and a new `DataTable` object. Creating the `SqlDataAdapter` object executes the defined command.

Finally, the code fills the `DataTable` object using the `SqlDataAdapter` object's `Fill` method and returns the resulting `DataTable` object.

8. BUILDING THE DATA ACCESS LAYER

NOTE: To modify this method to support a data provider different from SQL Server, change every data type prefixed with "Sql" to instead use the data provider data type, such as "OleDb" or "Odbc." For example, to work with an Access database using the OleDb provider, change the connection code as follows:

```
Using cnn As New _
    OleDbConnection(My.Settings.PTConnectionString)
```

If you want DAC code that can work with any data provider, you need to change the code more significantly. For example, to open an OleDb connection, the required code is as follows:

```
Dim df As DbProviderFactory = _
  DbProviderFactories.GetFactory("System.Data.OleDb")
Using cnn As DbConnection = df.CreateConnection
cnn.ConnectionString = My.Settings.PTConnectionString
cnn.Open()
```

See the "Additional Reading" section for more information on DbProviderFactory.

To make this `ExecuteDataTable` method easier to call when there are no stored procedure parameters, create an overloaded method that takes no stored procedure parameters:

```
Public Shared Function ExecuteDataTable( _
    ByVal storedProcedureName As String) As DataTable
    Return ExecuteDataTable(storedProcedureName, Nothing)
End Function
```

This method calls the original method, passing in `Nothing` as the second parameter.

To make it easy for the business objects to create the set of parameters that are passed to the method, define a `Parameter` method in the DAC that returns a `SQLParameter` object given the parameter name and value:

```
''' <summary>
''' Creates a Parameter
''' </summary>
```

```
'''   <param name="parameterName">Name of the parameter</param>
'''   <param name="parameterValue">Value of the parameter</param>
'''   <returns>SqlParameter object</returns>
'''   <remarks>The parameter name should be the same as the
'''   property name</remarks>
Public Shared Function Parameter(ByVal parameterName As String, _
    ByVal parameterValue As Object) As SqlParameter
    Dim param As New SqlParameter
    param.ParameterName = parameterName
    param.Value = parameterValue
    Return param
End Function
```

This method creates a `SqlParameter` object, assigns the defined name and value to that `SqlParameter` object, and returns it. Notice that the data type of the second parameter is `Object`. This allows the code to pass in any type of value, such as strings, integers, and dates.

NOTE: To modify this method to support a data provider different from SQL Server, change every data type prefixed with "Sql" to instead use the data provider data type, such as "OleDb" or "Odbc."

Now that the methods are complete, you can call them from the business object classes as described in the next section.

Building Along

For the Purchase Tracker sample application:

- Add the **ExecuteDataTable** method to the **DAC** class, as described in this section.
- Add the overloaded **ExecuteDataTable** method that has no stored procedure parameters to the **DAC** class, as described in this section.
- Add the **Parameter** method to the **DAC** class, as described in this section.

You now have the basics of a data access class. If desired, build a unit test for this class to test it.

Calling the DAC from the Business Objects

The DAC does not do anything until you add code to call it from the business objects. This section details the steps needed to call the DAC from your business object component.

Before you can access the DAC from the business object component, you need a reference between the business object component and the DAC, as detailed in Chapter 3.

You can then add code in the business object classes to call the DAC methods. For example, the `Create` method in a `ProductList` class can call the `ProductRetrieveList_sp` stored procedure as follows:

```
Public Shared Function Create() As DataTable
    Dim dt As DataTable
    dt = DAC.ExecuteDataTable("ProductRetrieveList_sp")
    Return dt
End Function
```

It is normally considered inappropriate programming practice to use hard-coded strings in your code, as in this code example. It is better to define the string names of your stored procedures as constants in the associated business object, or as resource strings in the business object Class Library project properties, as described in Chapter 4.

Building Along

For the Purchase Tracker sample application:

- You already have a reference in the business object Class Library project (**PTBO**) to the DAC Class Library component (**PTDAC**), as detailed in Chapter 3.
- In the business object Class Library project (**PTBO**), add a constant to the associated class or resource string to the project properties for each stored procedure name as follows:

Resource String/Constant Name	Stored Procedure Name
SP_CustomerRetrieveByID	CustomerRetrieveByID_sp
SP_CustomerRetrieveList	CustomerRetrieveList_sp
SP_CustomerSave	CustomerSave_sp
SP_ProductRetrieveByID	ProductRetrieveByID_sp
SP_ProductRetrieveList	ProductRetrieveList_sp
SP_ProductSave	ProductSave_sp
SP_PurchaseRetrieveByCustomerID	PurchaseRetrieveByCustomerID_sp

- Open the **ProductList** class in the Code Editor.
- In the **Create** method, remove the hard-coded data values, and insert a call to the DAC `ExecuteDataTable` method.

Pass in the appropriate resource string or constant for the stored procedure name:

```
dt = DAC.ExecuteDataTable( _
            My.Resources.SP_ProductRetrieveList)
```

- Open the **CustomerList** class in the Code Editor.
- In the **Create** method, remove the hard-coded data values, and insert a call to the DAC `ExecuteDataTable` method.

Pass in the appropriate resource string or constant for the stored procedure name:

```
dt = DAC.ExecuteDataTable( _
            My.Resources.SP_CustomerRetrieveList)
```

Run the application. It displays your splash screen and then shows the MDI parent form. Select **Products | Manage Products** to display the ProductWin form. When you drop down the list of products, you now see the products you defined as sample data in your database earlier in this chapter.

Then select **Customers | Manage Customers** to display the CustomerWin form. When you drop down the list of customers, you now see the customers you defined in your sample data.

List classes, such as `ProductList` and `CustomerList`, are easy to implement, because they bind directly to the resulting DataTable. In most cases, however, you need to populate the properties of the business object from the data in the DataTable. This requires a bit more code.

First, define constants in the associated business object or resource strings in the project properties for each column name in the DataTable. This provides type safety when retrieving the column values from the DataTable. For example, the constants for the Product table are as follows:

```
Private Const CN_ProductID As String = "ProductID"
Private Const CN_ProductName As String = "ProductName"
Private Const CN_ProductNumber As String = "ProductNumber"
Private Const CN_Description As String = "Description"
Private Const CN_Price As String = "Price"
Private Const CN_ProductType As String = "ProductType"
Private Const CN_StockType As String = "StockType"
```

The constants are defined with the `Private` modifier so that they can be used within the business object but not outside of it. The "CN_" prefix denotes that it is a column name. This makes it easier to find the column names using Intellisense and ensures that the names don't collide with the business object's property names.

You can either type all of these for each business object or use the same techniques defined for the stored procedure generator to generate these constants.

NOTE: To aid in defining the correct constants or resource strings, you can view the list of column names in each table using Server Explorer.

System fields are in every table. Instead of adding constants for them to each business object, add the constants to the base business object class:

```
Protected Const CN_LastUpdateUser As String = "LastUpdateUser"
Protected Const CN_RowState As String = "RowState"
```

The constants are defined with the `Protected` modifier, so they can be used in any class that inherits from the base business object class.

When the constants (or resource strings) are in place, the business object can call the `ExecuteDataTable` method to retrieve the DataTable and populate each business object property with its associated column value:

```
Public Shared Function Create(ByVal prodID As Integer) As Product
    Dim prod As Product

    ' Populate the object
    Dim dt As DataTable
    dt = DAC.ExecuteDataTable( _
            My.Resources.SP_ProductRetrieveByID, _
            DAC.Parameter(CN_ProductID, prodID))

    ' Create a new instance
    prod = New Product()

    With dt.Rows(0)
        prod.ProductID = CType(.Item(CN_ProductID), Integer)
        prod.ProductName = .Item(CN_ProductName).ToString
```

```
        prod.ProductNumber = .Item(CN_ProductNumber).ToString
        prod.Price = CType(.Item(CN_Price), Decimal)
        prod.Description = .Item(CN_Description).ToString
        prod.ProductType = CType(.Item(CN_ProductType), Integer)
        prod.StockType = .Item(CN_StockType).ToString
    End With

    ' Reset the state to unchanged
    prod.DataStateChanged(EntityStateEnum.Unchanged)
    Return prod
End Function
```

This code begins by calling the DAC's `ExecuteDataTable` method, passing it the name of the stored procedure and the `ProductID` parameter. Notice that the parameter is defined using the `Parameter` method created earlier in this chapter. The returned `DataTable` object contains all of the data for product with the defined product ID.

The code then creates a new instance of the `Product` class and assigns the value from each `DataTable` object column to the associated `Product` class property. Since this project has Option Strict On, each column value must be converted to the appropriate data type.

NOTE: If a column value could be null, take care when using the `CType` method. Check for a null before converting the column value as follows:

```
If .Item(CN_Price) IsNot DBNull.Value Then
    prod.Price = CType(.Item(CN_Price), Decimal)
End If
```

Each time a property is set, the `Property` statement setter is called. If the property is set to a different value, the `EntityState` is changed to `Modified`. (The `Property` setter code was detailed in Chapter 5.) So after all the properties are set, this code changes the `EntityState` back to `Unchanged`. This ensures that the application tracks the changes to the object that the user makes, not those made when populating the object in the `Create` method.

The populated `Product` business object is then returned from this method. Code detailed in Chapter 7, "Binding the User Interface to the Business Objects," demonstrated how to bind this resulting business object to the user interface so that the user interface displays the values of the business object properties.

8. BUILDING THE DATA ACCESS LAYER

In summary, the code to populate a business object from a DataTable is relatively straightforward. Call the DAC to get the DataTable, create the business object, and set the data from each column in the DataTable into a property of the business object. The data binding features take it from here and automatically populate the user interface controls from the business object properties.

Building Along

For the Purchase Tracker sample application:

- Open the base business object class (**PTBOBase**) in the Code Editor.
- Add constants for the system field column names to the base business object class.
  Or define the column names as resource strings.
- Open the **Product** class in the Code Editor.
- Add a constant for each column in the **Product** table, as detailed in this section.
- In the **Create** method, remove the hard-coded values, and insert a call to the ExecuteDataTable method in the DAC.
  Pass in the appropriate constant or resource string for the stored procedure name and the ProductID parameter:

```
dt = DAC.ExecuteDataTable(_
        My.Resources.SP_ProductRetrieveByID, _
        DAC.Parameter(CN_ProductID, prodID))
```

- In the **Create** method, add code to populate the business object properties from the DataTable columns, as detailed in this section.
- Open the **Customer** class in the Code Editor.
- Add a constant for each column in the **Customer** table.
- In the **Create** method, remove the hard-coded values, and insert a call to the ExecuteDataTable method. Populate the business object similar to the Create method in the Product class.
- Open the **Purchase** class in the Code Editor.
- Add a constant for each column in the **Purchase** table.
  Don't modify the Create method for this class yet. It will be covered in the next section.
- If you created unit tests in Chapter 6, "Class Tools and Techniques," you may need to change them to work with your test data instead of your hard-coded data.

Run the application. It displays your splash screen and then shows the MDI parent form. Select **Products | Manage Products** to display the ProductWin form. You can pick any entry from the Product drop-down list and see the values for all the properties appear in the form.

NOTE: Because of how decimal data is stored in the database, the price now has four places to the right of the decimal point. Since you defined the price with a `Property` statement, you can easily fix this by adjusting the getter for the `Price` property:

```
Return Decimal.Round(_Price, 2)
```

Then select **Customers | Manage Customers** to display the CustomerWin form. You can pick any entry from the Customer drop-down list and see the values for all the properties appear in the form.
This is so much more exciting than seeing hard-coded data!

Handling Object Collections

So far the business objects have used the DAC to handle two cases: single objects and lists of objects bound to a DataTable. The business object classes that manage a single object, like the `Product` and `Customer` classes, call the DAC and pass in the ID of the one item to retrieve. The business object classes that manage a list of objects by binding directly to a DataTable, like the `ProductList` and `CustomerList` classes, call the DAC to get the DataTable.

But what about the case where the business object class manages a set of business objects as a generic collection, such as the `PurchaseList` class? When working with object collections, you have two choices for populating the business object with the retrieved data.

The first option is to retrieve the data for all the objects in the collection with one query. Then loop through the results and create each individual object, passing in a row of data. The object then uses the data in the row to set its properties.

The second option is to retrieve just the keys for the objects in the collection with the query. Then loop through the set of keys and create each individual object, passing in the ID. The object then uses the ID to retrieve its own data and sets its properties from that data.

In most cases, the first option is more efficient, because there is only one call to the database. The second option is more encapsulated, because each object gets its own data.

Because of the efficiency of executing one query instead of one query for each object, this example uses the first option. The code required to retrieve all of the data for a list of objects and to use it to populate the individual objects is as follows:

```
Public Shared Function Create(ByVal custID As Integer) As _
    PurchaseList
    Dim purchList As PurchaseList

    Dim dt As DataTable
    dt = DAC.ExecuteDataTable( _
        My.Resources.SP_PurchaseRetrieveByCustomerID, _
        DAC.Parameter(Purchase.CN_CustomerID, custID))

    ' Create a new instance
    purchList = New PurchaseList

    ' Populate the objects
    For Each dr As DataRow In dt.Rows
        purchlist.Add(Purchase.Create(dr))
    Next
    Return purchList
End Function
```

The `Create` method begins by calling the DAC's `ExecuteDataTable` method, passing it the name of the stored procedure and the `CustomerID` parameter. The returned `DataTable` object contains all the purchases for the defined customer.

The code then creates a new instance of the `PurchaseList` class, adds entries to the collection for each row in the `DataTable` object, and returns the populated `PurchaseList`.

Notice that the code passes a `DataRow` object to the `Create` method of the `Purchase` class. No `Create` method in the `Purchase` class currently takes a `DataRow` object as a parameter, so you need to add one as follows:

```
Public Shared Function Create(ByVal dr As DataRow) As Purchase
    Dim purch As Purchase

    ' Create a new instance
    purch = New Purchase()

    ' Populate the object
    With dr
        purch.PurchaseID = CType(.Item(CN_PurchaseID), Integer)
        purch.ProductID = CType(.Item(CN_ProductID), Integer)
        purch.CustomerID = CType(.Item(CN_CustomerID), Integer)
        purch.PurchaseDate = CType(.Item(CN_PurchaseDate), Date)
        purch.Quantity = CType(.Item(CN_Quantity), Integer)
    End With

    ' Reset the entity's state
    purch.DataStateChanged(EntityStateEnum.Unchanged)
    Return purch
End Function
```

The `Create` method begins by creating a new instance of the `Purchase` class. It does not need to access the DAC, because the data is passed in to the method in the `DataRow` object.

The values of the columns in the `DataRow` object are then assigned to the `Purchase` business object properties.

After all the properties are set, this code changes the `EntityState` back to `Unchanged`. This ensures that the application tracks the changes to the object that the user makes, not those made when populating the object in the `Create` method.

The resulting `Purchase` object is returned from this method.

In summary, you can populate a generic collection of objects using one database query and then create each object from the resulting rows. Or you can use one query to retrieve the set of IDs and then pass the ID to the object's `Create` method so that it can retrieve its own data.

Building Along

For the Purchase Tracker sample application:

- Open the **PurchaseList** class in the Code Editor.
- In the **Create** method, remove the hard-coded values, and insert a call to the `ExecuteDataTable` method, as detailed in this section.

■ Open the **Purchase** class in the Code Editor.
■ Create an overloaded **Create** method to accept a `DataRow` object as a parameter, as shown in this section.

Run the application. It displays your splash screen and then shows the MDI parent form. Select **Purchase Tracker** | **View Purchases** to display the PurchasesWin form. You can select any customer from the list and view the associated purchases. If necessary, add more sample data to your database to fully test this feature.

Saving Data

Unless you are building a read-only application, you also need code to save the properties of the objects back to the database.

To save the properties of a business object, add a `Save` method that calls the same `ExecuteDataTable` method in the DAC but passes every property as a parameter. The code in a sample `Save` method is as follows:

```
''' <summary>
''' Saves the current object properties back to the database
''' </summary>
''' <returns>True if the save was successful;
'''     otherwise False</returns>
''' <remarks></remarks>
Public Function Save() As Boolean
    Dim success As Boolean = False
    ' Pass the properties back to the DAC
    Dim dt As DataTable
    dt = DAC.ExecuteDataTable(My.Resources.SP_ProductSave, _
        DAC.Parameter(CN_ProductID, ProductID), _
        DAC.Parameter(CN_ProductName, ProductName), _
        DAC.Parameter(CN_ProductNumber, ProductNumber), _
        DAC.Parameter(CN_Description, Description), _
        DAC.Parameter(CN_Price, Price), _
        DAC.Parameter(CN_ProductType, ProductType), _
        DAC.Parameter(CN_StockType, StockType), _
        DAC.Parameter(CN_LastUpdateUser, My.User.Name), _
        DAC.Parameter(CN_RowState, EntityState.ToString))

    ' If it was an add, update the product ID
    If EntityState = EntityStateEnum.Added Then
```

```
      ProductID = CType(dt.Rows(0).Item(CN_ProductID), Integer)
   End If

   ' Reset the entity's state
   Me.DataStateChanged(EntityStateEnum.Unchanged)
   success = True

   Return success
End Function
```

This method begins by calling `ExecuteDataTable` and passing every property value as a parameter. This assumes that the names of the columns in the table match the names of the parameters in the stored procedures.

The `ExecuteDataTable` returns a `DataTable` object, but the only time this method needs to access the returned `DataTable` object is when a row is added. In that case, SQL Server assigns a new ID value, so the returned ID is reassigned to the associated property.

The `EntityState` is then reset to `Unchanged`, because there are no longer any unsaved changes.

You then need to add code in the `ProcessSave` method of each form to call the business object's `Save` method:

```
Public Function ProcessSave() As Boolean _
   Implements IMDIChild.ProcessSave
   Dim success As Boolean
   Me.Validate()
   success = DirectCast(ProductBindingSource.Current, _
                                 PTBO.Product).Save()
   Return success
End Function
```

This code first calls the form's `Validate` method. Normally, validation for a control occurs when the user leaves the control. Calling the `Validate` method ensures that the current control is validated, even if the user does not leave the control. See Chapter 7 for more information on validation.

The code then uses the instance of the business object referenced by the `Current` property of the `BindingSource` component to call the `Save` method. The properties for the currently displayed business object are then saved.

Use defensive coding techniques in the `ProcessSave` function to ensure that it won't generate an error if there is no current product:

```
If ProductBindingSource.Current Is Nothing Then
    MessageBox.Show("Select a Product to save first, " & _
        "then select the Save option.", Me.Text)
    success = False
Else
    Me.Validate()
    success = DirectCast(ProductBindingSource.Current, _
                                    Product).Save()
End If
```

Or use `TryCast` as follows:

```
Dim prod As Product
prod = TryCast(ProductBindingSource.Current, Product)
If prod Is Nothing Then
    MessageBox.Show("Select a Product to save first, " & _
        "then select the Save option.", Me.Text)
Else
    Me.Validate()
    prod.Save()
End If
```

Use similar code whenever you need to save object data.

NOTE: The additional code required to support adding new items or deleting existing items is not detailed in this chapter. See the "Building Along" section at the end of this chapter for more information.

Building Along

For the Purchase Tracker sample application:
- Open the **Product** class in the Code Editor.
- Add a **Save** method, as detailed in this section.
- Open the **ProductWin** form in the Code Editor.
- Modify the **ProcessSave** method to call `Validate` and then the business object `Save` method, as defined in this section.

- Open the **Customer** class in the Code Editor.
- Add a **Save** method.
- Open the **CustomerWin** form in the Code Editor.
- Implement the **IMDIChild** interface, as described in Chapter 4.
- Add code to the **ProcessSave** method to call `Validate` and then the business object `Save` method.

Run the application. At this point, you can view or edit existing customers and products, save changes to customers and products, and view existing purchases for a customer. You have a functional application!

The base form class, base business object class, DAC, `Validation` class, and other reusable code can be extracted from this application and used as the basis of your reusable application framework.

This book has taken you through the process of building the user interface layer, business object layer, and data access layer. By dividing your application into logical layers, you have an application that is much easier to build and maintain. Enjoy!

Conclusion

What Did This Chapter Cover?

This chapter provided information on using the Visual Studio tools to create a database (or connect to an existing database) and build stored procedures. It then defined how to build a data access component and call that component from business objects.

This chapter covered several real productivity enhancers:

- Using the database tools provided within Visual Studio, you can quickly create, review, or edit your SQL Server database without leaving the comfort of your development environment.
- Using Server Explorer, you can connect to any database, including Microsoft Access, Oracle, and MySQL. You can then see the names of your tables, columns, and stored procedures or queries.
- The Query Builder helps you build the queries in your SQL Server stored procedures, but a stored procedure generator would make you even more productive.

- Using a database project makes it easier to manage your SQL Server stored procedures.
- Your data access component does not need to be as huge or full-featured as the data access block in the Enterprise Library (see the "Additional Reading" section of Chapter 2 for more information on the Enterprise Library). Keep it focused to your application's needs to stay productive.
- After you build your data access component, you can reuse it in every application you build.
- Adding common code, such as the system column constants, to the base business object class prevents the need to add it to each business object.
- Using a common pattern for the `Create` and `Save` methods in your business objects makes building your business objects very quick and easy. Consider writing a code snippet to generate these methods for even greater productivity.
- Building an application as a set of encapsulated components divided into logical layers lets you focus on each layer, helping you manage the complexity of your application and making the entire building process more efficient.

Building Along

If you are "building along" with the Purchase Tracker sample application, this chapter added all the code you need for your data access layer.

You can run the Purchase Tracker sample application and view and edit product and customer information and view purchase information.

When building production-level applications, consider enhancing the data access features as follows:

- Implement a New feature to create new products and customers. The user interface and `IMDIChild` programmatic interface are already set up to support creating new entries, such as products and customers. Add a business object method to handle creating new entries.
- Implement a Delete feature to delete a product or customer. The user interface and `IMDIChild` programmatic interface are already set up to support deleting entries, such as products and customers. Add a business object method to handle the delete.

- Implement features to handle concurrency issues.
  In a multiuser application, it is possible for two users to modify the same data. You need to add code to handle this situation. One way to handle concurrency is to use a TimeStamp field. See the "Additional Reading" section for references to database books that cover this topic.
- Create a stored procedure generator.
  One of the most tedious and error-prone tasks is creating all the stored procedures or queries required for your application. Implement a stored procedure generator to save time (see "Additional Reading").
- Implement parameter discovery.
  Probably the second-most tedious task in working with the data access layer is defining all the parameters for calling Save stored procedures. It would be better if the DAC could discover the parameters for you. If you are using SQL Server, you can use the following method to discover the parameters from the `SqlCommand` object:

```
SqlCommandBuilder.DeriveParameters(cmd)
```

  If you are not using SQL Server, but you did name the parameters using the same names as the columns, you can discover the parameters yourself. Pass the DataRow into the DAC method, and build the parameters from the column information accessible from the DataRow.
- Add more DAC methods.
  Add methods to the DAC similar to `ExecuteDataTable` that instead return a DataSet, DataReader, or any other type of data container that your application may want to use.

You now have an operational application and the beginnings of an application framework!

Additional Reading

Goldstein, Jackie. *Microsoft SQL Server 2005 Express Edition Step by Step*. Microsoft Press, 2006.

Teach yourself how to get a data-intensive application up and running quickly with SQL Server Express Edition—one step at a time. With this book, you work at your own pace through hands-on, learn-by-doing exercises. Whether you're new to database programming or new to SQL Server, you'll learn how, when, and why to use specific features of this simple but powerful database development environment. Each chapter puts you to work, building your knowledge of core capabilities and guiding you as you create actual components and working applications.

Kurata, Deborah. "Building a Stored Procedure Generator." *CoDe* magazine, September/October 2005.

Creating basic data access stored procedures is boring, time-consuming work. Relieve the tedium by writing code that writes these stored procedures for you. This article presents all the code you need to build your own stored procedure generator.

MSDN. "Writing Provider Independent Code for .NET Framework Data Providers." http://msdn2.microsoft.com.

This topic is an overview of building data-provider-independent code using DbProviderFactories. It provides links to more information on this topic. Since things seem to move around on MSDN, it did not seem useful to provide the direct link to this help topic. To quickly find this information, search on the title.

Vaughn, William R. *Hitchhiker's Guide to Visual Studio and SQL Server*, Seventh Edition. Addison Wesley, 2006.

This book is designed for the "ordinary" developer who wants to become an expert. It has chapters like "How Does SQL Server Work?" and information that can help developers build smarter, faster, and more robust applications more quickly. It talks about design principles, architecture, and best practices.

Try It!

Here are a few suggestions for trying some of the techniques presented in this chapter:

1. Add a SalesRep table to your database using Server Explorer.
2. Add sample data to the SalesRep table.
3. Add stored procedures to retrieve data from and save data to the SalesRep table.
4. Modify the `Create` method of the `SalesRep` class to call the DAC and display your sample data instead of the hard-coded data.
5. Add a `Save` method in the `SalesRep` class, and call the method from the UI as appropriate.
   You can then modify SalesRep data.
6. If you are up for a challenge, add a method to the DAC that takes a DataRow as a parameter and automatically builds the parameters for the save stored procedures based on data in the DataRow.

INDEX

THIS BOOK IS SAFARI ENABLED

INCLUDES FREE 45-DAY ACCESS TO THE ONLINE EDITION

The Safari® Enabled icon on the cover of your favorite technology book means the book is available through Safari Bookshelf. When you buy this book, you get free access to the online edition for 45 days.

Safari Bookshelf is an electronic reference library that lets you easily search thousands of technical books, find code samples, download chapters, and access technical information whenever and wherever you need it.

TO GAIN 45-DAY SAFARI ENABLED ACCESS TO THIS BOOK:

- Go to **http://www.awprofessional.com/safarienabled**
- Complete the brief registration form
- Enter the coupon code found in the front of this book on the "Copyright" page

If you have difficulty registering on Safari Bookshelf or accessing the online edition, please e-mail customer-service@safaribooksonline.com.